MACMILLAN
GENERAL
KNOWLEDGE
MANUAL
2010

MACMILLAN'S GENERAL KNOWLEDGE MANUAL 2010

Muktikanta Mohanty

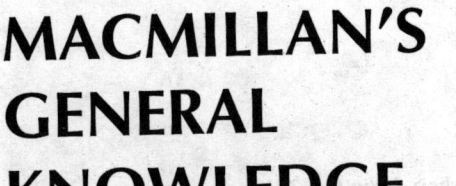

© *Macmillan Publishers India Ltd, 2010*

All rights reserved. No part of this publication may be reproduced or transmitted, in any form or by any means, without permission. Any person who does any unauthorised act in relation to this publication may be liable to criminal prosecution and civil claims for damages.

First published, 2010

MACMILLAN PUBLISHERS INDIA LTD
Delhi Bangalore Chennai Kolkata Mumbai
Bhopal Chandigarh Coimbatore Cuttack Guwahati
Hubli Hyderabad Jaipur Lucknow Madurai Nagpur
Patna Pune Raipur Thiruvananthapuram Visakhapatnam

Companies and representatives throughout the world

ISBN 10: 0230-32874-1
ISBN 13: 978-0230-32874-7

Published by Rajiv Beri for Macmillan Publishers India Ltd
2/10 Ansari Road, Daryaganj, New Delhi 110 002

Typeset by Arpit Graphics
Navin Shahadara, Delhi 110 032

Printed at Sanat Printers
312 EPIP, Kundli, Haryana 131 028

The views and content of this book are solely of the author(s). The author(s) of the book has/have taken all reasonable care to ensure that the contents of the book do not violate any existing copyright or other intellectual property rights of any person in any manner whatsoever. In the event the author(s) has/have been unable to track any source and if any copyright has been inadvertently infringed, please notify the publisher in writing for corrective action.

Preface

The study of General Knowledge has become very important. It is not only a major constituent of most competitive examinations but also aids professionals in general awareness.

The book *Macmillan's General Knowledge Manual 2010* is an endeavour, primarily towards the fulfillment of knowledge awareness covered in various competitive examinations.

The objective of this book is to provide the vast subject in a structured and concise manner to help students take the examinations with ease and score well.

It discusses all subjects in a lucid manner, keeping in view the various competitive examinations held every year, viz.:

- Civil Services
- Sate Civil Services
- Indian Engineering Services
- Bank PO
- Combined Defence Services (CDS), National Defence Academy (NDA)
- LIC, GIC AAO and other administrative examinations
- SSC (Preliminary and Mains)
- RBI Grade A & B
- Railway Recruitment Board
- MBA, MCA Entrance tests, etc.

All the chapters are structured into sections and sub-sections. Important questions are put at the end of the pages to acquaint you with the question pattern of competitive examinations. Important data and useful information are presented in tabulations for quicker revision. The latest events are put into the chapter on Current Affairs.

Environmental Science has been put as a separate chapter keeping in mind the latest trend of the examinations. This adds to the uniqueness of the book.

The recent General Election, State Elections, Union Budget, etc., are updated in the Current Affairs section for easy reference.

I hope the information provided in this book would be of immense help to the students appearing for various competitive examinations and for professionals to refresh their general awareness.

It would be required to constantly revise each edition of this book in order to keep it up to date. We will appreciate your sincere comments and suggestions for the development of chapters and expanding the scope of this book.

I would like express my gratitude to my parents – Ajaya Kumar Mohanty and Renuka Mohanty, without whose constant encouragement and inspirations, this book would not have been possible.

I also appreciate the efforts of my younger brother Sashikanta, who in fact helped me in writing the book.

I especially thank my sisters – Jharana, Aruna, Tapaswini and Payaswini – for their support and encouragement in the preparation of the book.

Last but not the least my wife Ritisnata has been most encouraging and helpful in this endeavour.

Finally I would like to thank my publishers, specially Ms. Dona Ghosh for her effort and commitment towards the project.

I wish each and every aspirant success in forthcoming examinations.

Muktikanta Mohanty

Contents

Preface   *vii*

1. HISTORY OF INDIA   1
    Ancient India   1
    Medieval India   11
    Modern India   14
    Indian Freedom Struggle   19
    Prominent Personalities   24
    Timelines in Indian History   27

2. WORLD HISTORY   32
    Ancient World   32
    Medieval World   34
    Modern World   35
    Timelines in World History   41

3. GEOGRAPHY OF INDIA   49
    Location   49
    Area and Dimensions   49
    Boundaries and Points   49
    Physical Presence   50
    River Systems of India   55
    Climate in India   56
    Forests in India   57
    Agriculture   57
    Minerals of India   60
    Transport and Communication   61
    Ports in India   65
    Demography   66
    Miscellanea   71
    State at a Glance I   79
    States at a Glance II   81

4. WORLD GEOGRAPHY   84
    The Universe   84

The Solar System	85
The Earth	87
Atmosphere	89
Hydrosphere	91
Lithosphere	92
Our World	97

5. INDIAN ECONOMY — 114

Planning in India	114
Indian Financial System	121
Industries	128
Economic Terminology	136

6. INDIAN POLITY — 139

Constitution of India	139
State Executive	158
The State Legislature	159
The High Court	160
Union State Relations	161
Political Process in India	163
The Election Commission	163
Panchayati Raj System	164
General Election 2004	165
Order of Precedence	166

7. INTERNATIONAL ORGANISATIONS — 169

United Nations Organisation (UN)	169
Other World Organisations	173

8. GENERAL SCIENCE AND TECHNOLOGY — 185

Branches of Science	185
Physics	186
Chemistry	192
Important Laws and Principles	198
Biology	199
Human Body	201
Various Systems of the Body	204
Glands of Human Body	210
Human Diet	211
Human Diseases	212
Principles of Medical Treatment	215
Common Drugs	216
Medical Technology	217
Scientific Explanations of Some Facts	219
Computer	220
Internet	225
Computer Terminology	226

9. ENVIRONMENTAL SCIENCE — 230

- Environment — 230
- Global Warming — 231
- Pollution — 233
- Acid Rain — 237
- Waste — 238
- Hazardous Waste — 239
- Disasters — 240
- Major Disasters — 240
- Global Oil Supply and Demand — 247

10. BASIC GENERAL KNOWLEDGE — 249

- Abbreviations — 249
- Famous Books and Their Authors — 261
- Great Personalities — 268
- Important Dates — 275
- Religions of the World — 277
- Awards, Honour and Prizes — 280
- The World of Sports — 284

11. NATIONAL INSIGNIA AND INDIAN MISCELLANEA — 293

- National Insignia — 293
- India's Defence System — 295
- Paramilitary and Reserved Forces — 301
- Defence Research — 302
- Chandrayaan – 1 — 306
- Atomic Research — 307

12. CURRENT AFFAIRS — 317

- General Elections 2009 — 317
- State Assembly Elections 2009 — 318
- National News — 319
- International News — 324
- Science and Technology — 327
- Economic and Business — 329
- Union Budget — 330
- Railway Budget — 336
- Economic Survey — 338
- Games and Sports — 341
- Prize and Honours — 346
- Who is Who — 353
- Appointments — 364
- Abbreviations — 365

1

HISTORY OF INDIA

History of India is broadly divided into three separate periods:
(i) Ancient India
(ii) Medieval India and
(iii) Modern India

ANCIENT INDIA

The ancient history of India spreads from Indus valley civilisation to coming of Muslims in India till around AD 1000.

Indus Valley Civilisation: (2500–1500 BC)

- The Indus valley civilisation belongs to Bronze Age, which flourished in India on the banks of river Indus.
- It extends from Manda (Jammu and Kashmir) in North to Dimabad (Maharashtra) in south and from Sutkagan Dor (Pakistan-Iran Border) in west to Alamgirpur (Uttar Pradesh) in the east.
- *Major Cities:*
- Mohenjedaro in Sindh, Harappa in West Punjab, Chanhudaro in Sindh, Kalibangan in Northern Rajasthan, Lothal in Gujarat, Banwali in Haryana, Surkatada in Gujarat.
- *Major Excavations*:
  Mohenjedaro   by R D Banerjee (1922)
  Harappa   by R B Dayaram Sahni (1921)
  Chanhudaro   by M G Majumdar
  Kalibangan   by B B Lal
  Lothal   by S R Rao
  Banwali   by R S Bisht
  Surkatada   by J Joshi
- Indus Valley civilisation had systematic town planning on the lines of grid system. Houses were made of bricks. There were no stone buildings, and with proper drainage system.
- *Main crops*: wheat, barley as well as rice. Other crops: dates, mustard, sesamum, cotton (first in the world). Food grains were stored in granaries.

- They were very fond of ornaments (of gold, silver, ivory, copper, etc.) and cotton fabrics.
- Tools were made of copper and bronze.
- There existed inter-regional trade and foreign trades with Mesopotamia or Sumeria, Bahrain, etc. Barter system was used for exchange of materials. 16 (16, 32, 64, 160, 320, etc.) was the unit of measurement.
- Main object of worship was mother Goddess symbolising fertility, proto Shiva (Pasupatinath) represented the male deity.
- There is evidence of the fact that they were also were worshipping tree (*pipal*), animal (bull), bird (dove, pigeon).
- Their script is not deciphered satisfactorily and there is no conclusive proof of its connection with the Dravidian language or Sanskrit.
- *Causes of Decline*: Possible causes are invasion of Aryans, recurring of floods, drying up of rivers, decreasing fertility, deforestation, ignoring of defence, decline of trade, limited use of script, etc. However, Indus Valley civilisation existed about 1000 years.

Vedic Period (1500–600 BC)

- The Vedic Period is the period during which the Vedas, the oldest sacred texts of the Indo-Aryans, were being composed.
- The Aryans were semi-nomadic pastoral people and believed to have originated from the area around Caspian Sea in Central Asia.
- They entered India around 1500 BC through Khyber Pass of Hindukush mountain. Some other sources (Zend-Avesta, holy book of Iran) say, they entered India through Iran.
- *Vedic period is broadly divided into*: Early Vedic Period and Late Vedic Period.

The Early Vedic Period

- They first settled in eastern Afghanistan, Punjab and western Uttar Pradesh called the land of seven rivers.
- They were living in family or *Kula*, headed by *Kulpas* or *grihapati*, *grama* or village headed by *grammi*. Sabha (Council of tribal leaders) and *Samiti* (general assembly of tribes) exercised deliberative or military power.
- Women held a respectable social status, participated in religious ceremonies and tribal assemblies.
- During this period four *Vedas* were composed: *Rig Veda*, *Sama Veda*, *Yajur Veda* and *Atharva Veda*.
- *Rig Veda* is considered to be the oldest religious text in the world, which contains 1028 hymns (*Sukta*), the prayer to God and also the *Gayatri mantra* (address to Sun).
- *Sama Veda* is derived from root *Saman*, which deals with music.
- *Yajur Veda* deals with procedures for the performance of sacrifices; it has two main texts: White *Yajur Veda* (contains mantras) and Black *Yajur Veda* (contains commentary in prose).
- *Atharva Veda* deals with medicines.
- The *Upanisads* are the main sources of

Q.1. 'War begins in the minds of men' is inscribed in which Veda?
Q.2. What are the prose explanations of the Vedas known?

philosophy. There are about 108 Upanisads. They condemn ceremonies and sacrifices.
- The *Brahmans* explains the hymns of *Vedas* in orthodox manner; it deals with socio-economic, political life of Aryans and their belief.
- The *Aranyakas,* known as forest books, was meant for hermits who live in forest. It deals with mysticism and philosophy, opposed to sacrifice and emphasise on meditation.
- Aryans worshipped the Sun, the Water, the Fire, etc; they did not believe in erecting temples or idol worship. They worshipped in open air through *Yajna*.

The Later Vedic Period (1000–600 BC)

- This age is also known as the Epic Age because the two great epics *Ramayana* and *Mahabharata* were written during this period.
- The Aryans expanded from Punjab to whole of west of Uttar Pradesh through Gangetic Valley.
- Several large kingdoms arose because of the increasing importance of land and long-distance trade.
- Kingdoms like Kosala, Videha, Kuru, Magadha, Kasi, Avanti and Panchala came into existence and big cities like Ayodhya, Mathura, etc., developed.
- Tiny tribal settlements were replaced with kingdoms; the position of the king was considerably high. The power of the king and the Kshatriyas greatly increased.
- The kings performed sacrifices like *rajasuya* (royal consecration), *vajapeya* (including a chariot race) and for supreme dominance over other kings, the *ashvamedha yogna* (horse sacrifice).
- The role of the people in political decision-making and the status of the Vaishyas as such were greatly decreased.
- Fourfold caste system came into existence: the Brahmins, Kshatriyas, Vaishyas and Shudras. The Brahmins were priests and teachers. The Kshatriyas were rulers and soldiers. They enjoyed high position in the society. The Vaishyas were traders, artisans and farmers. The Shudras were the uneducated workers who served the other three castes.
- There was a decline in the status and dignity of women. Women were subordinated. They were not allowed to participate in public affairs. They could not own property.
- The transition was marked by the emergence of agriculture as the dominant economic activity, corresponding decline in the significance of cattle rearing.
- Both internal and foreign trade flourished. Medicinal plants, medicine, clothing and leather products were exported to countries like Babylonia.
- Rice, wheat, barley, milk and milk products, fruit and vegetables were their diet. Fish was also eaten. The flesh of oxen, sheep and goats were eaten.
- People started worshipping Gods like Prajapathi, Pasupathi, Vishnu and Krishna. Prayers and sacrifices became important ways of worshipping God.
- There were six *Vedangas*: Shiksha, Kalpa, Vyakarana, Nirukta, Chhanda and Jyotisa.
- Shiksha deals with pronunciation, Kalpa deals with rituals, *Vyakarana*

> Q.3. Which Buddhist council was held during the reign of Ashoka?
> Q.4. To the court of which king did Dhanvantri, the renowned physician, belong to?

deals with grammar, *Nirukta* deals with etymology, *Chhanda* deals with metre and *Jyotisha* deals with astronomy.
- There were six school of Indian Philósophy called *Shad Darshana*.
- *There were four Upavedas:*
  Dhanur veda (of *Yajur Veda*) deals with art of warfare;
  Gandharva veda (of *Sama Veda*) deals with art and music;
  Shilpa veda (of *Atharva Veda*) deals with architecture and
  Ayurveda (of *Rig Veda*) deals with medicines.

Growth of Buddhism and Jainism

As the Brahmins monopolised over the society, other castes started revolution against them, which resulted into the rise of several schools of thought.

The movement was spearheaded by Kshatriyas of Royal families of Magadha, which helped in propagation of Buddhism and Jainism.

Buddhism

- Founder of Buddhism was Gautam Siddharth, who was a Saka prince.
- He was born in 563 BC on *Vaishakha Poornima* day at Lumbini (near Kapilavastu in Nepal). His father was Suddhodana (a Saka ruler) and mother Mahamaya, who died after seven days of his birth. He was brought up by step-mother Gautami.
- He married at the age of 16, to Yashodhara, a cousin of the same age, and had a son named Rahula.
- He left palace at the age of 29, in search of truth (or renunciation).
- He attained enlightenment at the age of 35, at Gaya in Magadha (Bihar), under a Pipal tree.
- He delivered the first sermon at Sarnath and attained *mahaparinirvana* (death) at Khushi Nagar (Gorakhpur dist.) in 483 BC at the age of 80.

Doctirine of Buddhism

Some of the fundamentals of the teachings of Gautama Buddha are:

- *The Four Noble Truths*: (i) suffering is an inherent part of existence; (ii) the origin of suffering is ignorance; (iii) the main symptoms of that ignorance are attachment and craving; (iv) attachment and craving can be ceased by following an eightfold path, which will lead to the cessation of attachment and craving.
- *The Noble Eightfold Path is*: right understanding, right thought, right speech, right action, right livelihood, right effort, right mindfulness and right concentration.
- Nirvana is the state of being free from both suffering and the cycle of rebirth by following the eightfold path.
- Buddhism believes in ahimsa, law of Karma and existence of God.
- Buddhism is scripted in different forms, written in pali language.
- *Vinaya Pitaka* deals with rules of disciplines in Buddhist monasteries. *Sutta Pitaka* is the largest one and deals with collection of Buddha's sermons. *Abhidhamma Pitaka* deals with explanations of the philosophical principles of Buddhist religion.

Q.5. Which king built the statue of Gomateshwara at Sravanabelagola?

Q.6. In which language did Babur write his autobiography Babur Namah?

History of India

- *Mahavansh* and *Deepvansh* are other Buddhist texts, which provide information about the then Sri Lanka.
- *Jataks* are also the Buddhist texts, which are fables about different births of Buddha.

Jainism

- Jainism was propagated by non-brahmins. It was founded by Rishabha, the father of king Bharat.
- Jainism became a major religion under Bardhaman Mahavir.
- The first Tirthankara (Prophet or Guru) was Rishabhanath (emblem-Bull), twenty-third was Pashwanath (emblem-Snake) and the twenty-fourth was Mahavir (emblem-Lion).
- The main teachings of Pashwanath were non-injury, non-lying, non-stealing and non-possession.
- Mahavir adopted one more along with all these which was 'Brahmacharya' (celibacy).
- Mahavir was born to King Siddhartha and Queen Trishala on the thirteenth day under the rising moon of *Chaitra*.
- He was married to Yashoda and had a daughter, whose husband became his first disciple.
- At the age of 30, Mahavira renounced his home, gave up his worldly possessions and spent twelve years as an ascetic.
- He attained supreme knowledge (*kaivalay*) at the age of 43 on the tenth day of Vaishakha, outside the town of Jrimbhikgrama.
- Then he was called *Jaina* or *Jitendriya* and his followers were known as Jain.
- He died at the age of 72, at Pava, near Patna in 527 BC.

Doctrine of Jainism

Jainism believed in the following principles:

(i) Rejected the authority of vedas
(ii) Rejected the existence of God
(iii) Discarded the sacrifice and rituals
(iv) Attainment of salvation by believing in penance and dying of starvation
(v) Universal brotherhood
(vi) Belief in *ahimsa* in word, thought, action towards all living beings.

Some of the fundamental teachings of Mahavir are:

– To liberate one's self, Mahavir taught the necessity of right faith (*samyak-darshana*), right knowledge (*samyak-gyana*) and right conduct (*samyak-charitra*).
– At the heart of right conduct (for Jains) lies the five great vows:
  (i) Non-violence (*Ahimsa*) – to cause no harm to any living being;
  (ii) Truthfulness (*Satya*) – to speak the harmless truth only;
  (iii) Non-stealing (*Asteya*) – to take nothing not properly given;

Q.7. Name the last of the European powers which competed for commercial gains in the East.
Q.8. Who was the last Mughal emperor to sit on the Peacock Thorne?

(iv) Chastity (*Brahmacharya*) – to indulge in no sensual pleasure;
(v) Non-possession/Non-attachment (*Aparigraha*) – to detach completely from people, places and material things.
- The teachings of Jainism were compiled in 14 books called *puranas*, later these were converted into 12 books called *angas*, written in ardh-magadhi and prakrit dialects.
- Jains were divided into two groups – Digambara (they remain nude) and Shvetambaras (they wear white clothes) – in first Jain council held at Pataliputra.

Magadha Empire (Sixth Century to Fourth Century)

Magadha formed one of the sixteen Mahajanapadas or regions in ancient India. The core of the kingdom was located in the area of Bihar of south of the Ganges; its first capital was Rajgriha (modern Rajgir) then Pataliputra (modern Patna).

Haryanka Dynasty

Bimbisara (544–492 BC): He was the founder of the Haryanka dynasty. He expanded the Magadha kingdom by conquering Agra (east Bihar) and entering into matrimonial relation with Kosala, Vaishali and Madra. His capital was Girivraja (Rajgiri).

Ajatashatru (492–460 BC): Ajatashatru imprisoned and killed his father Bimbisara. Under his rule the dynasty reached its largest extent.

He extended Magadha empire by annexing the Lichchavi kingdom. Buddha died during his reign. He arranged first Buddhist council at Rajgriha in 483 BC under the chairmanship of Mehakassaapa.

Udayabhadra

The Mahavamsa text tells that Udayabhadra eventually succeeded his father, Ajatashatru, moving the capital of the Magadha kingdom to Pataliputra, which under the later Mauryan dynasty would become the largest city in the world.

Shishunaga Dynasty

Shishunaga (also called King Sisunaka) was the founder of the Shishunaga dynasty. He established the Magadha empire (in 430 BC). This empire, had its original capital in Rajgriha, later shifted to Pataliputra (in Bihar). The Shishunaga dynasty in its time was one of the largest empires of the Indian subcontinent.

Shishunaga Dynasty Rulers

(i) Shishunaga (430 BC) established the kingdom of Magadha.
(ii) Kakavarna (394–364 BC)
(iii) Kshemadharman (618–582 BC)
(iv) Kshatraujas (582–558 BC)
(v) Kalasoka had arranged second Buddhist council at Vaishali in 383 BC under Sabakami.

This dynasty was succeeded by the Nanda dynasty.

Q.9. Who introduced the Civil Services in India?
Q.10. Who built the famous 'Kirtistambha' at Chittor?
Q.11. In which year did Raja Ram Mohan Roy lay the foundation of 'Brahmo Samaj'?

Nanda Dynasty (344–323 BC)

This dynasty was founded by Mahapadma Nanda; it was the first non-Kshatriya dynasty. He added Kalinga to his empire.

Dhana Nanda, the eighth son of the founder and the last Nanda ruler was overthrown by Chandragupta Maurya. Alexander invaded India during this period.

Foreign Invasions

Cyrus of Persia was the first foreign conqueror to invade India; Darius I (522–486 BC), the great grandson of Cyrus annexed Indus Valley in 518 BC.

Darius III enlisted the Indian soldiers to fight against Alexander. The control of Persia became weak on the eve of Alexander's invasion.

Greek Invasion
Invasion by Alexander

- Alexander (356–323 BC) ascended the throne of Macedonia after the death of his father Philips in 334 BC. By 329 BC he annexed Persia and up to Afghanistan.
- He crossed Hindukush on May 327 BC and invaded India. At that time north-west India was ruled by small independent states like Taxila, Punjab (King of Porus), Gandharas, etc.
- In the battle of Hydapses (326 BC), Alexander crossed Hydapses (Jhelum) river and took Porus by surprise. Only Porus put up a tough fight against Alexander and other kings submitted meekly.
- Alexander moved towards river Beas with a view of annexing Magadha, but his soldiers refused to cross the river. Failing to persuade the soldiers, he ordered to retreat.
- The retreat began on October 326 BC. After reaching Babylon (Baghdad) he fell seriously ill and died on June 323 BC at the age of 33 only.

Maurya Dynasty (300–200 BC)
Chandragupta Maurya (322–298 BC)

- Chandragupta Maurya, the exiled general, founded the Maurya dynasty after overthrowing the last Nanda king Dhana Nanda with the help of Chanakya (known as Kautilya or Vishnugupta) to establish the Mauryan empire in 321 BC.
- He expanded this empire not only to most of the Indian subcontinent, but also pushed its boundaries into Persia and Central Asia, conquering the Gandhara region.
- He fought a long battle with Seluscus Nikator (a general of Alexander, who acquired the throne of Babylon after the death of Alexander) and with the treaty of 303 BC, he won the battle and trans-Indus region.
- During his reign Meghasthenes (a Greek ambassador) was sent by Seluscus to his court.
- Chandragupta embraced Jainism towards the end of his life and stepped down from throne for his son Bindusara.

Q.12. Who came to Jahangir's Court in AD 1608 with letter from James I of England to obtain trade facilities?
Q.13. Who founded the Servants of Indian Society?

Bindusara (Born on 320 BC; Ruled: 298–272 BC)

- Bindusara was the second Mauryan emperor after Chandragupta Maurya. During his reign, the empire expanded southwards up to Mysore.
- He had two sons, Sumana and Ashoka, who were the viceroys of Taxila and Ujjain.
- The Greeks called Bindusara Amitrochates or Allitrochades (derived from Sanskrit word 'Amitraghata' meaning slayer of enemies). He was also called *ajathasetru* (which means man having no enemies) in Sanskrit.
- He conquered sixteen states and extended the empire from sea to sea. The empire included the whole of India, except the region of Kalinga (modern Orissa) and the Dravidian kingdoms of the south.
- Deimachus, the Greek ambassador, visited his court.

Ashoka the Great (Born on: 304 BC; Ruled 268–232 BC)

- Ashoka was finally crowned in BC 268, four years after the death of his father Bindusara, by winning over other princes.
- Ashoka ruled almost the entire Indian subcontinent. His empire stretched from present-day Pakistan, Afghanistan in the west, to the present-day Bangladesh and the Indian state of Assam in the east, and as far south as the brahmagiri in Karnataka and peninsular part of southern India.
- He conquered Kalinga in 261 BC.
- He embraced Buddhism after witnessing the mass deaths of the war of Kalinga, which he himself had waged out of a desire for conquest.
- He was later appointed as *Dharma Mahapatras* to propagate Buddhism across Asia and established monuments marking several significant sites in the life of Gautama Buddha.
- He sent the missionaries to Ceylon, Burma and also sent his son Mahindra and daughter Sanghamitra to Ceylon.
- His inscriptions were written in brahmi, kharoshthi, armaic and greek languages.
- The emblem of India has been adopted from the Lion Capital of the Ashokan Pillar at Sarnath (Uttar Pradesh).
- The last Mauryan king was Brihadratha, who was killed by Pushymitra Shunga in 185 BC, and started Shunga Dynasty in Magadha.

Kingdom After Mauryan Empire

In north-west India Mauryan empire were succeeded by some dynasties of central Asia.

The Indo-Greeks: Greeks were the first to invade India, who were also known as 'Bactrian Greeks' (they ruled Bactria). The most famous Indo-Greek ruler was Menander (165–145 BC) also known as Milinda.

The Shakas or Scythians: (A branch of Iranian Shakas).

The Greeks were followed by Shakas. Vikramaditya, the king of Ujjain defeated Shakas in 57 BC and with this victory commenced the era of *Vikram Samvat*.

Q.14. Which is said to be the fifth veda?
Q.15. To which dynasty did Menandar, also known as Milinda, belong to?

History of India

The Parthians: They invaded India at the beginning of the Christian era. Gondophernes was their famous king, during whose rule St Thomas said to had visited India to propagate Christianity.

Kushan Empire (1–3 Century)

The empire was created by the Kushan branch of the Yuezhi confederation.

Kanishka was their most famous king. He started *Saka* era in AD 78. He patronised Buddhism and held the fourth Buddhist council in Kashmir. In eastern, central and Deccan India, Mauryan were succeeded by dynasties like Shungas, Kanvas and Satavahanas.

Shunga Dynasty: (184–75 BC) The founder was Pushyamitra Shunga. He was succeeded by Agnimitra (central character of Kalidas's *Malavikagnimitra*). It was a period of revival of Bhagvatism. Patanjali's *Mahabhasya, Yugasutra* were composed during this period. The last ruler of this dynasty was Devabhuti.

Kanva Dynasty: (75–30 BC) The founder of this dynasty was Vasudeva. Satavahanas succeeded this dynasty.

Satavahana Dynasty: (60 BC–AD 250) Simukha was the founder of this dynasty. They ruled the Deccan in the central India. Gautamiputra Satakarni was the famous ruler of this dynasty.

Southern Kingdom (Sangam Age)

The history of the Southern kingdom can be learnt from the Sangam literature. Sangam was the assembly of Tamil poets held under the royal patronage.

The Pandyas: Their capital was located at Madurai. They had trade links with Roman Empire.

The Cholas: Kaveripattanam was their capital. Chola king Elara conquered Sri Lanka. They maintained a navy.

The Cheras: Vanji was their capital. The famous ruler of this dynasty was Senguttuvan, who was also known as Red Chera.

Gupta Dynasty (AD 320–550)

The Gupta dynasty is known as the golden age of the ancient India.

Chandragupta I (AD 319–335)

The coronation of Chandragupta in AD 319 marked the beginning of Gupta era. He acquired the title of *Maharajadhiraj*.

Samudragupta (AD 335–375)

Known as the Napoleon of India, Samudragupta was the son of Chandragupta I. He was also called *Kaviraj*, as he had composed many poems. He was presented as playing lute (*Vina*) on his coins.

Chandragupta II (AD 380–413)

He acquired the title of *Vikramaditya* by defeating Rudrasimha, the king of Ujjain. His court was adorned with 'Nine Gems' (*Navaratnas*). Fahien, the Chinese pilgrim, visited India during his reign.

Q.16. During whose reign did the Mongols appear for the first time on Indian Shore?

Q.17. Where was the first Indus valley civilisation site discovered?

Contributions of Gupta Dynasty

- They issued gold coins.
- The Buddhist monastery, Nalanda, was established during the reign of Kumaragupta.
- Bhagavad Gita was written and history was presented as 10 incarnation of Vishnu.
- The famous statue of Buddha at Bamiyan (Afghanistan) and Ajanta paintings belong to this period.
- Great poet and dramatist Kalidas belongs to this period. Some of his works are *Abhigyana Shakuntalam, Kumarasambhavam, Meghaduttam, Malavikagnimitram, Ritusamhara, Raghuvansham,* etc. Other authors were Sudraka (written *Mrichchakatikam*), Bhairavi (written *Kiratarjuniya*), Vishnu Sharma (written *Panchatantra*).
- The great Mathematician Aryabhata wrote *Aryabhatiya* and *Suryasiddhanta*. His greatest contributions are his mentioning of the value of first nine numbers, use of zero, calculating the value of 'pie' and inventing algebra.
- Varahamihira wrote *Panchasidhantika* and *Brihatsamhita*.
- Dhanvntari, the great physician, lived during this period.

Other Dynasties and Rulers

Harsha Vardhana (606–647)

The last hindu king of northern India, Harsha Vardhana belonged to Pushyabhuti family. Kannauj was the capital of his kingdom. He wrote three plays – *Priyadarshika, Ratnavali* and *Nagananda*. Banabhatta, his court poet, wrote *Harshacharita* and *Kadambari*.

Hieun Tsang, the Chinese traveller visited his court.

Chalukyas (AD 6–12 century)

The Chalukyas of Karnataka can be classified into three eras: (i) Chalukyas of Badami (early Western era), (ii) Chalukyas of Kalyani (later Western era), (iii) Chalukyas of Vengi (Eastern era).

Pulakesin I was the founder of Chalukya of Badami. Pulakesin II was its famous ruler.

Rashtrakutas (AD 735-973): They succeeded the Chalukyas. Its founder was Danti Durga. Their king Krishna I built the Kailash Temple at Ellora.

Pallavas: Shimhavishnu was the founder and their capital was Kanchi. Narasimhavarman founded the town Mamallapuram (Mahabalipuram).

Gangas (of Orissa): Narasimhadeva built the Sun temple at Konark and Anatavarman Ganga built the Jagannath temple at Puri.

Cholas: It was founded by Rajaraja I and its capital was Tanjore. He built Rajarajeshwari temple (Brihadeshwar Shiva Temple) there. The last ruler was Rajendra III. Modern concept of Panchayatiraj has been borrowed from the local self-government system of the Cholas. Nataraj, dancing figure of Lord Shiva, belongs to this period.

Palas (of Bengal): It was founded by Gopala and their capital was Monghyr. Other rulers of this dynasty were Dharmapala (he founded Vikramasila University and revived Nalanda University) and Mahipala.

Q.18. Who transformed the Sikhs into a military community?
Q.19. In which language Sangama Classics were written?

Pratiharas: Its founder was Nagabhatta I and their famous ruler was Bhoja.
Yadavas: Singhara and Ramachandra were its major ruler.
Hindu Kingdom of Vijayanagar: The kingdom lay in Deccan, Harihara and Bukka were its co-founders.
Krishnadeva Raj was their most famous ruler.
Rajputs: They were divided into four clans: (i) Pratihara (South Rajasthan), (ii) Chauhans (East Rajasthan), (iii) Chalukyas or Solankis (Kathiawar) and (iv) Parmars or Pawars (Malwa).
Chandalas built Mahadev Temple at Khuraho in AD 1000. Solankis of Gujarat built Dilwara Temple at Mount Abu.

MEDIEVAL INDIA

This includes the invasion of muslims, the establishment of Sultanate of Delhi to the Mughal Empire.

Invasion of Muslims

Md. Bin Quasim of Iraq was the first Arab to invade India. Mahmud of Ghazni raided India 17 times from AD 1001 to 1027. He attacked Somnath Temple in the year 1025. He patronised Firdaus, a Persian poet, who wrote *Shanama*, and Alberuni, a scholar who wrote *Tahqiq-I-Hind*.

Muhammad Ghori of Afghanistan fought the first battle of *Tarain* (1191) against Prithviraj Chauhan and was defeated. But in second battle of *Tarain* (1192), he defeated Prithviraj and captured Delhi, which led to the foundation of the Sultanate of Delhi, which is the beginning of Muslim rule in India.

Delhi Sultanate

Five dynasties ruled Delhi over a period of more than 300 years. These are:

1. Ilbari or Slave Dynasty (1206–90)
2. Khalji Dynasty (1290–1320)
3. Tughlaq Dynasty (1320–1414)
4. Sayyid Dynasty (1414–51)
5. Lodhi Dynasty (1451–1526)

Slave Dynasty (1206–1290)

The founder was Qutab-ud-din Aibak (1206–10) who laid the foundation of Qutab Minar and built 'Adhai-Din-Ka Jhopra' (Ajmer). Iltutmish (1210–36) formed Chalisa, a group of 40 Turkish nobles and introduced S*ilver Tanka* and *Copper Jitat*. Raziya Sultan (1236–39) was the first and only women ruler. Balban (1266–86) was a member of Chalisa, who introduced *Sijah* or *Paibos* practice and started the festival of *Nauraj*.

Khalji Dynasty (1290–1320)

The founder, Jalaluddin Khalji (1290–96), was killed and succeeded by his nephew Alauddin Khalji. He had a permanent army and introduced market control.

Q.20. In Medieval India for what purpose was **Mansabdari** *System introduced?*
Q.21. What does the first discourse of Buddha at Deer Park in Sarnath called?

The poet, musician and historian **Amir Khusrau** served seven rulers of Delhi sultanate. He invented *sitar* and was given the tittle *Tuti-I-Hind*.

Tughlaq Dynasty (1320–1414)

Ghiyasuddin Tughlaq (1320–25) was the founder of this dynasty. Muhammad Bin Tughlaq (1325–51) introduced token coins of brass and copper; he set up department of agriculture – Dewan-i-Kohi. Famous traveller Iban Batuta came to Delhi during his period and had written *Satarnamah*.

Firoz Shah Tughlaq (1351–88) imposed four new taxes: *Kharaj* (a land tax), *Jaziya* (a tax by non muslim), *Zakat* (tax on property) and *Khams* (one-fifth booty captured wars).

He built the towns of Hissar, Firozabad, Firozshah Kotla. Barani, his court historian wrote *Tarikh-i-Firozshahi* and *Fatwa-i-Jahandari*.

Timur the Lame, a mongol leader, invaded Delhi (in December 1398) during the rule of Nasiruddin Muhmmad Tughlaq.

Sayyid Dynasty (1414–51)

Khizr Khan was its founder and its other rulers were Mubarak Shah, Muhammad Shah and Alauddin Alam Shah.

Lodhi Dynasty (1451–1526)

Its founder was Bahlol Lodhi (1451–88).

Sikandar Lodhi (1489–1517) and Ibrahim Lodhi (1517–26) were its other rulers. Babur defeated Ibrahim Lodhi in the Battle of Panipat in 1526 and that was the end of the Sultanate of Delhi.

Religious Movements

The Sufis: The Chishti, the Suharawadi and the Silsilah of Firdausi were three major orders of Sufis in India. The relationship between the teacher or *Pir* and his disciple or *Murid* was an important aspect of Sufism.

The Chishti: It was established by Khwaja Muinuddin Chishti (Ajmer). Its other saints were Nizamuddin.

Auliya, Nasiruddin *Chirag-I-Delhi*, Barani and Amir Khusrau.

The Suharawadi: Its famous saints were Shaikh Shihabuddin and Hamid-ud-din-Nagry. It was popular in Punjab and Sindh region.

The Silsilah: It was established by Firdausi and was popular in Bihar.

The Bhakti Movement (Fifteenth century): Ramananda, a worshiper of Lord Rama, was the first Bhakti saint. Others were Namadeva (a tailor), Kabir (a weaver), Sadhana (a butcher), Ravidas (a cobbler) and Sena (a barber).

Chaitanya popularised the Krishna cult. Tulsi Das was born in 1532 in Varanasi. He wrote *Rama Charita Manas*, *Vinay Patrika*, *Gitawali*, etc.

The Mughal Empire

Babur (1526–30)

- He defeated Ibrahim Lodhi in the first Battle of Panipat in 1526 and established the Mughal empire.

Q.22. What title did Harsh assume after coming to the throne?

Q.23. The Lucknow Pact was concluded in December 1916 between...?

History of India 13

- He defeated Rana Sang of Mewar in Battle of Khanua in 1527.
- He died in 1530 and was buried in Aram Bagh (Kabul).
- His autobiography *Tazuk-i-Baburi* was written in Turkish language.

Humayun (1530–40 and 1555–56)

- He was defeated by Sher Shah in the Battle of Chausa (1539) and again in the Battle of Bilgram (also known as Battle of Kanauj in 1540), and remained exiled from India till 1555.
- He regained the throne in 1555 and died in 1556. His tomb is the prototype of Taj Mahal. His sister Gulbadan Begum wrote *Humayun-nama*.

Akbar (1556–1605)

- Born at Amarkot in 1542, Akbar was coronated at the age of 14.
- He fought the second *Battle of Panipat* in 1556 against Hemu, and emerged victorious.
- He defeated the Rajputs led by Rana Pratap in the *Battle of Haldighati* in 1576. He conquered Malwa (1561), Gandwana (1564) and Gujarat (1573), and built the Buland Darwaza at Fathepur Sikri to commemorate this victory.
- Akbar constructed the royal city of Fatehpur Sikri in 1570 and served as the empire's capital from 1571 until 1585.
- He introduced Mansabdari system (under this system the army and bureaucracy were organised in order of rank), Zabti system (for land revenue) which is also known as Todar Mal Bandobast and Dahasals system (a revenue on crops). He abolished Jiziya (1564) and formulated a new order *Tauhit-e-Illahi (Din-e- Illahi)* or universal religion. He built Agra Fort and his own tomb at Sikandara (Agra). Abul Fazal wrote *Ain-I-Akbari* and *Akbarnama*.

Jahangir (1605–27)

- He executed fifth Sikh guru Arjun Dev, who helped Khusro (Jahangir's son, later known as Sahajahan) in the rebellion against him.
- He married Merh-un-Nisa (Nur Jahan) in 1611. Captain Hawkins (1608–11) and Sir Thomas Roe (1615–19) visited his court and he allowed British to establish factories at Surat.
- Jahangir built Moti Masjid at Agra and his Mausoleum at Shahdara (Lahore).
- He wrote his memoir *Tuzuk-I-Jahangiri* in Persian language.

Shahjahan (1627–58)

- He annexed Ahmadnagar (1633) and concluded treaties with Bijapur and Golkonda (1636). He was defeated and imprisoned by his son Aurangzeb (1658) and later died in 1666.
- He built Taj Mahal (Agra), Moti Masjid (Agra), Jama Masjid (Delhi), Red Fort (Delhi) and Shalimar Bagh (Lahore).
- He built the famous Peacock throne.

Aurangzeb (1658–1707)

- He came to power by murdering his three brothers (Dara, Shuja and Murad) and imprisoning his father Sahajahan.

Q.24. To probe which incident was the Hunter Commission appointed by the British?
Q.25. With whom the Indus Valley people had trade relation?

- Various rebellions took place during his reign. He reimposed *Jaziya* and banned *Nauraz* (singing and dancing in court). He was called as Zinda Pir or Darvesh.
- He built Moti Masjid (Delhi) and Bibi-Ka- Mokbara (Aurangabad).

Later Mughal Rulers
- Aurangzeb's successors were weak and incapable rulers, which led to the fall of the Mughal empire.
- Nadir Shah, a Persian king, invaded India during the rule of Mohammed Shah and took away the 'Peacock thorne' and Kohinoor diamond.
- Bahadur Shah II (1837–57) was the last Mughal ruler. He was deported to Rangoon after the 1857 revolt.

Regional Uprising

The Sikhs
- Guru Angad was the successor of Guru Nanak and he invented the gurumukhi script.
- Guru Ramdas was the founder of Amritsar city.
- Guru Arjun Dev compiled Adigranth and built the Swarna Mandir. Aurangzeb executed Guru Teg Bahudur (the ninth Guru) in 1675.
- Guru Govind Singh (tenth and last Guru) organised sikhs into a military force and called them *khalsa* (1699); later he was killed by an Afghan.

The Marathas
- Marathas became powerful under the rule of Shivaji. Shivaji was imprisoned by Aurangzeb, but he managed to escape and was coronated in 1674 at Raigarh. He died in 1680 and was succeeded by his son Sambhaji, who was executed by Aurangzeb.
- Rajaram, brother of Sambhaji became the ruler. After death of Rajaram, Shivaji II (son of Rajaram, who was a minor at that time) was declared ruler by his mother Tarabai.

Peshwas
- Balaji Vishwanathan became powerful and established the Peshwas as hereditary.
- Baji Rao came to power and Maratha power reached its zenith. He began the system of confederacy and there by several Maratha families became powerful in different parts of India: (i) Gaekwad at Baroda, (ii) Bhasale in Nagpur, (iii) Holkar in Indore, (iv) Scindia in Gwalior and (v) Peshwa at Pune.

MODERN INDIA

The history of modern India begins with the ascent of Europeans to the British rule leading to the Independence of India.

Portuguese: They were the first to discover the sea route to India. Vasco da Gama reached Calicut via the Cape of Good Hope on 17 May 1498. Alfonso d' Albuquerque captured Goa.

Q.26. Which is the first month of Saka Calender?
Q.27. Which battle led to the firm foundation of Muslim Rule in India?
Q.28. Who is referred to as the 'father of local self-government'?

Dutch: In 1602 Dutch East India Company was formed and they set their first factory in Masulipatnam in 1605, followed by more factories in Pulicat, Surat, etc. They were defeated by British in the Battle of Bedera in 1759.

English: The English East India Company was established in 1600 and they set up their first factory at Surat in 1608. Later they established their trading centre at Bombay, Calcutta and Madras.

Danish: In 1616 Danish East India Company was formed and they established their settlements at Serampur (Bengal).

French: They established their first factory at Surat in 1664. They were defeated by British in Carnatic wars.

British Conquest of India

At the beginning the British had to face challenges from the Dutch and French to establish their rule in India. It was Robert Clive who laid the British foundation in India.

Carnatic Wars

There were three Carnatic wars fought between the French and British.

In the first Carnatic war (1745–48), the French were defeated and Madras was restored to the English.

In the second Carnatic war (1749–54), Arcot was captured by the British.

In the third Carnatic war (1758–63), the French were defeated in the Battle of Wandiwash and British gained the control over south India.

Conquest of Bengal

In 1756 Colonel Robert Clive and Admiral Watson captured Calcutta. But it was the Battle of Plassey and Battle of Buxar that led to the British conquest of Bengal.

Battle of Plassey (1757): The British led by Robert Clive defeated Bengal ruler Siraj-ud-Daula. This marked the 'drain of wealth' from India to British.

Battle of Buxar (1764): It was fought between the British and the triple alliance of Nawab Mir Qasim of Bengal, Nawab Shuja-ud-Daula of Awadh and Mughal Emperor Shah Alam. The alliance was defeated.

Anglo-Mysore War

First War (1766–69): The British in the alliance with the Nizam and Marathas fought against Haider Ali (ruler of Mysore). The war ended in a draw and a Defensive Treaty was concluded.

Second War (1780–84): Haider Ali allied with Nizam and Marathas and fought against the British. Haider Ali died and Tipu Sultan succeeded him at the throne. The war ended with a draw and Treaty of Mangalore was concluded by Tipu and Lord McCartney.

Third War (1790–92): Tipu Sultan defeated British in 1790 and Treaty of Seringapatam (1792) was signed between Tipu Sultan and Lord Cornwallis.

Fourth War (1799): Tipu was defeated and killed in the war of 1799. Major part of Tipu's kingdom was annexed to British India.

Q.29. When did British shift their capital from Calcutta to Delhi?
Q.30. In which session of Congress, it split into Moderates and Extremists?
Q.31. Who laid the foundation of the Forward Block?

Anglo-Maratha War: There were three Anglo-Maratha war fought over a period of 1775 to 1818.

All the territories of Peshwa were annexed by British and Bombay Presidency was created.

British Rule
Governor Generals

Warren Hastings (1773–85): He was the first Governor General of India. He introduced Regulating Act of 1773, thereby ending the Dual government of Bengal and also introduced Pitt's India Act of 1784.

He founded the Asiatic Society of Bengal with Sir William Jones in 1744. He wrote the introduction of the English translation of *The Gita* by Charles Wilkins.

Lord Cornwallis (1786–93): He introduced the permanent revenue settlement or Zamindari System in Bengal in 1793. He also introduced the system of Civil Service in India.

Sir John Shore (1793–98): He played an important role in the introduction of the Permanent Settlement in 1793.

Lord Wellesley (1798–1805): He introduced the system of Subsidiary Alliance (1798), fought fourth Mysore war and established the Madras Presidency.

Lord Minto I (1806–13): Vellore Mutiny (1806) took place during his time. He concluded the Treaty of Amritsar with Ranjit Singh in 1809.

Lord Hastings (1813–23): During his tenure the third Maratha war was fought. He also created the Bombay Presidency in 1818. He introduced Ryotwari Settlement in Madras Presidency in 1820.

Lord Amherst (1823–28): During his time in India the first Burmese war (1824–26) was fought and Bharatpur (1826) came under the British Empire.

Lord William Bentinck (1828–35): He brought about social reform by prohibition of *Sati* in 1829 and suppression of *Thuggee* (1829–35). He introduced English as the medium of higher education in 1833 on Macaulay's recommendation. Charter Act of 1833 was introduced.

Sir Charles Metcalf (1835–36): He abolished all restriction on press.

Lord Auckland (1836–42): First Afghan War was fought while he was the Governor General.

Lord Ellenborough (1842–44): First Sikh war took place (1845-46) during his regime.

Lord Hardinge I (1844–48): He prohibited female infanticide.

Lord Dalhousie (1848–56): He introduced Charter Act of 1853 and applied the Doctrine of Lapse. He introduced the first Railway in India (first train line between Bombay and Thane), first telegraph line (Calcutta-Agra) and Postal System in 1853. He established the Public Works Department and introduced Widow Remarriage Act, 1856.

Viceroys of India

Lord Canning (1858–62): He was the last Governor General and first Viceroy.

Sepoy Mutiny took place during his time and the empire of India was passed on to the Crown in1858. The universities of Calcutta, Bombay and Madras were established in 1857.

Q.32. In which region did the Moplah rebellion of 1921 break out?

Q.33. In which session of Indian National Congress, the Non-Cooperation Movement was adopted?

History of India

Lord Elgin I (1862–63): He died in 1862; Sir Napier and Sir Denison carried out his administration.

Lord Lawrence (1863–69): He established the High Courts at Calcutta, Bombay and Madras in 1865.

Lord Mayo (1869–72): The Rajkot College in Kathiawar and the Mayo College of Ajmer were established by Lord Mayo. He organised the Statistical Survey of India. He was assassinated in office by a convict in the Andamans in 1872.

Lord Northbrook (1872–76): When he was in the office, Prince of Wales visited India in 1875.

Lord Lytton (1876–80): He organised the Delhi Durbar in 1877 to entitle Queen Victoria *Kaiser-i-Hind*. He passed the Vernacular Press Act and Arms Act of 1878.

Lord Ripon (1880–84): First census of India took place in 1881 (254 million). He introduced local self-government; removed the Vernacular Press Act; appointed Educational Commission under Sir William Hunter in 1882 and passed the Ilbert Bill in 1883.

Lord Dufferin (1884–88): Indian National Congress was founded in 1885 during his tenure.

Lord Lansdowne (1888–94): He appointed Durand Commission to define the line between British India and Afghanistan (now between Pakistan and Afghanistan) in 1893.

Lord Elgin II (1894–99): Two British officers were assassinated by the Chapekar brothers in 1897.

Lord Curzon (1899–1905): Many things happened during his tenure which include passing of Indian University Act, 1904 on the recommendation of Thomais Raleigh Commission; passing of Indian Coinage and Paper Currency Act, 1899 and Ancient Monument Preservation Act, 1904. Last, but not the least, in 1905 Bengal Partition also took place while Curzon was in the office.

Lord Minto II (1905–10): Morley-Minto Reform or Indian Council Act, 1909 was passed; it envisaged a separate electorate for Muslims.

Lord Hardinge II (1910–16): Partition of Bengal was cancelled in 1911; Delhi was made capital in place of Calcutta in 1912; coronation Durbar of King George (V) and Queen Marry at Delhi in 1911.

Lord Chelmsford (1916–21): During the span of these five years August Declaration (1917) and Government of India Act, 1919 or Montagu-Chelmsford reforms were declared; Rowlatt Act, 1919 was passed; and Jallianwala Bagh Massacre took place on 13 April 1919.

Lord Reading (1921–26): Major events that took place during his tenure are – cancellation of Rowlatt Act, withdrawal of Non-Cooperation Movement by Gandhi due to the 'Chauri Chaura' incident on 5 February 1922.

Lord Irwin (1926–31): Simon Commission visited India in 1928 and first Round Table Conference was held in England in 1930.

Lord Willingdon (1931–36): Three major events that took place during Lord Willingdon's time are second and third Round Table Conference being held in 1931 and 1932 respectively, and passing of Government of India Act, 1935.

Lord Linlithgow (1936–43): The Forward Block was formed by Subhas Bose in 1939; outbreak of World War II (1939); August Offer

Q.34. 'A safety valve for the escape of great and growing forces generated by our own actions was urgently needed' – who said this regarding Indian National Congress?

Q.35. Who founded the Gaddar Party?

was made by Linlithgow in 1940 and was rejected by the Congress and Gandhiji started 'Satyagraha'. Cripps Mission (1942) offered dominion status to India and Quit India Movement (1942) Resolution was passed.

Lord Wavell (1944–47): He organised the 'Shimla Conference' in 1945. INA trials and the Naval Mutiny took place in 1946. Cabinet Mission Plan was set up on 16 May 1946 and Interim Government was formed by the Congress in 1946.

Lord Mountbatten (March 1947– June 1948): He was the first Governor General of free India. Partition of India was declared by the June 3 Plan of Mountbatten on 4 July 1947. He was succeeded by C Rajagopalachari as the last Governor General of free India.

Constitutional Developments

Regulating Act of 1773: With the passing of this Act Dual Government of Bengal ended. Governor of Bengal became the Governor General of British India.

The Supreme Court was established in Calcutta.

Pitt's India Act of 1784: A Board of Control, constituting of six members, was established to supervise and control of India.

Charter Act of 1830: It threw open Indian trade to all British subjects. But company's monopoly of trade in Tea and trade with China was not distributed.

Charter Act of 1833: Free trade was established and company's monopoly in Tea and trade with China was ended.

The Governor General-in-Council was given the power to make laws for British India.

Charter Act of 1853: Direct recruitment to the ICS began through a competitive examination. Additional members included in Governor General's Council, which act as the Legislative Council.

Government of India Act of 1858: Rule of British crown began in India with passing of this Act. A post of Secretary of States for India was created with a 15 men council to assist him. Governor General of India was made the Viceroy and he was assisted by an executive council.

Indian Council Act of 1861: The portfolio system was introduced in Viceroy's executive Council. Legislative Councils were established in various provinces like Madras, Bombay and Bengal.

Morley Minto Act or Indian Council Act, 1904: Direct election was introduced to the Legislative Council. Separate electorates introduced for Muslims.

Government of India Act, 1919: With the introduction of this Act Dyarchy system was introduced in the provinces; provincial subjects were divided into 'Reserved Subjects' (like police, jails, land revenue, Irrigation, etc., to be administered by Governor and its executive Council) and 'Transport Subjects' (Like education, local self government, public health, etc., to be looked after by Governor and his ministers).

The central legislature was made bi-cameral.

The High Commissioner of India was appointed at London.

Government of India Act, 1935: This act made the provision for the establishment of 'All India Federation' consisting of British provinces and princely states. Provincial autonomy was introduced; Provincial legislatures were made bi-cameral in six provinces (Bengal, Madras, Bombay, UP, Bihar and Assam).

Q.36. In which session, did INC declare Complete Independence as its goal?

Q.37. Name the place from where the first war of Independence in 1857 started.

Separate electorate extended to Sikhs, Europeans, Indian-Christians and Anglo-Indians. A federal Court was established at Delhi in 1937.

Socio-cultural Reforms

- Raja Ram Mohan Roy founded *Brahmo Samaj* in 1828. He opposed *Sati Pratha*, casteism and advocated Widow Remarriage.
- Keshab Chandra started *Sangat Sabha* and *Prathana Samaj*.
- MG Ranade founded the *Prathana Sabha*.
- Swami Dayanand founded *Arya Samaj* in 1875.
- Swami Vivekananda (1863–1902) founded Ramakrishna Mission in 1897. He attained the Parliament of Religion at Chicago in 1893.
- Young Bengal Movement was founded by Henry Louis Vivian Derozio.
- *Satya Shodhak Samaj* was founded by Jyotiba Phule in 1873.
- Madam HP Blavatsky began the movement of Theosophical Society in US in 1875. In India it was popularised by Annie Besant (who was also the president of this society in 1907) and she founded the Central Hindu College in 1898.

INDIAN FREEDOM STRUGGLE

Revolt of 1857

India's first war of Independence is also famously known as Sepoy Mutiny.

Causes

- Through Doctrine of Lapse, many states were annexed to British, and Tittles and pensions of royals were suspended.
- Sepoys were mistreated and discriminated in payment and promotions.
- Levying of heavy taxes, eviction and destruction of handicrafts industry due to one-way free trade policy of the British caused dissatisfaction among the Indians.
- But the most immediate cause that caused the mutiny was the introduction of the new Enfield riffle with greased cartridges (supposedly having a coating made of fat from cows and pigs).

Revolution

- Revolution in Delhi was led by the leadership of Bahadur Shah II and General Bakht Khan.
  Revolt was suppressed by John Nicholson and Lt Hudson.
- In Kanpur, leaders were Nana Saheb, Rao Sahib and Tantia Tope. Here Campbell and Havelock suppressed the revolt.
- Begum of Awadh (Hazrat Mahal) and Ahmadullah led the revolt in Lucknow, and was suppressed by Campbell and Havelock.
- Rani Lakshmibai of Jhansi was defeated by Sir Hugh Rose.
- The revolt was completely suppressed by the end of 1858.

Q.38. To protest against what Gandhiji founded Satyagraha Sabha in 1919?
Q.39. Who established the Indian Independence League?

Causes of Failure

Hostility of many native rulers; non-participation of Bengal and Madras; lack of discipline, common plan of action and centralised leadership were some of the causes of the failure of the mutiny.

Result

The direct result of the revolt was the end of the company's rule and the administration was transferred to the British Crown.

National Movements

Indigo Revolt of Bengal (1859–60): The peasants of Bengal were forced to grow indigo plants by the Europeans. Bishnucharan Biswas and Digambar Biswas played prominent role in the resistance against the planters.

The Indian National Congress (INC): It was formed by A O Hume, an English retired civil servant, in 1885 with a purpose to provide 'a safety valve' to the growing discontent of the educated Indians. First session of the INC was held in Bombay under the presidentship of W C Banerjee.

Swadeshi Movement (1905): In the Banaras session of INC in 1905, which was chaired by president G K Gokhale, the first call for Swadeshi Movement was made. Lal, Bal, Pal and Aurobindo Ghosh played important role.

Muslim League (1906): Aga Khan, Nawab Salimullah of Dhaka and Nawab Mohsin-ul Mulk set up the league in 1906.

Swaraj (1906): The INC under Dadabhai Naoroji called for Swaraj (Self-Government) in December 1906 at Calcutta Session.

Division in INC (1907): In 1907, the INC split into two groups – the Extremists and the Moderates – at the Surat session. Extremists were led by Lal, Bal and Pal, while the moderates were by G K Gokhale.

Moderates: Important leaders of this group were Dadabhai Naoroji, M G Ranade, Surendranath Banerjee, Badruddin Tyabji, G K Gokhle, Rash Behari Bose, etc. Their objectives were to raise the issue of reform in the legislative council, opportunity for Indians in the Public Service, imposition of import duties on cotton goods, grant of self-government within the British rule, etc.

Their method of revolution was peaceful struggle. They worked through meetings, resolutions and petitions.

Extremists: Bal Gangadhar Tilak in Maharashtra, Bipin Chandra Pal and Aurobindo Ghosh in Bengal and Lala Lajpat Rai in Punjab led the extremist group. Their objective was attainment of Swaraj or complete Independence. They resorted to non-cooperation, boycott of foreign goods and promotion Swadeshi.

They gave importance to the inclusion of mass in the national movement for that they emphasized on the promotion of national education among the masses.

Ghadar Party (1913): It was formed by Lala Hardayal, Sohan Sing Bhakkna and Tarakanath Das. Its Head Quarter was at San Francisco.

Home Rule Movement (1916): It was started by B G Tilak and Annie Besant with the objective of self-government for India in the British Empire.

Q.40. Who was the first woman president of Indian National Congress?

Q.41. Who was the Congress President when India became free?

During this movement Tilak gave the slogan: 'Swaraj is my birth right and I will have it.'

Revolutionary Activities:
- Revolutionaries like Sachindra Nath Sanyal, Jogesh Chandra Chartterjee, Ramprasad Bismil, Bhagat Singh, Sukhdev and Chandrasekhar Azad set up Hindustan Socialist Republic Association (HSRA).
- They carried out a dacoity on the Kakori bound train on the Saharanpur- Lucknow railway line on 9 August 1925.
- Bhagat Singh with his colleagues shot dead Saunders (who had ordered the Lahore lathicharge, where Lala Lajpat Roy died) on 17 December. On 8 April 1929, Bhagat Singh and Batukeshwar Dutt threw a bomb in Central Assembly.
- On 23 March 1931 Bhagat Singh, Rajguru and Sukhdev were hanged.
- In 1929, Jatin Das died in Lahore jail after 63 days of fasting in protest against horrible conditions in Jail.
- Surya Sen master minded the Chittagong Armoury in 1930. In 1931 Chandrasekhar Azad shot himself at Alfred Park in Allahabad.

Lucknow Pact (1916): Signed by INC and ML, both demanded dominion status for India.

Rowlatt Act (1919): This Act empowered Government to arrest an imprison suspects without trial.

Jallianwala Bagh Massacre (1919): On 13 April 1919, General O' Dyer fired at the people who were assembled in the Jallianwala Bagh, Amritsar over protest against the arrest of the local leaders.

Hunter Commission was appointed to inquire into it.

Sardar Udham Singh killed O' Dyer on 13 March 1940 at London.

Khilafat Movement (1920): Mohammed Ali and Shaukat Ali started the movement in protest against the mistreatment of British on Turkey.

Non-Cooperation Movement (1921–22): INC in its Calcutta session passed the resolution in September 1920 to start the Non-Cooperation Movement. The movement started in January 1921.

Moplah Rebellion (1921): The Muslim Moplah peasants of Malabar (Kerala) rebelled against the Hindu Zamidaars and the British Government. As many as 2,337 rebels were killed and many were injured.

Chauri Chaura Incident (1922): Congress decided to launch Civil Disobedience Movement at the Allahabad Session in December 1921. But a mob attacked the police and burnt 22 policemen at Chauri-Chaura (near Gorakhpur) on 5 February 1922. Gandhiji withdrew Non-Cooperation movement on 12 February 1922 due to this incident.

Swaraj Party (1923): Motilal Nehru, C R Das and N C Kelkar formed Swaraj Party on 1 January 1923. The party dissolved in 1926 with the death of C R Das.

Simon Commission (1927): Indian leaders opposed the Simon Commission which came to India in order to introduce further reforms and extensions of Parliamentary democracy. While protesting against the commission, Lala Lajpat Rai died in a lathicharge at Lahore.

Q.42. Which Acts gave representation to Indians for the first time in legislature?
Q.43. Who is known as 'Sher-e-Punjab'?

Bardoli Movement (1928): It was a 'No Revenue' Campaign by the Bardoli (a district in Gujarat) peasants under the leadership of Sardar Vallabhbhai Patel.

Lahore Session (1929): Under the presidentship of J L Nehru, the INC declared 'Purna Swaraj'.

The newly adopted Tricolour flag was unfurled on 31 December 1929, and 26 January 1930 was fixed as the first Independence Day to be celebrated every year.

Dandi March (1930): On 12 March 1930, Gandhiji started his March from Sabarmati Ashram to Dandi to break the Salt Law imposed by the British. On 6 April 1930, he picked a handful of salt and started the Civil Disobedience movement. When he was arrested, Sarojini Naidu led the movement.

First Round Table Conference (1930): It was held on 12 November 1930 in London to discuss Simon Commission report.

Gandhi-Irwin Pact (1931): A pact was signed between Gandhji and the Governor General Lord Irwin in March 1931. As a result Congress withdrew Civil Disobedience Movement and Government on its parts released Political prisoners and permitted to make salt for the persons residing within the certain distance of the sea coast.

Second Round Table Conference (1931): It was held between Gandhiji and British P M Ramsay Mcdonald.

Poona Pact (1932): According to this pact, seats reserved for the depressed classes in the Provincial Legislature were increased. Third Round Table Conference was held in 1932, which did not bring out any result.

Government of India Act, 1935: It was passed on the basis of Simon Commission report. A federal type government was introduced.

Demand for Pakistan (1940): Muslim League in its Lahore session raised a demand for Pakistan in March 1940 under Jinnah's leadership.

Quit India Movement (1942): On 8 August 1942, the resolution of Quit India Movement was passed in Bombay. Gandhi asked the British to quit India and gave the slogan 'Do or die' to his country men.

Indian National Army (INA): In 1942 Subhas Chandra Bose formed Azad Hind Fauj (Indian National Army) in Singapore and gave the call 'Dilli Chalo'. INA had three fighting brigades, named after Gandhi, Azad and Nehru and one women force named after Rani Jhansi. Its headquarters were at two places: Singapore and Rangoon.

Cabinet Mission Plan (1946): The Cabinet mission comprising Lord Lawrence, Sir Stafford Cripps and A V Alexander visited India. The election of Constituent Assembly was held in July 1936. On 2 September 1946, an interim Government was formed.

Formation of Constituent Assembly (1946): On 9 December 1946, the Constituent Assembly met and Dr Rajendra Prasad was elected its President.

Mountbatten Plan (3 June 1947): The conflict between INC and ML was solved with the 'Mountbatten Plan'. He laid down the detailed plan regarding the partition of India. British Government passed the Indian Independence Act in July 1947.

Partition of India (1947): India was partitioned on 15 August 1947 into India and Pakistan on the basis of Mountbatten Plan. Lord Mountbatten was appointed Governor General of free India and M A Jinha as first Governor General of Pakistan.

Q.44. Who introduced 'Permanent Settlement' in Bengal?
Q.45. Between whom the first Battle of Panipat was fought?
Q.46. With whom did Gandhi sign the Poona Pact?

India after Independence: Pt Nehru became the first Prime minister of India. On 30 January 1948 Gandhiji was assassinated by Nathuram Vinayak Godse.

On 26 January 1950 India became republic and Dr Rajendra Prasad became the first President and Dr S Radhakrishnan the first Vice-President.

SESSIONS OF INDIAN NATIONAL CONGRESS

Year	Venue	President
1885	Bombay	W C Banerjee
1886	Calcutta	Dadabhai Naoroji
1887	Madras	Badruddin Tyabji
1888	Allahabad	George Yule
1889	Bombay	Sir William Wedderburn
1890	Calcutta	Sir Pherozeshah Mehta
1891	Nagpur	P Anandacharlu
1892	Allahabad	Womesh Chandra Bonnerjee
1893	Lahore	Dadabhai Naoroji
1894	Madras	Alfred Webb
1895	Poona	Surendranath Banerjea
1896	Calcutta	Rahimtulla M Sayani
1897	Amraoti	Sir C Sankaran Nair
1898	Madras	Ananda Mohan Bose
1899	Lucknow	Romesh Chunder Dutt
1900	Lahore	Sir Narayan Ganesh Chandavarkar
1901	Calcutta	Sir Dinshaw Edulji Wacha
1902	Ahmedabad	Surendranath Banerjea
1903	Madras	Lalmohan Ghosh
1904	Bombay	Sir Henry Cotton
1905	Benares	Gopal Krishna Gokhale
1906	Calcutta	Dadabhai Naoroji
1907	Surat	Rashbihari Ghosh
1908	Madras	Rashbihari Ghosh
1909	Lahore	Pandit Madan Mohan Malaviya
1910	Allahabad	Sir William Wedderburn
1911	Calcutta	Pandit Bishan Narayan Dar
1912	Bankipur	Rao Bahadur Raghunath Narasinha Mudholkar
1913	Karachi	Nawab Syed Muhammad Bahadur
1914	Madras	Bhupendra Nath Bose
1915	Bombay	Lord Satyendra Prasanna Sinha
1916	Lucknow	Ambica Charan Mazumdar
1917	Calcutta	Annie Besant
1918	Delhi	Pandit Madan Mohan Malaviya
1918	Bombay (Special Session)	Syed Hasan Imam
1919	Amritsar	Pandit Motilal Nehru
1920	Calcutta (Special Session)	Lala Lajpat Rai
1920	Nagpur	C Vijayaraghavachariar
1921	Ahmedabad	Hakim Ajmal Khan

1922	Gaya	Deshbandhu Chittaranjan Das
1923	Kakinada	Maulana Mohammad Ali
1923	Delhi (Special Session)	Maulana Abul Kalam Azad
1924	Belgaum	Mahatma Gandhi
1925	Kanpur	Sarojini Naidu
1926	Gauhati	S Srinivasa Iyengar
1927	Madras	Dr M A Ansari
1928	Calcutta	Pandit Motilal Nehru
1929 & 30	Lahore	Pandit Jawaharlal Nehru
1931	Karachi	Sardar Vallabhbhai Patel
1932	Delhi	Pandit Madan Mohan Malaviya
1933	Calcutta	Pandit Madan Mohan Malaviya
1933	Calcutta	Nellie Sengupta
1934 & 35	Bombay	Dr Rajendra Prasad
1936	Lucknow	Pandit Jawaharlal Nehru
1936 & 37	Faizpur	Pandit Jawaharlal Nehru
1938	Haripura	Netaji Subhash Chandra Bose
1939	Tripuri	Netaji Subhash Chandra Bose
1940–46	Ramgarh	Maulana Abul Kalam Azad
1947	Delhi	Acharya J B Kripalani
1948 & 49	Jaipur	Dr Pattabhi Sitaraimayya

PROMINENT PERSONALITIES

Mohandas Karamchand Gandhi: Mahatma Gandhi popularly known as 'Father of the Nation' was born in Porbandar, Gujarat on 2 October 1869.

In 1891, Gandhi went to London to study law but after having admitted to British bar he returned to India and began law practice in Bombay. In 1893, he went to South Africa and stayed there till 1914, opposing discrimination against Indians.

After his struggle in South Africa he returned to India in 1915 and started Non-Cooperation movement in 1919, Civil Disobedience Movement (1930) and Quit India Movement in 1942. Finally, in August 1947, the British were forced to leave India.

Mahatma Gandhi was assassinated by Nathuram Godse on 30 January 1948.

Mangal Pandey: Born on 19 July 1827 in the village of Nagwa, district Ballia, Uttar Pradesh, Mangal Pandey was the first freedom fighter and martyr of 1857.

The main reason of Sepoy Mutiny was the Pattern 1853 Enfield rifled musket. To load a new rifle, the soldiers had to bite the cartridge and open to pour gunpowder into the rifle's muzzle.

He was sentenced to death on 8 April 1857 in Barrackpore.

Lal Bahadur Shastri: He was the second Prime Minister of India and was born on 2 October 1904. Influenced by Non-Cooperation Movement launched by Gandhi in 1921, he joined the freedom struggle at the age of 17. Later he actively participated in the Civil Disobedience Movement, Salt Stayagraha and Quit India movement for which he was sentenced to imprisonment several times.

Q.47. Who raised the slogan 'Inquilab Zindabad'?
Q.48. Who was the founder of Amritsar city?

He coined a slogan 'Jai Jawan, Jai Kisaan' to bring unity within the country. He died on 10 January 1966 at Tashkent after he had signed the Joint Declaration with President Agha Khan of Pakistan.

Bal Gangadhar Tilak: Born in a Brahmin family on 23 July 1856 in Ratangari, Maharashtra, he was a multifaceted personality. He was a scholar of Indian history, Sanskrit, mathematics, astronomy and Hinduism. He organised Extremist Party within Congress.

He is called 'Father of Indian Unrest' by the British. He launched Swadeshi Movement and called for 'Swaraj is my birth right and I shall have it', which inspired millions of Indians to join the freedom struggle. With the goal of Swaraj, he also built 'Home Rule League'. He died on 1 August 1920.

Dr Rajendra Prasad: He was the first President of free India, who was born on 3 December 1884 in Ziradevi village in Bihar's Siwan district. In 1905, Dr Rajendra Prasad plunged headlong into the Swadeshi Movement and later on joined the Dawn Society run by Satish Chandra Mukherjee and Sister Nivedita.

He was actively involved in the Non-Cooperation Movement, Salt Satyagraha and Champaran Agrarian Agitation. In 1934, he was elected as the President of Indian National Congress and in 1950 as President of independent India. He was honoured with the Bharat Ratna Award and died on 28 February 1963.

Chakravarti Rajagopalachari: Popularly known as 'Rajaji' or 'CR', he was born in a village of Salem district in Tamil Nadu in a Brahmin family on 10 December 1878.

Rajaji actively participated in Home League Rule under Bal Gangadhar Tilak. Later in 1919 and being influenced by Gandhi he joined in the freedom struggle. Later, in 1937 he was selected as the Chief Minister of Madras.

In 1948, he was honoured with the title 'First Indian Governor General of India'. In 1957, Rajaji found the Swatantra Party. He also published the Hindu Epic Mahabharata that was translated from Sanskrit to Tamil and then to Hindi. He was awarded Bharat Ratna in 1954. He died on 26 December 1992.

Gopal Krishna Gokhale: He was born on 9 May 1866 in Kothapur, Maharashtra. He was the political guru of Gandhi. Gokhale was one of the first Indians who completed graduation. In 1905 he founded Servants of Indian Society.

Gokhale was actively involved in the Morley-Minto reforms of 1909 that gave Indians right to access highest posts in the government. He also wrote articles for Tilak's weekly paper.

He died on 19 February 1915.

Jawaharlal Nehru: First Prime Minister of India, born on 14 November 1889 in Allahabad, was the only son of Motilal Nehru and Swarup Rani.

Being highly influenced by Gandhiji, he joined the freedom struggle. He is said to be the architect, the maker of modern India. As Congress president at the Lahore Session of 1929, he declared that complete Independence was the aim of Congress. He wrote *Discovery of India* and *Glimpses of World History* among other books. He took his last breath on 27 May 1964.

Annie Besant: He was born in London on 1 October 1847. During her stay in India she was actively involved in the Indian Nationalist Movement and Home Rule League. She founded CentrSal Hindu College at Banaras and was elected President of Theosophical Society in 1907.

Q.49. By the introduction of which Act, Dyarchy system was introduced?

Q.50. Who was the founder of 'Young Bengal Movement'?

She expired in India on 20 September 1933.

Lala Lajpat Rai: He was born on 28 January 1865 in Jagraon in Ludhiana.

His political career started in 1888 with the Indian National Congress Session at Allahabad. Famously known as 'Lion of Punjab', he was the founder and editor of *Bande Mataram*. He died of head injury caused by police lathicharge while leading a demonstration against Simon Commission at Lahore on 17 November 1928.

Maulana Abul Kalam Azad: He was born on 11 November 1888 in Mecca. He was a distinguished scholar, a great poet, a true freedom fighter and independent India's first Education Minister. He actively participated in Khilafat Movement, Non-Cooperation Movement and Salt Stayagraha.

In 1947, Maulana Azad was appointed as the Minister of Education in the cabinet of Jawaharlal Nehru. He served the country till 1958 and on 22 February 1958 died of a stroke.

Subhas Chandra Bose: He is popularly known as Netaji. He was born on 23 January 1897 in Cuttack, Orissa. Under the influence of Mahatma Gandhi he joined the Indian National Congress and actively participated in Civil Disobedience Movement in 1930.

In 1938, Subhas Bose was elected as the President of All India Congress. He founded the Indian National Army with the soldiers of the prisoners of war at Singapore in 1943. He is reportedly killed in an air crash on 17 August 1945.

Dadabhai Naoroji: Born on 4 September 1825 in Bombay, he was fondly known as 'the promise of India' in his youth and later known as 'the grand old man of India'. Naoroji started with his political career in 1852.

Naoroji was the driving spirit of Indian National Congress and was elected three times as the President of the Congress in 1866, 1893 and 1906. He was the first Indian to become a member of British Parliament. He died on 30 June 1917.

Sardar Vallabhbhai Patel: Popularly known as a 'Man of Steel', he was born on 31 October 1875 at Nadiad, Gujarat.

Inspired by the work and philosophy of Mahatma Gandhi, he decided to join the freedom struggle. He was also involved in Salt Satyagraha in Nagpur and Quit India Movement in 1942. In 1931, he was elected as the President of Indian National Congress.

After independence he was appointed as the first Home Minister and Deputy Prime Minister of India. He died on 15 December 1950.

Sarojini Naidu: She was born on 13 February 1879. She was known as Nightingale of India.

She joined the Indian independence movement in 1905. In 1925, she presided over the annual session of Indian National Congress and later participated in the Civil Disobedience Movement.

She was the first Indian woman to become the Governor of the state, Uttar Pradesh. She wrote Golden Threshold, Bird of Time and Broken Wing. She died in her office on 2 March 1949.

Madan Mohan Malviya: Born at Prayag (Allahabad) in 1861, he was a leading nationalist leader and prominent educationalist. He founded Hindu MahaSabha (1906) and Banaras Hindu University in 1916. He died in 1946.

Q.51. On whose recommendation English language was introduced as the medium of higher education in India?

History of India

Names of Mausoleum of Indian Leaders

Person	Place	Person	Place
Mahatma Gandhi	Raj Ghat	Charan Singh	Kisan Ghat
Jawahar Lal Nehru	Shanti Van	Gianni Zail Singh	Ektasthal
Lal Bahadur Shastri	Vijaya Ghat	Rajiv Gandhi	Veerbhoomi
B R Ambedkar	Chaithrabhoomi	Morarji Desai	Abhayghat
Indira Gandhi	Shaktisthal	Gulzarilal Nanda	Narayanghat
		Jagjivan Ram	Samtasthal

TIMELINES IN INDIAN HISTORY

Ancient India

BC

2500–1500: Beginning of the Indus Valley Civilisation.

1000: One of the earliest Holy Scripture, Rig-Veda is composed; Iron Age India started during this time.

750: Indo-Aryans rule over 16 Mahajanapadas (16 Great States) in northern India, from the Indus to the Ganges.

600: The Upanishads are composed in Sanskrit.

527: Prince Siddhartha Gautama attains enlightenment and becomes the Buddha.

500: The ascetic prince Mahavira establishes Jainism in northern India.

327: Alexander the Great of Macedonia invades the Indus valley; fights the famous Battle of the Hydaspes with Porus.

300: *Ramayana*, a famous epic is composed.

273: Ashoka the Great becomes the emperor of the Mauryan Empire.

261: Kalinga War takes place between Ashoka and the kingdom of Kalinga.

200: *Mahabharata*, another famous epic is composed.

100: *Bhagavata Gita* is composed.

AD

50: Thomas, an apostle of Jesus, visits India.

78: Beginning of Saka Era.

320: Chandragupta I ascend to the throne of Gupta empire.

606: Harshavardhana crowned king.

761: First Muslim, Md. Bin Qasim defeats King Dahir.

997: Mahmud of Ghazni raids northern India.

1000: Invasion of Mahmud of Ghazni.

1191: First Battle of Tarain between Mohammed Ghauri and Prithviraj III takes place in which the former is defeated.

1192: Second Battle of Tarain fought between Ghauri and Prithiviraj Chauhan III and the latter is defeated by Mohammed Ghauri.

Medieval India

1206: The Ghurid prince Qutub-ud-din Aibak became the first Sultan of Delhi.

Q.52. Which Act envisaged a separate electorate for Muslims?
Q.53. In which year was Muslim League set up?

General Knowledge Manual

1290: Jalal ud-Din Firuz established the Khilji sultanate at Delhi.
1325: Muhammad bin Tughlaq becomes sultan of Delhi.
1490: Guru Nanak Dev established Sikhism and the city of Amritsar.
1497: Babur, a ruler of Afghan, established the Mughal dynasty in India.
1497-99: Vasco da Gama completed the first voyage in sea route from Europe to India and back.
1526: First Battle of Panipat fought in which Babur defeats Ibrahim Lodhi and establishes the Mughal Dynasty.
1556: Akbar won in second Battle of Panipat and goes on to become one of the greatest rulers of India.
1600: East India Company is formed in England, which gets exclusive trading rights with India.
1611: East India Company is established in India by the British.
1627: Shivaji establishes the Maratha kingdom.
1631: Shah Jahan builds the world famous Taj Mahal.
1707: Aurangzeb dies destabilising the Mughal Empire.

Modern India

1757: British defeat Siraj-ud-daulah at the Battle of Plassey.
1761: The Marathas are defeated in the Third battle of Panipat by Ahmed Shah Abdali.
1764: Battle of Buxar is fought in which the English defeat the triple alliance of Nawab Mir Qasim of Bengal, Nawab Shuja-ud-daula of Awadh and Mughal emperor Shah Alam.
1769: A famine kills ten million people in Bengal and the East India Company does nothing to help them.
1799: British defeat Tipu Sultan in fourth Anglo-Mysore war.
1829: Prohibition of Sati by law.
1853: Railway, postal services and telegraph line introduced in India.
1857: First War of Indian Independence, also known as Revolt of 1857 or Sepoy Mutiny broke out.
1877: Queen of England is proclaimed as the Empress of India.
1885: First meeting of the Indian National Congress held in Bombay.
1905: The First Partition of Bengal takes place.
1906: Muslim League is formed.
1912: The Imperial capital shifted to Delhi from Calcutta.
1919: The cruel Jallianwala Bagh massacre takes place due to protests against the Rowlatt Act.
1920: Non-Cooperation Movement launched.
1922: Chauri-Chaura violence takes place due to Civil Disobedience Movement.
1928: Simon Commission comes to India and is boycotted by all parties.
1930: Salt Satyagraha is launched as an agitation against salt tax. First Round Table Conference takes place.
1931: Second Round Table Conference takes place and Irwin-Gandhi Pact is signed.
1934: Civil Disobedience Movement is called off.
1942: Quit India Movement is launched; Indian National Army is formed.
1946: Cabinet Mission Plan and Formation of Interim Government at the centre proposed.

Q.54. What was the name of women force of Indian National Army (INA)?

History of India

3 June 1947: Lord Mountbatten's plan for partition of India comes into light.
15 August 1947: India Independence from the British rule and the country is also divided into two.

Post-Partition (1947 –)

1948: Muhammad Ali Jinnah, the first governor general of Pakistan, dies.
1950: India became a republic.
1951: First five year plan implemented.
1952: First General Election held.
1954: 'Panchsheel' agreement between India and China.
1959: Dalai Lama exiled, seeks shelter in India.
1962: Chinese attack on India.
1965: War between Pakistan and India breaks out.
1971: East Pakistan attempts to secede, leading to civil war; India intervenes in support of East Pakistan; Pakistan fights another war with India; East Pakistan breaks away to become Bangladesh; Yahya Khan resigns.
1972: Shimla Agreement signed between India and Pakistan.
1974: First nuclear tests in Pokhran.
1975: India's first satellite Aryabhatta launched; National Emergency declared.
1979: Mother Teresa won the Noble Peace Prize.
1982: Ninth Asian Games held in Delhi.
1984: Rakesh Sharma goes into space; 'Operation Blue Star' in Punjab after the assassination of Indira Gandhi; Bhopal gas tragedy occurs.
1989: Foundation stone for the Rama Janmabhoomi temple at Ayodhya was laid.
1991: Rajiv Gandhi was killed in bomb blast.
1992: Babri Masjid is demolished.
1993: Bombay bomb blast; Panchayati Raj came into effect.
1997: Mother Teresa passes away.
1998: India concluded five nuclear tests; Amartya Sen won the Nobel Prize.
1999: Indian Airlines plane IC-814 hijacked; Devastating cyclone in Orissa.
2000: Karnam Malleshwari won bronze medal in the Olympic games; states of Chhattisgarh, Uttarakhand and Jharkhand were formed.
2001: Indo-Pak summit in Agra; Gujarat hit by an earthquake; terrorist attack on Indian Parliament.
2002: Godhra incident in Gujarat; India and Russia sign Delhi Declaration.
2003: First Afro-Asian games held in Hyderabad.
2004: Tsunami in the Indian Ocean hits south India.
2005: Devastating flood and landslide at Bombay.
2006:
- President of the United States, George W Bush visited India;
- USA signs landmark nuclear deal with India pending approval from the US Congress and Indian Parliament;
- A series of coordinated bomb attacks strikes several commuter trains in Mumbai during the evening rush hour;
- Shehnai musician and Bharat Ratna winner, Bismillah Khan, died.

Q.55. What is the name of the Sufi Saint who was the founder of the order of Chisti?

2007:
- Prathiba Patil is elected as the first female President of India;
- India won the first Twenty-20 World Cup in South Africa;
- Tata Steel acquired Corus Steel to become one of the largest steel makers;
- Vijay Mallya acquired Whyte & Mackay (W&M), the fourth-largest Scotch Whisky producer in the world.
- Aditya Birla Group took over Novelis and became the world's largest aluminium rolling company.
- Miss India-Earth Pooja Chitgopekar wins in Miss Earth 2007 beauty pageant as 1st-runner up held in Manila, Philippines.

2008:
- 10 states go to assembly polls;
- Blasts rocked cities of Jaipur, Bangalore, Ahmedabad and New Delhi claiming many lives;
- Suicide attack on the Indian embassy in Kabul kills 58 people along with two Indian diplomats, while injuring 170;
- Vishwa Hindu Parishad (VHP) leader Swami Lakshmanananda Saraswati and four disciples are killed by unidentified assailants at his ashram at Jalespata and violence against Christians in Orissa's Kandhamal district follows;
- In a biggest ever terrorist attack, 183 persons were killed in Mumbai;
- Baba Amte (94) passes away at Anandvan, Warora in Maharashtra;
- Field Marshal Sam Manekshaw passes away at 94 in Ooty;
- Former PM Chandra Shekhar dies battling blood cancer;
- Former PM V P Singh passes away at 77. He was battling blood cancer for the past 17 years;
- Kalka-Shimla Railway line is included in UNESCO Heritage list;
- Aravind Adiga becomes the fourth debut novelist to win the coveted Man Booker Prize for his novel, *The White Tiger*;
- Chandrayaan-I successfully launched on 22 October from Satish Dhawan Space Centre at Sriharikota;
- India decides to go ahead with Iran-Pakistan-India Gas pipeline;
- India and France sign pact for civilian nuclear technology;
- India and the United States signed the Nuclear Deal, popularly called 123 agreements on 11 October 2008.
- Russian President Medvedev visits New Delhi for the annual Indo-Russia summit and the formal conclusion of the 'Year of Russia'. Year 2009 is decided to be the 'Year of India' in Russia.
- HDFC Bank and Centurion Bank of Punjab announced their merger, creating India's largest bank in terms of branches.
- Tata group is world's sixth most reputed company in 'Global: 200' compiled by Reputation Institute, USA.
- India's Parvathy Omanakuttan finished first runner up in Miss World 2008;
- Abhinav Bindra wins gold at Olympics also Sushil Kumar and Vijender Singh capture bronze in wrestling and boxing at Olympics;
- Virender Sehwag joins Lara and Bradman to be the only players to score two test triple hundreds;
- India's U19 team won ICC U19 World Cup beating South Africa.

ANSWERS

1. Atharva Veda
2. Brahmanas
3. The third Buddhist was held
4. Chandragupta Vikramaditya
5. Chamundaraya
6. Turki or Turkis
7. The French
8. Mohammad Shah
9. Lord Cornwallis
10. Rana Kumbh
11. In 1828
12. Thomas Roe
13. Gopal Krishna Gokhale
14. Tirukkural
15. Indo-Greeks
16. Iltutmish
17. Harappa
18. Guru Har Govind
19. Tamil
20. Recruitment for army
21. Dharmachakrapravartana
22. Sila ditya
23. Congress and Muslim League
24. Jallianwala Bagh Tragedy
25. Mesopotamia
26. Chaitra
27. Second Battle of Tarain
28. Lord Dalhousie
29. 1911
30. Surat
31. Subash Chandra Bose
32. Kerala
33. September 1920 in Calcutta Session
34. A O Hume
35. Lala Hardayal
36. Lahore Session of 1929
37. Meerut
38. Rowlatt Act
39. Rash Behari Bose
40. Annie Besant
41. J B Kripalini
42. Government of India Act, 1935
43. Lala Lajpat Rai
44. Lord Cornwallis
45. Babur and Ibrahim Lodhi
46. Harijana Leaders
47. Bhagat Singh
48. Guru Ramdas
49. Government of India Act, 1919
50. Henry Louis Vivian Derozio
51. Lord Macaulay
52. Morley-Minto Reform
53. 1906
54. Rani Jhansi
55. Khwaja Moinuddin

2
WORLD HISTORY

ANCIENT WORLD

Human civilisation came of age between fourth and third millennium BC, in different areas: between Tigris and Euphrates river, in Mesopotamia and Nile river in Egypt, the Indus river in India and Hwang Ho in China.

The first city to have developed was Mesopotamia. Harappa and Mohenjedaro civilisation in the Indus Valley in India was next to witness development of city and then it happened in Egyptian civilisation.

Mesopotamia Civilisation

The word 'Mesopotamia' comes from the Greek words 'mesos' meaning 'middle' and 'potamos' meaning 'river'. Hence, the word Mesopotamia means 'land between the rivers'. Mesopotamia was the alluvial plain lying between the Tigris and Euphrates rivers, comprising parts of modern day Iraq and Syria.

Several groups, such as Sumerians, Akkadians, and Babylonians, etc., conquered it one after another.

Sumerians worshipped God in temples called *Ziggurat*. They were also first to develop writing known as Cuneiform script.

First empire was made by Sargon, an Akkad (a city of Mesopotamia) ruler, which lasted for 100 years.

Hammurabi (1792–1750 BC) of Babylonia later ruled Mesopotamia. It was during his rule a set of written law was adopted for the first time in the history.

Other contributions of the Mesopotamians:

(i) They made lunar calendar with a week of seven days; they also had the knowledge of the existence of five planets, a Sun and a Moon;
(ii) They developed a number system based on 60, and from this system the concept of circles of 360 degree and 60 minutes in an hour were deduced;
(iii) They also developed the tables of division, multiplication, square roots, quadratic equations and formulated equivalent of zero.

Hebrew originated in Sumeria (lower part of Mesopotamia). Its history is written in the five books of Old Testaments, the Torah. Hebrews had great influence on Judaism, Christianity and Islam.

Egyptian Civilisation

This civilisation flourished on the banks of river Nile. Egypt's first golden age is known as Pyramid age. Egyptian rulers are called 'Pharaohs'. They believed in life after death and built huge pyramids to save their mummified dead bodies.

Egyptians believed and worshipped many gods. Osiris was their god of after-life and Isis was the goddess of female fertility. Ancient Egyptians used pictographs instead of letters; the signs are known as 'hieroglyphics'.

Chinese Civilisation

It developed in the valleys of the Hwang Ho and the Yangtze rivers. First known dynasty of Chinese civilisation was the Hsia dynasty (2000–1500 BC). Cheng (founder of Chin dynasty) known as Shin Hung Ti, built the Great Wall of China (1400 miles). China derived its name from this dynasty.

Greek Civilisation

This civilisation developed from a combination of two earlier cultures: Minoan and Mycenaean. Two major Greek cities that developed during this period are Sparta and Athens.

Athens was among the first cities in the world to introduce democracy.

Pericles (460–429 BC) was a great Athenian ruler and strong believer of democracy.

The Athenian period saw lots of development in the field of art and science. Many great poets like Homer, Aeschylus, Sophocles, Euripides and Aristophanes belong to this period. Athenians were the first to write history in a critical fashion. Herodotus (considered father of History) and Thucydides were famous historian of this time. They were the first to believe in natural laws. In the field of mathematics and science, Pythagoras formulated the Pythagorean Theorem which gives the relation between the sides of a right angle triangle.

Aristotle (384–322 BC), Plato (427–347 BC), Socrates (469–399 BC) and Hypocrites were other philosophers of this period, who made significant contributions.

Sparta invaded Athens in 431 BC and fought for 27 years; known as Peloponnesian war (431–404 BC).

Macedonian Empire

This empire was founded by King Philip, after whose assassination his son Alexander the Great, took over at the age of 20 in 336 BC. Aristotle was his teacher and was appointed by his father. Alexander expanded his empire from Asia Minor, Egypt to Mesopotamia and Persia.

He never lost a battle and died at the age of 33. His kingdom was got dividedinto three parts: Egypt, Asia and Macedonia.

Roman Civilisation

Rome was named after Romulus. In 509 BC Romans overthrew the Etruscan king, Tarquin. Roman had no king, and they elected two Consuls to hold office for one year.

There were three Punic wars fought between Rome and Carthage and in 146 BC Rome defeated Carthage in the third Punic War.

Q.1. Which two countries fought Crimean War?
Q.2. What is the place of worship of Sumerians called?

Romans occupied Macedonia by 196 BC and entire Greece by 133 BC.

Julius Caesar took over in 60 BC; Gaul (France) came under Caesar's rule after the Gallic war.

Augustus Caesar (27 BC–AD 14), the adopted son of Julius Caesar, defeated Antony and Cleopatra and took over the charge of Rome as dictator. It was during his reign Jesus was born and was crucified in Judea during the reign of another Roman emperor named Tiberius (14–37 BC).

Theodosius (AD 392–395) was the last Roman emperor, after whose reign Roman Empire was divided into Eastern and Western empires with Constantinople and Rome as their capitals respectively.

There are many reasons for the decline of Roman Empire:
  (i) Due to internal political and economical weakness and external threats posed by foreign invaders;
  (ii) All rulers were dictators;
  (iii) Growing corruption, high taxes charged by the empires led to disturbance in the provinces.

MEDIEVAL WORLD

Byzantine Empire

The period of AD 500 to 1000 is called the early middle ages or late antiquity. Crucial features of early middle age were a unique blending of three distinct traditions: Greco-Roman, Judeo-Christian and Germanic tradition. Constantine the Great, rebuilt the Byzantium (Eastern part of Roman) and renamed it Constantinople in AD 330.

Byzantium empire remained in existence until it was defeated by the Turks in 1453. Justinian (AD 482–565), the greatest of all the eastern emperors, was a reformer like Augustus Caesar. He formed a 16 men commission to codify all laws, which produced *Corpus Juris Civilis* (body of Civil law), written in Latin. Byzantines were major conduit of classical learning and science into West, down to Renaissance.

Islamic Arab Empire

Islamic Civilisation (Seventh to Twelfth Century): Islam absorbed and added its culture to the heritage of Greece and Rome, and also from Judaism, Christianity and near east.

The home of Islam was the Arabian Peninsula.

All Arabs worshipped an object in common – the *Kabba,* a large black stone enshrined at Mecca.

Life of Mohammed (570–632): Prophet Mohammed was born at Mecca but he left Mecca and lived in life of isolation in the desert. At the age of 40 he received his revelations and began to preach in AD 610. These revelations were compiled in the Quran by his followers between 650 to 651.

Tenets of Islam: Basic belief of Islam:
(i) God is good and Omnipotent; (ii) God will judge all men on the last day and assign them

Q.3. Ancient Egyptians used pictographs instead of letters. What are these known as?

their place in either heaven or hell; (iii) Men should thank God for making the world as it is; (iv) God expects men to be generous with their wealth; (v) Mohammed was the Prophet sent by God to teach men and warn them of the last judgement.

Since his teachings were rejected by both the Authorities and Merchants of Mecca; to avoid a showdown he left for Medina in 622. This journey was called *Hejira*. He died in AD 632.

Abu Bakr (Father-in-law of Mohammed) was selected as *Calipha,* or new leader. In 636 Muslims defeated Byzantine army, Syria fell in 640 and a decade later they conquered the entire Persian Empire. In 732, Muslim army was defeated at the Battle of Tours and expansion of Islamic empire ended there.

Crusades (Eleventh to Thirteenth Century): The people of Western Europe launched a series of holy wars, called crusades, against the East and Constantinople to free the holy lands from Islamic influence.

There were several crusades, some of the major crusades are:

First Crusade (1096–99), Second Crusade (1144–49), Third Crusade (1189–92), Fourth Crusade (1202–04), Fifth Crusade (1218–21), Sixth Crusade (1228–29). There were also two Children Crusade in 1212.

Feudalism: It refers to a social system of right and duties based on land tenures and personal relationships, in which the land is held in 'fief' by vassals from lord. The lord would protect the smaller landlords. It first developed in medieval period in Western Europe. This socio-economic and political system is called 'feudalism'.

It had three phases: Formative Phase (sixth to eleventh century), Mature Phase (eleventh to thirteenth century) and Later Phase (fourteenth to fifteenth century).

Geographical Discoveries: Prince Henry of Portuguese discovered many island on west coast of Africa.

Bartholomew Diaz reached the southern tip of Africa in 1487 and named it 'Cape of Storm', later renamed as 'Cape of Good Hope'.

Vasco-da-Gama's voyage to India (Calicut) in 1498 opened the new water route to east. Cabral discovered Brazil in 1500. Columbus discovered some islands in 1492 and named as 'Indies', thinking that these were part of India. Amerigo Vespucci explored the 'New World' already discovered by Columbus. Magellan was the first to circumnavigate the world between the years 1519 to 1522. Jacques Cartier explored parts of modern Canada.

MODERN WORLD

Modern world witnessed the developments that had mainly originated in Europe and resulted in positive impact on the human civilisation across the world.

MAIN REVOLUTIONS AND WARS OF INDEPENDENCE

Renaissance in Western Europe

Renaissance in Latin means revival or rebirth. However, it has become a term to describe an intellectual literary, artistic and scientific movement and roughly expands to a span of 250 years in European history that started in mid-fourteenth century.

Q.4. The journey of Muhammed from Mecca to Medina in 622 BC is called?

Reasons:

   (i) It largely began in Italy during the Roman reign, when the Eastern and Western parts were engaged in trade;
   (ii) The tendency of middle class towards secular attitude gained importance;
   (iii) Greek scholars migrated to Italy with their manuscripts (containing wisdom of ancient Greeks), when attacked by Turkish in 1453. They spread the learning throughout Western Europe and the movement reached to other European countries such as England, France and Germany.

Results of the Renaissance were evident in literature, arts and science:

   (i) Rise of new languages and authors like Machiavelli, Dante and Petrarch in Italy; Chaucer, Shakespeare and Ben Johnson in England; Erasmus in Holland; Camoens of Portugal; De Vena and Calderon in Spain.
   (ii) Rise of painters like Michelangelo, Raphael and Leonardo Da Vinci in Italy; Durer and Holbein in Germany; Murillio and El Greco in Spain; Rubens and Van in Holland, etc.
   (iii) Advancement made in science and astronomy saw the rise of astronomers, like Copernicus (Poland), John Kepler (Germany), Galileo (Italy), Newton (Britain); chemists, like Vasalius, Harvey and Helmont; physicists, like Gilbert, Steven; mathematicians, like Tartaglia, Ferrari, Descartes and Napier.

French Revolution (1787–99)

The revolutionary movement that shook France between the years 1787–99 and reached its first climax in 1789 is called the 'French Revolution', which is also known as 'Revolution of 1789'.

Reasons:

   (i) Poor conditions of peasants due to over population and overcrowding of agriculture, backward method of farming, uneconomical landholding, steep increase of industrial goods over agricultural goods and payment of several taxes to the states;
   (ii) Inequality of privileges of the first two estates (especially higher clergy and higher nobility led to dissatisfaction amongst the middle class;
   (iii) Participation of France in the American Revolution had driven the government to the brink of bankruptcy;
   (iv) Crop failures in many parts of the country in 1788 and a long period of economic difficulties made the population particularly restless;
   (v) Inefficiency of King Louis XVI, supplemented with weak administrative capability;

Influence of Philosophers: Voltaire, Rousseau and Montesquieu echoed the words 'Liberty, Equality and Fraternity', which fuelled the revolution.

Course of Revolution: The French Revolution began with the meeting of the States General in May 1789. On 14 July 1789 Bastille

> *Q.5. Who discovered Cape of Good Hope?*
> *Q.6. What are the three words that became the guiding principles of French Revolution...?*

was stormed, and on 6 October 1789 Louis XVI and the Royal Family were removed from Versailles to Paris, thus legitimising the National Assembly.

A Legislative Assembly sat from October 1791 to September 1792, later it was replaced by the National Convention, which proclaimed the Republic. The King XVI and Queen Antoinette were brought to trial in December 1792, and executed on 21 January 1793.

Success of the revolution resulted in abolition of feudalism. The Constitution was born in 1791, which paved the way for reorganisation of Central Government and local government.

Napoleon Bonaparte (1799–1814) was the product of French Revolution, though he did not take active part in the revolution but gained prestige through the influence of one of the directors named Barras.

Industrial Revolution in Europe

This period, marked with the increase in industrial productivity, began in late eighteenth century and has continued to the present day.

It was observed in two stages: the first stage included the mechanisation of industries and development of steam engine and its application in industry and transportation; second stage characterised by direct application of science to industry and developing the techniques for mass production.

The possible causes:

(i) Commercial revolution provided large-scale capital and raw materials not only from within but also from 'New World'.
(ii) Agricultural revolution generated enough surpluses through growth in agricultural productivity and early availability of labour forces due to the growth of population, etc.

The Industrial Revolution resulted into inventions of new machines and processes, such as fly shuttle developed by John Kay for weaving, spinning jenny by James Hargreaves, steam engine by New Comen and later developed by James Watt, steam locomotives by Stephenson, development of postal services, telephone, etc.

Industrial revolution had multifaceted impacts:

(i) Industrialisation diffused from England to Belgium, France, Germany, Austria, etc.;
(ii) Growth of population due to economic and medical reasons;
(iii) Unprecedented increase in productivity and human resources;
(iv) Unprecedented growth of urbanisation;
(v) Enhancement of living standard of Europeans;
(vi) Colonisation of Asia and Africa by European countries.

American Civil War

12 April 1861–69 April 1865 (last battle ended on 13 May 1865)

- The American Civil War is also known as the 'War Between the States' of the United States of America.
- Eleven of Southern slave states declared their secession from the US

Q.7. With which incident in history is 'Fall of Bastille' related?

Q.8. Where was Napoleon imprisoned?

and formed the Confederate States of America, led by Jefferson Davis. They fought against the US federal government, which was supported by all the free states and the five border slave states in the North.
- In the Presidential Election of 1860, the Republican Party (led by Abraham Lincoln) had campaigned against the expansion of slavery beyond the states in which it already existed.
- The seven Southern States declared their secession from the Union even before Lincoln took office on 4 March 1861.
- Hostilities began on 12 April 1861, when Confederate forces attacked a US military installation at Fort Sumter in South Carolina.
- Lincoln responded by calling for a volunteer army from each state, leading to declarations of secession by four more Southern slave states.
- In September 1862, Lincoln's Emancipation Proclamation to end slavery made into a goal for going to war in South and it dissuaded the British from intervening.
- Confederate commander Robert E Lee won battles in the east, but in 1863 his northward advance was turned back at Gettysburg and in the west, the Union gained control of the Mississippi River at the Battle of Vicksburg, thereby splitting the Confederacy.
- Confederate resistance collapsed after Lee surrendered to Grant at Appomattox Court House on 9 April 1865.
- The American Civil War was the deadliest war in American history, causing the death of 6, 20,000 soldiers and an undetermined number of civilian casualties.
- Its legacy includes ending slavery in the United States, restoring the Union and strengthening the role of the federal government.

World War I (1914–18)

- It was a global military conflict which involved the majority of the world's great powers organised into two opposing military alliances: the Entente Powers and the Central Powers.
- Over 70 million military personnel were mobilised. In a state of total war, the major forces fully placed their scientific and industrial capabilities at the war. Over 15 million people were killed, making it one of the deadliest conflicts in human history.
- The proximate cause for the war was the assassination of Archduke Franz Ferdinand of Austria, heir to the Austro-Hungarian throne, by a Serbian nationalist, Gavrilo Princip.
- Austria-Hungary's resulting demands against the Kingdom of Serbia led to the activation of a series of alliances which within weeks saw all of the major European powers at war.
- As a consequence of the involvement of global empires of many European nations, the war soon spread worldwide.
- At the end of War, four major imperial powers – Germany, Russia, Austria-Hungary and the Ottoman Empire had been defeated with the latter two ceasing to exist as autonomous countries.

Q.9. Name the nations between whom the Hundred-year War was fought?
Q.10. Where was America's Declaration of Independence issued?

- The League of Nations was formed in the hope of preventing another such conflict.

Russian Revolution

- The Russian Revolution is the series of revolutions in Russia in 1917 which destroyed the Tsarist autocracy and led to the creation of the Soviet Union.
- The February Revolution (on March 1917) was a spontaneous popular revolution which resulted in setting of a Provisional Government by Duma and abdication of Czar.
- In the October Revolution (on November), the Bolshevik party, led by Vladimir Lenin and the workers' soviets overthrew the Provisional Government in Petrograd.
- The Bolshevik leadership signed a peace treaty with Germany in March 1918.
- Soon a civil war erupted between the Red and White (all non-Bolshevik) factions, which was to continue for several years, with the Bolsheviks ultimately emerging victorious.
- In this way the Revolution paved the way for the formation of the USSR.

World War II (1939–45)

- It was the largest war in the world history, fought between September 1939 and September 1945, which involved a majority of the world's nations, including all of the great powers, organised into two opposing military alliances: the Allies and the Axis.
- More than 40 million men and women were serving in the armed forces by 1944, and civilian and military deaths exceeded 70 million. The major battles involved millions of men and thousands of tanks and aircraft.
- The immediate cause of the conflict was the German's demand for the return of Danzig and part of the Polish 'corridor' granted to Poland from German territory in the Treaty of Versailles of 1919.
- The failure of League of Nations to maintain International peace, rise of dictatorship in Germany and Italy and Isolation policy of the USA (since it did not join League), are some other causes for the eruption of the war.
- The war began with the German invasion of Poland and subsequent declarations of war on Germany by most of the countries in the British Empire and Commonwealth and France on 1 September 1939; later on other nations joined the war.
- Some of the main events of the War are the Marco Polo Bridge Incident (between China and Japan), the start of Operation Barbarossa (German invasion of the Soviet Union) and the attacks on Pearl Harbor (by Japan).
- With the dropping of two atom bombs on Hiroshima (on 6 August 1945) and Nagasaki (on 9 August 1945) by America, Japan surrendered on 2 September 1945 and the war ended with a victory for the Allies.
- The Soviet Union and the United States subsequently emerged as the superpowers of the world; with this began the era of the Cold War, which lasted for the next 45 years.
- The United Nations was formed in the hope of preventing another such conflict.

> **Q.11. When was the Treaty of Versailles signed?**
> **Q.12. Who led the October Revolution?**

General Knowledge Manual

- The acceptance of self-determination accelerated decolonisation movements in Asia and Africa and Western Europe began moving towards integration.

Important Battles

Battles	Time Period	Fought Between/Results
Battle of Marathon	490 BC	Athens and Persia/Persia was defeated
Peloponnesian War	431–404 BC	Sparta and Athens/Sparta won
Battle of Issus	333 BC	Macedonia and Persian army in northern Syria/Macedonia won.
Battle of Arabia	331 BC	Greek and Persia/Greek won
Battle of Magnesia	190 BC	Syria and Rome/Syria defeated
Battle of Iron Bridge	AD 637	Khalid ibn al-Walid defeats Roman army under Heraclius in final battle against the Roman Empire.
100 Years War	1337–1453	France and England
Anglo-Spanish War	1588	Spain and Britain/Spain defeated
Civil War of England	1642–49	Cavalier (Supporters of King Charles) and the Parliament led by Oliver Cromwell/King Charles executed.
Battle of Gibraltar Bay	1607	Between Dutch, Spanish and Portuguese/Dutch won
Seven Year War	1756–63	Britain and France against Austria and Prussia/ British alliance won
Battle of Autarlitz	1805	Britain, Austria, Russia and Prussia against France/ France Won
Battle of Borodino	1812	France and Russia/France led by Napoleon was defeated
Battle of Leipzig	1813	Germany, Austria, Prussia and Russia against France/ France defeated
Battle of Waterloo	1815	British force led by Duke of Wellington defeated French force led by Napoleon/Napoleon abdicated and was exiled to Island of St. Helena, where he died in 1821.
First China War	1840	China and Britain/China defeated. It was a trade war also known as 'Opium War'.
American Civil War	1861–65	Northern versus Southern states of America/Northern states led by Abraham Lincoln defeated the Southern states.
Russo-Japanese War	1904–05	Between Russia and Japan/Russia was defeated also called the Battle of Port Arthur or Battle of Yalu.
Battle of Jutland	1916	Naval war between Germany and England/Germany was defeated.
Korean War	1954	North Korea invaded South Korea and was forced back by UN forces.
Israel-Arab War (Shortest War- 6 days)	1967	Arab forces led by Egypt, Syria and Jordan were defeated by Israel.
Pakistan-Bangladesh War	1971	Mukti Bahini forces aided by India against the Pakistani forces stationed at Bangladesh/Pakistan were defeated and Bangladesh came into existence.

World History

Gulf War	1991	US led multinational forces attacked Iraq to drive them away from Kuwait.
US-Afghanistan War	2001	US led coalition forces attacked Afghanistan/Taliban was defeated in Afghanistan.
Gulf War II	2003	US led coalition forces defeated the Iraqi President Sadam Hussein.

TIMELINES IN WORLD HISTORY

BC
6000:
- Neolithic settlements at Mehrgarh, Baluchistan and Indus Valley built around this time.
- Copper was discovered.

5000:
- Sumerian civilisation arises in between the reverse of Tigris and Euphrates.
- Invention of first phonetic writing.
- Invention of the wheel.
- Neolithic settlement in Egypt.

3000: Role of Pharos begins in Egypt.
2680: The construction of the Great Pyramid of Giza.
2500:
- Building of Mohenjedaro.
- Sumerians evolve a numerical system and develop lunar calendar.

2300:
- The Babylonians, Egyptians and Chinese built observatories and this was the beginning of astrology.
- The Neolithic age continues in Northern Europe.

2400:
- The Aryan migrators from the bank of the Danube and South Russia spread southwards.
- Evolution of the Aryan language.

2205–1122:
- Rise of the Chinese civilisation along the banks of river Hwang Ho.

2200:
- The beginning of Iron Age.
- The rise of Babylon City in ancient Mesopotamia.
- The Bronze Age reaches Europe.

1500:
- Compilation of the Rig Veda.
- Rise of civilisation around the river Ganges; Aryans reached Ganges.

1480: Moses leads Israelites out of Egypt.
1000:
- Beginning of epic civilisation in India; composition of the *Ramayana* and the *Mahabharata*.

Q.13. When did the Russian Revolution take place?
Q.14. With which historical event in history Boston Tea Party associated with?

General Knowledge Manual

	• The writing of the book *Old Testament* of Bible begins.
900–800:	
	• Phoeninians established Carthage.
	• The *Iliad* and the *Odyssey* were composed.
776:	The first Olympics in the city of Olympia in Greece were held.
753:	Rome was built by Romulus.
660:	Birth of Zorasthushtra or Zoroaster, the founder of Zoroastrianism in Medea (Iran).
616:	End of Assyrian empire.
604:	The birth of Lao-Tse (China), founder of Taoism.
586:	Babylon destroys Jerusalem.
560:	Birth of Lord Buddha.
551–479:	Confucius developed his social philosophy in China.
553:	Work of Pythagoras.
509:	Foundation of the Roman Republic.
500:	Building of the Theatre at Delphi.
490:	The battle of Marathon; Athens defeat Persia.
447:	The Parthenon is built in Athens for goddess Athena.
399:	Socrates, the Athenian philosopher executed.
387:	Plato, a disciple of Socrates who founded 'the academy' in Athens and wrote *The Republic*.
347:	Plato died in this year.
323:	Euclid's work on geometry, 'Elements of Geometry' is composed.
300–280:	Creation of the Colossus of Rhodes; A statue of Helios (Apollo), the Sun God.
279:	Pharos Light House at Alexandria is built.
264:	Ashoka becomes the Emperor of India.
215:	The Great Wall of China was built by Shih Hunga Ti.
149–146:	Rome destroys Carthage.
100:	Chinese developed the use of paper.
73:	Slaves revolt in Rome.
58:	Caesar conquers Gaul (modern France).
55:	Invasion of Britain by Julius Caesar.
44:	Julius Caesar murdered by Brutus.
31:	Augustus Caesar, the adopted son of Julius Caesar, defeated Mark Antony and Cleopatra at the Battle of Actium and established Roman empire as Emperor Augustus.
4:	Birth of Jesus Christ.
AD	
29:	Crucification of Jesus Christ.
64:	Burning of Rome; the great fire continues for six days.
70:	Jews revolted against Rome; Jerusalem is destroyed.
71–80:	Colosseum built in Rome.
570:	Birth of Prophet Mohammed.
1138:	Civil war in England.
1163:	Oxford University founded.
1215:	Magna Carta signed.
1348:	Plague in England.
1400:	Welsh war on independence.

> *Q.15. When was the first atom bomb dropped in Hiroshima?*
> *Q.16. Under which famous Treaty League of Nations was formed in 1920?*

World History

1438:	Rule of the Incas in Peru.
1492:	Columbus discovers the West Indies.
1504:	Mona Lisa painted by Leonardo Da Vinci.
1556:	Akbar becomes the ruler of Mughal Empire.
1558:	Queen Elizabeth I ascends the throne in England.
1582:	Pope Gregory XIII implements the Gregorian calendar.
1614:	John Napier discovered logarithm.
1642:	Civil war in England.
1660:	Restoration of Monarchy in England under King Charles II.
1689:	Establishment of constitutional Monarchy in England.
1756:	Seven-year war between combined forces of Britain and Prussia against Austria, France and Russia.
1776:	American declaration of Independence.
1789:	

- French revolution.
- The fall of Bastille.

1792:	France becomes a Republic.
1804:	Napoleon Bonaparte takes over as Emperor of France.
1815:	Battle of Waterloo.
1821:	

- Napoleon dies in St Helena.
- Greeks launch war of independence against Turks.

1830:	Greeks gain Independence.
1833:	Abolition of Slavery in Britain.
1840:	

- Opium war between Britain and China.
- Antarctica discovered.

1848:

- *Communist Manifesto* is written by Karl Marx and Friedrich Engels.
- February revolution in France.
- European revolution.

1861:	American Civil war.
1663:	

- Slavery abolished in the US by President Abraham Lincoln.
- International Football Association formed.

1865:	American Civil War ends; Abraham Lincoln was assassinated.
1883:	Egypt occupied by Britain.
1889:	The Eiffel Tower is built in Paris.
1893:	New Zealand becomes the first country in the world to grant women the right to vote.
1896:	First modern Olympic Games were held in Athens, Greece.
1901:	The first Nobel Prizes are awarded.
1909:	Discovery of North Pole by Robert Peary.

Q.17. Who wrote Communist Manifesto?
Q.18. Who led the Confede-rate States of America in the American Civil War?
Q.19. Who is the first woman Prime Minister of Bangladesh?

1914:
- First World War begins.
- Panama Canal is officially opened.

1917:
- US enters the World War.
- Outbreak of Russian Revolution.

1918:
- Tzar Nicholas II and his family executed by Bolsheviks.
- First World War ends.

1920:
- League of Nations formed under Treaty of Versailles.

1924:
- Death of Lenin.
- First Labour government established in Britain.
- Adolf Hitler writes *Mein Kampf*.

1934: Hitler becomes President of Germany.

1939:
- Germany annexes Austria and Czech Republic.
- Second World War begins.

1941: Japan attacks Pearl Harbor.

1943: Italy surrenders.

1945:
- Germany and Japan Surrender.
- Hiroshima and Nagasaki are bombed.
- Formation of the UNO.

1949:
- NATO is formed.
- German republic is established.

1952: Accession of Queen Elizabeth II of England.
1955: First Afro-Asian conference of heads of states held in Bandung, Indonesia.
1957: Sputnik-I launched by the former USSR.
1960: Africa Year, 16 African countries achieved independence.
1961: Yuri Gagarin of Russia became the first man to go the space.
1964: Nelson Mandela is sentenced to Life Imprisonment.

1968:
- Martin Luther King assassinated.
- UN approves Nuclear Non-Proliferation Treaty.

1969: US astronauts Neil Armstrong and Edwin Aldrin land on the moon.

1971:
- Eruption of war between India and Pakistan.
- Mujibur Rahman declares Bangladesh Independence.
- China admits to UN; Taiwan expelled.

1973: Vietnam War ends.
1974: Indian conducts first nuclear blast at Pokhran in Rajasthan.

1975:
- Margaret Thatcher elected first woman leader of the British Conservative party.

Q.20. Who was the founder of Macedonian Empire?
Q.21. During the reign of which king the French Revolution took place?

World History

1979:
- India enters space with the launch of satellite 'Aryabhata'.
- Margaret Thatcher becomes the first woman Prime Minister of the Britain.
- China invades Vietnam.
- Zulfikar Ali Bhutto, former Prime Minister of Pakistan, is executed.

1980: Eight Year Iraq-Iran war begins.

1982: Israel invades Lebanon in an attack on PLO.

1984: Soviet Union and its allies withdraw from the summer Olympic Games in Los Angeles.

1985: Pakistan's first civilian government in eight years, headed by Prime Minister Mohammed Khan Junejo sworn in.

1987:
- US space shuttle Challenger explodes just after launch from the Cape Canaveral in Florida, killing all seven on board.
- Major Nuclear accident in Soviet Union's Chernobyl power plant.

1988:
- Pakistan President Zia-ul-Haq killed in a plane crash.
- PLO chairman Yasser Arafat declares State of Palestine, with Jerusalem as its capital.
- Benazir Bhutto sworn in PM of Pakistan.

1989:
- Yasser Arafat elected President of Palestine.
- The Dalai Lama wins the Nobel Prize for Peace.

1990:
- Nelson Mandela freed from Prison after 27 years.
- Iraq invades Kuwait.
- West and East Germany united.
- Lithuania, Latvia, Belarus and Kazakhstan declare their independence from the USSR.

1991:
- The USSR divided into 15 republics.
- Begum Khaleda Zia appointed first woman Prime Minister of Bangladesh.
- US and allies go on war against Iraq.

1992:
- Yugoslavia expelled from the UNO.
- The Earth summit, UN Conference Environment and Development (UNCED), held in Rio De Janeiro, Brazil.

1993:
- Czechoslovakia breaks up into Czech Republic and Slovakia.
- President of Sri Lanka, Ranasinghe Premadasa is assassinated.

1994:
- NAFTA comes into effect.
- Nelson Mandela becomes the first black President of South Africa.
- First Communist government formed in Nepal.

Q. 22. What are the religious wars by the European Christians to liberate the holy land called?

Q. 23. When did the Bolshevik Revolution take place?

General Knowledge Manual

1995:
- World Trade Organization (WTO) is established replacing GATT.
- Austria, Finland and Sweden enter the European Union.
- The Bose-Einstein condensate is created for the first time.
- Doctor Bernard Harris Jr becomes the first African-American astronaut to walk in space.

1996:
- Russia becomes member of European Union.
- Dolly, the sheep is the first mammal to be successfully cloned from an adult cell.
- Martina Hingis becomes the youngest person in the history (age 15 years and 282 days) to win the singles' lawn tennis title in women's category at Wimbledon.
- The US signs the CTBT.

1997:
- Civil war in Cambodia breaks out.
- IBM's chess computer 'Deep Blue' defeats Grandmaster Garry Kasparov.
- US Mars Pathfinder transmits first images from Mars.
- Tony Blair of Labour Party elected the Prime Minister of UK.

1998:
- Nuclear test conducted by India and Pakistan.
- Indonesian President Suharto resigns after his 32 years in presidency.

1999:
- The EU common currency, Euro is introduced.
- Kosovo crisis deepens as Russia moves warship into Mediterranean.
- Pakistan's Army General Pervez Musharraf ousts the government of Prime Minister Nawaz Sharif and takes control of Pakistan.
- Human population in the world crosses six billion.

2000:
- Vladimir Putin wins the presidential election of Russia.
- The Constitution of Finland is written.
- Republican candidate George W Bush defeats candidate of the Democratic Party Vice President Al Gore in the US Presidential Election.

2001:
- Cricket legend Sir Donald Bradman passes away.
- Tony Blair re-elected the Prime Minister of UK.
- World Trade Center in New York City was hit by two planes hijacked by terrorists on 11 September.
- American war against terrorism begins in Afghanistan.
- Taliban surrenders Kandahar.

2002:
- The NASA space probe Mars Odyssey finds signs of ice deposits in the planet.
- SARS (Severe Acute Respiratory Syndrome) outbreaks in China and spreads all over the world killing thousands.
- Introduction of Euro bank notes and coins in 12 member state of the EU.
- Quaoar is discovered, which is a Trans-Neptunian object orbiting the sun in Kuiper belt.

Q.24. When was the Battle of Waterloo fought?
Q.25. What was the capital city of King Hammurabi in 1800 BC?

World History

2003:
- The American space shuttle Columbia disintegrates on re-entry into earth's atmosphere, killing all seven astronauts on board, including Indian born Kalpana Chawla.
- US forces seize control of Bagdad which marks the end of Saddam Hussein.
- Zimbabwe withdraws from the Commonwealth of Nations.

2004:
- The first of the NASA's Mars exploration Rovers Spirit successfully lands.
- Brian Lara becomes the first cricketer to score 400 runs in a Test innings against England.
- Tsunami hits South-East Asian nations and around Indian Ocean.
- The Chechen terrorists seize a school in Beslan, Russia.
- George W Bush wins presidential election for a second time.
- Yasser Arafat dies in Paris.

2005:
- Condoleezza Rice becomes the first African American woman to serve as US Secretary of State.
- Kyoto Protocol on global warning comes into effect.
- Tony Blair becomes the first Labour Party Prime Minister to lead his party to three election victories in the UK.
- The International Red Cross and Red Crescendo movement adopt a red crystal design to allow Israel to join as a fully participating member.

2006:
- Former Yugoslavian President Slobodan Milosevic is found dead in his prison cell in the Hague, Netherland.
- UN General Assembly votes to establish the United Nations Human Rights Council.
- Saddam Hussein is executed in Baghdad.

2007:
- Ban-ki-Moon is elected as the new Secretary General of UN.
- US astronauts Sunita Williams sets a new record in space walking of 22 hours and 27 minutes.
- Bulgaria and Romania join the European Union.
- Boris Yeltsin, former Russian President, passes away.
- British troops leave Northern Ireland after 38 years stays as part of 'Operation Banner'.
- The UN marks Mahatma Gandhi's birthday as the First International Day of Non-Violence.
- Political crisis begins in Pakistan after the suspension of Supreme Court Chief Justice Iftikhar Muhammad Chaudhry by General Pervez Musharraf.
- The former Pakistani Prime Minister Benazir Bhutto is assassinated in a suicide attack in Rawalpindi.

2008:
- Kosovo declares independence from Serbia.
- Fidel Castro resigns as President of Cuba; his brother, Raul Castro, succeeds him.

Q.26. From which dynasty China derives its name?

- Nepal holds historic election and becomes republic following the end of its 239 years old monarchy. Narayanhiti Palace in Kathmandu becomes a National Museum.
- Cyclone Nargis ravages the Irrawaddy Delta and Yangon, killing 78,000 people and leaving up to a million homeless.
- The Nuclear Suppliers Group (NSG), comprised representatives from 45 countries, votes to allow India to buy nuclear fuel for its reactors as long as it uses the fuel for civilian purposes only.
- Lehman Brothers declares bankruptcy.
- Zhai Zhigang steps out of the *Shenzhou VII* spacecraft and enters outer space, thus becoming the first Chinese astronaut to walk on space.
- Bhutan's first ever General Election is held on 24 March and Jigme Yoser Thinley becomes Bhutan's first elected Prime Minister.
- CERN begins Large Hadron Collider (LHC) experiment on 10 September in Geneva near the Swiss-French Border.
- World's largest sea bridge inaugurated in the Yangtze River delta in China.
- In Beijing Olympic, Michael Phelps of the USA wins eight gold medals with seven World records and surpassing Mark Spitz's record of winning seven gold medals in single edition of the Olympic Games.
- Usain Bolt of Jamaica becomes the fastest man on earth by completing 100 meter sprint with the record timing of 9.69 seconds; he won three gold medals with three World records in the Beijing Olympic.
- Spain beat Germany 1-0 in the final of Euro 2008 held in Vienna.

ANSWERS

1. Russia and Turkey
2. *Ziggurat*
3. Hieroglyphics
4. Hejira
5. Bartholomew Diaz
6. Liberty, Equality and Fraternity
7. French Revolution
8. St Helena
9. France and England
10. Philadelphia
11. 1919
12. Vladimir Lenin
13. 1917
14. American Independence
15. 6 August 1945
16. Treaty of Versailles
17. Karl Marx
18. Jefferson Davis
19. Begum Khaleda Zia
20. King Philip
21. King Louis XVI
22. Crusades
23. 1917
24. 1815
25. Babylon
26. Chin Dynasty

3
GEOGRAPHY OF INDIA

LOCATION

- India is a part of Asian Continent that lies in Northern hemisphere, from latitude 8° 4' N to 37° 6' N and from longitude 68° 7' E to 97° 25' E.
- It is the seventh largest country in the world, accounts 2.4 per cent of total world surface.

AREA AND DIMENSIONS

- The total area is   32,87,263 sq km
- Distance between North to South   3214 km
- Distance between East to West   2933 km
- Total length of coastline   7516.6 km
- The largest coastline in Gujarat; second largest coast-line in Andhra Pradesh.
- Total length of land frontier   15200 km
- India accounts 2.4 per cent of total world surface and 16.7 per cent of total world population.

BOUNDARIES AND POINTS

East: Myanmar (Burma) and Bangladesh
West: Pakistan, Afghanistan and Arabian Sea
North: The Himalayas, Nepal, Bhutan and China
South: Sri Lanka and Indian Ocean. Gulf of Mannar and Palk Strait separates India from Sri Lanka.

The Southernmost point of Indian Territory is Indira Point (Nicobar Islands – 6.74°N 93.84°E).

Island of India – Andaman and Nicobar in Bay of Bengal and Lakshadweep, Minicoy, Amindive Islands in the Arabian Sea.

INDIA : POLITICAL

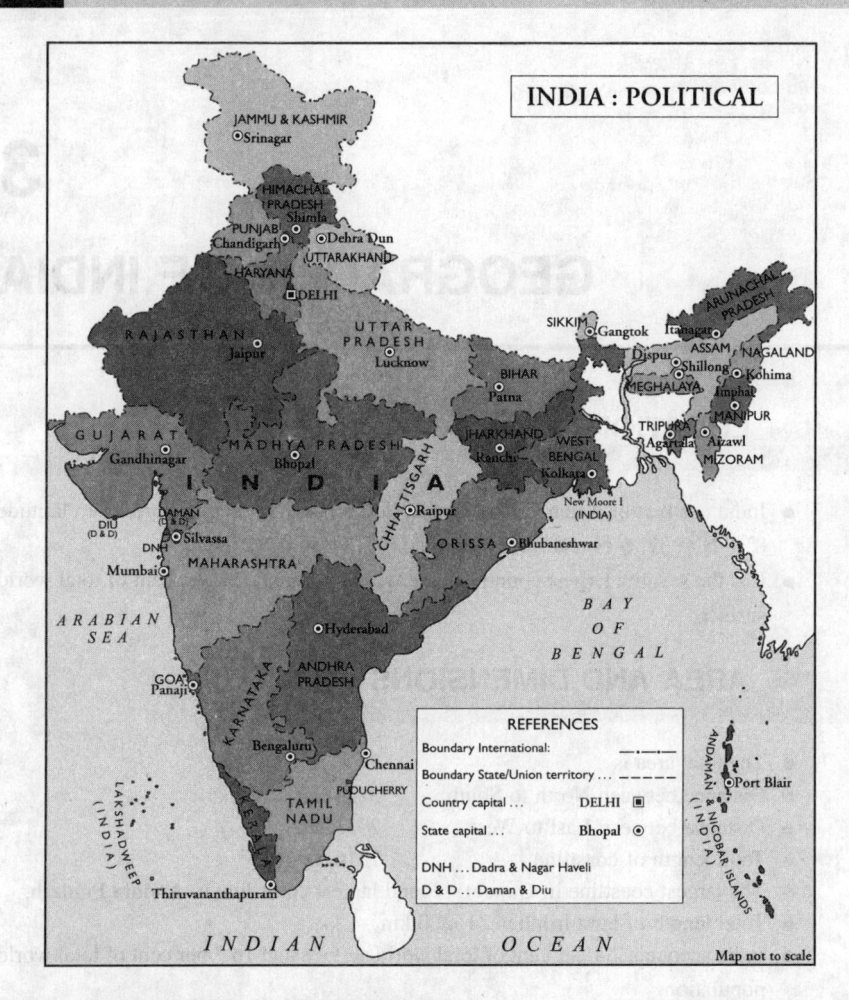

Map not to scale

PHYSICAL PRESENCE

The main land broadly divided into:

A. The Mountains
B. The Plains
C. The Plateau
D. The Desert

The Mountains

The mountains extended for more than 2400 km

  (a) The Himalayas
  (b) The Peninsular Mountains

Q.1. Which is the Indian state that has the longest coastline?
Q.2. Where is the southernmost point of Indian Territory located?

The Himalayas

It borders on the North, North-West and North-East. It comprises three parallel ranges:
- *The Greater Himalayas or the Himadri*: The average altitude of the zone varies from 4,800 metres to 6,000 metres. It contains highest mountains on Earth – Mount Everest (8848 m) in Nepal, Mount Godwin Austin or K2 (8611 m), Kanchenjunga (8580 m), Mount Makalu (8411 m), Mount Dhaulagiri (8177 m).
- *The Lesser Himalayas or the Himachal*: Their average altitude is 1,500 metres to 2,700 metres and of the valley bottoms between 500 metres and 1,200 metres. Important ranges: Dhauladhar, Pir Panjal, Nag Tibba, etc. Important Hill stations: Simla, Chhail, Ranikhet, Chakrata, Mussoorie, Nainital, Darjeeling.
- *The Outer Himalayas or Shiwaliks*: A long chain of narrow and low hills, from 300 metres to 600 metres in elevation lie almost parallel to the main ranges of the Himachal. Important ranges: Korakoram range, Zanskar range, Patkai range, Garo range, Lushai, etc.

The Peninsular Mountains

- *The Aravallis (Rajasthan)*: The oldest mountain range in the World. The highest peak is Guru Shikhar, where Mount Abu (1722m) is situated.
- *The Vindhyas*: It separates Indo-Gangetic plains from Deccan Plateau.
- *The Satpuras Range*: It lies between rivers Narmada and Tapti.
- *The Western Ghats or Sahyadri*: The average height is 915–1220 metres Southern part is separated from main Sahyadri by Palghat (between Tamil Nadu and Kerala)
- *The Eastern Ghats*: The average height is about 610 metres. It lies in the eastern coast and from the boundary of east Coast plains. The highest peak is Mahendra Giri (1501m).
- *The Nilgiris or the Blue Mountains*: The junction of Eastern Ghats and the Western Ghats. The highest peak is Dodda betta.

India's Top 20 Mountain Peaks

S. No	Name of Peaks	Height Above Sea Level (Metres)
1	K2	8611
2	Kanchenjunga	8580
3	Dhaulagiri	8177
4	Nanda Parbat	8126
5	Gasher Brum	8068
6	Brad Peak	8047
7	Disteghil Sar	7885
8	Masher Brum-E	7820
9	Nanda Devi	7818
10	Masher Brum-W	7806
11	Rakapushi	7788
12	Kamet	7756

13	Saser Kangri	7672
14	Skyang Kangri	7544
15	Sia Kangri	7422
16	Chaukhamba (Badrinath Peak)	7138
17	Trishul-West	7138
18	Nunkun	7135
19	Pauhunri	7128
20	Kangto	7090

Glaciers of India

A glacier is a large, slow-moving mass of ice, formed from compact layers of snow. There are two main types of glaciers:

Alpine glaciers, which are a highland glacier that flow slowly down a valley in a mountainous region like a river of ice, and Continental glaciers which are ice sheets and can cover larger areas.

Some of the Important Glaciers

- Siachen glacier is the largest glacier outside the Polar regions and largest in the Himalayas-Karakoram range.
- Gangotri glacier (source of the Ganga) is located in Uttarkashi district, Uttarakhand.
- The Rathong glacier is an important glacier situated in Sikkim.

The Plains

These are formed by the valleys of the rivers Ganga, Yamuna, Brahmaputra, Indus, Godavari, Kaveri, etc. It consists of four divisions:

- Bhabar lies along the foot hills of outer Himalayas. It is highly fertile.
- Tarai and Bhanger have older alluvium deposited by the flow of rivers.
- Khadar is the new alluvium soil.
- The Great Northern Plain is formed by the deposits of three major rivers: Indus, Ganga and Brahmaputra and their tributaries. It's average width is 150–300 km.

Punjab-Haryana Plain: Plain in Haryana is formed by the Yamuna. Punjab plain is made up of Doabs (land between two rivers), formed by the rivers Beas, Ravi, Chenab, Jhelum and Indus.

Gangetic Plains: It forms the largest part of northern plain covering Uttar Pradesh, Bihar, and West Bengal. These are formed by the Ganga and its tributaries.

Upper Ganga Plain is formed by Ganga and its tributaries – the Yamuna, the Gomati and the Ghaghra river.

Middle Ganga Plain is formed by Ghagra, Gandak and Kosi rivers. The delta occupies most of the lower Ganga plain. The Ganga is divided into several channels in this region. A large part of this delta is covered by tidal forest, also called Sunderbans.

Brahmaputra Plains: These plains are formed by the deposits of Brahmaputra and its tributaries. This plain is also known as Assam Valley.

The West-Coastal Plain: It extends from Kanyakumari to Surat. The northern part of

Q.3. Which is the oldest mountain range in India?

Q.4. Which is the largest brackish water lake in India?

western coastal plain is known as Kokan and the southern part of it is known as Malabar Coast.

The East-Coastal Plain: It extends from the West Bengal-Orissa border to Kanyakumari. These are much wider than the west-coastal plains. Most of it is formed by the deltas formed by rivers Mahanadi, Godavari, Krishna and Cauvery. The eastern coastal plain is also called Coromandal Coast.

The Plateau

A plateau is a large, flat area of land that is higher than the surrounding land. In India it lies in south of Indo-Gangetic plains, surrounded by sea in three sides.

Important Plateaus: The Malwa Plateau, The Deccan Plateau, Chhota Nagpur Plateau.

The Malwa Plateau: It is a region in West-Central Northern India, and has volcanic origin. Average elevation is 500 mt.

The Deccan Plateau: The Deccan Plateau, also known as the Peninsular Plateau or the Great Peninsular Plateau, is located between three mountain ranges and extends over eight Indian states. The Peninsular Plateau is flanked on the one side by the Eastern Ghats where average elevation is about 610 metres and on the other by the Western Ghats where it is generally from 915 to 1,220 metres.

It is the largest plateau in India, made up of lava that flowed from fissure eruption. It lies south of the Indo-Gangetic plain.

Chhota Nagpur Plateau: It lies in eastern India. It is made up of three smaller plateaus: the Ranchi, Hazaribagh and Kodarma Plateaus. The Ranchi plateau is the largest of the plateaus, with an average elevation of 700 metres. The total area of Chhota Nagpur is approximately 65,000 km^2.

The Desert

The desert region lies in the western and northern part of India.
It can be divided into two parts:
The Great Desert: It extends from Rann of Kuchch, beyond the Luni River northwards.
The Little Deserts: It extends from Luni River, between Jaisalmar and Jodhpur up to northern-west.

Islands of India

There are two groups of Island:

I. Andaman and Nicobar Group: The Andamans comprise a group of 204 islands at the northern cluster and the Nicobar comprise 19 islands at southern cluster (Great Nicobar is the largest one).

Highest peak in North Andaman is Saddle peak.

II. Lakshadweep: It is a group of 27 coral islands in Arabian Sea, comprising the Lakshadweep Island, 300 km west of Kerala.

- 10° channel separates Andaman from Nicobar.
- Duncan passes separates South Andaman and Little Andaman.
- 9° channel separates Kavaratti from Minicoy Island.
- 8° channel separates Minicoy Island from Maldives.

Q.5. Which type of soil has the maximum water retaining capacity?

Q.6. In which state is the Zaskar and Pir Panjal mountain ranges located?

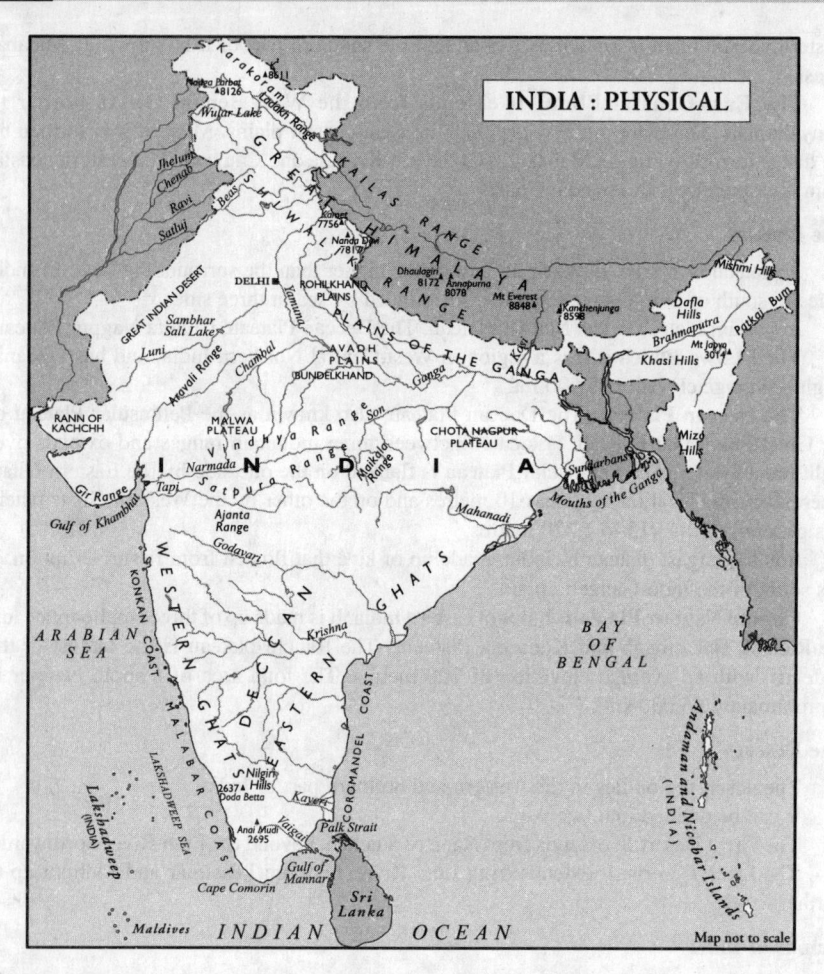

Soils in India

These are broadly divided into following groups:

Alluvial Soil: It is composed of sediments deposited by rivers and waves.

It covers major part of the total soil. Found in Indo-Gangetic Plains, in Punjab, Haryana, Uttar Pradesh, Uttarakhand, Bihar and West Bengal.

Black Soil: It is composed of rich mineral soil (iron and aluminum) formed by deposition of lava ejected by volcanoes and is ideal for Cotton cultivation. It is found in Deccan Plateau – Maharashtra, Madhya Pradesh, Gujarat, Chhattisgarh, Orissa, Andhra Pradesh, Karnataka and Tamil Nadu.

Red Soil: It is formed by weathering of metamorphic and crystalline rocks, having high iron content, ideal for cultivation of pulses. It is found in Andhra Pradesh, Chhattisgarh, Madhya Pradesh, Orissa and Karnataka.

> Q.7. Which is the junction of Eastern Ghats and Western Ghats?
> Q.8. Which is the highest mountain peak in southern India?

Laterite Soil: It is formed by weathering of lime of rocks and is found in Andhra Pradesh, Maharashtra, Eastern Ghats, Orissa and Karnataka.

Forest Soil: It is formed by plantation of tea, coffee, spices and tropical fruits. It is found in Himalayas and other ranges in north and in peninsular region.

RIVER SYSTEMS OF INDIA

The rivers in India are classified as:

(a) The Himalayan River System
(b) The Peninsular River System

The Himalayan River System: The Himalayan rivers are formed by melting of snow and glaciers and therefore they are perennial.

River Indus (3180 km): It originates from Mansarovar lake (western Tibet) and flows through India and thereafter through Pakistan and finally falls in the Arabian sea near Karachi.

Main Tributaries are: Jhelum (725 km) which originates from Virinag, Chenab (1800 km) from Bara Lacha pass, Ravi (720 km) from Kullu Hills near Rohtang pass in Himachal Pradesh, Beas (470 km) from near Rohtang pass and Satluj (1050 km) from Mansarovar lake.

(i) *River Ganga (2510 km):* Originating from Gangotri glacier in the Uttarakhand and it forms the Sunderbans delta before falling in the Bay of Bengal.

The rivers Bhagirathi and Alakananda meet at Debprayag to form the river Ganga.

The river Bhagirathi rises at the foot of Gangotri glacier, at Gaumukh; river Alakananda from Badrinath and Mandakini from Kedarnath.

Yamuna (1375 km) is the largest tributary of the Ganga, which meets it at Allahabad. Other tributaries are: Ghaghra, Gandhak, Kosi, Gomiti, Damodar.

In Bangladesh it is known as Padma.

(ii) *Brahmaputra River (2900 km):* Originates from Mansarovar Lake (western Tibet). In Tibet it flows in the name of Tsangpro and when it enters in India, it is known as Dihang.

Main tributaries are: Sibansiri, Dhansiri, Manas, Teesta and Kameng.

Before it enters Bay of Bengal it is known as 'Meghna'.

The Peninsular River System: These are seasonal rivers, as their flow depends mainly on rainfall. They carry about 30 per cent of total discharge.

These can be divided into following categories:

(a) East-Flowing Rivers
(b) West-Flowing Rivers

East-Flowing Rivers

Mahanadi (890 km) rises from north-west of Deccan Plateau and enters into Bay of Bengal.

Godavari (1450 km) rises from Western Ghats and is the longest peninsular river system. It is also called Vriddha Ganga or Dakshina Ganga.

Krishna (1290 km) rises from Western Ghats, near Mahabaleswar and enters into Bay of Bengal. It is the second largest peninsular river system.

Q.9. Across which river is the Vidyasagar setu built?

Q.10. Which Indian state has the largest forest area cover?

Cauvery (760 km) rises from Western Ghats and enters into Bay of Bengal.
Pennar (560 km) rises from Western Ghats and enters into Bay of Bengal.

West-Flowing Rivers

Narmada (1290 km) rises from Amarkantak Plateau (north-west of Deccan Plateau) and enters into gulf of Khambat.
Tapti (724 km) rises from north-west of Deccan plateau and flows into Arabian Sea.
Sabarmati (416 km) rises from Aravallis and flows into Arabian Sea.
Periyar (300 km) rises from Western Ghats and enters into Arabian Sea.
Sharavati rises from Sahyadri. It forms the famous jog or Gersoppa falls (289 m).

Some rivers in Rajasthan do not reach the sea and make inland drainage. The Ghaggar is an inland drainage river.

Water Bodies of India

1. Chillika Lake is the largest lake of India and is in the state of Orissa. It is also the largest brackish water lake of India.
2. Wular Lake is the largest fresh water lake of India, present in Jammu and Kashmir.
3. Sambhar Lake is in Rajasthan. Salt is produced from this lake.

Some other important lakes are Dal Lake in Jammu and Kashmir, Pulicat and Kolleru in Andhra Pradesh and Vembanad in Kerala.

Important Gulfs in India

Gulf of Kutch (Gujarat) has the highest potential of tidal energy generation.
Gulf of Cambay (Gujarat) Rivers Tapti, Narmada, Sabarmati and Mahi rivers drain into it.
Gulf of Mannar (Tamil Nadu) is the first marine biosphere in Asia.

CLIMATE IN INDIA

In broad terms India experiences four seasons:
(i) Winter (January-February)
(ii) Summer (March-May)
(iii) Monsoon (June-September)
(iv) Post-monsoon, also known as north-east monsoon in the southern Peninsula (October-December)

However, the monsoon is the main season. India experiences rain during following monsoons:

1. South-West Monsoon lasts for four months, from June to September and is known as summer monsoon. It blows from sea to land after crossing the Indian Ocean, the Arabian Sea and the Bay of Bengal. India receives 86 per cent of the rain during South-West Monsoon.

2. North-East Monsoon stretches from the month of November to December. It is also called winter monsoon and blows from land to sea. It is

Q.11. How many separate islands does the group Lakshadweep consists of?

Q.12. On which state does the retreating monsoon has the most effect?

effective in smaller areas: Tamil Nadu, Kerala, sometimes Andhra Pradesh and Karnataka.

During the monsoon several regions experience rainfall above 200 cm – Assam, Meghalaya, Sikkim, and West Bengal. Some areas experiences lesser rain fall (below 50 cm) are – western Rajasthan, south-east Punjab, Ladakh, and southern Haryana.

FORESTS IN INDIA

India covers about two per cent of the World's total forest area. The total area under forest land in India is 20.64 per cent and Madhya Pradesh have the largest forest area.

India has six types of forests. They are:

1. Evergreen forests (Tropical Forests) are found in the areas that receive an average 200 cms to 300 cms of rainfall. Average annual temperature is 20° C to 27° C and average humidity is more than 80 per cent. It is found in Western Ghats and sub-Himalayan regions. Trees that grow in these forests are teak, rose wood, ebony and bamboos.

2. Deciduous forests (Monsoon Forests) are found in places that receive lesser rainfall between 150 cms to 200 cms, have an average temperature of 24° C to 28° C and humidity is about 75 per cent. Trees found in these forests are sal and sandal wood, and are spread across Maharashtra, Madhya Pradesh and Karnataka.

3. Dry forests are found in those areas which receive scant amount of rainfall between 75 cms to 100 cms, have an average annual temperature between 23° C to 29° C and humidity 50 to 60 per cent. Trees found are palm and acacias.

4. Hill forests are found in Southern India and Himalayas. Trees found are oak, pine, deodar, walnut, maple and chestnut.

5. Tidal forests (Mangrove) are found in coastal submerged plains of Ganges (Sundarban), Delta of Mahanadi and Godavari.

6. Grasslands are found in hilly areas of Himalayas, Deccan hills above 100 metres, lowlands as in Punjab, Haryana, Uttar Pradesh, Bihar and riverine grassland.

AGRICULTURE

About 60–70 per cent people in India live on agriculture and about 50 per cent (approx. 142.42 million hectares) of total land is under cultivation. There are two major crop seasons: Kharif and Rabi

Kharif crops are sown in June-July and harvested in September-October. Main cultivations are rice, jawar, bajra, ragi, maize, cotton and jute.

Rabi crops are sown in October-December and harvested in April-May. Main cultivations are wheat, barley, peas, rap seed, mustard and gram.

Q.13. Which Indian state is the largest producer of natural rubber?
Q.14. Which river is known as Dakshin Ganga?

General Knowledge Manual

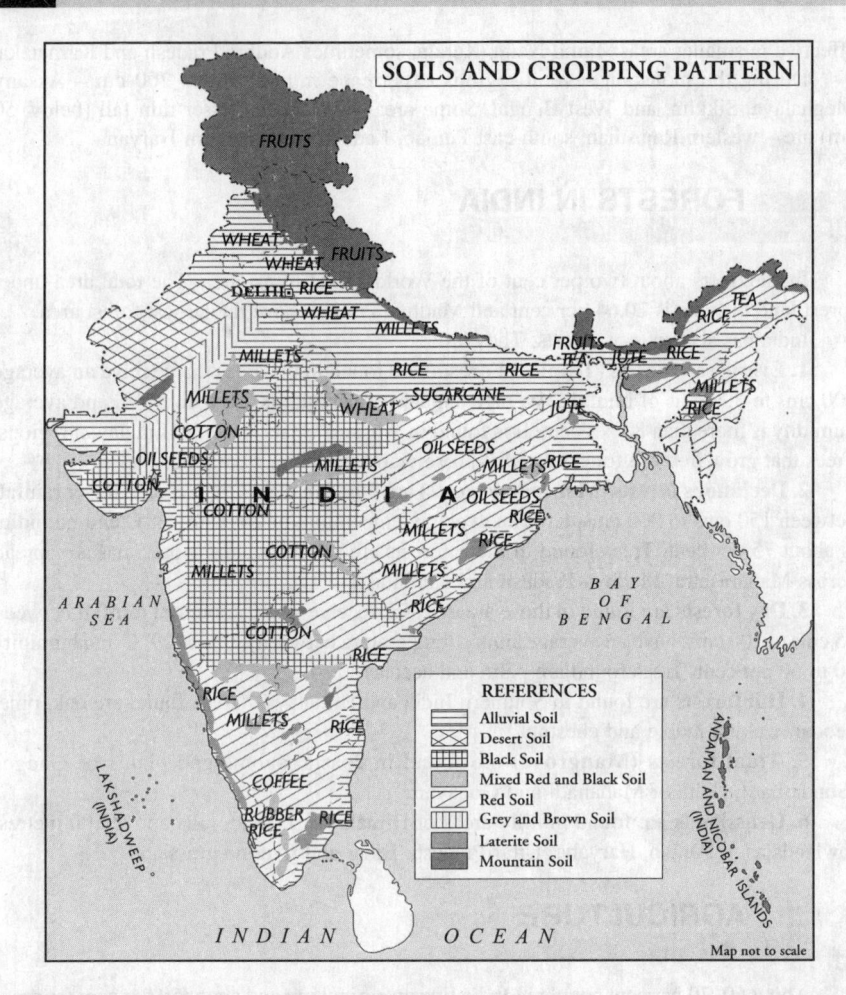

SOILS AND CROPPING PATTERN

Map not to scale

Some Important Crops and Major Producing States

Crops	Major States
Rice	West Bengal, Tamil Nadu, Uttar Pradesh, Andhra Pradesh, Punjab
Wheat	Uttar Pradesh, Punjab, Haryana, Madhya Pradesh, Rajasthan
Maize	Uttar Pradesh, Bihar, Punjab
Bajra	Rajasthan, Gujarat, Uttar Pradesh, Maharashtra
Barley	Maharashtra, Uttar Pradesh, Rajasthan
Sugar cane	Uttar Pradesh, Maharashtra, Tamil Nadu, Andhra Pradesh
Cotton	Gujarat, Maharashtra, Punjab, Tamil Nadu, Haryana

Q.15. By which name does the Brahmaputra enter into India?
Q.16. What are the Satpura ranges an example of?

Jute	West Bengal, Jharkhand, Bihar, Orissa, Assam
Silk	Karnataka, Kerala
Oilseeds	Madhya Pradesh, Gujarat, Rajasthan, Tamil Nadu
Groundnut	Andhra Pradesh, Gujarat, Tamil Nadu
Coconut	Kerala, Tamil Nadu
Sunflower	Maharashtra, Karnataka
Sesame	Uttar Pradesh, Rajasthan
Coffee	Karnataka, Kerala, Tamil Nadu
Tea	Assam, West Bengal, Himachal Pradesh, Tripura, Manipur, Kerala
Rubber	Kerala, Karnataka
Tobacco	Gujarat, Andhra Pradesh, Karnataka, Tamil Nadu, Maharashtra, Madhya Pradesh
Pepper	Kerala, Karnataka, Tamil Nadu
Ginger	Kerala, Uttar Pradesh
Turmeric	Andhra Pradesh, Orissa
Chillies	Maharashtra, Andhra Pradesh
Cloves	Kerala
Saffron	Jammu and Kashmir, Karnataka, Tamil Nadu

Some Landmarks in Indian Agriculture

Green Revolution: To increase agricultural output, green revolution was launched in 1967–68. First green revolution took place mainly in the states of Punjab, Haryana and Uttar Pradesh to increase wheat production. Second green revolution (1983–84) happened mainly in eastern states including Orissa, Bihar, Madhya Pradesh and eastern part of Uttar Pradesh. Due to the impact of green revolution the wheat production got doubled and rice production increased by 53 per cent.

Operation Flood was launched in 1970–81 in collaboration with World Bank to increase the milk market in urban areas.

Operation Flood II was launched in 1981 and was extended to all states.

Operation Flood III (1985–90) was launched in 1985 during the seventh Five-Year Plan. These programmes were implemented under National Dairy Development Board (NDB) and Indian Dairy Corporation (IDC). Banking on these programmes, India became the second largest producer of milk in the world, only next to the USA.

Irrigation and Agriculture

Due to climatic positions, agriculture in India mainly depends on rains. However, rain water is not sufficient to meet the requirements of the agriculture. There are other methods used for providing water for cultivation, called irrigation.

Methods of Irrigation

Wells accounts for about 47 per cent of the total irrigated land in the country. It is mainly used in Uttar Pradesh, Punjab, Tamil Nadu and Maharashtra.

Tanks supply water to about 10 per cent of the total irrigated areas. It is mainly used in central and southern India.

Q.17. Which is the world's longest river bridge?
Q.18. Which is India's largest manmade lake?

Canals account for about 40 per cent of the total irrigated areas. It is mainly used in Uttar Pradesh, Punjab, Haryana and Orissa.

Multi-Purpose River Project

Name of the Project	River	State	Purpose
Bhakra-Nangal	Sutlej	Punjab	Power and Irrigation
Beas	Beas	Punjab	Power and Irrigation
Chambal	Chambal	Madhya Pradesh & Rajasthan	Power and Irrigation
Damodar Valley (First in India)	Damodar	Bihar	Power, Irrigation, Flood Control
Farakka	Ganga	West Bengal	Power and Irrigation
Hirakud	Mahanadi	Orissa	Power and Irrigation
Kakrapara	Tapti	Gujarat	Power and Irrigation
Kosi	Kosi	Bihar	Power, Irrigation, Flood
Matatilla	Betwa	Uttar Pradesh & Madhya Pradesh	Power and Irrigation
Mayurakshi	Mayurakshi	West Bengal	Power and Irrigation
Nagarjunsagar	Krishna	Andhra Pradesh	Power and Irrigation
Ramaganga	Ramaganga	Uttar Pradesh	Power and Irrigation
Rihand	Rihand	Uttar Pradesh	Hydroelectricity
Tungabhadra	Tungabhadra	Karnataka	Power and Irrigation
Ukai	Tapti	Gujarat	Power and Irrigation

MINERALS OF INDIA

India is a rich source of minerals, such as iron, mica, manganese, bauxite, etc. Other minerals are also found here.

Some Important Minerals

Mineral	Found in	Facts
Iron	Orissa, Bihar, Jharkhand, AP, TN, Karnataka, Maharashtra, Goa	India has the World's largest reserves (about 25 per cent)
Coal	Bihar, WB, Orissa, MP, Maharashtra, AP, Assam	Third largest producer
Manganese	Orissa, MP, Maharashtra, Gujarat, Karnataka, Jharkhand, AP	Third largest producer
Mica	Jharkhand, Rajasthan, AP, Tamil Nadu	Largest reserves in World
Bauxite (Aluminium Ore)	Jharkhand, Gujarat, Chhattisgarh, TN, Karnataka, Maharashtra, J&K, Orissa	Third largest producer

Q.19. Where is Ellora cave located?
Q.20. To which state does the Garos tribal groups belong to?

Crude Oil	Assam, Tripura, Manipur, WB, Himachal Pradesh, Kutch, Maharashtra, Gujarat
Gold	Karnataka, AP
Gypsum	Rajasthan, J&K, TN
Zinc	AP, Gujarat, Maharashtra, Meghalaya, TN, Orissa, Sikkim, Rajasthan
Chromite	Orissa, Jharkhand, Karnataka, TN, AP, Maharashtra, Manipur
Dolomite	MP, Orissa, Gujarat, UP, Maharashtra, WB, Arunachal Pradesh
Diamond	MP, Bihar, Orissa

TRANSPORT AND COMMUNICATION

There are four transport systems in India. They are: Railways, Road, Air and Water Transport.

Railway Transport

- Indian Railway system is the third largest in the World after US and Canada and largest in Asia.
- It is the biggest Public Undertaking in the country also the biggest employer in the world (1.54 million employees).
- On 16 April 1853, first train in India ran between Bombay and Thane, a distance of 34 km. Second train ran between Howrah and Hoogly in 1854.
- In 1929, first electric train, Deccan Queen ran between Bombay and Pune.
- The electrified system of Indian Railways is the second largest in the World next to Russia.
- The fastest train in India is 'Bhopal Shatabdi Express', which runs at a maximum speed of 140 km per hour.
- Total railways network is 63,465 km.
- Total number of railway stations in India is 7133.
- The longest railway platform in India is in Kharagpur (West Bengal).
- The longest train route is Jammu-Tavi to Kanyakumari, a distance of 3,726 km, which stretches across 10 states. The Himsagar Express runs on this route.
- The highest number of trains terminates in Mumbai.
- First metro rail started in Kolkata on 24 October 1984, commuting between Dumdum and Balgachhia.

Q.21. Which is the smallest of all Union Territories?
Q.22. Where is the earth satellite station located in India?
Q.23. On which river is the Rana Pratap Sagar dam located?

Rail Tracks of Indian Railways

Rail Tracks	Distance Between Rails	Route (km)	Running Tracks (km)	Total Tracks (km)
Brad Gauge	1.676 m	47,749	67,932	89,771
Metre Gauge	1.00 m	12,662	13,271	15,684
Narrow Gauge	0.762 m/.61 m	3,054	3,057	3,350
Total		63,465	84,260	1,08,805

Indian Railways is divided into 16 zones and each zone is headed by General Manager.

Zone	Date of Creation	Head Quarters
Southern	14 Apr 51	Chennai
Northern	14 Apr 51	New Delhi
Western	5 Nov 51	Mumbai
North-Eastern	14 Apr 52	Gorakhpur
Eastern	1 Aug 55	Kolkata
South-Eastern	1 Aug 55	Kolkata
Central	5 Nov 55	Mumbai (CST)
North-East-Frontier	15 Jan 58	Malegaon-Guwahati
South Central	2 Oct 66	Secunderabad
East Central	1 Oct 02	Hajipur (Bihar)
North-Western	1 Oct 02	Jaipur
East Coast	1 Apr 03	Bhubaneswar
North Central	1 Apr 03	Allahabad
South-East Central	1 Apr 03	Bilaspur (Chhattisgarh)
South-Western	1 Apr 03	Hubli (Karnataka)
West Central	1 Apr 03	Jabalpur (Madhya Pradesh)

- Northern Railway is the largest railway zone and accounts for 10,995 km.
- North-East-Frontier is the smallest Railway zone and accounts for 3,860 km.
- First Hospital on Wheel in the world started in Mumbai on 16 July 1991, known as Jeevan Rekha or Life Line Express. It caters to the medical needs of people in rural areas.

Railway Manufacturing Units

Name	Location	Established in	Items Manufactured
Chittaranjan Locomotive Works	Chittaranjan (WB)	1950	Locomotives
Integral Coach Factory	Perambur (TN)	1955	Coaches
Diesel Locomotive Works	Varanasi (UP)	1964	Locomotives
Diesel-Loco Modernization Works	Patiala (Punjab)	1981	Components of Diesel engine
Rail Coach Factory	Kapurtala (Punjab)	1988	Coaches, Wagons and Special containers
Rail Wheel Factory	Bangalore	2004	Wheels and axles

Geography of India

Road Transport

India has a vast road network of about 3.34 million kilometres, which includes National highways, State Highways, Major District Roads (MDR) and rural roads.

National highways and border roads are maintained by Central Government, state highways by State Governments and district roads and rural roads by respective districts administratives.

Types of Road	Total Length (km)
National Highways	66,590
State Highways	1,28,000
District roads	4,70,000
Rural roads	26,50,000

Roads carry about 60 per cent of the freight traffic and about 80 per cent of the total passenger traffic in the country. National Highways carry about 40 per cent road traffic in the country. Maharashtra has the maximum length of roads in India. NH-7 is the longest one.

National Highways	From	To
NH-1	New Delhi	Amritsar
NH-2	New Delhi	Kolkata
NH-3	Agra	Mumbai
NH-4	Thane (Maharashtra)	Chennai
NH-5	Kolkata	Chennai
NH-6	Kolkata	Dhule (Maharashtra)
NH-7	Varanasi	Kanyakumari
NH-8	Delhi	Mumbai
NH-9	Mumbai	Vijayawada
NH-10	Delhi	Fazilaka (Punjab)

Work on Golden Quadrilateral Project which will connect the four metropolitan cities: Delhi, Mumbai, Chennai and Kolkata and will cover a distance of 5952 km is still going on.

Air Transport

History: Jahangir Ratanji Dadabhoy Tata was the first person to take a flight from Mumbai to Karachi in 1931. Tata Airlines started its operation between Mumbai and Thiruvananthapuram in 1935 and between Mumbai and Delhi in 1937.

Developments

- In 1953, Private Airlines were nationalised and Indian Airlines and Air India were formed.
- Ministry of Civil Aviation is responsible for:
  (a) Formulation of National Policies and programmes for development and regulation of Civil Aviation;
  (b) Devising and implementing schemes for orderly growth and expansion of civil air transport;

Q.24. Where is Chinnar wildlife sanctuary located?
Q.25. Which state is the largest producer of pulses in India?

(c) Oversee the provision of airport facilities, air traffic services and carriage of passengers and goods by air.

Public Sector Undertakings under Ministry of Civil Aviation
- Airports Authority of India (AAI).
- Indian Airlines and its subsidiary.
- The AAI was formed on 1 April 1995 by merging the National Airports Authority (NAA) and the International Airports Authority of India (IAAI). The corporate headquarters (CHQ) is at New Delhi.
- Air India manages International operations, while Indian Airlines manages domestic operations.
- AAI manages and operates 127 airports including 12 international airports, 90 domestic airports and 26 civil enclaves at Defence airfields.
- AAI controls and manages the entire Indian airspace of 2.8 million Nautical Miles on land, 1.75 million nautical miles of ocean space and restricted land area of 0.37 million nautical miles square.
- AAI has a Civil Aviation Centre in Fursatgarh, near Allahabad to provide ground training to the pilots along with other services.
- Pawan Hans Limited operates helicopter services to oil sector, hill stations and remote areas.
- A number of private airlines also operate in India – Jet Airways, King Fisher Airlines, Indigo Airlines, etc.
- There are about 370 fleets operating in India presently and it is expected to reach about 500–550 by the end of 2010.
- India ranks third in the World, only next to China and the US, in terms of number of flights.
- The number of Air travellers is about 0.8 per cent of the total population.

International Airports of India

1.	Amritsar International Airport (Rajasansi Airport)	Amritsar
2.	Bangalore International Airport	Bangalore
3.	Chennai International Airport (Meenambakkam Airport)	Chennai
4.	Chhatrapati Shivaji International Airport	Mumbai
5.	Cochin International Airport	Kochi
6.	Goa Airport	Vasco da Gama
7.	Hyderabad International Airport	Hyderabad
8.	Indira Gandhi International Airport	New Delhi
9.	Lokpriya Gopinath Bordolio International Airport	Guwahati
10.	Netaji Subashchandra Bose International Airport	Kolkata
11.	Sardar Vallabhbhai Patel International Airport	Ahmedabad
12.	Thiruvananthapuram International Airport	Thiruvananthapuram

Air Traffic Management

Airports Authority of India (AAI) manages one of the biggest airspace in the world which encompasses huge area of oceanic airspace in the Bay of Bengal and Arabian Sea.

Q.26. What was the first multi-purpose project of Independent India?
Q.27. Which river originates at Amarkantak?

Total Air space: 6.0 Million sq km (approx.)
Land area: 2.2 Million sq km (approx.)
Oceanic area: 3.8 Million sq km (approx.)

Water Transport

- India has about 14500 km of navigable waterways, which comprise rivers, canals, back waters, creeks, etc., out of which 3700 km is navigable by boats.
- About 44 million tonnes of cargo is moved annually through the water ways.
- Inland Water Authority of India (IWAI) came into existence in 27 October 1986.
- The objective of IWAI is to develop and regularise the inland waterways for shipping and navigation. Head office of IWAI is in Noida.
- It has regional offices: Patna, Kolkata, Guwahati, and Kochi, sub-offices in Allahabad, Varanasi, Bhagalpur, Farakka and Kollam.

Three waterways have been declared as National waterways (NW). They are:

1. NW-1: Allahabad – Haldia stretch (1620 km) of Ganga, Bhagirathi and Hoogly river system.
2. NW-2: Sadiya – Dhubri stretch (819 km) of Brahmaputra River.
3. NW-3: Kuttupuram – Kollam stretch (205 km) of west coast canal along with Champakara and Udyogmandal canal.

PORTS IN INDIA

- India with a coastline of 7617 km has 12 major ports. There are about 187 minor and intermediate ports.
- While the Central Shipping Ministry administer the major ports, the minor and intermediate ports are administered by the relevant departments or ministries in the nine coastal states of West Bengal, Orissa, Andhra Pradesh, Tamil Nadu, Kerala, Karnataka, Goa, Maharashtra and Gujarat.
- India has 28 shipyards; out of which seven shipyards are under the control of the central government, two shipyards are controlled by state governments, and nineteen are privately owned shipyards.
- About 95 per cent of the India's foreign trades by volume and 70 per cent by value moves through ports.

Twelve Major ports are:

Name	State	Sea
Chennai	Tamil Nadu	Bay of Bengal
Cochin	Kerala	Arabian Sea
Ennore	Tamil Nadu	Bay of Bengal
Jawahar Lal Nehru (JNPT)	Maharashtra	Arabian Sea
(Fifth fastest growing port in the world)		

Q.28. Which is the fastest train in India?
Q.29. Which channel separates Andamans from Nicobar?

Kandla	Gujarat	Arabian Sea
Kolkata	West Bengal	Bay of Bengal
Maormugoa	Goa	Arabian Sea
Mumbai (Busiest Port)	Maharashtra	Arabian Sea
New Mangalore	Karnataka	Arabian Sea
Paradip	Orissa	Bay of Bengal
Tuticorin	Tamil Nadu	Bay of Bengal
Vishakhapatnam (*Deepest port*)	Andhra Pradesh	Bay of Bengal

Communication System of India

Postal Service

- The British East India Company established the first post office in Bombay followed by similar ones in Calcutta and Madras from 1764-66, each serving the Bombay, Madras and Calcutta presidencies.
- Indian Post Office was established on 1 October 1837.
- The usage of the stamps began on 1 July 1852 in Scinde/Sindh district.
- Independent India's first stamp was issued on 21 November 1947, depicting the national emblem.
- Mahatma Gandhi was the first person to be depicted on Free India's Stamp (1948).
- India has been divided into 22 postal circles.
- The Indian Postal Service, with 155,516 post offices, is the most widely distributed post office system in the world (China is next, with 57,000).
- Money Order service was started in 1880.
- Pin code in India was introduced on 15 August 1972.

Telephone Service

- In 1850, the first experimental electric telegraph line was started between Kolkata and Diamond Harbour. In 1851, it was opened for the British East India Company.
- First telephone service and also telephone exchange was started in Kolkata in 1881.
- First International telephone line was started between London and Mumbai in 1870.
- In 1960, first subscriber trunk dialing (STD) route commissioned between Kanpur and Lucknow.
- First automatic telephone exchange was established in Shimla in 1913, with a capacity of 700 lines.
- In 1985, first mobile telephone service started on non-commercial basis in Delhi.

DEMOGRAPHY

Demography is the scientific study of human population, its size, structure, and development.

India's population reached one billion marks on 11 May 2000.

Q.30. What is the name of the place where most of India's iron and steel industries are located?

Q.31. In which state is the Jog Fall located?

India accounts a meagre 2.4 per cent of world area, which supports 16.7 per cent of world population.

Factors Influencing Demography

Populations can change through three processes: Birth, death, and migration.

Birth: The ratio of total live births to total population in a specified community or area over a specified period of time. The birth rate is often expressed as the number of live births per 1,000 of the population per year.

Death: It is expressed in mortality rate, which is defined as a measure of the number of deaths (in general, or due to a specific cause) in some population, scaled to the size of that population, per unit time. Mortality rate is typically expressed in units of deaths per 1000 individuals per year.

Migration: Migration refers to the movement of people from an origin place to a destination place across some pre-defined, political boundary.

Populations in a Geographical Area: If population of a country is 'X', at time 'T', then the size of the population at time T + 1 is

Size of Population = X + Natural-increase + Netmigration
Natural increase from time T to T + 1:
Natural-increase = Births – Deaths
Net migration from time T to T + 1:
Net migration = Immigration* – Emigration**
* Immigration is the arrival of new individuals in a geographical area.
** Emigration is the act of leaving one's native country or region to settle in another.

Facts About Census 2001

Census: Census is the process of collecting, compiling, analysing and publishing demographic, social and economic data pertaining to specific point of time to all persons in a country.

Total Population:	1028610328
Population Density** (per Sq km):	324
Sex Ratio*:	933
Literacy Rate (%):	65.38
Urban Population (%):	27.78
Life Expectancy (yr):	68.59
Birth Rate (%):	2.2
Death Rate (%):	0.65
Total Fertility Rate:	2.81/women
Unemployment Rate (%):	7.8

Note: * Sex Ratio: It is defined as the number of females per thousand males.
** Population Density: It is defined as the number of persons per sq km.

Q.32. In which season is the Kharif crop harvested?
Q.33. Give the name of the islands between which Duncan Pass is located.

Progress of Literacy in India, 1901 To 2001

Year	Total (%)	Male (%)	Female (%)
1901	5.53	9.83	0.69
1911	5.92	10.56	1.05
1921	7.16	12.21	1.81
1931	9.5	15.59	2.93
1951	18.33	27.16	8.86
1961	28.3	40.4	15.35
1971	34.45	45.96	21.98
1981	42.57	56.38	29.76
1991	52.21	64.13	39.29
2001	65.38	75.85	54.16

Sex Ratio In India (1901–2001)

Year	Sex Ratio	Year	Sex Ratio
1901	972	1961	941
1911	964	1971	930
1921	955	1981	934
1931	950	1991	927
1941	945	2001	933
1951	946		

Rural-Urban Distribution

Total Rural Population:	742,490,639 (72.2%)
Total Urban Population:	286,119,689 (27.8%)
State with Highest percentage of Urban Population:	Goa (49.76%)
State with Lowest percentage of Urban Population:	Himachal Pradesh (9.3%)
UT with highest percentage of Urban Population:	Delhi (93.18%)
UT with lowest percentage of Urban Population:	Dadra and Nagar Haveli (22.89%)

State-wise Statistics

Literacy Rate (%):

First Five		Last Five	
Kerala	90.92	Bihar	47.53
Mizoram	88.49	Jharkhand	54.13
Goa	82.32	Jammu & Kashmir	54.46
Maharashtra	77.27	Arunachal Pradesh	54.74
Himachal Pradesh	77.13	Uttar Pradesh	57.36

Q.34. Where is the Head Office of Inland Water Authority of India located?
Q.35. Which is the largest railway zone of India?

Sex Ratio

First Five		Last Five	
Kerala	1058	Haryana	861
Chhattisgarh	990	Punjab	874
Tamil Nadu	986	Sikkim	875
Andhra Pradesh	978	Jammu & Kashmir	890
Manipur	978	Uttar Pradesh	898

Area-wise Position of States

First Five (Area in sq km)		Last Five (Area in sq km)	
Rajasthan	342,239	Goa	3,702
Madhya Pradesh	308,144	Sikkim	7,096
Maharashtra	307,713	Tripura	10,492
Uttar Pradesh	294,000	Nagaland	16,579
Andhra Pradesh	275,045	Mizoram	21,081

Population-wise Position of States

First Five		Last Five	
Uttar Pradesh	166,197,921	Sikkim	540,851
Maharashtra	96,752,247	Mizoram	891,058
Bihar	82,878,796	Arunachal Pradesh	1,091,117
West Bengal	80,221,171	Goa	1,343,998
Andhra Pradesh	75,727,541	Nagaland	1,988,636

Population Density

First Five		Last Five	
West Bengal	904	Arunachal Pradesh	13
Bihar	880	Mizoram	42
Kerala	819	Sikkim	76
Uttar Pradesh	689	Manipur	107
Punjab	482	Himachal Pradesh	109

Percentage of Total Population

First Five		Last Five	
Uttar Pradesh	16.6	Sikkim	5.4
Maharashtra	9.7	Mizoram	8.9
Bihar	8.3	Arunachal Pradesh	10.9
West Bengal	8	Goa	13.4
Andhra Pradesh	7.6	Nagaland	19.8

Q.36. Between which two places was the first international telephone line in India started?
Q.37. How many PIN Code zones are there in India?

Area-wise Position of Union Territories (sq km)

Andaman and Nicobar Island:	8,249
Delhi (NCT):	1,483
Pondicherry:	492
Dadra and Nagar Haveli:	491
Chandigarh:	114
Daman & Diu:	112
Lakshadweep:	32

Population-wise Position of Union Territories

Delhi (NCT):	13,850,507
Pondicherry:	973,829
Chandigarh:	900,914
Andaman and Nicobar Island:	356,265
Dadra and Nagar Haveli:	220,451
Daman & Diu:	158,059
Lakshadweep:	60,650

Population-wise Positions of Districts in India

First Five		Last Five	
Medinipur (West Bengal)	9,610,788	Yanam (Pondicherry)	31,394
North 24 Pargonas (West Bengal)	8,930,295	Upper Siang (Arunachal Pradesh)	33,146
Mumbai Suburban (Maharashtra)	8,587,561	Lahul & Spiti (Himachal Pradesh)	33,224
Thane (Maharashtra)	8,128,833	Tawang (Arunachal Pradesh)	34,705
Pune (Maharashtra)	7,224,238	Mahe (Pondicherry)	36,823

Largest District: Kachchh (Gujarat)   45,652 sq km
Smallest District: Mahe (Pondicherry)   9 sq km

Most Literate (in %) Districts in India (Top Five)

Aizawl (Mizoram):	96.64
Serchhip (Mizoram):	96.18
Kotayam (Kerala):	95.90
Mahe (Pondicherry):	65.78
Pathanamthitta (Kerala):	95.09

Population-wise Top Cities in India

1. Greater Mumbai   16,368,084
2. Kolkata   13,216,546
3. Delhi   12,791,458
4. Chennai   6,424,624

Q.38. Indian Railway is divided into how many zones.
Q.39. On which river is Dibrugarh situated?

5. Bangalore	5,686,844	
6. Hyderabad	5,533,640	
7. Ahmedabad	4,519,278	
8. Pune	4,519,278	
9. Surat	2,811,466	
10. Kanpur	2,690,486	
11. Jaipur	2,324,319	
12. Lucknow	2,266,933	
13. Nagpur	2,122,965	
14. Patna	1,707,429	
15. Indore	1,639,044	

- State with maximum forest area: Madhya Pradesh
- State with highest mineral output: Jharkhand
- State producing maximum sugar: Uttar Pradesh
- State producing maximum wheat: Uttar Pradesh
- State producing maximum rice: West Bengal
- State producing maximum tea: Assam
- State producing maximum cotton: Gujarat
- State producing maximum sugar cane: Uttar Pradesh

MISCELLANEA

National Parks: 89; covers about 37526.90 sq km (about 1.14 per cent of India's total area)

Wildlife Sanctuaries: 501; covers about 1,07,310 sq km (about 4.5 per cent of India's total land area)

Name	Location	Reserve for
Kaziranga National park	Jorhat (Assam)	Rhinoceros, Buffalos, Hog
Manas National Park	Manas (Assam)	Rhinoceros
Sonairupa Sanctuary	Tezpur (Assam)	Elephant, Sambar, Wild Boar, Rhinoceros
Namdapha National Park	Arunachal Pradesh	Tiger
Pakhal Sanctuary	Warangal (AP)	Tiger, Panther, Nilgai
Dachigam	Kashmir	Kashmir Stag
Corbet National Park	Nainital (Uttarakhand)	Tiger, Elephant
Achanakmar Sanctuary	Bilaspur (MP)	Tiger, Bear, Chital, Sambar, Bison
Kanha National Park	Madhya Pradesh	Tiger
Shivpuri National Park	Madhya Pradesh	Leopards, Jackals, Wild Boar, Sloth Bears
Gandhi Sagar Sanctuary	Mandsaur (MP)	Chital, Sambar, Chinkara
Chandraprabha Sanctury	Uttar Pradesh	Lion
Dudhwa National Park	Uttar Pradesh	Barasingha (12-pointed deer)
Sariska Sanctuary	Alwar (Rajasthan)	Tiger, Panther, Chinkara, Sambar
Ranthambhor National Park	Sawai Madhopur (Rajasthan)	Tiger, Leopard, Sloth Bear, Crocodile
Ghana Bird Sanctuary Or Keoladeo	Bharatpur (Rajasthan)	Water birds, Black Buck, Chital, Sambar

Gir Forest (Biggest wild-life sanctuary in India)	Junagarh (Gujarat)	Lion
Wild Ass Sanctuary	Little Rann of Kutch (Gujurat)	Wild Ass, Wolf, Nilgai, Chinkara
Hazaribagh National Park	Bihar	Wild Boar, Sambar, Nilgai, Chital
Palamu Tiger Projects	Bihar	Tiger
Sundarban Tiger Reserve	South 24 Parganas (West Bengal)	Tiger, Deer, Wild Boar, Leopard
Similipal National Park	Mayurbhanj, Orissa	Tigers, Leopards, Elephants, Hill Maynah
Nokrek National Park	Garo Hills (Meghalaya)	Fishing Cat, Tiger
Keibul Lamjao (Only Floating Park in the World)	Bishnupur (Manipur)	Dancing Deer
Vedanthangal Bird Sanctuary	Tamil Nadu	Birds
Mudumalai Sanctuary	Tamil Nadu	Tigers, Golden, Jackle, Stripped Hyena
Bandipur Sanctuary	Boarder of Karnataka and Tamil Nadu	Elephants, Tiger, Sambar, Panther
Ranganthittoo Bird Sanctuary	Mysore (Karnataka)	Birds
Nagarhole National Park	Karnataka	Elephant, Tigers, Leopards, Wild Dogs
Sharaswathy Sanctuary	Shimoga (Karnataka)	Elephant, Tigers, Panther
Tungabhadra Sanctuary	Ballary (Karnataka)	Four Horn Antelope, Sloth Bear
Periyar Sanctuary	Idukki (Kerala)	Elephant, Tigers, Panther, Nilgai, Sambar

Geographical Epithets

Nick Name	Places
Sorrow of Bengal	Damodar River
Sorrow of Bihar	Kosi River
Golden city	Amritsar
Garden of India	Bangalore
Silicon Valley of India	Bangalore
Electronic city of India	Bangalore
City of seven Islands	Mumbai
Gateway of India	Mumbai
Queen of Arabian Sea	Cochin
Venice of East	Cochin
Queen of Mountains	Mussoorie
Sacred River	Ganga
Pink City	Jaipur
City of Festivals	Madurai
City of Nawabs	Lucknow
Dakshin Ganga	Godavari
Deccan Queen	Pune
City of Buildings	Kolkata
City of Castles	Kolkata
Egg bowl of Asia	Andhra Pradesh

Q.40. Which is the state with largest urban population?
Q.41. Which is the deepest port in India?

State of five rivers	Punjab
City of temples	Varanasi
Heaven of India	J&K
City of Rallies	New Delhi
Abode of God	Prayag (Allahabad)
City of Lakes	Srinagar
City of Weavers	Panipat
Manchester of North	Kanpur

Indian Cities on River Banks

Cities	River	State
Agra	Yamuna	Uttar Pradesh
Ahmedabad	Sabarmati	Gujarat
Allahabad	Confluence of Ganga, Yamuna and Saraswati	Uttar Pradesh
Alwaye	Periyar	Kerala
Ayodhya	Sarayu	Uttar Pradesh
Badrinath	Gangotri	Uttarakhand
Bareilly	Ram Ganga	Uttar Pradesh
Bhagalpur	Ganges	Bihar
Buxor	Ganges	Bihar
Kolkata	Hoogly	West Bengal
Cuttack	Mahanadi	Orissa
Delhi	Yamuna	Delhi
Dibrugarh	Brahmaputra	Assam
Guwahati	Brahmaputra	Assam
Haridwar	Ganges	Uttarakhand
Howrah	Hoogly	West Bengal
Hyderabad	Musa	Andhra Pradesh
Jabalpur	Narmada	Madhya Pradesh
Jamshedpur	Subarnarekha	Jharkhand
Kanpur	Ganges	Uttar Pradesh
Kota	Chambal	Rajasthan
Leh	Indus	Jammu & Kashmir
Lucknow	Gomti	Uttar Pradesh
Ludhiana	Satluj	Punjab
Mathura	Yamuna	Uttar Pradesh
Moradabad	Ran Ganga	Uttar Pradesh
Monghyr	Ganges	Uttar Pradesh
Nashik	Godavari	Maharashtra
Panji	Mandavi	Goa
Patna	Ganges	Bihar
Sambalpur	Mahanadi	Orissa
Srinagar	Jhelum	Jammu & Kashmir
Srirangapatnam	Cauvery	Karnataka
Surat	Tapti	Gujarat
Tiruchirapalli	Cauvery	Tamil Nadu
Ujjain	Shipra	Madhya Pradesh

| Vijayawada | Krishna | Andhra Pradesh |
| Varanasi | Ganges | Uttar Pradesh |

Tribal Groups in India

Tribal Groups	Found in
Abhors	Assam, Arunachal Pradesh
Angami	Manipur
Ao	Nagaland, Assam
Apatamis	Arunachal Pradesh
Badagas	Tamil Nadu
Baiga	MP, Chhattisgarh
Bhils	MP, Rajasthan, Gujurat
Bhotias	Uttarakhand
Birhors	MP, Bihar
Chenchus	AP, Orissa
Chutia	Assam
Gaddis	Himachal Pradesh
Gallongs	North-East
Garos	Meghalaya
Gonds	MP, Bihar, AP, Orissa
Guzzar	J&K, HP
Jaintias	Meghalaya
Kanikar	Tamil Nadu
Khonds	MP, Orissa
Khasis	Assam, Meghalaya
Kol	MP, Chhattisgarh
Kolam	Andhra Pradesh
Kotas	Tamil Nadu
Koki	Manipur
Lahura	Nagaland, Assam
Lahaulas	HP
Lepchas	Sikkim
Sushais	Tripura
Minas	Rajasthan
Monpa	Arunachal Pradesh
Moplash	Kerala
Nagas	Nagaland
Oraons	Jharkhand, Orissa
Onges	Andaman & Nicobar
Santhals	WB, Jharkhand, Orissa
Sema	Nagaland, Assam
Sentinelese	Andaman & Nicobar
Shomens	Andaman & Nicobar
Tangkhul	Nagaland, Assam
Todas	Tamil Nadu
Uralis	Kerala
Wancho	North-east
Warlis	Maharashtra

Important Hill Stations

Name	Height (From Sea Level in m)	State
Almora	1650	Uttarakhand
Coonoor	1860	Tamil Nadu
Delhousie	2035	Himachal Pradesh
Darjeeling	2135	West Bengal
Gangtok	1850	Sikkim
Kalimpong	1250	West Bengal
Kodai Canal	2120	Tamil Nadu
Kullu Valley	1362	Himachal Pradesh
Kasauli	1895	Himachal Pradesh
Lansdowne	2120	Uttarakhand
Mahabaleswar	1370	Maharashtra
Mount Abu	1220	Rajasthan
Mukteshwar	1975	Uttarakhand
Moossorie	2006	Uttarakhand
Manali	1830	Himachal Pradesh
Mannar	1160	Kerala
Nainital	1940	Uttarakhand
Ooty (Ootacamund)	2290	Tamil Nadu
Panchagani	1200	Maharashtra
Panchmarhi	1065	Madhya Pradesh
Pahalgam	2200	Jammu & Kashmir
Ranikhet	1830	Uttarakhand
Simla	2210	Himachal Pradesh
Shillong	1500	Meghalaya
Srinagar	1770	Jammu & Kashmir

Important Site and Monuments of India

Name	Location	Built by/Famous for
Ajanta Caves	Aurangabad	Gupta Rulers-Buddhist Cave Temple
Agra Fort	Agra (UP)	Akbar
Akbar's Mausolaum	Sikandra (UP)	Jahangir
Amarnath Caves	Kashmir	Naturally formed Ice Shiv Linga
Anand Bhawan	Allahabad	Motilal Nehru-Ancestral house of Nehru Family
Bibi-ka-Makbara	Aurangabad	Aurangzeb; Mausoleum of his wife – Rabiadurrani
Buland Darwaza	Fatehpur Sikri	Akbar; to commemorate his victory against Deccan
Charminar	Hyderabad	Quli Qutab Shah
Dargha Ajmer Sharif	Rajasthan	Sutan Shyasuddin
Dilwara Temple	Mount Abu	Siddharaja
Diwani-e-Khas	Agra fort	Sahajahan
Elephant Caves	Mumbai	Rashtrakuta ruler; for rock cut temple
Ellora Cave	Aurangabad	Buddhist temple

Gandhi sadan	Delhi	Birla House; Gandhiji was assassinated in 1948
Gateway of India	Mumbai	British Government; erected in 1911 to welcome King George-V in India
Gol Gumbaz	Bijapur	Largest Dome in India
Gomotiswar	Mysore	Statue of a jain sage carved out of a single stone
Hawa Mahal	Jaipur	Maharaja Pratap Singh; a pink castle of air
Humayun's Tomb	Delhi	Humayun's Wife
Jantar Mantar	Delhi	Maharaja jai Singh II of Ajmer; Observatory
Jama Masjid	Delhi	Shahjahan; Biggest Moshque in India
Jagannath Temple	Puri, Orissa	Gangadev
Jim Corbett Park	Nainital	Sir Malcom Haillery
Jodhpur Fort	Rajasthan	Rao Jodhaji
Konheri's Fort	Mumbai	Buddhist temple
Konark Temple	Konark, Orissa	Narsingha Dev I; Sun Temple
Khajuraho Temple	Bhopal, MP	Chandellas Ruler; Mahadev Temple
Lalbagh	Bangalore	Hyder Ali
Meenakshi Temple	Madurai	Hindu (Lord Shiva) temple
Moti Masjid	Agra	Shahjahan;
Nishat Garden	Srinager	Asaf Ali
Purana Qila	Delhi	Sher Shah Suri
Qutab Minar	Delhi	Qutubuddin Aibak; Largest Minaret
Red Fort	Delhi	Shahjahan
Sabarmati Ashram	Ahmedabad	Gandhji's Ashram
Sarnath	Vananasi	Lord Buddha sermons after enlightenment
Shanti Niketan	Kolkata	Rabindranath Tagore; University
Sanchi	Sarnath,MP	Ancient Buddhist monument
Swarna Mandir (Golden Temple)	Amritsar	Guru Ramdas; Largest Gurudwar
Taj Mahal	Agra	Shahjahan
Vellure Math	Kolkata	Swami Vivekananda
Victoria Memorial	Kolkata	British Government; Museum
Vijayastambha	Cittorgarh	Maharana Kumbh

Largest, Longest and Highest in India

Longest River	Ganges
Longest Tributary River	Yamuna
Longest River of the South	Godavari
Longest Road	Grand Trunk Road
Longest Coastline of a State	Gujurat
Longest Beach	Marina Beach, Chennai (Tamil Nadu)
Longest Rail Route	Jammu-Tavi to Kanyakumari
Longest Tunnel	Jawahar Tunnel (Jammu & Kashmir)
Longest National Highway	NH-7 (Varanasi-Kanyakumari)
Longest Dam	Hirakud (Orissa)
Longest River Bridge	Mahatma Gandhi Setu (Patna)

Geography of India

Longest Road Bridge	Sone Bridge (Patna)
Longest Railway Platform	Kharagpur (West Bengal)
Longest Electric Railway Line	Delhi to Kolkata
Longest Corridor	Rameshwaram Temple Corridor
Largest Cave Temple	Ellora (Maharashtra)
Largest Gurudwara	Golden Temple (Amritsar)
Largest Church	St John's Cathedral (Goa)
Largest Mosque	Jama Masjid (Delhi)
Largest Dome	Gol Gumbuz (Karnataka)
Largest Residence	Rashtrapati Bhawan
Largest Cinema Hall	Thangam (Madurai)
Largest Museum	Indian Museum (Kolkata)
Largest River Barrage	Farakka (West Bengal)
Largest Canti Lever	Howrah Bridge (West Bengal)
Largest Delta	Sundarbans (West Bengal)
Largest Auditorium	Srishanmukhanda Hall (Mumbai)
Largest Lake	Wular Lake (Jammu & Kashmir)
Largest Saline water Lake	Chilika (Orissa)
Largest Manmade Lake	Govind Vallaabh Pant Sagar (Riahn dam), UP
Largest Planetarium	Birla Planatarium (Kolkata)
Largest Zoo	Zoological Garden, Alipur (Kolkata)
Largest Desert	Thar (Rajasthan)
Largest River Island	Majuli (Assam)
Largest no of Cities in a State	Uttar Pradesh
Largest Stadium	Salt Lake Stadium (Yuva Bharti), Kolkata
Largest Port	Mumbai
Highest Mountain Peak	Godwin Austin (K2)
Highest Dam	Bhakra Dam (Punjab)
Highest Bridge	Chambal Bridge (MP)
Highest Waterfall	Gersoppa (Karnataka)
Highest Lake	Devatal (Garhwal)
Highest Battle Field	Siachen Glacier (J&K)
Highest Airport	Leh (Ladakh)
Highest Statue	Gomateshwar (Karnataka)
Highest Gateway	Buland Darwaja, Fatehpur Sikri (Agra)
Highest Tower	Pitampura (Delhi)
Highest Civilian Award	Bharat Ratna
Highest Gallantry Award	Paramveer Chakra
Deepest River Valley	Bhagirathi-Alakananda
Place with Heaviest Rainfall	Mausinran (Meghalaya)
Biggest Hotel	Oberoi Sheraton (Mumbai)

World Records Held by India

Largest exporter/producer of tea	Largest manufacturer of cycles
Largest exporter of cut diamond	Largest exporter of spices
Largest producer of millet	Largest producer of turmeric
Largest producer of ginger	Largest producer of sugar cane

Largest producer of grapes	Largest producer of pulses
Largest reserves of iron and mica	Highest yield of potatoes
Highest yield of rice	
Banks having maximum number of branches:	State Bank of India
Largest employer in the World:	Indian Railways
Companies having maximum number of share holders:	Reliance Group of Companies
World's highest road (5602m):	Khardungla Road in Leh-Manali
World's longest river bridge:	Mahatma Gandhi Setu (Patna) over Ganga
World's longest railway platform:	Kharagpur (West Bengal)
World's largest delta:	Sundarbans
World's largest open university:	Indira Gandhi National Open University (IGNOU)
World's largest school:	South Point High School, Kolkata

ANSWERS

1. Gujarat
2. Nicobar Island
3. Aravallis
4. Sambhar Lake (Rajasthan)
5. Regur Soil
6. Jammu and Kashmir
7. The Nilgiris
8. Anaimudi
9. Hoogly
10. Madhya Pradesh
11. 27
12. Tamil Nadu
13. Kerala
14. Godavari
15. Dihang
16. Residual Mountain
17. Mahatma Gandhi Setu
18. Govind Vallabh Pant Sagar
19. Aurangabad
20. Meghalaya
21. Lakshadweep
22. Arvi
23. Chambal
24. Kerala
25. Madhya Pradesh
26. Damodar Valley Project
27. Narmada
28. Bhopal Shatabdi Express
29. 10°
30. Chhota Nagpur Region
31. Karnataka
32. September/October
33. South Andaman & Little Andaman
34. Noida
35. Northern Railway
36. London and Mumbai
37. 8
38. 16
39. Brahmaputra
40. Maharashtra
41. Vishakhapatnam

States at a Glance – I

Sl. No.	State	Capital	No. of Districts	Chief Minister	Governor	Area ('000 km^2)	Population	Population Density	Literacy Rate (%)	Sex Ratio
1.	Andhra Pradesh	Hyderabad	23	K Rosiah	N D Tiwari	275.1	76210007	275	61.11	978
2.	Arunachal Pradesh	Itanagar	13	Dorjee Khandu	General (Rtd.) J J Singh	83.7	1097968	13	54.74	901
3.	Assam	Dispur	23	Tarun Gogoi	Katteekal Sankaranarayanan	78.4	26638407	340	64.28	932
4.	Bihar	Patna	37	Nitish Kumar	Devanand Konwar	94.1	82878796	880	47.53	921
5.	Chhattisgarh	Raipur	16	Dr Raman Singh	E S L Narasimhan	136.0	20795956	154	65.18	990
6.	Goa	Panaji	2	Digambar V Kamat	Shivender Singh Sidhu	3.7	1343998	363	82.32	960
7.	Gujarat	Gandhinager	25	Narendra Modi	Navalkishore Sharma	196.0	50671017	258	82.32	921
8.	Haryana	Chandigarh	20	Bhupinder Singh Hooda	Dr A R Kidwai	44.2	21144564	477	68.59	861
9.	Himachal Pradesh	Shimla	12	Prem Kumar Dhumal	Smt. Prabha Rau	55.7	6077900	109	77.13	970
10.	Jammu & Kashmir	Srinagar Jammu	14	Omar Abdullah	N N Vohra	222.2	10069987	99	54.46	900
11.	Jharkhand	Ranchi	22	Shibu Soren	Syed Sibtey Razi	79.7	26909428	338	54.13	941
12.	Karnataka	Bangalore	27	B S Yeddyurappa	H R Bhardwaj	191.8	52850562	275	67.04	964
13.	Kerala	Thiruvananthapuram	14	V S Achutha Nandan	R S Gavai	38.9	31841374	819	90.92	1058
14.	Madhya Pradesh	Bhopal	48	Shivraj Singh	Balaram Jhakar Chauhan	308.0	60385118	196	64.11	920
15.	Maharashtra	Mumbai	35	Ashok S Chvan	S C Jameer	307.7	96752247	314	77.27	922
16.	Manipur	Imphal	9	Okram Ibobi Singh	Gurbachan Jagat	22.3	2293896	107	68.87	978
17.	Meghalaya	Shilong	7	Dr D D Lapang	Ranjit Shekhar Mooshahary	22.4	2318822	103	63.31	975
18.	Mizoram	Aizawl	8	Pu Lalthanhawla	Lt. Gen. (Retd) M M Lakhera	21.1	891058	43	88.49	938

(Contd...)

Sl. No.	State	Capital	No. of Districts	Chief Minister	Governor	Area ('000 km²)	Population	Population Density	Literacy Rate (%)	Sex Ratio
19.	Nagaland	Kohima	8	Neiphiu Rio	K Sankaranarayan	16.6	1988636	120	67.11	909
20.	Orissa	Bhubaneswar	30	Naveen Patnaik	Syed Sibtey Razi	155.7	36804660	236	63.61	972
21.	Punjab	Chandigarh	19	Prakash Singh Badal	Lt Gen (Retd) S F Rodrigues	50.4	24358999	482	69.95	874
22.	Rajasthan	Jaipur	32	Ashok Gehlot	Shilendra Kumar Singh	342.2	56473122	165	61.03	922
23.	Sikkim	Gangtok	4	Pawan Chamling	Balmiki Prasad Singh	7.1	540493	76	69.68	875
24.	Tamil Nadu	Chennai	30	M Karunanidhi	S S Barnala	130.1	62405679	478	73.47	986
25.	Tripura	Agartala	4	Manik Sarkar	Dinesh Nandan Sahaya	10.5	3199203	304	73.66	950
26.	Uttar Pradesh	Lucknow	70	Mayawati	T V Rajeshwar Rao	240.8	166052859	689	57.36	898
27.	Uttarakhand	Dehradun	13	Dr Ramesh Pokhariyal Nishank	Maj Gen (Retd) B L Joshi	53.4	8489349	159	72.28	964
28.	West Bengal	Kolkata	18	Buddhadeb Bhattacharjee	Gopal Krishna Gandhi	88.8	80176197	904	69.22	934
Union Territories
1.	Andaman & Nicobar Islands	Port Blair	3	—	Lt Gen (Retd) Bhopinder Singh	8.2	356152	43	81.18	846
2.	Chandigarh	Chandigarh	1	—	Lt Gen (Retd) S F Rodrigues	0.1	900635	7902	81.76	773
3.	Dadra & Nagar Haveli	Silvassa	1	—	Rajni Kant Verma	0.5	220490	449	60.03	811
4.	Daman & Diu	Daman	2	—	Rajni Kant Verma	0.1	158204	1444	81.09	709
5.	Delhi (NCT)	New Delhi	1	Sheila Dixit	Tejendra Khanna	1.4	13782976	9294	81.82	821
6.	Lakshadweep	Kavaratti	1	B V Selvaraj	B V Selvaraj	0.03	60650	1894	87.52	947
7.	Puducherry	Puducherry	4	Thiru V Vaithilingam	Iqbal Singh	0.5	974345	2029	81.49	1001

State at a Glance – II

Sl.	States	Major Cities	Principal Languages	Major Crops	Main Rivers	Chief Industries	Tourist Spots
1.	Andhra Pradesh	Vizag, Guntur Vijayawada	Telugu, Urdhu	Rice, Jawar, Bajra, Ragi, Maize	Godavari, Krishna	Iron, Steel, Jute, Ship-building, Aircraft, Pharmaceuticals	Tirupati, Tirumalai
2.	Arunachal Pradesh	Alom, Teju, Khonsa Wancho	Munpa, Adi, Nishi, Mizi,	Rice, Maize, Wheat, Mustard	Dibang	Plywood, Handicraft	Twang, Pasighat
3.	Assam	Guwahati, Diburgarh	Assamese	Rice	Brahmaputra	Tea, Oil Refinery Fertiliser, Jute, Paper	Kaziranga Manas
4.	Bihar	Gaya, Bhagalpur	Hindi	Rice, Wheat Maize, Pulses	Ganga, Sone	Cootton, Jute, Sugar, Paper, Silk, Leather	Bodh Gaya Nalanda, Vaishali, Sasaram
5.	Chhattisgarh	Bilaspur, Jabalpur	Hindi	Rice, Wheat, Maize, Pulses	Indravati, Mahanadi	Mining, Iron Jute, Cement	Raipur
6.	Goa	Marmagao Vascodagama	Kookni, Marathi	Rice, Ragi	Mandvi Fisheries Zuari	Old Goa, Ship-building	Ponda, Paula
7.	Gujarat	Ahmedabad Surat, Vododara	Gujurati	Rice, Wheat Bajra	Sabarmati Narmada	Cotton, Woollen Cement, Paper	Junagarh Gir Park
8.	Haryana	Ambala, Gurgaon, Rohtak	Hindi	Rice, Wheat	Yamuna Ghaggar	Dairy, Automobile Engg. Sugar	Kurukshetra Surajkund
9.	Himachal Pradesh	Mondi, Kulu	Pahari, Hindi	Wheat, Maize	Sutlej, Beas	Forest products	Manali, Kulu, Simla, Dharmsala, Delhousie, Lahul
10.	Jammu & Kashmir	Jammu, Leh Anatnag	Urdhu, Dogori	Rice, Wheat Bajra, Maize	Jhelum, Chenab	Woollen, Silk	Ladakh, Pahalgam Gulmarg
11.	Jharkhand	Bokaro, Hindi Jamshedpur		Rice, Maize	Subarnarekha Barnamani	Iron & Steel Cement, Paper	Dhanbad

(Contd...)

Sl.	States	Major Cities	Principal Languages	Major Crops	Main Rivers	Chief Industries	Tourist Spots
12.	Karnataka	Mysore, Mangalore	Kannada	Rice, Wheat Tobacco, Sunflower	Krishna, Cauvery	Silk, Aircraft, glass Cotton	Bijapur, Udipi Hampi, Halebid Bandipur
13.	Kerala	Kochi, Allepy	Malayalam	Rice	Periyar Pamba	Shipbuilding Paper	Thiruvananthapuram Periyar Park
14.	Madhya Pradesh	Gwalior, Indore	Hindi	Rice, Wheat	Chambal Tapti, Mahanadi	Silk, Suger, Cement	Panchmari, Ujjain Khajuraho, Sanchi
15.	Maharashtra	Pune, Nagpur	Marathi Hindi	Wheat, Rice	Bhima, Krishna	Cotton, leather Automobile, Aircraft Pharmaceutical	Aurangabad, Siridi
16.	Manipur	Bishnupur, Chandel	Manipuri	Rice, Maize	Lril, Thoubal	Handicraft	Mao, Ukhrul, Taminglong
17.	Meghalaya	Tura, Jowoi	Khasi, Garo English	Rice, Maize	Manda Damring	Handicraft	Wards lake Elephant falls
18.	Mizoram	Chhimtuipui	Mizo, English	Rice	Dhaleswari Tuivawal	Handicraft	Aizwal
19.	Nagaland	Mon, Dimapur	English, Ao, Chang, Konyak,	Rice	Doyang, Dikhu, Dhansiri	Paper, Ply wood	Wokha, Phek Intaki
20.	Orissa	Rourkela, Cuttack Berthampur	Oriya	Rice	Mahanadi, Baitarani	Iron & steel Aluminium	Puri, Konark Gopalpur, Chilika
21.	Punjab	Ludhiana, Jalandhar	Punjabi, Hindi	Wheat, Rice	Sutlej, Beas	Bicycle, sports goods Sugar, Paper, Woollen	Amritsar, Nangal
22.	Rajasthan	Jodhpur, Ajmer Kota	Hindi, Rajasthani	Wheat, Bajra Jowar	Banas, Chambal	Marble, Textile, Cement, Sugar	Udaipur, Mt Abu, Bharatpur, Puskar Ranthambore
23.	Sikkim	Gyalshingh Yoksum	Lepcha, Nepali Bhutia	Wheat, Rice Millets	Ranjit, Tista	Leather, Food Product	Gangtok, Bakkhim

(Contd...)

Sl.	States	Major Cities	Principal Languages	Major Crops	Main Rivers	Chief Industries	Tourist Spots
24.	Tamil Nadu	Coimbatore, Trichy, Madurai	Tamil	Rice, Pulses	Cauvery, Vaigai	Leather, Automobile Iron & Steel, Cement Handloom,	Ooty, Rameswaram Kodai kanal
25.	Tripura	Kilas Nagar, Kamalpur	Bengali, Kokborak	Rice	Deo, Gomti		Dimboor, Jampuai Sericulture
26.	Uttar Pradesh	Kanpur, Varanasi Allhabad	Hindi	Rice, Wheat, Maize, Barley	Ganga, Yamuna	Sugar, Leather, Cement Locomotive, Jute	Agra, Mathura Vrindavan
27.	Uttarakhand	Roorki, Nainital	Hindi	Barley	Bhagirathi Ganga, Yamuna	Food processing Forest Products	Haridwar, Rishikesh Badrinath, Almora Dehradun, Mussoorie
28.	West Bengal	Durgapur Asansol	Bengali	Rice, Wheat	Ganga, Hoogly amodar	Jute, Paper Iron & steel	Darjeeling Sunderbans
1.	Andaman & Nicobar	Diglipur Rangat	Nicobarese Bengali	Rice, Pulses	—	Plywood, Handicraft	Port-Blair
2.	Chandigarh	Chandigarh	Hindi, Punjabi	Wheat, Rice	Chandigarh	Machineries	Rock Garden
3.	Dadra & Nagar Haveli	Khadoli, Massat	Bhili, Bhilodi, Gujurati	Rice, Ragi Pulses	Daman Ganga	Fisheries	Devka Beach Nagao Beach
4.	Daman & Diu	Daman, Diu	Gujurathi, Marathi	Rice, Pulses	—	Fisheries	Beach
5.	Delhi (NCT)	New Delhi	Hindi	Wheat, Bajra	Yamuna	Electronics, Plastics Pharmaceuticals	Qutab Minar Red Fort, Rajghat
6.	Lakshadweep	Androth, Minicoy	Malayalam	Rice	—	Handicrafts, Fisheries	Cheriyam Suheli
7.	Puducherry	Karaikal	Telugu, Tamil French, English	Rice, Ragi	—	Textile, Paper	Puducherry, Koraikal

4

WORLD GEOGRAPHY

Eratosthenes coined the term 'Geography' and defined as 'the study of earth as the home of man'. Geography literary means 'description of earth'.

THE UNIVERSE

The Universe encompasses everything that physically exists – the entirety of space and time, all forms of matter, energy and momentum, and the physical laws and constants that govern them. The study of universe is called 'Cosmology'.

Galaxies were formed 12 billion years ago; solar system evolved five billion years ago and life evolved on earth about 3.8 billion years ago.

The earth lies in difference between Space and Outer Space. The outer space is vast. The dimensions could be measured by 'light year' and Astronomical Unit (AU).

'Light year' is the distance travelled by light in one year at the speed of 2.99792.5 km/sec. Distance between Sun and the Earth is less than one light year.

Astronomical Unit (AU) represents the mean distance between the sun and the earth. Light from the sun takes approximately 8.3 minutes to reach earth.

    1 AU = 1, 49,597,870 km

    1 Light Year = 60,000 AU

Astronomy is the branch of physics that deals with the study of celestial objects in the universe.

Galaxies: These are huge congregation of stars which are held together by the force of gravity. There may be 1.3 billion galaxies in the visible universe. Galaxies are of three forms: spiral, elliptical and irregular.

The Milky Way: The Milky Way is the galaxy where our solar system is located. It forms a part of a cluster of about 24 galaxies. It is a spiral galaxy, which consists of billions of stars. The galactic nucleus is about 3200 light years from the sun.

Stars: There are millions of stars in the sky. However, about 6000 stars are brighter enough to be visible. Stars contribute about 98 per cent in a galaxy and rest two per cent includes interstellar or galactic gas and dust.

Nearest stars to earth: Sun at a distance of less than one light year; Proxima Centauri 4.2 light year; Alpha Centauri A&B is about 4.3 light years.

Red Giants: These are dying stars. When hydrogen in a star is depleted, it's outer region swell and redden; hence it is called Red Giants. For example, Mira near the river at Ephesus Betelgeuse.

Novae and Super Nova: These are the stars whose brightness increases suddenly, about 10-20 times, and fades gradually into normal brightness. This brightness is attributed to partial or outright explosion. In Novae, the outer shells of a star explode, while in Super Nova the entire star explodes.

Pulsars: These are visible stars, which emit regular pulses of electro-magnetic waves of very short duration.

Black Hole: Strange things happen to a star at the end of its life. If its mass is more than three times the mass of the sun, it transforms into a black hole. US Physicist, John Wheeler first time used the term 'black hole' in 1967.

Age of Universe: The age of universe is estimated to be 13 billion years. Its size is not known, however some class of thought describes it as finite but unbound (e.g. Einstein).

THE SOLAR SYSTEM

The **Solar System** consists of the only star Sun and those celestial objects bound to it by gravity, which were formed from the collapse of a giant molecular cloud approximately 4.5 billion years ago.

Composition of the Solar System

The Sun contains 99.85 per cent of all the matter in the solar system. The planets, which condensed out of the same disk of material that formed the Sun, contain only 0.135per cent of the mass of the solar system. Jupiter contains more than twice the matter of all the other planets combined together. Satellites of the planets, comets, asteroids, meteoroids and the interplanetary medium constitute the remaining 0.015 per cent.

The Sun

Sun is at the centre of the solar system. Its mass is about 740 times as much as of all the components of the solar system combined together.

Sun moves almost in circular orbit around the galactic centre at the speed of 250 km/sec.

It takes about 250 million years to complete one revolution around the centre; the period is called cosmic year.

Glowing surface of Sun is called photosphere (about 400 km thick), and its temperature is 4226° to 5276°C. The gases (about 2500km thick) extending from the photosphere make up the chromospheres. Chromosphere (10,000 km thick) is called so because it is reddish in colour. Average temperature ranges from 4226° to 9726°C. The chromosphere merges into corona, the outermost region of the Sun's atmosphere. The corona is visible during solar eclipse. The visible white light of corona is made up of a continuum of colours such as violet, indigo, blue, green, yellow, orange and red (VIBGYOR). The bright spots on the surface of Sun are called plages and the dark spots called sunspot.

Sun's energy is generated by the nuclear fusion reactions occurring in its interior. Sun consumes four million tonnes of hydrogen every second. It will last about five billion years and then will turn into a red giant.

Q.1. In which unit is the mean distance between the Sun and the Earth measured?

Q.2. What is the shape of the Milky Way Galaxy?

Facts about the Sun

Distance from Earth:	149.8 million km
Diameter:	1,384,000 km
Age: (approximately)	5 billion years
Mass:	3, 30,000 times that of earth
Chemical composition:	Hydrogen = 71%, Helium = 26.5%, other elements = 2.5%

There are two Polar Auroras: the Aurora Borealis or Northern lights and the Aurora Australis or Southern lights.

There are eight known planets: Mercury, Venus, Earth, Mars, Jupiter, Saturn, Uranus and Neptune. There are 162 satellites in the solar system.

The descending order of the size of the planets is Jupiter, Saturn, Uranus, Neptune, Earth, Venus, Mars and Mercury.

Pluto is a special case as its orbit is most inclined (18 degrees) and most elliptical of all the planets. Because of this, Pluto is closer to the Sun than that of Neptune.

The axis of rotation for most of the planets is nearly perpendicular to the ecliptic. The exceptions are Uranus and Pluto, which are tipped on their sides.

Some facts about Planets

Fastest Planet	Mercury
Brightest object in the sky (Other than the Sun and the Moon)	Venus
Planet that rotates backward	Venus
Red planet	Mars
Plant having maximum number of satellites	Jupiter
Planet having largest satellite	Jupiter
Planet with strongest magnetic field	Jupiter
Planet having shortest (synodic) day	Jupiter
Planet having lowest average density	Saturn
Planet with deepest ocean	Jupiter

From 1930 to 2006, Pluto was considered as the ninth planet. However in 2006, the International Astronomical Union (IAU), created an official definition of the term 'planet' and under this definition Pluto is reclassified as 'dwarf planet'. Also IAU recognises three more dwarf planets: Charon, Eris and Ceres. These four dwarf planets have four satellites (Pluto's 3 +Eris's 1).

Asteroids are a series of planets or fragments of planets lying between the orbits of Mars and Jupiter. There are about 1,00,000 known asteroids and the largest one is Ceres (diameter 940 km).

Meteors or shooting stars are the burning fragments often seen in the sky. They burn due to friction with atmosphere. They often burn up and fall on earth surface in the form of dusts or fragments called 'meteorites'.

Comets are the fragments of planets that revolve around the Sun in highly elliptical orbits. Examples: Hailey's, Borrelly, Finlay, Faye, Smith Tuttle, etc.

Moon is the natural satellite of earth. It's about one-sixth of the size of the earth. About 59 per cent of the moon's surface is visible from earth. Its distance from earth is 3, 82,200 km. Moon light takes 1.3 seconds to reach earth. It takes 27 days 7 hours 43 minute and 11.47 seconds to complete one revolution around earth.

Neil Armstrong and Edwin Aldrin were the first to set foot on moon on 21 July 1967 on Apollo XI.

Planets, natural satellites, thousand small planets (asteroids) and large number of comets, meteors and plasma form the Solar System.

Q.3. What does a star whose outer shell explode is known as?
Q.4. Which planet has the strongest magnetic field?

The following table lists statistical information for planets.

Planets	Revolution Period (Days)	Radius (of Earth's)	Mass (of Earth's)	Rotation (Days)	No. of Satellites	Density (Water=1)
Mercury	88	0.38	0.05	58.8	0	5.43
Venus	224.7	0.95	0.89	244	0	5.25
Earth	365	1.00	1.00	1.00	1	5.52
Mars	687	0.53	0.11	1.029	2	3.95
Jupiter	4333	11	318	0.411	63	1.33
Saturn	10759	9	95	0.428	47	0.69
Uranus	30686	4	17	0.748	27	1.29
Neptune	60188	4	17	0.802	13	1.64
Pluto	92611	0.18	0.002	0.267	1	2.03

THE EARTH

Study of the earth, its shape and size is called Geodesy. The shape of earth is spheroid or geoid. Earth is the fifth largest planet in the solar system. It is also called 'Blue planet'. Perigee is the nearest position from earth's surface to moon, while the farthest position is called apogee.

The nearest position from earth's surface to sun is called perihelion and the epihelion is the farthest position.

Different layers of earth are (chemical sub-division):
 (i) Crust (32–35 km thickness), also known as SIAL or Silicon and Aluminium.
 (ii) Mantle (thickness is 2900 km) also known as SIMA or Silicon and Magnesium.
 (iii) Outer core (thickness is 2100 km)
 (iv) Inner core (thickness is 1370 km), it is solid and made up of Iron and Nickel, and is responsible for earth's magnetism.

Composition of Earth

Earth is made up of more than 100 elements, out of which some important elements are:

Oxygen	46.5%
Silicon	27.72%
Aluminium	8.13%
Iron	5.01%
Calcium	3.63%
Sodium	2.85%
Potassium	2.62%
Magnesium	2.09%

Quick Facts about Earth

Equatorial diameter:	12757 km
The Polar diameter:	12714 km
Total surface area:	5,09,700,000 sq km
Total land area (29%)	1,48,400,000 sq km
Total water area (71%)	3,61,300,000 sq km
Mean distance from sun	1,49,407,000 km
Estimated weight (Mass)	5.94×10^{19} metric tonnes

Earth's Movements

Earth has two types of movements:

Rotation: Earth moves on its imaginary axis from west to east which is known as rotation. It takes 23 hours, 56 min, 4.09 second or approximately 24 hours. This movement causes days and nights.

Q.5. What is the time taken by moonlight to reach earth?
Q.6. What is the time of the year, when difference between length of days and nights is the largest called?

At equator days and nights are equal throughout the year. In northern hemisphere, the longest day is June 21 and shortest day is December 21. Whereas in Southern hemisphere, December 22 is the longest day, June 21 is the shortest day.

Revolution: Time taken by earth to revolve around the sun is called revolution. For one revolution, earth takes 365 days 6 hours 9 minutes and 9.54 second. Revolution results into change of season.

Important Terms

Equator: It refers to an imaginary line which is equidistant from both the poles (0° to 10° North and 100° South).

Tropical: There are two tropics – the Tropic of Cancer is the 23½ degree North parallel to Equator and the Tropic of Capricorn 23½ degree South parallel to Equator.

Subtropical: The zones between 23½ degree North and 40° North and between 23½ degree South and 40° South.

Arctic Circle: It refers to the parallel of 66½ degree north.

Antarctic Circle: It refers to the parallel of 66½ degree south.

Equinox: These are dates when days and nights are equal – March 21(vernal equinox) and September 23 (autumnal equinox).

Solstice: The time of the year when difference between length of days and nights is the largest. June 21 is the summer solstice while December 22 is the winter solstice.

Latitude: It's imaginary line which is drawn parallel to equator. Equator represents 0° latitude, while North Pole is 90°N and South Pole is 90°S.

Parallel: A line connecting all points of the same latitude is called 'Parallel', as it is parallel to all other lines of the latitude.

Each degree is divided into 60 minute and each minute into 60 seconds.

One degree latitude is equal to 111km.

Longitude: It is measured in degree from west to east of Greenwich from 0° to 180° meridian.

Meridian: It is a line connecting all points on the same longitude. Meridians are not parallel to one another, except where they cross equator (0° Parallel). Meridians cross all the parallels at right angle. At equator 1 degree is equal to 111 km.

Earth is divided into 24 longitudinal zones, each being 15° or one hour apart in time.

Local time: Local time of a place is determined with reference to the sun's path in the sky. Local time varies, from GMT (London) at the rate of four minutes per degree of longitude. It is presented as AM and PM for before noon and after noon respectively.

Standard time: It is the fixed time for a country, generally based on a central meridian, on which most important city is located. It does not vary like that of local time. The central meridian is chosen in such a way that it is divisible by 7½° so that standard time differs from GMT in multiple of half an hour.

Greenwich meridian Time (GMT): It is the standard time in UK, which is based on the local time of the meridian passing through Greenwich near London.

International Date Line (IDL): The International Date Line is an imaginary line which runs from the North Pole to the South Pole and is 180° away from the Greenwich Meridian. The

> **Q.7. Which layer of earth's atmosphere protects earth from falling meteorites?**
> **Q.8. What are the lines drawn parallel to the equator called?**

International Conference in 1884 deemed that there would be a single Universal Day and that this would begin at midnight at Greenwich, near London.

The 180° meridian running over the Pacific Ocean deviating at Fiji, Samoa and Gilbert islands also deviated at the land of masses so that travellers do not feel inconvenient. Travellers crossing the IDL from west to east repeat a day while travellers crossing it from east to west lose a day.

ATMOSPHERE

Earth's atmosphere is composed of colourless, odourless, tasteless gases, moisture and fine dusts. It is about 700 km in vertical extent.

The composition of gases: Nitrogen = 78.09 per cent, Oxygen = 20.95 per cent, Argon = 0.93 per cent and Minor gases = 0.03 per cent.

Atmosphere acts as the shield to protect earth's surface from harmful rays emitted from the Sun during the day. It also prevents excessive loss of heat during night.

Atmosphere is divided into following layers according to the way temperature changes with height. These are:

    (i) Troposphere
   (ii) Stratosphere
  (iii) Mesosphere
  (iv) Ionosphere
   (v) Exosphere

Troposphere: It is the layer nearest to earth's surface and contains 90 per cent of the total mass of the atmosphere. It extends up to 8 km at poles and about 16 km in equator. Temperature declines with the height at the rate of 6.4°/6.5°C per km ascent, called the lapse rate.

Stratosphere: It extends from 20 km to 50 km. Temperature increases with height. Ozone (O_3) is the main gas in this layer, which absorbs ultraviolet light and radiates energy at lower wavelengths as infrared energy. It is free from water vapour, clouds and dust.

Mesosphere: It extends up to 50 to 80 km. Temperature decreases with height. Its upper boundary, the Mesopause, is the coldest portion of the atmosphere (average temperature -90°C).

Ionosphere: It extends from 500–800 km. It is composed of those particles which acquire electrical charges when it absorbs solar radiations. The charged atoms are called the ions and give the 'Ionosphere' its name. It also protects earth from falling meteorites (dust fragment of meteors) as most of the meteors burn out in this layer.

Exosphere: The upper limit is uncertain and the upper part is called magnetosphere. Heavier gases like nitrogen and oxygen are present in troposphere and stratosphere. However lightest elements hydrogen and helium are present in case of other layers.

Winds

Trade Wind: Most regular of all planetary winds blow with great force and in constant direction. Since they blow from the cooler sub-tropical latitude (30° North and 30° South) to warmer tropics, they have great capacity for

Q.9. What is Willy-Willies?
Q.10. The wind that blows from sub-tropical high pressure to sub-polar low pressure is called?

holding moisture. While passing across oceans, they gather more moisture and bring heavy rainfall to the east coast of the continents.

Westerlies: These blows from sub-tropical high pressure to sub-polar low pressure. These are much less constant and consistent than trade winds. It is usual for seafarers to refer to the westerlies as Raring forties, Furious fifties and Shricking sixties according to the varying degree of storminess.

Easterlies: These blows from polar high pressure belt towards the temperate low pressure belt. They are typically cold and dry winds and are quite variable.

Local winds:
Foehn: Hot, dry wind in Alps.
Khamsin: Hot, dry wind in Egypt.
Sirocca: Hot, moist wind from Sahara to Mediterian Sea.
Bora: Cold dry wind flowing outward from Hungary to the north of Italy.
Mistral: Very cold wind blows down from Alps over France.
Punas: Cold, dry wind blowing towards western side of Andes.
Brick fielder: Hot wind blowing in Australia.
Levanter: Cold wind in Spain.
Norwester: Hot wind in New Zealand.
Santa Ana: Hot wind in South California.

Cyclones and Anticyclones

Cyclones: It is a system of low pressure region surrounded by increasingly high pressure outwards. In this condition wind blows in a circular manner. In Northern hemisphere it blows in anticlockwise direction and in southern hemisphere it blows in clockwise direction. These are having different names in different regions – cyclones in the Indian Ocean; Hurricanes in the West Indies; typhoons in the China; Willy-Willies in the North-West Australia; tornado in the coastal US, etc.

Anticyclones are the regions of high pressure and are opposite to that of cyclones.

Types of Climates

Tropical Rain Forest Climate: It is also known as equatorial type of climate or 'selvas', found in the region of 5° to 10° north and south of equator. In this region day and night are equal. Average monthly temperature is 24°–27° C. Average annual rainfall is 250 cm. Broad-leaf ever green dense forests and trees are found in abundance. It is found in Amazon basin, Congo basin and Indonesia.

Monsoon Climate: Annual average rainfall is 200 cm. Deciduous types of forests, i.e. trees shed leaves in a particular season of the year, are found in here. Rainfall is seasonal. Average temperature is 30° C.

Tropical Savanna Climate: Average annual rainfall is 150 cm. Rainfall is seasonal. Temperature is constantly high. Fire resistant and trees with longer roots are found in this region. Grass land type of forests with scattered trees and bushes are found.

Tropical-subtropical hot desert: Situated in the trade wind belt, found in the western belt of the continents between 35°–45° north and south. It experiences dry summer and humid winter. Average summer temperature is 25° C and winter temperature is 4° to 10° C. Olive, grapes and fruits of citrus family are found in abundance.

Q.11. What is the average salinity of the oceanic water?

Q.12. Himalayas are example of which kind of mountains?

Taiga Climate: Taiga means snow forest or coniferous forests; needle leaf composed of evergreen fir and pine are found here. Average summer temperature 10° C and winter is very cold (temperature below 0° C). Total annual rainfall is 50 cm.

Tundra Climate: Rainfall is less than 30 cm. Lichens and mosses are commonly found.

Clouds

Clouds are formed when air happens to cool to dew point and vapour condenses into water droplets. General classification of clouds was proposed by Luke Howard in 1803.

Clouds can be classified as:
  (i) High Clouds: founds at an elevation above 6000 m.
  (ii) Middle Clouds: exist between 2000 to 6000 m.
  (iii) Low Clouds: found at the elevation below 2000 m.
  (iv) Clouds with great vertical extent may grow low bases to heights up to 15 km.

HYDROSPHERE

Oceans

The earth surface is covered up to 71 per cent by water and contains five oceans, including the Arctic, Atlantic, Indian, Pacific and Southern. For many years only four oceans were officially recognised, and then in 2000, the International Hydrographic Organisation established the Southern Ocean, and determined its limits. Those limits include all water below 60 degrees south, and some of it, like the Arctic Ocean, is frozen.

Oceans by size:

Name	Area (sq km)
Pacific	155,557,000
Atlantic	76,762,000
Indian	68,556,000
Southern	20,327,000
Arctic	14,056,000

Oceanic Floor

The oceanic floor is very irregular, which can be divided into the following classes: continental shelf, continental slope, continental rise, ridges and trenches. Oceanic water is saline in taste; the average salinity of the oceanic water is 35 per cent, i.e. 35 gm of salt is present in 1 litre of water.

Water of Lake Van (Turkey) is the most saline (330 per cent) and Dead Sea stands at second place with 240 per cent salinity.

Ocean Currents

These are the large scale movements of water from one part of ocean to another. It circulates clockwise in northern hemisphere and anticlockwise in southern hemisphere.

Ocean currents are classified as warm and cold currents.

Q.13. What is the point of origin of earthquake called?
Q.14. Which is the largest sea in the world?

Warm currents: North Equatorial current, South Equatorial current, North pacific drift, Brazil current, Florida current, Gulf Stream, Caynne current, etc.

Cold Current: East Greenland current, West wind drift, Benguela current, Peru current, Falkland current, Canaries current.

On the basis of volume of water, velocity and dimensions, the ocean currents are classified as Drifts, Currents and Streams.

Drifts refer to slow motion of the surface layer having velocity between 16–24 km per day.

Current refers to the surface movement which is more rapid and defined, velocity in between 6–8 km per hour.

Stream refers to surface motion, which is still and not definite.

Pacific Ocean Currents: Kuroshio, Okhotsk, Alaskan, Californian in north Pacific, east Australian currents in South pacific.

Atlantic Ocean Currents: Antills, Florida, Gulf Stream, Labrador, North Atlantic drift in north Atlantic and Brazilian, Falkland and Benguela in South Atlantic.

Indian Ocean Currents: These currents change their direction from season to season. In winter season, currents flow in the anticlockwise direction in North Indian Ocean. Mozambique and Agulhus are important currents of south Indian Ocean.

LITHOSPHERE

The Continents of the World

Continent is used to differentiate between the various large areas of the earth into which the land surface is divided into. So, a continent is 'a large, continuous area of land on Earth'.

All continents together constitute less than one-third of the earth's surface that means more than two-thirds of the earth's surface are covered with water.

Two-thirds of the continental land mass is located in the northern hemisphere.

They are:

Continents (by Area size)

Continent	Area (sq. km)	Continents	Population (2006 est.)
Asia	44,579,000	Asia	3,879,000,000
Africa	30,065,000	Africa	877,500,000
North America	24,256,000	Europe	727,000,000
South America	17,819,000	North America	501,500,000
Antarctica	13,209,000	South America	379,500,000
Europe	9,938,000	Australia/Oceania	32,000,000
Australia/Oceania	7,687,000	Antarctica	—

Mountains

Fold Mountains: They are formed when rocks of the crust of earth get folded due to forces of compressions, which results into earthquakes. For example, all the big mountains, Himalayas, Alps, Andes, Atlas, etc.

Q.15. Which is the largest fresh water lake in the world?
Q.16. What is the parliament of Japan being referred to as?

Block Mountains: They are formed when great blocks of earth's crust may get raised or lowered. For example, Narmada, Tapti and Damodar valley in India, Meseta (Spain), Black forest to the east of Rhine in Germany and France boarder.

Volcanic Mountains: These are formed by the accumulation of volcanic eruptions and out flow of lava. For example, Catopaxi in Andes, Fuji Yama (Japan), Vesuvius and Etna (Italy).

Rocks

Igneous Rocks: It is most abundant of three rocks (95 per cent). It is formed by solidification of magma from interior of the earth. Since all types of rocks originate from these, hence they are called 'Primary rocks'. For example, granites, basalt and volcanic rocks.

Sedimentary Rocks: They are formed from weathered remains of igneous rocks and also contain matter from remains of marine organisms. For example, gypsum, chalk, lime stones, pebble, sandstone etc.

Metamorphic Rocks: Sometimes igneous rocks or sedimentary rocks get metamorphosed or change due to great pressures, intense temperatures or action of water and chemical. For example, quartzite from sand stone, gneiss from granites, anthracites from coal, etc.

Earthquakes

The sudden movements snaps the rocks on each side of the faults (a fissure in a rock along which blocks of the rock slip past each other) back into their original shape, which produces an earthquake.

Earthquakes vary from a tremor to great shocks, which reflect its magnitude.

The amount of shaking of the ground as the quake passes are measured by 'Seismograph'. The magnitude is assessed on the Richter scale, which was developed by C F Richter. The point of origin of earthquake is called 'seismic focus'. The point on the earth's surface, vertically above the earth surface below is called 'epicenter'. There are two types of earthquakes:

   (i) Tactonic Earthquake (associated with faulting)
   (ii) Volcanic Earthquake (associated with volcanic eruptions)

Tactonic earthquakes are of three types:

(a) Shallow (where focal depth is 70 km)
(b) Intermediate (where focal depth is 70–300 km)
(c) Deep (where focal depth is 300–700 km)

Volcanoes

These are the gigantic safety valves through which nature releases the tremendous pressures that build up inside earth. Volcanoes are of three types:

   (a) *Active*: for example Mona Lua (Hawaii Islands), Etna (Sicily), Catopaxi (Ecuador)
   (b) *Dormant*: for example, Fuji Yama (Japan), Krakatoa (Indonesia)
   (c) *Extinct*: for example, Kopa Mountain (Myanmar), Mount Kilimanjaro (Africa)

Q.17. What is the currency of Saudi Arabia?

Q.18. Which country is known as Land of Thunder Bolt?

Important Mountain Peaks

Name	Height (m)	Location
Mt Everest	8848	Nepal-Tibet
K2 (Godwin Austen)	8611	India
Kanchenjunga	8598	Nepal-India
Lhotse	8501	Nepal-China
Makalu	8481	Tibet-Nepal
Dhaulagiri	8172	Nepal
Nanga Parbat	8126	India
Nanda Devi	7817	India
Illampu	7014	Bolivia (S. America)
Mc Kingley	6194	Alaska (N. America)
Mont Blanc	4810	France

Major Plateaus of the World

Name	Location
Tibetan Plateau	between Himalayas & Quinloo Mountains
Deccan Plateau	Southern India
Arabian Plateau	South-West Asia
Plateau of Brazil	Central-Eastern South America
Plateau of Mexico	Mexico
Plateau of Colombia	USA
Plateau of Madagascar	Madagascar
Plateau of Alaska	North-west North America
Plateau of Bolivia	Andes Mountain
Great Basin Plateau	South of Colombia Plateau, USA
Colorado Plateau	South of Great Basin Plateau, USA

Island

Most populated island: Java (Indonesia)
Largest island of India: Middle Andaman

Major Islands

Name	Area (km^2)	Location
Australia	7,617,930	Southern Ocean
Kalaalit Nunaat (Greenland)	21,75,597	North Atlantic Ocean
New Guinea	8,20,033	South-west Pacific Ocean
Borneo	7,43,197	West-Central Pacific Ocean
Malagasy (Madagascar)	5,87,042	Indian Ocean
Baffin	4,76,068	North-Atlantic Ocean
Sumatra	4,73,605	Northern Indian Ocean
Newzealand	2,70,000	South Pacific Ocean
Honshu	2,30,316	Western Pacific Ocean
Great Britain	218,100	North-Atlantic Ocean

Q.19. What is the location of Arctic Circle?
Q.20. Gypsum is an example of which type of rock?

World Geography

Important Seas

Name	Area (km²)	Name	Area (km²)
South China Sea	29,74,600	Sea of Japan	10,07,700
Caribbean Sea	27,53,170	Andaman Sea	7,97,600
Mediterranean Sea	25,03,900	North Sea	5,75,300
Bering	22,68,200	Black Sea	4,62,000
Gulf of Mexico	15,43,000	Red Sea	4,37,000
Sea of Okhotsk	15,27,000	Baltic Sea	4,22,300
East China Sea	12,49,000	Gulf of St. Lawrence	2,37,760
Hudson Bay	12,32,200	Gulf of California	1,62,000

Major Lakes (by Size)

Name	Area (sq km)	Location
Caspian Sea (Largest lake/saline Water Lake)	3,94,299	Turkmenistan, Kazakhstan Ajaerbaijan and Iran
Superior (Largest Fresh Water Lake)	82,414	USA-Canada
Victoria	69,485	Uganda, Tanzania and Kenya
Aral	66,457	Kazakhstan and Uzbekistan
Huron	59,596	USA and Canada
Michigan	57,800	North America
Tanganyika	32,893	Tanzania, Zaire (Congo)
Baikal (Deepest Lake)	31,500	Russia
Great Bear	31,080	Canada
Malawi	28,900	Africa
Great Slave	28,568	Canada
Erie	25,667	North America
Winnipeg	24,387	Canada
Ontario	19,529	North America
Balkhash	18,300	Kazakhstan
Lake Titicaca (Highest Lake)	8,372	Bolivia

Important Canals

Kiel Canal (98 km): Between London and Baltic Ports, links North Sea with Baltic Sea.

Panama Canal (58 km): Links the Atlantic Ocean and Pacific Ocean, first time opened in 1914.

Suez Canal (169 km): Connects the Mediterranean Sea and Red Sea.

Beloye-More is the Longest Canal in the World with the length of 227 km, located in the Baltic Sea.

Q.21. Which is the longest canal in the world?
Q.22. Which seas are joined by the Strait of Gibraltar?
Q.23. Who discovered China?
Q.24. Where is Grand Canyon located?

Important Straits of the World

Straits	Water Bodies Joined	Area
Bab-al-Mandeb	Red sea & Arabian sea	Arabia & Africa
Bering	Arctic Ocean & Bering sea	Alaska & Asia
Bosphorus	Black Sea & Marmara sea	Turkey
Dover	North Sea & Atlantic Ocean	England & Europe
Florida	Gulf of Mexico & Atlantic Ocean	Florida & Bahamas Island
Gibralter	Mediterranean sea & Atlantic Ocean	Spain & Africa
Malacca	Java Sea & Bay of Bengal	India & Indonesia
Palk	Bay of Bengal & Indian Ocean	India & Sri Lanka
Magellan	South Pacific & South Atlantic Ocean	Chile
Sunda	Java Sea & Indian Ocean	Indonesia

Major Gulfs of the World

Names	Area (sq km)
Gulf of Mexico	15, 44,000
Gulf of Hudson	12, 33,000
Arabian Gulf	2, 38,000
Gulf of St. Lawrence	2, 37,000
Gulf of California	1, 62,000
English Channel	89,900

Important Rivers in World

River	Located at	Length	Source	Enters into
Amazon	S. America & Brazil	6448	Andes (Peru)	Atlantic Ocean
Amur	Asia & Siberia	4510	Pamirs	Pacific Ocean
Brahmaputra	Asia & India	2960	Tibet	Bay of Bengal
Congo	Africa & Zaire	4800	Lualuba and Luapula	Atlantic Ocean
Danube	Europe & Austria Hungary	2820	Near Baden (Germany)	Black Sea
Hwang –Ho	Asia & China	4840	Tibet	Pacific Ocean
Indus	Asia, India & Pakistan	3180	Mt. Kailash	Arabian Sea
Lena	Europe & Russia	4800	Lake Baikal	Laptev Sea (Arctic Ocean)
Missouri-Mississippi	N. America & US	6300	Red Rock Montana	Gulf of Mexico
Murray	Australia	3720	Alps	Indian Ocean
Nile	Africa & Egypt	6670	Lake Victoria	Mediterranean Sea
Niger	Africa & Nigeria	4800	Sierra Leone	Gulf of Guinea (Atlantic Ocean)
Ob	Asia & Siberia	4150	Altai Mountains	Gulf of Ob (Pacific Ocean)

Q. 25. What is the name of the parliament of Russia?
Q. 26. Sickle and Hammer is the national emblem of which country?

World Geography

Yangtze-Kiang	Asia & China	5490	Tibetan Plateau	China Sea
Yenisei	Asia & Siberia	5300	Mt. Tannuola	Arctic Ocean
Volga	Asia & Russia	3700	Valdia Plateau (Moscow)	Caspian Sea

OUR WORLD

The Countries of the World

Our world comprises 203 sovereign states, of which 192 countries are the recognised by the United Nations.

| Largest Countries (by Area-wise) || Population-wise ||
Country	Area (sq km)	Country	Population (2006 est.)
Russia	17,075,400	China	1,306,313,800
Canada	9,330,970	India	1,080,264,400
China	9,326,410	USA	295,734,100
USA	9,166,600	Indonesia	241,973,900
Brazil	8,456,510	Brazil	186,112,800
Australia	7,617,930	Pakistan	162,419,900
India	2,973,190	Bangladesh	144,319,600
Argentina	2,736,690	Russia	143,420,300
Kazakhstan	2,717,300	Nigeria	128,772,000
Sudan	2,376,000	Japan	127,417,200

Richest Countries (GNP in USA $)		Poorest Countries (GNP in USA $)	
Luxembourg	45,360	Mozambique	80
Switzerland	44,355	Somalia	100
Japan	41,010	Eritrea	100
Liechtenstein	40,000	Ethiopia	100
Norway	34,515	Congo, DNC	100

| Countries with Highest Urbanisation (2001) || Countries with Lowest Urbanisation (2001) ||
Country	Urbanisation	Country	Urbanisation
Bermuda	100.0	Rwanda	6.3
Cayman Inland	100.0	Bhutan	7.4
Hong Kong	100.0	Burundi	9.0
Singapore	100.0	Nepal	12.2
Guadeloupe	99.6	Uganda	14.5
Macau	98.9	Malawi	15.1
Belgium	97.4	Ethiopia	15.9
Kuwait	96.1	Burkino Faso	16.9

Q.28. Forty-ninth Parallel is the boundary between which two countries?
Q.29. Where is Merdeca Palace is located?
Q.30. What is the new name of Abyssinia?

Martinique	95.2	Cambodia	17.5
Qatar	92.9	Papua New Guinea	17.6
Iceland	92.7	Eritrea	19.1
Bahrain	92.5	Laos	19.7
Andorra	92.2	Thailand	20.0
Uruguay	92.1	Niger	21.1
Luxembourg	91.9	Afghanistan	22.3

Countries with Highest Life Expectancy (On 2004–05)

Countries with Lowest Life Expectancy (On 2004–05)

Country	Life Expectancy (in yrs)	Country	Life Expectancy (in yrs)
Andorra	83.5	Zambia	32.4
Japan	81.6	Zimbabwe	33.1
Sweden	80.1	Sierra Leone	34.2
Hong Kong	79.9	Swaziland	34.4
Iceland	79.8	Lesotho	35.1

Countries and Their Parliaments

Country	Name of the Parliament	Country	Name of the Parliament
Afghanistan	Shora	Israel	Knesset
Australia	Parliament	Iran	Majlis
Bangladesh	Jatiya Parliament	Japan	Diet
Bhutan	Tsongdu	Malaysia	Majlis
Bulgaria	Narodna Subranie	Maldives	Majlis
Canada	Parliament	Mongolia	Khural
China	National People Congress	Nepal	National Panchayat
Denmark	Folketing	Netherlands	States General
Egypt	People's Assembly	Norway	Storting
England	Parliament	Pakistan	National Assembly
Ethiopia	Shergo	Poland	Sejm
Finland	Eduskusta	Spain	Cortes
France	National assembly	Sweden	Riksdag
Germany	Bundestag (lower House)	South Africa	Parliament
	Bundestrat (Upper House)	Surinam	Staten
Greenland	Landstraad	Switzerland	Federal Assembly
Iceland	Althing	Russia	Duma
India	Lok Sabha (Lower House)	Taiwan	Yuan
	Rajya Sabha (Upper House)	USA	Congress

Q.31. Which country is known as the Sick Man of Europe?
Q.32. Who was the first woman in the world to scale Mount Everest?

World Geography

National Emblem of some Countries

Country	National Emblem	Country	National Emblem
Australia	Kangaroo	Italy	White Lily
Bangladesh	Water Lily	Japan	Chrysanthemum
Canada	White Lily	Norway	Lion
Denmark	Beach	Pakistan	Crescent
France	Lily	Spain	Eagle
Germany	Corn Flower	Sri Lanka	Sword and Lion
India	Replica of Lion Capital	Russia	Sickle & Hammer
Iran	Rose	UK	Rose
Ireland	Shamrock	USA	Golden Rod

National Monuments of Some Countries

Monument	Country	Monument	Country
Emperial Palace (Tokyo)	Japan	Great Wall of China	China
Eiffel Tower	France	Kinder Disk	Denmark
Tajmahal (Agra)	India	Kremlin (Moscow)	Russia
Leaning Tower of Pisa	Italy	Opera House (Sidney)	Australia
Pyramid (Giza)	Egypt	Statue of Liberty (New York)	USA

Major Geographical Discoveries

Discover	Discoverer	Discover	Discoverer
America	Christopher Columbus	North Pole	Robert Peary
Sea Route to India	Vasco-de-Gama	China	Marco Polo
Solar System	Copernicus	Hudson Bay	Henry Hudson
Planets	Kepler	Cape of Good Hope	Bartholomew Diaz
South Pole	Amundsen		

Major Political Parties in the World

Political Parties	Country
Liberal Party, Labour Party	Australia
Bangladesh National Party, Awami league, Jatiya Party	Bangladesh
Chinese Communist Party	China
Socialist Party, National Front, Union for French Democracy	France
Indian National Congress, Bhatiya Janata Party	India
Nepali Congress, Nepali Communist party	Nepal
Muslim League, Pakistan People's Party	Pakistan
Liberal Democratic Party, Communist Party	Russia
African National Congress, National Party	South Africa
Freedom Party, United National Party	Sri Lanka
Labour Party, Conservative Party, Liberal Democratic Party	UK
Democratic Party, Republican Party	USA

Q.33. Which is the largest Artificial Lake in the world?
Q.34. On which river is world's largest waterfall Victoria located?

General Knowledge Manual

Important Sites and Their Locations

Site	Location	Site	Location
Bastille Prison	Paris	Kremlin	Moscow
Brandenburg Gate	Berlin	Leaning Tower	Pisa (Italy)
Broadway	New York	Louvre	Paris
Buckingham Palace	London	Merdeca Palace	Jakarta
Colosseum	Rome	Pentagon	Washington DC
Downing Street (PM Residence)	London	Porcelain Tower	Nanjing (China)
		Potala	Lhasa
Eiffel Tower	Paris	Red Square	Moscow
Empire State Building	New York	Scotland Yard	London
Fleet Street	London	Dragon Pagoda	Yangon
Grand Canyon	Arizona (USA)	Sphinx	Egypt
Harley Street	London	Wall Street	New York
Hyde Park	London	Wailing Wall	Jerusalem
India House	London	Wambley	London
Jodrell Bank	Manchester (UK)	White Hall	London
Kabba	Mecca (Saudi Arabia)		

Important Boundaries

Durand Line: It was established in 1893 and it marked the border between Afghanistan and Pakistan. It was drawn by Sir Mortimer Durand, who induced Abdor Rahman Khan (Amir of Afghanistan).

Hindenburg Line: This line divides Germany and Poland. The Hindenburg Line resisted all Allied attacks in 1917 and was not breached until late in 1918.

McMahon Line: This line demarcates the boundary between India and China. It was named after Sir Henry McMahon. However China does not recognise it and violated in 1962.

Mannerheim Line: This line divides Russia and Finland and was drawn by General Mannerheim.

Order-Neisse Line: It is the border between Poland and Germany, drawn along the rivers Order and Neisse, adopted on August 1945 at the Poland Conference after the World War II.

Radcliffe Line: This line demarcates the boundary between India and Pakistan which was drawn up by Sir Cyril Redcliff.

Siegfried Line: It is the border line laid by Germany with France.

Forty-ninth Parallel: It is the boundary between USA and Canada.

Thirty-eighth Parallel: It is the boundary between North Korea and South Korea.

Twenty-fourth Parallel: This line has been claimed by Pakistan as its border line with India, which is not accepted by India.

Seventeenth Parallel: It defined the boundary between North and South Vietnam before their unification.

Q.35. Which country is the biggest producer of mica in the world?

Q.36. Philadelphia is located on which river bank?

World Geography

Most Populous Cities of the World (on 08/07)

	City	Population (million)	Country
1.	Tokyo	33.2	Japan
2.	New York	30.1	USA
3.	Mexico City	22.65	Mexico
4.	Seoul	22.25	South Korea
5.	Sao Paulo	20.2	Brazil
6.	Jakarta	18.2	Indonesia
7.	Osaka-Kobe-Kyoto	17.6	Japan
8.	New Delhi	17.36	India
9.	Mumbai	17.34	India
10.	Los Angeles	16.7	USA
11.	Cairo	15.86	Egypt
12.	Kolkata	14.3	India
13.	Manila	14.1	Philippines
14.	Shanghai	13.9	China
15.	Dhaka	13.6	Bangladesh

Important Cities of the World on River Banks

	City	River		City	River
1.	Antwerp	Scheldt	16.	Glasgow	Clyde
2.	Baghdad	Tigris	17.	Lisbon	Tagus
3.	Bangkok	Chao Phraya	18.	London	Thames
4.	Basra	Shatt-al-Arab	19.	Madrid	Manzanares
5.	Belgrade	Danube	20.	Montreal	St. Lawrence & Ottawa
6.	Bonn	Rhine	21.	Moscow	Moskva
7.	Bristol	Avon	22.	New York	Hudson
8.	Brussels	Seine	23.	Paris	Seine
9.	Budapest	Danube	24.	Philadelphia	Delaware
10.	Cairo	Nile	25.	Prague	Vltava
11.	Canton	Chu-Kiang	26.	Rotterdam	Nieuwe Maas
12.	Chittagong	Karnafuli	27.	Shanghai	Yangtze-Kiang
13.	Cologne	Rhine	28.	Sydney	Darling
14.	Dublin	Liffey	29.	Warsaw	Vistula
15.	Dresden	Elbe	30.	Washington DC	Potomac

Major Crops Producing Countries

Crop	Nations
Coffee	Brazil, Columbia, Indonesia, India
Cocoa	Cote D'Ivore, Indonesia, Ghana, Nigeria
Cotton	China, USA, India, Pakistan
Cereals	China, USA, India, Russia
Coarse Grains	USA, China, Brazil, Russia

Q.37. Which is the longest day in the Northern Hemisphere?
Q.38. In the structure of planet Earth, what is the core made up of?

General Knowledge Manual

Cloves	Tanzania
Jute	Bangladesh, India, China, Japan
Maize	USA, China, Brazil, Argentina
Oil Seed	USA, Brazil, China, Argentina, India
Rubber	Thailand, Malaysia, Indonesia, China
Rice	China, India, Indonesia, Bangladesh
Sugar	Brazil, India, China
Silk	Japan, China, Korea, India, Turkey
Tea	India, China, Sri Lanka, Kenya
Tobacco	USA, Russia, China, India, Egypt
Wheat	China, Russia, USA, India

Major Mineral Producing Countries

Mineral	Nations
Aluminium	China, Russia, Canada, USA
Copper	Chile, Indonesia, USA, Australia
Coal	USA, Russia, China, Germany
Gold	South Africa, USA, Australia, China
Iron Ore	Russia, USA, Australia, Canada, India
Lead	Australia, China, USA, Peru
Magnesium	India, Russia, Mexico, Ivory Coast
Mica	India
Natural Gas	Russia, USA, Canada, UK, Algeria
Nickel	Russia, Australia, Canada, Indonesia
Platinum	South Africa, Russia
Petroleum	Saudi Arabia, Kuwait, Iran, Iraq, Quarter, UAE
Silver	Canada, Russia, Mexico, USA
Tin	Indonesia, China, Peru, Brazil
Thorium	India, Brazil, USA
Uranium	Zaire, South Africa, USA, Canada, Germany, India
Zinc	China, Australia, Peru, Canada

Major Industrial Countries

Industry	Nations
Automobiles	USA, Japan, Germany
Aircraft Industry	USA, EU, France, Brazil
Chemicals	USA, Germany, UK, Russia, Japan, Canada, Australia, India
Iron and Steel	USA, Russia, Japan, Germany, UK, France, India
Paper	USA, Canada, Japan, UK, Germany, Sweden, Norway, Finland, Russia, India
Pharmaceuticals	USA, EU, Japan, India
Rubber	USA, UK, Germany, France, Netherlands, Australia, Canada, Brazil, Indonesia
Sugar	Brazil, India, China, Australia, Thailand

Q.39. What is the traditional Tibetan name for Mount Everest meaning 'Goddess Mother of the Earth'?
Q.40. In the northern hemisphere, December 22 is known as..... .

World Geography

Textiles	USA, China, India, Japan, Russia, UK, France, Italy
Tea	India, China, Sri Lanka, Bangladesh, Indonesia, Japan
Coffee	Brazil, Columbia, Venezuela, Jamaica, Haiti, Indonesia
Oil	Iraq, Saudi Arabia, Kuwait, Iran, UAE, Qatar, Bahrain, USA, Venezuela, Mexico, Russia
Natural Gas	USA, Netherlands, Canada, Indonesia, UK

Major Newspapers in the World

Newspaper	Place/Country	Newspaper	Place/Country
Al-Ahram	Cairo (Egypt)	Izvestia	Moscow
Bangladesh Observer	Dhaka (Bangladesh)	Pravada	Moscow
Daily News	New York (USA)	Le Monde	Paris
New York Times	New York	Le Republica	Rome (Italy)
Daily Mail	London (UK)	Merdeka	Jakarta (Indonesia)
Daily Mirror	London (UK)	People's Daily	Beijing (China)
Financial Times	London	Star	Johannesburg (S.Africa)
Guardian	London	The Island	Colombo (Sri Lanka)
Independent	London	The Times of India	India
The Times	London	The Hindu	India
Dawn	Karachi (Pakistan)	Washington Post	Washington DC
Eastern Sun	Singapore	Khalij Times	Dubai (UAE)

Major News Agencies in the World

News Agencies	Country	News Agencies	Country
AAP	Australia	PTI, UNI, Univarta, Sanchar Bharti	India
XINHUA	China		
MENA	Egypt	Antara	Indonesia
A.F.P.	France	IRNA	Iran
ANSA	Italy	APP	Pakistan
ITIM	Israel	WAFA	Palestine
KYODO	Japan	Tass, NOVOSTI	Russia
BERNAMA	Malaysia	REUTER	UK
D.P.A.	Germany	AP, UPI	USA

Old and New Names in the World

New Name	Old Name	New Name	Old Name
Ethiopia	Abyssinia	Myanmar	Burma
Ankara	Angora	Cape Kennedy	Cape Canaveral
Belize	British Honduras	Sri Lanka	Ceylon
Jakarta	Batavia	Oslo	Christiana
Botswana	Bechuanaland	Zaire	Congo
Lesotho	Basutoland	Istanbul	Constantinople

Q.41. *In which sea the direction of ocean currents is reversed with season?*
Q.42. *What is the phenomenon of Midnight Sun in Norway result of?*

New Name	Old Name	New Name	Old Name
Dhaka	Dacca	Zambia	Northern Rhodesia
Benin	Dahomey	Malawi	Nyasaland
Indonesia	Dutch of East Indies	Beijing	Peking
Surinam	Dutch Guiana	Leningrad	Petrograd
Bangladesh	East Pakistan	Iran	Persia
Loro Sea	East Timer	Guinea Bissau	Portuguese Guinea
United Arab Republic	Egypt	Yangon	Rangoon
Tuvalu	Ellice Island	Zimbabwe	Southern Rhodesia
Taiwan	Formosa	Ho Chin Men city	Saigon
Mali	French West Africa	Harare	Salisbury
Ghana	Gold Coast	Hawaiian Islands	Sandwich Islands
Kalaallit Nunaat	Greenland	Thailand	Siam
Cambodia	Kampuchea	Namibia	South West Africa
Kinshasa	Leopoldville	Equatorial Guinea	Spanish Guinea
Malagasy	Madagascar	Volgograd	Stalin grad
Malaysia	Malaya	Tanzania	Zanzibar & Tanganyika
Manchuria	Manchukuo	United Arab Emirates	Trucial Oman
Iraq	Mesopotamia	Burkina Faso	Upper Volta
Vanuatu	New Hebrides	Mauritania	West French Africa
Japan	Nippon		

Geographical Epithets

Epithet	Names	Epithet	Names
Battlefield of Europe	Belgium	Garden City	Chicago
Britain of the South	New Zealand	Garden of England	Kent
Bengal's Sorrow	Damodar River	Gate of Tears	Babel-Mandeb, Jerusalem
Blue Mountains	Nilgiri Hills		
City of the Golden Gate	San Francisco	Granite City	Aberdeen, Scotland
City of Dreaming Spires	Oxford		
City of Magnificent Distances	Washington DC	Great White Way	Broadway, New York
City of Popes	Rome	Gift of Nile	Egypt
City of Seven Hills	Rome	Golden City	Johannesburg
City of Skyscrapers	New York	Gibraltar of Indian Ocean	Aden
City of Eternal Springs	Quito (South America)	Hermit Kingdom	Korea
		Herring Pond	Atlantic Ocean
China's Sorrow	Hwang Ho	Holy Land	Palestine
Cockpit of Europe	Belgium	Island of Cloves	Madagascar
Dark Continent	Africa	Island Continents	Australia
Dairy of Northern Europe	Denmark	Island of Pearls	Bahrain
Emerald Island	Ireland	The Isle of Spring	Jamaica
Empire City	New York	Key to the Mediterranean	Gibraltar
Eternal City	Rome	Land of Cakes (Oat Cakes)	Scotland
Forbidden City	Lhasa (Tibet)	Land of the Flying Fish	Barbados

World Geography

Epithet	Names	Epithet	Names
Land of the Golden Fleece	Australia	Rich Coast	Costa Rica
Land of the Golden Pagoda	Myanmar	Rich Port	Puerto Rico
Land of Kangaroos	Australia	Roof of the World	Pamir (Tibet)
Land of Lilies	Canada	The Sea of Mountains	British Columbia
Land of Maple Leaf	Canada	The Saw Mill of Europe	Sweden
Land of Midnight Sun	Norway	Sick Man of Europe	Turkey
Land of Milk & Honey	Canada	Sugar Bowl of the World	Cuba
Land of Morning Calm	Korea	The Store House of the world	Mexico
Land of Rising Sun	Japan	The Down under	Australia
Land of a Thousand Lakes	Finland	Venice of the North	Stockholm
Land of Thunderbolt	Bhutan	Venice of the East	Bangkok, Allepey (India)
Land of White Elephants	Thailand		
Lady of Snow	Canada	Yellow River	Hwang Ho
Little Venice	Venezuela	White City	Belgrade
Loneliest Island	Tristan De Gunha (Mid-Atlantic)	Windy City	Chicago
		White Man's Grave	Guinea Coast (West Africa)
Mother-in-Law of Europe	Denmark		
Never, Never Land	Prairies (North Australia)	Workshop of Europe	Belgium
		World's Bread Basket	Prairies of North America
Pearl of Antilles	Cuba		
Playground of Europe	Switzerland	The Spice Island of the West	Grenada
Pillars of Hercules	Straits of Gibraltar	The Mother Colony	St Kitts (West Indies)
Pearl of the Pacific	Guayaquil Port (Ecuador)	City of Arabian Nights	Baghdad
Powder Keg of Europe	Balkans	Twin City	Budapest
The Promised Land	Canada	The Imperial City	Rome
Quaker City	Philadelphia	The Modern Babylon	London
Queen of the Arabian Sea	Kochi (India)	Valley of Kings	Thebes
Queen of the Adriatic	Venice		

First in the World

1.	First person to climb Mount Everest	Sherpa Tenzing Norgay (Nepal)
2.	First woman to climb Mt Everest	Junko Tabei (Japan)
3.	First person to climb Mt Everest twice	Nawang Gombu
4.	First person to reach North Pole	Robert E Peary (USA)
5.	First person to go to space	Yuri Gagarin (Russia)
6.	First person to set foot on Moon	Neil Alden Armstrong (USA)
7.	First person to walk in Space	Alexi Leonov (Russia)
8.	First person to reach South Pole	Roald Amundsen (Norway)
9.	First woman to reach North Pole	Mrs Karoline Mikkelsen (Norway)
10.	First woman to reach South Pole	Mrs Fran Phipps (Canada)
11.	First woman Cosmonaut in Space	Valentina Tereshkova (Russia)

Q.43. What is a narrow strip of land separating two seas called?
Q.44. What does equinox refers to?

12.	First woman to cross the Strait of Gibraltar	Arti Pradjan (India)
13.	First woman Prime Minister of a Country	Mrs S. Bandaranaike (Sri Lanka)
14.	First woman Bishop	Rev. Barbara C Harris (USA)
15.	First woman President of Country	Maria Estela Peron (Argentina)
16.	First handicapped person to cross Strait of Gibraltar	Taranath Shenoy (India)
17.	First person to Circumnavigate the Poles	Sir Ranulph Fiennes and Charles Burton (Britain)
18.	First foreigner to invade India	Alexander the Great (Greece)
19.	First person to sail around the World	Ferdinand Magellan (Portugal)
20.	First chinese traveller to India	Fahien
21.	First religion in the World	Hinduism
22.	First country to print book	China
23.	First country to issue Paper Currency	China
24.	First country to win Soccer World Cup	Uruguay
25.	First country to host NAAM Summit	Belgrade
26.	First president of USA	George Washington
27.	First president of China	Dr Sun Yat-Sen
28.	First prime Minister of Britain	Sir Robert Walpole
29.	First woman Prime minister of Britain	Margret Thatcher
30.	First muslim Prime Minister of a Country	Benazir Bhutto (Pakistan)
31.	First Spacecraft to reach on Mars	Columbia
32.	The first Muslim woman to receive Nobel Prize	Shirin Ebadi (Nobel Peace Prize 2003)

New Seven Wonders of the World

The following sites always will remain official new Seven Wonders of the World Finalists, which were nominated from hundreds of sites around the world. The results include worldwide online, SMS and telephone voting.

Name of the Wonder	Country
The Pyramid at Chichén Itzá (before AD 800)	Yucatan Peninsula, Mexico
Christ Redeemer (1931)	Rio de Janeiro, Brazil
The Roman Colosseum (AD 70–82)	Rome, Italy
The Great Wall of China (220 BC and AD 1368–1644)	China
Machu Picchu (1460–1470)	Peru
Petra (9 BC–AD 40)	Jordan
The Taj Mahal (AD 1630)	Agra, India

Seven Wonders of Ancient Times

One of the first known lists was made by Antipater of Sidon, who lived in the first half of the second century.

Name of the Wonder	Location
Light house of Alexandria (280 BC)	Ancient island of Pharos (modern Alexandria, Egypt)
Phidias' statue of Zeus in Olympia (437 BC)	Olympia

The hanging gardens of Babylon (6th century BC)	East bank of Euphrates, South of Baghdad in Iraq
The Colossus of Rhodes (325-292 BC)	City of Rhodes (Eastern part of Mediterranean Sea)
The Pyramids of Egypt (c.2630 and c.1640)	Egypt
The Mausoleum of Halicarnassus (325 BC)	Eastern side of Aegean Sea in Turkey
The temple of Artemis of Ephesus (800 BC)	Asia Minor at Ephesus (now a vanished city)

COUNTRY, THEIR CAPITAL AND CURRENCY

Country	Capital	Currency
1. Afghanistan	Kabul	Afghani
2. Albania	Tirana	Lek
3. Algeria	Algiers	Algerian Dinar
4. Andorra	Andorra la Vella	Euro
5. Angola	Luanda	New Kwanza
6. Antigua and Barbuda	Saint John's	East Caribbean Dollar
7. Argentina	Buenos Aires	Peso
8. Armenia	Yerevan	Dram
9. Australia	Canberra	Dollar
10. Austria	Vienna	Euro (Earlier Schilling)
11. Azerbaijan	Baku	Manat
12. Bahamas	Nassau	Bahamian Dollar
13. Bahrain	Manama	Bahrain Dinar
14. Bangladesh	Dhaka	Taka
15. Barbados	Bridgetown	Barbados Dollar
16. Belarus	Minsk	Ruble
17. Belgium	Brussels	Euro
18. Belize	Belmopan	Belize Dollar
19. Benin	Porto-Novo	Franc CFA
20. Bhutan	Thimphu	Ngultrum
21. Bolivia	La Paz (administrative) Sucre (judicial)	Boliviano
22. Bosnia and Herzegovina	Sarajevo	Convertible Marka
23. Botswana	Gaborone	Pula
24. Brazil	Brasilia	Real
25. Brunei	Bandar Seri Begawan	Brunei Dollar
26. Bulgaria	Sofia	Lev
27. Burkina Faso	Ouagadougou	Franc CFA
28. Burundi	Bujumbura	Burundi Franc
29. Cambodia	Phnom Penh	Riel
30. Cameroon	Yaounde	Franc CFA
31. Canada	Ottawa	Canadian Dollar
32. Cape Verde	Praia	Cape Verde Escudo
33. Central African Republic	Bangui	Franc CFA
34. Chad	N'Djamena	Franc CFA
35. Chile	Santiago	Chilean Peso

#	Country	Capital	Currency
36.	China	Beijing	Renminbi Yuan
37.	Colombia	Bogota	Colombian Peso
38.	Comoros	Moroni	Comoros Franc
39.	Congo, Republic of the	Brazzaville	Franc CFA
40.	Congo, Democratic Republic of the	Kinshasa	Congo Franc
41.	Costa Rica	San Jose	Costa Rican Colon
42.	Croatia	Zagreb	Kuna
43.	Cuba	Havana	Cuban Peso
44.	Cyprus	Nicosia	Cyprus Pound
45.	Czech Republic	Prague	Koruna
46.	Denmark	Copenhagen	Danish Krone
47.	Djibouti	Djibouti	Djibouti Franc
48.	Dominica	Roseau	East Caribbean Dollar
49.	Dominican Republic	Santo Domingo	Peso
50.	East Timor (Timor-Leste)	Dili	US Dollar
51.	Ecuador	Quito	US Dollar
52.	Egypt	Cairo	Egyptian Pound
53.	El Salvador	San Salvador	Colon
54.	Equatorial Guinea	Malabo	Franc CFA
55.	Eritrea	Asmara	Nakfa
56.	Estonia	Tallinn	Kroon
57.	Ethiopia	Addis Ababa	Birr
58.	Fiji	Suva	Fiji Dollar
59.	Finland	Helsinki	Euro (Earlier Marka)
60.	France	Paris	Euro (Earlier Franc)
61.	Gabon	Libreville	CFA Franc
62.	The Gambia	Banjul	Dalasi
63.	Georgia	Tbilisi	Lari
64.	Germany	Berlin	Euro (Earlier Deutsche Mark)
65.	Ghana	Accra	Cedi
66.	Greece	Athens	Euro (Earlier Drachma)
67.	Grenada	Saint George's	East Caribbean Dollar
68.	Guatemala	Guatemala City	Quetzal
69.	Guinea	Conakry	Guinea Franc
70.	Guinea-Bissau	Bissau	Franc CFA
71.	Guyana	Georgetown	Dollar
72.	Haiti	Port-au-Prince	Gourde
73.	Honduras	Tegucigalpa	Lempira
74.	Hungary	Budapest	Forint
75.	Iceland	Reykjavik	Krona
76.	India	New Delhi	Rupee
77.	Indonesia	Jakarta	Rupiah
78.	Iran	Tehran	Rial
79.	Iraq	Baghdad	Iraqi Dinar
80.	Ireland	Dublin	Euro (Earlier Punt)
81.	Israel	Jerusalem	Shekel

#	Country	Capital	Currency
82.	Italy	Rome	Euro (Earlier Lira)
83.	Jamaica	Kingston	Jamaican Dollar
84.	Japan	Tokyo	Yen
85.	Jordan	Amman	Jordan Dinar
86.	Kazakhstan	Astana	Tenge
87.	Kenya	Nairobi	Shilling
88.	Kiribati	Tarawa Atoll	Australian Dollar
89.	Korea, North	Pyongyang	Won
90.	Korea, South	Seoul	Won
91.	Kosovo	Pristina	Euro (Earlier Serbian Dinar)
92.	Kuwait	Kuwait City	Kuwait Dinar
93.	Kyrgyzstan	Bishkek	Som
94.	Laos	Vientiane	Kip
95.	Latvia	Riga	Lats
96.	Lebanon	Beirut	Lebanese Pound
97.	Lesotho	Maseru	Loti
98.	Liberia	Monrovia	Liberian Dollar
99.	Libya	Tripoli	Libyan Dinar
100.	Liechtenstein	Vaduz	Swiss Currency
101.	Lithuania	Vilnius	Litas
102.	Luxembourg	Luxembourg	Euro (Earlier Franc)
103.	Macedonia	Skopje	Denar
104.	Madagascar	Antananarivo	Malagasy Franc
105.	Malawi	Lilongwe	Kwacha
106.	Malaysia	Kuala Lumpur	Ringgit
107.	Maldives	Male	Rufiyaa
108.	Mali	Bamako	Franc CFA
109.	Malta	Valletta	Maltese Lira
110.	Marshall Islands	Majuro	Atoll US Dollar
111.	Mauritania	Nouakchott	Ouguiya
112.	Mauritius	Port Louis	Mauritius Rupee
113.	Mexico	Mexico City	Mexico Peso
114.	Federated States of Micronesia	Palikir	US Dollar
115.	Moldova	Chisinau	Leu
116.	Monaco	Monaco	Euro
117.	Mongolia	Ulaanbaatar	Tugrik
118.	Montenegro	Podgorica	Yugoslav New Dinar
119.	Morocco	Rabat	Dirham
120.	Mozambique	Maputo	Metical
121.	Myanmar (Burma)	YangonNaypyidaw or Nay Pyi Taw (administrative)	Kyat
122.	Namibia	Windhoek	Namibia Dollar
123.	Nauru	No official capital; Yaren District (government offices)	Australian Dollar
124.	Nepal	Kathmandu	Nepalese Rupee

125.	Netherlands	Amsterdam; (Seat of government) The Hague	Euro (Earlier Guilder)
126.	New Zealand	Wellington	New Zealand Dollar
127.	Nicaragua	Managua	Cordoba Oro
128.	Niger	Niamey	Franc CFA
129.	Nigeria	Abuja	Naira
130.	Norway	Oslo	Norwegian Krone
131.	Oman	Muscat	Rial Omani
132.	Pakistan	Islamabad	Pakistan Rupee
133.	Palau	Melekeok	US Dollar
134.	Panama	Panama City	Balboa, US Dollar
135.	Papua New Guinea	Port Moresby	Kina
136.	Paraguay	Asuncion	Guarani
137.	Peru	Lima	Nuevo Sol
138.	Philippines	Manila	Peso
139.	Poland	Warsaw	Zloty
140.	Portugal	Lisbon	Euro (Earlier Escudo)
141.	Qatar	Doha	Qatari
142.	Romania	Bucharest	Leu
143.	Russia	Moscow	Ruble
144.	Rwanda	Kigali	Rwanda Franc
145.	Saint Kitts and Nevis	Basseterre	East Caribbean Dollar
146.	Saint Lucia	Castries	East Caribbean Dollar
147.	Saint Vincent and the Grenadines	Kingstown	East Caribbean Dollar
148.	Samoa	Apia	Tala
149.	San Marino	San Marino	Euro
150.	Sao Tome and Principe	Sao Tome	Dobra
151.	Saudi Arabia	Riyadh	Rial
152.	Senegal	Dakar	Franc CFA
153.	Serbia	Belgrade	Dinar
154.	Seychelles	Victoria	Seychelles Rupee
155.	Sierra Leone	Freetown	Leone
156.	Singapore	Singapore	Singapore Dollar
157.	Slovakia	Bratislava	Slovak Koruna
158.	Slovenia	Ljubljana	Tolar
159.	Solomon Islands	Honiara	Solomon Islands Dollar
160.	Somalia	Mogadishu	Somali Shilling
161.	South Africa	Pretoria (administrative); Cape Town (legislative); Bloemfontein (judiciary)	Rand
162.	Spain	Madrid	Euro (Earlier Peseta)
163.	Sri Lanka	Colombo; Sri Jayewardenepura Kotte (legislative)	Sri Lankan Rupee
164.	Sudan	Khartoum	Sudanese Pound
165.	Suriname	Paramaribo	Suriname Guilder
166.	Swaziland	Mbabane	Lilangeni

World Geography 111

167.	Sweden	Stockholm	Krona
168.	Switzerland	Bern	Swiss Franc
169.	Syria	Damascus	Syrian Pound
170.	Taiwan	Taipei	New Taiwan Dollar
171.	Tajikistan	Dushanbe	Tajik Ruble
172.	Tanzania	Dar es Salaam; Dodoma (legislative)	Tanzania Shilling
173.	Thailand	Bangkok	Baht
174.	Togo	Lome	Franc CFA
175.	Tonga	Nuku'alofa	Paanga
176.	Trinidad and Tobago	Port-of-Spain	Trinidad and Tobago Dollar
177.	Tunisia	Tunis	Tunisia Dinar
178.	Turkey	Ankara	Turkish Lira
179.	Turkmenistan	Ashgabat	Manat
180.	Tuvalu	Vaiaku village, Funafuti province	Australian Dollar
181.	Uganda	Kampala	Uganda Shilling
182.	Ukraine	Kyiv	Hryvna
183.	United Arab Emirates	Abu Dhabi	Dirham
184.	United Kingdom	London	Pound Sterling
185.	United States of America	Washington DC	Dollar
186.	Uruguay	Montevideo	Uruguayan Peso
187.	Uzbekistan	Tashkent	Soum
188.	Vanuatu	Port-Vila	Vatu
189.	Vatican City (Holy See)	Vatican City	Euro
190.	Venezuela	Caracas	Bolivar
191.	Vietnam	Hanoi	Dong
192.	Yemen	Sana'a	Rial
193.	Zambia	Lusaka	Kwacha
194.	Zimbabwe	Harare	Zimbabwe Dollar

WORLD MISCELLANEA

Largest Continent	Asia
Largest Strait	Tartar (Between Russia and Sakhlin Island)
Largest Island	Greenland
Largest Delta	Sundarbans
Largest Sand Island	Fraser (East Coast of Australia)
Largest Peninsula	Arabia
Largest Gulf	Gulf of Mexico
Largest Bay	Hudson Bay
Largest Estuary	Orb (Russia)
Largest Lake	Caspian Sea
Largest Fresh Water lake	Lake Superior
Largest Artificial Lake	Lake Mead (USA)
Largest Salt Lake	Caspian Sea
Largest Town	Mt Isa (Queensland, Australia)
Largest Temple	Angkor Wakt (Cambodia)
Largest Dome	Astro Dome (USA)

Largest Mosque	Shah Faisal Mosque (Islamabad)
Largest Barrier Reef	Great Barrier Reef (Australia)
Largest Sea	South China Sea
Largest Gorge	Grand Canyon (Colorado River, Arizona)
Largest Archipelago	Indonesia
Largest Reservoir	Brats Lake (Angara River)
Largest River	Amazon
Largest Ocean	Pacific
Largest Dam	Grand Coulee (USA)
Largest Rain Forest	Amazon River Basin (South America)
Largest Glacier	Lambert Glacier (Antarctica)
Largest Waterfall	Victoria (Zambezi river, Zimbabwe & Zambia)
Largest Desert	Sahara
Largest Temperate Desert	Gobi
Largest Ice Desert	South Polar Region
Largest Zoo	Kruger National Park (South Africa)
Longest River (6,670 m)	Nile
Longest Road (27,387 km)	Pan-American Highway (North-west Alaska to Southernmost Chile)
Longest Coastline	Canada
Longest Mountain Range	Andes
Longest Canal	Beloye-More Canal (Baltic Sea)
Highest Mountain Peak (8,848 m)	Mt Everest
Highest Active Volcano	Ozos del Salado (Chile & Argentina)
Highest Extinct Volcano	Cerro Sconcagua (Argentina)
Highest Dormant Volcano	Llullaillaco (Chile)
Highest dam	Rohunsky (Tadzikstan)
Highest Waterfall	Angel Fall (Venezuela)
Highest Town	Wenzhuan (Tibet)
Highest Plateau	Pamirs (Tibet)
Highest Capital	La Paz (Bolivia)
Highest City	Van Chuan (China)
Smallest Continent	Australia
Smallest Ocean	Arctic Ocean
Smallest Republic	Nauru
Smallest Country	Vatican
Smallest Colony	Gibraltar
Deepest Ocean	Pacific Ocean
Deepest Lake	Baikal
Deepest George	Hell's Canyon (USA)
Deepest Ocean Depth	Challenger Deep, Mariana Trench (Pacific Ocean)
Lowest Point on the Earth	Dead Sea
Lowest Populated City	Vatican City
Lowest Temperate Region	Verkhoyansk (Siberia)
Shortest River	Roe River (Montana)
Driest Place	Atacama Desert (Chile)
Hottest Place	Aziza (Libya)
Rainiest Place	Mawsynram (Meghalaya, India)
Northern-most Town	Ny Alesun (Norway)

World Geography

Southern-most Town	Ushuaia (Argentina)
Country with Maximum Volcanoes	Indonesia
Country with Maximum rivers	China
Country with Longest Road Network	USA
Country with Densest Road Network	Macau
Country with Longest Railway Network	USA
Country with Highest Forest Cover	Russia
Country with Having most Number of Nuclear Reactors (104)	USA
Country with Producing Maximum Energy in Percentage of Its Total Energy (80%)	France
Country with Largest Number of Refugees	Iran

ANSWERS

1. Astronomical Unit
2. Spiral
3. Nova
4. Jupiter
5. 1.3 seconds
6. Solstice
7. Ionosphere
8. Latitudes
9. It is a tropical cyclone of the North West Australia
10. Westerlies
11. 35 per cent, i.e. 35 grams of salt is present in 1 litre of water
12. Fold Mountain
13. Seismic Focus
14. South China Sea
15. Lake Superior
16. Diet
17. Rial
18. Bhutan
19. 23° 27' south of equator
20. Sedimentary rocks
21. Beloye-More canal
22. Mediterranean sea and Atlantic Ocean
23. Marco Polo
24. Arizona
25. Duma
26. Russia
28. The USA and Canada
29. Jakarta
30. Ethiopia
31. Turkey
32. Junko Tabei
33. Lake Mead
34. Zambezi
35. India
36. Delaware
37. 21 June
38. Iron
39. Chomolungma
40. Winter Solstice
41. Mediterranean Sea
42. It is the result of: location of the place, rotation and revolution of earth
43. Isthmus
44. Two periods in the year when the days and nights are equal.

5
INDIAN ECONOMY

The economy of India is the twelfth largest (US$M 1,209,686) in the world by market value and the fourth largest in the world by GDP (US$M 3,288,345), measured on purchasing power parity (PPP) basis. (*Source: IMF: 2008*)

- India is the second fastest growing major economy in the world, with a GDP growth rate of 8.1 per cent.
- Per capita income of India was Rs 38,084 in 2008-09 (ranked 136th in the world) at PPP and is expected to grow by 14.4 per cent during the current fiscal.

Sectorial Contribution to Employment

Agriculture sector: 60%
Service sector: 28%
Industrial sector: 12%

Sectorial Contribution in GDP

Agricultural sector: 17%
Service sector: 54%
Industrial sector: 29%

PLANNING IN INDIA

Planning is the key to development for a developing country. The aim of the planning process is to offer quality of life to its citizens. In a welfare state equal opportunity in terms of education and employment, equitable distribution of wealth, health and social security are crucial.

Planning Commission of India

In March 1950, Planning Commission of India was constituted with Prime Minister as its Chairman.

It is composed of Prime Minister (as Chairman), Deputy Chairman, and few full-time members as experts of various fields like economics, industry, science and general.

Indian Economy

Present Planning Commission

Chairman: Dr Manmohan Singh (Prime Minister)
Dy Chairman: Dr Montek Singh Ahluwalia
Shri V Narayanasamy (Minister of State)

Members

- Dr Kirit Parikh
- Prof Abhijit Sen
- Dr V L Chopra
- Dr Bhalchandra Mungekar
- Dr (Ms) Syeda Hameed
- Shri B N Yugandhar
- Shri Anwar-ul-Hoda
- Shri B K Chaturvedi
- Member Secretary: Dr Subas Pani

Functions

(i) Formulation of Five Year Plans for effective use of resources.
(ii) Formulate plans for the most effective and balanced utilization of resources of the country.
(iii) Determination of priorities, and allocation of resources and implementation of the Plans.
(iv) Periodical appraisal of the progress of the Plan.
(v) To indicate the factors which are hampering economic development.

National Planning Council: It was established in 1965.

National Development Council (NDC): National Development Council was constituted in 1952.

Chief Ministers and Finance Ministers of all states, Lt Governors of Union Territories are the members of NDC. The Prime Minister is the Ex-officio Chairman of NDC.

Five-Year Plans

- The Five-Year Plan is drawn by Planning Commission of India.
- Basic objectives of five-year plans are to formulate economic policies, draft plans and monitor its implementation.
- There have been three Annual Plans –
  - ☐ 1966–67 to 1968–69: Plan holiday during war against China and Pakistan.
  - ☐ 1978–79 to 1979–80: During the Janta Party Government, this is also known as Rolling Plan.
  - ☐ 1990–91 to 1991–92: To bring about a maximum employment and social transformation.

> *Q.1. What is the contribution of industrial sector (in percentage) in the GDP of the Indian Economy?*

Five-Year Plans in Figures

Five-Year Plan	Period	Outlay (cr) Centre	State	UT	Total	Growth (%)
First Plan	1951–56	1241.00	828.00	—	2069.00	3.6
Second Plan	1956–61	2559.12	2240.88	—	4800.00	4.3
Third Plan	1961–66	3600.00	3725.00	175.00	7500.00	2.8
Fourth Plan	1969–74	8870.00	6606.47	425.00	15902.16	3.3
Fifth Plan	1974–79	19954.10	18265.08	634.06	38853.24	4.8
Sixth Plan	1980–85	47250.00	48600.00	1650.00	97500.00	6.0
Seventh Plan	1985–90	95534.00	80698.00	3768.00	180000.00	6.0
Eighth Plan	1992–97	247865.00	179985.00	6250.00	434100.00	6.8
Ninth Plan	1997–2002	489361.00	369839.00*	—	859200.00	5.5
Tenth Plan	2002–07	893183.00	632456.00	—	1525639.00	7.2
Eleventh Plan	2007–12	2156571.00	1488147.00	—	3644718.00	

* State outlay for Ninth Five year plan includes the figures for UTs.
Source: Planning Commission

First Five-Year Plan (1951–56)

The priority was to give agriculture and irrigation maximum attention.

Objectives

- To rectify the disequilibrium in the economy due to influx of refugees, severe food shortage and high inflation.
- To develop an all-round process to ensure a rising National Income and improvement in living standard.

Second Five-Year Plan (1956–61)

The priority was given to the development of basic and heavy industries, such as iron and steel, heavy chemicals, etc. Agriculture sector was not given much attention.

Third Five-Year Plan (1961–66)

It was aimed at long-term development to make India 'self-reliant'. Agriculture was again a top priority. During this plan Chinese aggression and Indo-Pak war occurred.

Fourth Five-Year Plan (1969–74)

It introduced the uses of scientific methodology in agriculture; objective was – 'growth with stability'.

Fifth Five-Year Plan (1974–79)

The objectives were to eliminate the poverty and increase self-reliance. The plan was terminated in (1978), one year earlier by the Janta Dal Government with the introduction of 'Rolling Plan'.

Q.2. Who is the Chairman of the Planning Commission of India?
Q.3. When was National Development Council constituted?

Indian Economy

Sixth Five-Year Plan (1980–85)

The objectives were to increase national income, induction of new technology and population control.

The original plan (devised by the Janta Dal Government) was abandoned by the Congress government, and it revised the plan.

Seventh Five-Year Plan (1985–90)

The objectives were to increase food production, generate employment and to raise productivity.

Eighth Five-Year Plan (1992–97)

The objectives – faster economic growth; faster growth in manufacturing, agricultural and allied sectors; growth in export and imports; reduction of fiscal deficit and trade deficit.

It was late by two years due to political upheavals at centre.

Ninth Five-Year Plan (1997–2002)

Objectives – Prioritising agriculture sector and rural development; accelerate the growth of economy; population control through family planning; empowering women and socially backward classes; promoting economic development of village through the institution of Panchayati Raj, self-help groups, etc.

Initially the target of GDP growth was set was at 7 per cent; however, it attained only 5.35 per cent.

Tenth Five-Year Plan (2002–07)

The main objectives of the tenth Five-Year Plan were:

- Reduction of poverty ratio by 5 per cent points by 2007.
- Reduction in gender gaps in literacy and wage rates by at least 50 per cent by 2007.
- Reduction in the decadal rate of population growth between 2001 and 2011 to 16.2 per cent.
- Increase in literacy rate to 75 per cent within the period of Tenth Plan (2002 to 2007).
- Reduction of Infant mortality rate (IMR) to 45 per 1000 live births by 2007 and to 28 by 2012.
- Increase in forest and tree cover to 25 per cent by 2007 and 33 per cent by 2012.
- Cleaning of all major polluted rivers by 2007 and other notified stretches by 2012.
- Economic Growth further accelerated during this period and crossed over 8 per cent by 2006.

Eleventh Five-Year Plan (2007–12)

The eleventh plan has the following objectives:

Income and Poverty

- Accelerate GDP growth from 8 per cent to 10 per cent, and then maintain at 10

> **Q.4.** Who gives the final approval to Five-Year Plan?
> **Q.5.** The Sensex is a market capitalisation weighted index of how many component stocks?

per cent in the Twelfth Plan in order to double per capita income by 2016-17.
- Increase agricultural GDP growth rate to 4 per cent per year to ensure a broader spread of benefits.
- Create 70 million new work opportunities.
- Reduce educated unemployment to below 5 per cent.

Education
- Reduce dropout rates of children from elementary school from 52.2 per cent in 2003-04 to 20 per cent by 2011-12.
- Increase literacy rate for persons of the age group of seven years or more to 85 per cent.

Health
- Reduce infant mortality rate to 28 and maternal mortality ratio to one per 1000 live births.
- Reduce Total Fertility Rate to two.
- Provide clean drinking water for all by 2009 and ensure that there are no slip-backs.

Women and Children
- Raise the sex ratio for the age group of 0-6 years to 935 by 2011-12 and to 950 by 2016-17.
- Ensure that at least 33 per cent of the direct and indirect beneficiaries of all government schemes are women and girl children.

Infrastructure
- Ensure electricity connection to all villages and BPL households by 2009 and round-the-clock power.
- Ensure all-weather road connection to all habitation with population 1000 and above (500 in hilly and tribal areas) by 2009, and ensure coverage of all significant habitation by 2015.
- Connect every village by telephone by November 2007 and provide broadband connectivity to all villages by 2012.

Environment
- Increase forest and tree cover by five percentage points.
- Attain WHO standards of air quality in all major cities by 2011-12.
- Treat all urban waste water by 2011-12 to clean river waters.
- Increase energy efficiency by 20 percentage points by 2016-17.

Measurement of Economic Welfareness

Poverty

Poverty line is defined on the basis of nutritional standards and Income levels.

Q.6. Under which Five-Year Plan did industrial growth recorded the highest growth?

Indicators	For Rural Population	For Urban Population
Daily Calorie intake (1991-92)	2400	2100
Per capita Expenditure (2004-05) Per month	Rs 559.00	Rs 1052.00
Annual Household Expenditure per month (2004)	Rs 565.00	Rs 1060.00

- People below these nutritional and income standards are considered to be Below Poverty Line.
- Presently 24.4 per cent population in India is Below Poverty Line; 24.36 per cent in rural and 24.5 per cent in urban population is Below Poverty Line.
(*Source*: National Sample Survey Organisation)

Unemployment

It is a situation which is characterised by availability of able person (capable of working), but having no job.

Different forms of Unemployment

(i) *Open Unemployment*: Lack of resources (primarily capital), results into having no job.
(ii) *Under Employment*: Unavailability of jobs for able person, throughout the year.
(iii) *Disguise Unemployment*: More persons are employed to complete a work, which could have been completed by fewer persons.

National Income

It is calculated as follows:
National Income = Net National Product (at market price) – Indirect taxes + subsidiaries
Per Capita Income = National Income/Population
National Statistical Organisation (NSO) calculates the National Income.

Flagship Programmes

(*a*) *Jawahar Gram Samridhi Yojana* (*JGSY*): It was introduced in place of Jawahar Rozgar Yojana in April 1999. Under this scheme the proportion of cost sharing between Centre and State is 7 per cent and 25 per cent respectively.

(*b*) *National Rural Employment Guarantee Act* (*NREGA*): It was introduced in February 2006, in all 596 rural districts in India, with the assistance of Central Government with the provision of Rs 16000 crore. This is renamed as Mahatma Gandhi National Rural Employment Guarantee Act from October 2009.

(*c*) *Swarnjayanti Gram Swarozgar Yojana* (*SGSY*): It was launched in April 1999 in place of the following programmes:
- Integrated Rural Development Programme
- Development of women and children in rural areas,
- Training rural youth for self-employment and Million Wells Scheme.

Q.7. Which government had introduced the Rolling Plan?
Q.8. Who estimates the National Income?

Proportion of cost sharing between Centre and state is again 75 per cent and 25 per cent respectively.

(d) *Jawaharlal Nehru National Urban Renewal Mission (JNNURM)*: The programme was run by Central Government with the allocation of Rs 6866 crore for 2008–09.

(e) *National Social Assistance Scheme*: The programme was introduced by Central Government from August 1995.

(f) *Food for Work Programme*: It was introduced in February 2001, in drought affected areas for providing food assistance through work.

(g) *Indira Awas Yojana*: This programme was launched to provide free house to poor family or to convert raw house to semi-pucca house.

(h) *Annapurna*: It was started by Central Government in April 2000 to provide food security to senior citizens.

(i) *Krishi Shramik Samajik Suraksha Yojana*: It was launched in July 2001, to provide security benefit to hired agricultural labourers.

Interim Union Budget 2009–10

Salient Features

- The Gross Domestic Product increased by 7.5 per cent, 9.5 per cent, 9.7 per cent and 9 per cent in the first four years from the fiscal year 2004–05 to 2007–08 recording a sustained growth of over 9 per cent for three consecutive years for the first time.
- The growth drivers for the period were agriculture, services, manufacturing along with trade and construction.
- Fiscal deficit was down from 4.5 per cent in 2003–04 to 2.7 per cent in 2007–08 and revenue deficit from 3.6 per cent to 1.1 per cent in 2007–08.
- The domestic investment rate as a proportion of GDP increased from 27.6 per cent in 2003–04 to 39 per cent in 2007-08. Gross Domestic savings rate shot up from 29.8 per cent to 37.7 per cent during this period.
- The tax to GDP ratio increased from 9.2 per cent in 2003–04 to 12.5 per cent in 2007-08.
- Exports grew at an annual average growth rate of 26.4 per cent (in US dollar) in the period 2004–05 to 2007–08. Foreign trade increased from 23.7 per cent of GDP in 2003–04 to 35.5 per cent in 2007–08.

Budget Estimates

- Total expenditure for fiscal 2009–10 is estimated at Rs 9,53,231 crore. Plan expenditure is estimated at Rs 2,85,149 crore and Non-Plan expenditure at Rs 6,68,082 crore.
- Rs 30,100 crore allocated for National Rural Employment Guarantee Scheme for the year 2009–10. In 2008–09 employment of 138.76 crore person days covering 3.51 crore household have already been generated.
- About 98 per cent habitations covered by primary schools under Sarva Shiksha Abhiyan.

Q.9. Under which flagship programme Central Government provides food security to senior citizens?

- Rs 8,000 crore allocated for Mid-day Meals Scheme for the year 2009–10.
- Proposal for allocation of Rs 6,705 crore for Integrated Child Development Scheme (ICDS) for the year 2009–10. New WHO child growth standards adopted for monitoring growth of children under ICDS.
- Rs 7,400 crore allocated for Rajiv Gandhi Rural Drinking Water Mission, Rs 1,200 crore for Rural Sanitation Programme, Rs 12,070 crore for National Rural Health Mission, Rs 40,900 crore allocated for Bharat Nirman for the year 2009–10.
- Major subsidies including food, fertiliser and petroleum estimated at Rs 95,579 crore.
- Allocation for Defence increased to Rs 1,41,703 crore which includes Rs 54,824 for Capital Expenditure.
- For the fiscal year 2009–10, with Centre's net tax revenue estimated at Rs 5,00,096 crore and revenue expenditure at Rs 8,48,085 crore, revenue deficit is estimated at 4 per cent of GDP and fiscal deficit at 5.5 per cent of GDP.

INDIAN FINANCIAL SYSTEM

1. Currency System

During the reign of Gupta Empire, gold coins were issued for the first time. And metal currency (the first Rupee, the silver coin) was minted in India during the empire of Sher Shah Suri.

- The first coins were introduced in 1950s. They were 1 pice, 1/2, 1 and 2 annas, 1/4, 1/2 and 1 rupee denominations.
- The Reserve Bank of India began note production in 1938, issuing 2, 5, 10 rupee notes, while the Government of India continued to issue one rupee notes.
- After independence the government introduced new designs in bank notes. In 1970s, 20 and 50 notes were introduced.
- In 1987, 500 rupee note was introduced followed by 1000 rupees in 2000.
- The language panel on the Indian rupee banknotes has 15 of the 22 national languages of India.
- All notes above one rupee are issued by Reserve Bank of India, therefore they bear the signature of the Governor of Reserve Bank of India. And one rupee bears the signature of the Secretary, Ministry of Finance.

2. Banking System

Background

Banks in India started, following the British pattern, in the beginning of the nineteenth-century, as joint stock banks. First bank managed by any Indian was the 'Oudh Commercial Bank' in 1881.

In 1894, Punjab National Bank was established. However, banking crisis began during 1913–17, which resulted into failure of many banks.

Q.10. How many times has the Indian currency been demonitised so far?

Q.11. On whose recommendations Reserve Bank of India was set up?

Post Independence the Government stepped in and enacted the Banking Companies Act in 1949 (subsequently renamed as Banking Regulation Act) to strengthen the weaker banks and to revive public confidence in banking system.

A new Section 45 was inserted in Banking Regulation Act in September 1960, which empowered the Government to compulsorily amalgamate weaker units with stronger ones on the recommendation of Reserve Bank of India (RBI).

Regulatory Authority (RBI)

- The Reserve Bank of India (RBI) is the Central Bank of India, and was established on 1 April 1935 in accordance with the provisions of the Reserve Bank of India Act, 1934, with a paid up share capital of five crore.
- It was set up on the recommendations of the Hilton Young Commission.
- The Central Office of the Reserve Bank was initially established in Kolkata but was permanently moved to Mumbai in 1937.
- RBI has been fully owned by the Government of India since nationalisation in 1949 (originally it was private owned).
- RBI's affairs are governed by a central board of directors. The board is appointed (for four years) by the Government of India in keeping with the Reserve Bank of India Act.
- It has 22 regional offices; most of them are in state capitals.

Functions of RBI

- It acts as regulator and supervisor of the financial system of the country.
- Regulating the issue of bank notes (above one rupee) and keeping of reserves with a view to secure monetary stability in the country.
- It regulates currency and credit system of the country.
- It maintains public confidence in the banking system; protects depositors' interest and provides cost-effective banking services to the public.
- It acts as banker to the union and state governments, commercial and co-operative banks.
- It formulates and administers the Monetary Policy.
- It facilitates external trade and payment and maintenance of foreign exchange market in India.

Classification of Bank: Banks are broadly classified into two groups:
1. Scheduled Commercial Banks
2. Non-Scheduled Commercial Banks

Scheduled Commercial Banks

Banks are included in the Second Schedule of the Reserve Bank of India Act 1934. In terms of Section 42 (6) (a) of Reserve Bank of India Act, a bank should fulfil certain conditions, stipulated by RBI, such as they must have paid up capital and reserves of an aggregate of not less than five lakh rupees. Those banks have privileges like approaching RBI for financial assistance,

Q.12. How many Public Sector Banks are now in India?
Q.13. When was the Securities and Exchange Board of India established?

refinance, etc. They in turn maintain certain obligations like submission of timely returns (Audit Compliance), certain cash Reserves prescribed by RBI.

SBI and its associates (8), other nationalised banks (19), foreign banks, private sector banks, co-operative banks and regional rural banks are Scheduled Commercial Banks.

Non-Scheduled Banks

These are joint stock banks, which are not included in the Second Schedule of the RBI Act 1934, on account of failure to comply with the minimum requirements for being Schedule Commercial Bank.

Since May 1997, there are no non-scheduled commercial banks existing.

Nationalisation of Banks

- On 19 July 1969, the Government of India nationalised 14 major banks with deposits over 50 crores.
- On 15 April 1980, six more commercial private sector banks were nationalised, with deposits over 200 crores.
- Now there are 27 Public Sector Banks, viz., State Bank of India and its six associate banks and 19 commercial banks. These are:

1. Bank of India	11. Syndicate Bank
2. Union Bank of India	12. United Commercial Bank
3. Bank of Baroda	13. Allahabad Bank
4. Bank of Maharashtra	14. United Bank of India
5. Punjab National Bank	15. Dena Bank
6. New Bank of India	16. Andhra Bank
7. Indian Bank	17. Corporation Bank
8. Indian Overseas Bank	18. Oriental Bank of Commerce
9. Central Bank of India	19. Punjab and Sind Bank
10. Canara Bank	20. Vijaya Bank

- In July 1993, New Bank of India was merged with Punjab National Bank.

State Bank of India (SBI)

- In the first half of nineteenth century, East India Company established three banks – The Bank of Bengal, The Bank of Bombay and The Bank of Madras. These three banks are known as Presidency Bank.
- In 1920, these three banks were amalgamated and Imperial Bank was formed.
- In 1955, by the State Bank of India Act, the Imperial bank of India was nationalised.
- In 1959, State Bank of India (Subsidiary banks) Act was passed, by which other eight banks –

The Bank of Bikaner,	The Bank of Patiala,
The Bank of Jaipur,	The Bank of Hyderabad,
The Bank of Indore,	The Bank of Sourashtra,
The Bank of Mysore,	The Banks of Travancore

– were made subsidiaries of SBI.
- In 1963, the State Bank of Bikaner and the State Bank of Jaipur were amalgamated to form the State Bank of Bikaner and Jaipur.

Q.14. What does IFCI stand for?
Q.15. When was Life Insurance sector nationalised?

124 General Knowledge Manual

- SBI is the largest bank in terms of number of branches (10836 branches).

Post-Nationalisation Period

- In order to cater to the needs of the customers and greater competition, private sector banks were allowed to operate.
- In 6 February 2003 'Kotak Mahindra Bank', was granted licence by RBI, which started its operation from 22 March 2003.
- In 24 May 2004 'Yes Bank Ltd' was granted licence by RBI to start operation.

Composition of Banking System

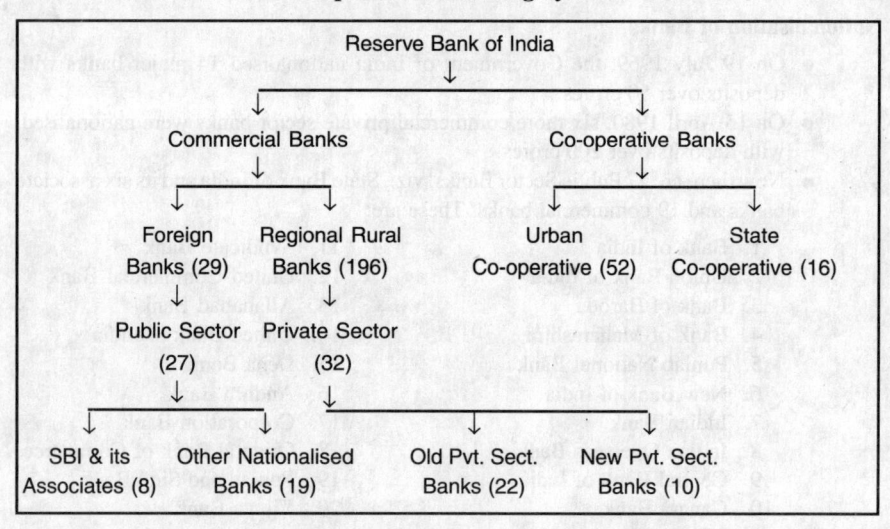

```
                        Reserve Bank of India
                                ↓
              ┌─────────────────┴─────────────────┐
              ↓                                   ↓
       Commercial Banks                    Co-operative Banks
              ↓                                   ↓
       ┌──────┴──────┐                    ┌──────┴──────┐
       ↓             ↓                    ↓             ↓
    Foreign      Regional Rural         Urban          State
   Banks (29)    Banks (196)        Co-operative (52)  Co-operative (16)
       ↓             ↓
  Public Sector  Private Sector
      (27)          (32)
       ↓             ↓
   ┌───┴───┐     ┌───┴───┐
   ↓       ↓     ↓       ↓
 SBI & its  Other Nationalised  Old Pvt. Sect.  New Pvt. Sect.
Associates (8)   Banks (19)     Banks (22)      Banks (10)
```

The public sector banks hold over 75 per cent of total assets of the banking industry, with the private and foreign banks holding 18.2 per cent and 6.5 per cent respectively. (*Source*: ICRA Limited, a rating agency)

Non-Bank Financial Institutions

Securities and Exchange Board of India (SEBI)

- The Securities and Exchange Board of India was established on 12 April 1992 in accordance with the provisions of the Securities and Exchange Board of India Act, 1992.
- The main function of SEBI is to protect the interests of investors in securities and to promote the development of and to regulate the securities market and for matters related with it.

Industrial Finance Corporation of India (IFCI)

- It was established in 1948.
- 50 per cent share is held by IDBI and rest with Banks and Insurance companies.

Q.16. IRDA was established on which committee's recommendation?

- It provides the finance to large and medium sized private and public sector companies.

Export Import (EXIM) Bank

Export Import Bank of India is also known as EXIM Bank of India and was established by an Act passed by the Parliament in September 1981, which started its operations in March 1982. The major objectives are to provide economic assistance to importers and exporters and to act as the apex financial institution.

National Bank for Agriculture and Rural Development (NABARD)

It was established in November 1982. Its main purpose is to provide credit for the development and publicity of small-scale industries, handicrafts, rural crafts, village industries, cottage industries, agriculture, etc.

Insurance Sector

- Oriental Life Insurance Company started by Europeans in Kolkata is the first Life Insurance Company of India in 1818.
- First Indian Life Insurance Company was Bombay Mutual Life Assurance Society.
- Life Insurance Sector was nationalised in 1956. And Life Insurance Corporation of India (LIC) came into existence in the same year, i.e. 1956.
- First General Insurance Company was set up India was Triton Insurance Company Ltd in1850 in Kolkata.
- General Insurance was nationalised in 1972.
- Currently there are 21 (20 + 1) General Insurance Companies and 21 (20 + 1) Life Insurance companies are operating in the country.
- Permitted limit of FDI in Insurance sector is 26 per cent.
- Insurance in India is divided into two categories:
  - *Life Insurance*: transacts life insurance business;
  - *General Insurance*: transacts the business regarding other forms of business.
  - State Life Insurer (1): Life Insurance Corporation of India (LIC)
  - State General Insurer and Reinsurer (1): General Insurance Corporation of India (GIC)

Insurance Regulatory and Development Authority (IRDA)

It was established in 1999 on the recommendation of the Malhotra committee; in the year 2000 IRDA was given statutory status.

Mutual Fund: The Mutual fund industry in India started in 1963 with setting up of Unit Trust of India (UTI). First Private Sector Mutual Fund started in 1993 with Kothari Pioneer Mutual Fund (Now merged with Franklin Templeton). The mutual fund Industry assets were estimated over Rs 306, 000 crore in August 2006. This industry had recorded a growth of nearly 8 per cent.

Types of Mutual Fund Schemes

(a) Open-Ended Schemes
(b) Close-Ended Schemes
(c) Interval Scheme

Q.17. How many Stock Exchanges are now in India?

Type of Investment Options
  (i) Growth Scheme
  (ii) Income Scheme
  (iii) Balanced Scheme
  (iv) Money Market Scheme

Other Schemes

Tax Saving Scheme
Special Scheme
Index Scheme
Sector Specific Scheme

Unit Trust of India (UTI)

- UTI was created by RBI in accordance with 'UTI Act' passed by the Parliament in 1963.
- In 1978, UTI was separated from RBI and its control was transferred to Industrial Development Bank of India (IDBI).
- First scheme of UTI was Unit Scheme 1964 (US-64).
- SBI mutual fund from State Bank of India became the first non-UTI mutual fund of India in 1978.

Stock Exchange of India

- Stock exchange is a corporation, which provides 'trading' facilities for stock brokers and traders to trade stocks, shares and other securities.
- First Stock Exchange of India was established in Mumbai in July 1875, later Ahmedabad Stock Exchange was established in 1894.
- Now there are 23 Stock Exchanges in India (North Zone: 4 + East Zone: 4 + West Zone: 9 + South Zone: 6)
- The Bombay Stock Exchange (BSE) or Sensex consists of 30 largest and most actively traded stocks, which are representative of various sectors.

3. Taxes

Taxes are of two types:

Direct Taxes: Personal Income Tax, Corporate Tax, Estate Duty and Wealth Tax come under Direct Taxes.

Indirect Taxes: These are Sales Tax, Excise Duty, Custom duty, etc.

Value Added Tax (VAT)

- VAT is based on the value addition to goods.
- It is introduced by Government for about 10 years in respect of Central Excise duties.
- There are two basic VAT rates of 4 per cent and 12.5 per cent and also a special VAT rate of 1 per cent for gold and silver ornaments, etc.
- VAT covers about 550 goods.
- Four per cent VAT rate is applicable for

Q.18. In which state VAT was first implemented?

Q.19. What is Trade Deficit?

about 270 items, common for all states, which comprises medicines and drugs, all agricultural and industrial inputs, capital goods, declared goods.
- The rest commodities fall under 12.5 per cent VAT common for all states.
- VAT was first implemented in Haryana on 1 April 2003.
- It is not implemented in Tamil Nadu, Uttar Pradesh and Puducherry.

4. Inflation

- Inflation is a rise in the general level of prices of goods and services in an economy over a period of time.
- A chief measure of general price-level inflation is the general inflation rate, which is the percentage change in the Consumer Price Index (CPI) over time.

5. Exports and Imports

- Exports and Imports in India are governed by Ministry of Commerce, which derives the policies pertaining to exports and imports.
- India's share in total global exports is 0.67 per cent in 2000–01.
- US, Canada, Japan and EU have been major trade destinations.
- India's exports as percentage of imports has gradually increased from 75.36 per cent (1990–91) to 88.17 per cent (2000–01).

Major Exports: Mineral fuels and their by-products, precious and semi-precious stones, apparels, jems and jewellary, iron and steel, jute products, leather goods, etc.

Major Imports: Capital goods and fuels – each account for about a quarter of Indian imports, edible oils, fertilisers, food grains, chemicals, industrial machinery, etc.

The latest release of commerce ministry shows exports in February 2009 slide by 21.7 per cent; imports also shrunk by 23 per cent for the same period, thus demonstrating limited consumption in the domestic economy.

Trade Deficit: is the gap between the value of exports and imports. Exports stood at Rs 274,313 crore (Apr-Jan. 2004–05), which registered 23.1 per cent growth in terms of rupees, in the corresponding period of previous year. At the same period import also registered a growth of 32.1 per cent, which figures Rs 376, 815 crore (Apr- Jan. 2004–05).

6. Foreign Investments

- India has been a good investment option for many countries in the world due to political stability, bureaucratic process involved and market-friendly environment for foreign players.
- The service sector attracts the maximum foreign investment, followed by construction, including roads and highways, housing and real estate, and computer hardware and software.
- Mauritius remained the top investing country, followed by Singapore, the US and the Netherlands.
- The total foreign direct investment till February 2009 was US$ 31 billion as compared to US$ 25 billion in the same period of the previous year.

Q.20. What is the Human Development Index comprised other than literacy rates and life expectancy at birth?

General Knowledge Manual

Foreign investments Inflows since 2000 (US$ million)

2000–01	4,029	2005–06	8,961
2001–02	6,130	2006–07	22,826
2002–03	5,035	2007–08	34,362
2003–04	4,322	2008–09	27,426
2004–05	6,051	(Apr-Dec'08)	

(*Source*: RBI's Bulletin March 2009)

INDUSTRIES

1. Agriculture Industry

India has gone through a Green Revolution, Yellow Revolution, Blue Revolution and Operation Flood for the increase of food production in the country. Today India holds the following ranks in the World:

- Largest producer of milk, fruit, cashew nuts, coconut and tea;
- Second largest producer of wheat, vegetables, sugar and fish; and
- Third largest producer of tobacco and rice.

Agricultural sector provides 60 per cent of the total employment.

FDI is not directly allowed in agriculture, however in food processing up to 100 per cent technology agreement within specified norms is allowed.

Major Food Grains Production (Million Tonnes)

Crop/Year	2003–04	2004–05	2005–06
Rice	88.3	85.3	73.8
Wheat	72.1	72.0	–
Coarse Cereals	38.1	33.9	26.4
Pulses	14.9	13.4	5.0
Food Grains	213.4	204.6	–

2. Iron and Steel Industry

The history of iron and steel industry in India is about 4000 years old. The first steel plant, TISCO, was established in Jamshedpur on 1911. In 1936 Mousier Iron and steel work was established (later named as Visveswarya Iron and Steel Work). In 1919 Indian Iron and Steel Company (IISCO) was started at Burnpur (Burdwan in West Bengal), now a subsidiary of SAIL.

At the time of Independence India had steel capacity of 1.3 million tonnes (mt) annually. Today India is tenth largest producer of steel (27.82 million tones finished annually). This industry employs 0.5 million people with 9000 crore turn over.

The world's largest steel producer is China (107 mt), followed by Japan (104 mt) and USA (97 mt). India's per capita consumption of steel is

Q.21. How much 'textile' sector accounts for India's Total Exports?

Q.22. What is reverse repo rate?

24 kg as compared to the USA, Germany, Russia and China who have per capita consumption of 422 kg, 417 kg, 107 kg and 87 kg respectively.

Tata Steel has acquired Dutch Steel maker Corus to become the fifth largest steel maker in the world.

Arcelor Steel merged with Mittal Steel in 2006 to become the largest steel maker in the world.

Production and Exports of Finished Steel and Pig Iron (mt) since 2004–05

Year	Production (In Million Tonnes)		Exports (In Million Tonnes)	
	Finished Steel	Pig Iron	Finished Steel	Pig Iron
2004–05	40.055	3.228	4.381	0.393
2005–06	44.544	4.695	4.478	0.440
2006–07	49.391	4.960	4.750	0.350
2007–08P (April–June)	12.088	1.165	1.310	0.120

P = Provisional Estimate

Public Sector Steel Plant: Public sector steel plants are managed by Steel Authority of India Ltd. (SAIL). SAIL has following plants operating under it:

Bhilai Steel Plant (BSP), Chhattisgarh, Durgapur Steel Plant (DSP), West Bengal, Rourkela Steel Plant (RSP), Orissa, Bokaro Steel Plant (BSP), Jharkhand.

SAIL has three special steel plants – Alloy Steel Plant (ASP) in West Bengal, Salem Steel Plant (SSP) in Tamil Nadu and Visvesvaraya Irion and Steel Plant (VISL) in Karnataka.

SAIL has three subsidiaries which are Indian Iron and Steel Company (IISCO) in West Bengal, Maharashtra Elektrosmelt Ltd. (MEL) in Maharashtra and Bhilai Oxygen Ltd. (BOL) in New Delhi.

Private Sector Steel Plant: Tata Iron and Steel Company (TISCO), Jamshedpur, Essar Steel, Jindal Vijaya Nagar Steels Ltd., Jindal Strips Ltd., Lloyds Steel Industries, Ispat Industries Ltd., Mahindra Ugine Steel Company, Tata SSL Ltd., Usha Ispat Ltd., etc.

3. IT & ITES/BPO Industry

- Information Technology and Information Technology Enabled Services (better known as Business Process Outsourcing – BPO) in the recent times has become one of the fastest growing industry in India.
- In 2004–05, this sector contributed more than a quarter of India's total service exports.
- IT Industry sector-wise breakup in 2008 (US$ billions)

IT Services	31
ITES/BPO	12.5
Engineering Services And R&D, Software Products	8.5
(a) Total Software and Services Revenues	52.1
(b) Hardware	12.0
Total IT Industry (a + b)	64.1

Q.23. 'Interest Rate Policy' is a component of ....

Q.24. What is US-64?

4. Telecom Industry

- Ministry of Telecommunication, Government of India concerned about the availability and effective communication for citizens.
- In 1999, Government of India authored National Telecom Policy (NTP-1999), which aimed at the growth of the Telecom Industry.
- *Organisation Concerned:* Telecom Regulatory Authority of India (TRAI) was established in 1997 by Government of India, whose main objective is to regulate the telecommunications business in India.
- Government has allowed 74 per cent FDI in this sector. India has second largest telecommunication network, which is only next to China and before USA.
- India is adding 8.5 to 10 million subscribers to the network every month. Tele-density is 26.89 per cent till June 2008.

FDI inflows in last few years (rupees in millions)

Year	Amount
2004	6004
2005	7062
2006	41,702
2007 (Till October)	45,963

5. Textile Industry

- It is one of the largest, most important sectors in terms of output, foreign exchange earnings and employment.
- It contributes 20 per cent of the total industrial output, 9 per cent of the excise collection, 18 per cent of the total employment in industrial sector, about 20 per cent of the total exports and 4 per cent of the GDP.
- Industry expected to achieve US$ 85 billion by 2010 (estimated by CRISIL).
- During 2005–06, the industry's growth rate was 8 per cent against last year's, share in FDI was 1.02 per cent (in terms of amount) and share in investment was 27.71 per cent.

6. Petroleum and Natural Gases

History: First oil well was found in 1867; however first well was successfully sunk in 1889 at Digboi, Assam. Assam has been the main oil producing state in the country; recently Hindustan Oil Exploration Company has found some other oil sources in Cambey Basin in Gujarat. Mumbai High is the richest oilfield of the country.

Organisations Involved: Department of Petroleum, under Ministry of Petroleum, is concerned about exploration, production and distribution of petroleum and natural gases in the country.

Oil and Natural Gas (ONGC) was set up in 1956 to explore the resources of oil and natural gases in India.

Oil India Limited (OIL) was started in 1959 in Duliajan (Assam), in collaboration with Burmah Oil Company. In 1981, government purchased the shares of Burmah Oil Company, so that it became a public limited company. It explores the crude oil as well as natural gases and transports it to the government refineries.

Q.25. 'A flame that has stood the test of time'– which company has used this punch line?

Indian Oil Corporation (IOC) was established in 1964 by the amalgamation of Indian Refinery Limited and Indian Oil Company. It has three divisions – Marketing (HO: Mumbai), Refining and Pipelines (HO: Delhi), Assam Oil (HO: Digboi).

Bharat Petroleum Corporation Limited (BPCL) came to the existence with the acquisition of Burmah Shell in 1976. In 1977 it was renamed as BPCL. It operates as refining Unit (HO: Mumbai) and marketing company all over India.

Hindustan Petroleum Corporation Limited (HPCL) came into existence by the amalgamation of ESSO and Caltex in 1974, and it became a public limited company in 1976. It is one of the Navratnas. Its main activities are refining of crude oil, manufacturing of petroleum products, marketing and distribution of its products.

Gas Authority of India Limited (GAIL) was set up by the Government of India in August 1984. It processes, distributes and markets the natural gas. It is the largest natural gas transportation company in the country.

Major Oil Refineries

Company	Location	Capacity (Million Metric Tonnes per Annum)
IOC	Barauni	4.20
	Koyali	12.50
	Haldia	3.75
	Mathura	7.50
	Panipat	6.00
HPCL	Mumbai	5.50
	Visakh	4.50
BPCL	Mumbai	6.90
Madras Refineries Ltd.	Chennai	6.50
Cochin Refineries Ltd.	Kochi	7.50
Manager Refinery and Petrochemicals Ltd (MRPL)	Mangalore	9.69
Reliance Petroleum Ltd.	Jamnagar	27.00
Others		6.91
Total		109.04

7. Pharmaceutical Industry

Indian Pharmaceutical now stands at $ 4.5 billion, in addition to over 3.1 billon exports. India has been a top player in world in generic market along with Brazil and China. The US and Russia are the major export destinations. Seventy per cent of the market share is acquired by to 250 companies. In global market India's share is 1.2 per cent and growing at 10 per cent annually.

India's biotech accounts for about two per cent of global market (US$ 41 billion), which ranks third in Asia-Pacific region and ninth in the world.

Q.26. What is India's major source of power generation?
Q.27. By what measure inflation can be checked temporarily?

Major Pharmaceutical Companies

Ranbaxy Laboratories Ltd.
Cipla Ltd.
Dr Reddys Laboratories Ltd.
Nicolas Piramal India Ltd.
Glaxo smithKiline Ltd.
Lupin Laboratories Ltd.
Cadila Healthcare Ltd.
Sun Pharmaceuticals Ltd.

8. Power Sector

Private participation was allowed in early 1990s. In March 2002, India had around 104,000 MW power generating capacity. Major source of power generation comes from thermal power (about 80 per cent), while Hydro-Electric accounts for 16 per cent and nuclear plants for the remaining capacity.

Unconventional energy source (solar energy and wind power) contribute only a relatively small percentage.

Overall Power Generation (Thermal + Hydro + Nuclear) in Public Utilities

Year	Generation (Billion Units)
2003–04	558.3
2004–05	587.4
2005–06	617.5
2006–07	662.5
2007–08 (up to Jan'08)	586.0

Power Supply Position

Year	Energy Requirement (MU)	Energy Availability (MU)	Energy Shortage (%)
2003–04	559,264	519,398	7.1
2004–05	591,373	548,115	7.3
2005–06	631,554	578,819	8.4
2006–07	690,587	624,495	9.6
2007–08 (Up to Jan'08)	608,804	554,248	9.0

Public Sector Undertakings (PSU): Public Sector Undertaking (PSU) is a term used for a government-owned corporation (company in the public sector). The term is used to refer to companies in which the government (either the Union Government or state or territorial governments, or both) owns majority (51 per cent or more) of the company's equity.

Navratnas: Navratnas was the title given originally to nine Public Sector Enterprises (PSE) identified by the Government of India in 1997, as it's the most prestigious PSEs, which allowed them greater autonomy to compete in the global

Q.28. What is Statutory Liquidity Rate (SLR)?
Q.29. Which is not a quantitative credit control technique?

market. The number of PSEs having navratna status has now been raised to 18; the most recent addition being Coal India Limited.

List of Navratnas
1. Bharat Electronics Limited
2. Bharat Heavy Electricals Limited
3. Bharat Petroleum Corporation Limited
4. Coal India Limited
5. GAIL (India) Limited
6. Hindustan Aeronautics Limited
7. Hindustan Petroleum Corporation Limited
8. Indian Oil Corporation Limited
9. Mahanagar Telephone Nigam Limited
10. National Aluminium Company Limited
11. NMDC Limited
12. NTPC Limited
13. Oil and Natural Gas Corporation Limited
14. Power Finance Corporation Limited
15. Power Grid Corporation of India Limited
16. Rural Electrification Corporation Limited
17. Shipping Corporation of India Limited
18. Steel Authority of India Limited

Miniratnas: The Government created another category called Miniratna. Miniratnas can also enter into joint ventures, set subsidiary companies and overseas offices but with certain conditions. It has two categories, which depends upon the type of autonomy.

Category I: 29 companies and Category II: 15 companies; in total there are 44 miniratnas.

Important Industries and Locations

Industry	Location
Aircraft Industry	Bangalore and Kanpur
Aluminium	Alwaye (Kerala), Asansol (West Bengal), Belur (Karnataka), Hirakud (Orissa), Renukoot (UP), Muri (Jharkhand), Korba (Chhattisgarh)
Automobiles	Mumbai, Burnpur (West Bengal), Kolkata, Jamshedpur (Jharkhand), Chennai
Cables	Rupnarainpur (West Bengal), Rajpur (Punjab)
Cement	Bhadravati (Karnataka), Churk (UP), Dalmianagar (Bihar), Surajpur (Punjab), Sahabad (Karnataka), Okha (Gujarat), Gwalior, Kymor (MP)
Coir Goods	Alleppey and Kalavoor (Kerala)
Cotton Textiles	Ahmedabad, Mumbai, Bangalore, Kolkata, Indore (MP), Kanpur (UP), Ludhiana and Amritsar (Punjab), Chennai, Madurai, Coimbatore (TN)
Cycles	Ludhiana (Punjab)
DDT	Alwaye (Kerala)
Glass Items	Firozabad (UP), Belgaum (Karnataka), Kolkata, Naini (UP), Amritsar (Punjab), Jabalpur (MP), Mumbai, Hyderabad, Chennai, Bangalore
Fertiliser	Nangal, Sindri (Jharkhand), Gorakhpur (UP), Rourkela (Orissa), Trombay (Maharashtra), Nuyveli (TN)

General Knowledge Manual

Hosiery Goods	Amritsar, Ludhiana (Punjab), Kanpur (UP)
Jut Goods	Kolkata, Gorakhpur, Kanpur (UP)
Lac	Jhalda, Kossikpur (WB), Mirzapur, Bareilly (UP)
Leather Goods	Kanpur, Agra (UP), Batanagar (WB), Mumbai, Chennai, Kolkata, Delhi
Locomotives	Chittaranjan (WB), Varanasi (UP), Jamshedpur (Jharkhand)
Match Boxes	Ahmedabad, Bareilly (UP), Mumbai, Chennai, Kolkata, Pune, Srinagar (J&K)
Paper	DalmiaNagar, Jagadhari (Haryana), Lucknow, Saharanpur (UP), Bhadravati and Dandali (Karnataka), Rajahmundry and Sirpur (AP), Brajrajnagar (Orissa), Amalai (MP)
Penicillin	Pimpri (Maharashtra)
Rail Coaches	Perambudur (TN), Pune, Kapurthala (Punjab)
Resin	Bareilly (UP), Nahan (HP)
Rubber Goods	Ambapur (TN), Mumbai, Bareilly (UP), Thiruvananthapuram (Kerala)
Salt	Kuchchh (Gujarat), Sambhar Lake (Rajasthan)
Sewing Machines	Kolkata, Delhi, Ludhiana (Punjab)
Ship Building	Visakhapatnam (AP), Kochi, Mumbai, Kolkata
Silk	Bangalore, Bhagalpur (Bihar), Srinagar (J&K)
Sports Material	Agra and Meerut (UP), Batala and Jalandhar (Punjab), Delhi
Sugar	Gorakhpur, Sitapur, Rampur, Bijor, Saharanpur, Meerut (UP), Zira and Jagraon (Punjab)
Telephone	Bangalore, Naini and Rai Bareilly (UP)
Watches	Pinjore (Haryana), Bangalore

Cities and Towns associated with Industries

Town	Industries
Agra	Shoes and Leather Goods
Ahmedabad	Cotton Goods
Aligarh	Locks
Alwaye	Rare earths Factory
Ankleshwar	Oil
Bangalore	Cotton Goods, Aircraft, Telephone, Motors, Machine Tools
Bareilly	Resin Industry and Wood Work
Bhilai	Steel Plant
Bokaro	Steel Plant
Chittaranjan	Locomotive
Delhi	Textiles, DDT
Dhariwal	Wool and Goods
Digboi	Oil
Durgapur	Steel Plant
Gwalior	Pottery and Textiles
Jaipur	Embroidery, Pottery
Jamshedpur	Iron and Steel
Jharia	Coal

Q.30. When the last time Indian currency was was demonetised?
Q.31. With which bank did the New Bank of India merged with?

Indian Economy

Kolkata	Jute, Electric Bulbs and Lamps
Kanpur	Leather Goods
Khetri	Copper
Ludhiana	Hosiery, Sewing Machines, Cycles
Mumbai	Cotton Textiles, Films
Mysore	Silk
Nangal	Fertilizer
Permbudur	Rail Coach Factory
Pinjore	Machine Tool
Pimpri	Penicillin Factory
Raniganj	Coal Mining
Rourkela	Steel and Fertilizers
Sindri	Fertilizers
Singhbhum	Copper
Surat	Textiles
Trombay	Atomic Power Station
Vishakhapatnam	Ship Building

State associated with Industries

States	Industries
Andhra Pradesh	Automobile and auto components, IT, Pharmaceuticals
Arunachal Pradesh	Timber based, Tourism
Assam	Petroleum and Refineries, Tea Industry
Bihar	Agro based, Oil refineries
Chhattisgarh	Forest and Agro based, Biotechnology
Goa	Fisheries, Tourism
Gujarat	Petrochemical and Engineering, Textile
Haryana	Automobile Industry, Agriculture
Himachal Pradesh	Chemical, Textile
Jammu & Kashmir	Handicrafts, Tourism
Jharkhand	Heavy engineering, Coal Mining & Steel
Karnataka	Electronics and Telecommunication, IT
Kerala	Textiles and Garments, Tourism
Madhya Pradesh	Agriculture, Tourism
Maharashtra	Automobile, Food Processing
Manipur	Tourism, Spinning mills
Meghalaya	Tourism, Iron & Steel
Mizoram	Handloom & Handicrafts, Bamboo Products
Nagaland	Arts and Handicrafts, Metal Work
Orissa	Agriculture, Iron & Steel
Punjab	Agriculture, Engineering & Pharmaceuticals
Rajasthan	Textile, Agriculture
Sikkim	Liquor, Tourism
Tamil Nadu	Agro based & Textile, Chemical and Petrochemical

Q.32. Which was the first Indian bank?
Q.33. The one rupee note bears the signature of...

Tripura — Jute, Tourism
Uttar Pradesh — Agriculture, Sugar and Derivatives
Uttarakhand — Wool, Agro based and Food processing
West Bengal — Agriculture, Chemicals and Cotton textiles

ECONOMIC TERMINOLOGY

Amalgamation: Amalgamation means to combine or unite into one firm. In commercial context it is used when two firms or companies unite to form a single entity.

Amortisation: The running down or payment of a loan by instalments.

Annuity: A fixed amount paid once in a year or at interval of a stipulated period.

Appreciation: A rise in the value of an Asset. When the value of a currency rises relative to another, it appreciates.

Assets: Things that have earning power or some other value to their owner.

Balance of Trade: The balance of trade is the difference between the monetary value of exports and imports in an economy over a certain period of time.

Balance of Payment: Balance of Payment (BOP) is a systematic record of economic transactions conducted by a country with rest of the world at a certain period of time.

Banker's Cheque: A cheque by one Bank on another.

Bank Rate: It is the rate of interest charged by Reserve Bank of India for lending money to commercial banks.

Bear: An investor who thinks that the price of a particular security or class of securities or shares is going to fall.

Bill of Exchange: A written, dated and signed three-party instrument containing an unconditional order by a drawer that directs a drawee to pay a definite sum of money to a payee on demand or at a specified future date.

Black Money: It means unaccounted money, concealed income and undisclosed wealth. In order to evade taxes some people do not record all transactions in their books. The money which thus remains unaccounted is called black money.

Bond: A certificate of debt issued by a government or corporation in order to raise money; the bond issuer is required to pay a fixed sum annually until maturity and then a fixed sum to repay the principal.

Breakeven Point: This is a term used to describe a point at which revenues equal costs (fixed and variable).

Budget: A summary of intended expenditures along with proposals for how to meet them. A budget can provide guidelines for managing future investments and expenses.

Budget Deficit: It is the amount by which government spending exceeds government revenues during a specified period of time, usually a year.

Bull: An investor with an optimistic market outlook; an investor who expects prices to rise and so buys now for resale later.

Call money: Price paid by an investor for a call option. The rate depends on the type of stock, its performance prior to the purchase of the call option and the period of the contract.

Q.34. When did India become a member of International Monetary Fund (IMF)?

Cash Reserve Ratio (CRR): It is a bank regulation that sets the minimum reserves each bank must hold to customer deposits and notes. These reserves are designed to satisfy withdrawal demands, and would normally be in the form of fiat currency stored in a bank vault (vault cash), or with a central bank.

Cartel: An organisation of producers seeking to limit or eliminate competition among its members, most often by agreeing to restrict output to keep prices higher than would occur under competitive conditions.

Closed Economy: A closed economy is one in which there are no foreign trade transactions or any other form of economic contacts with the rest of the world.

Collateral Security: Additional security that a borrower supplies to obtain a loan.

Credit Crunch: When banks suddenly stop lending, or bond market liquidity evaporates, usually because creditors have become extremely risk-averse.

Customs Duty: Duty levied on the imports of certain goods. It includes excise equivalents; unlike tariffs, customs duties are used mainly as a means to raise revenue for the government rather than protecting domestic producers from foreign competition.

Deflation: Deflation is a reduction in the level of national income and output, usually accompanied by a fall in the general price level.

Depreciation: Depreciation is an economic term that refers to the decline in the value of assets through the passage of time.

Devaluation: Official reduction in the foreign value of domestic currency. It is made to encourage the exports and reduce the imports.

Direct Tax: A tax that you pay directly, as opposed to indirect taxes, such as tariffs and business taxes. The income tax is a direct tax, as are property taxes.

Duopoly: A market structure in which two producers of a commodity compete with each other.

Exchange Rate: The price of one currency stated in terms of another currency, when exchanged.

Exports: The value of all goods and nonfactor services sold to the rest of the world; they include merchandise, freight, insurance, travel, and other non-factor services.

Fiscal Deficit: It is the gap between the government's total spending and the sum of its revenue receipts and non-debt capital receipts. The fiscal deficit represents the total amount of borrowed funds required by the government to completely meet its expenditure.

Fiscal Policy: It is the use of government expenditure and taxation to try to influence the level of economic activity.

Foreign Direct Investment (FDI): Overseas investments by private multinational corporations.

Free Trade: Free trade in which goods can be imported and exported without any barriers in the forms of tariffs, quotas, or other restrictions.

Gross Domestic Product (GDP): It is the total of goods and services produced by a nation over a given period (usually 1 year). Gross Domestic Product measures the total output from all the resources located in a country, wherever the owners of the resources live.

Gross National Product (GNP): It is the value of all final goods and services produced within a nation in a given year, plus income earned by its citizens abroad, minus income earned by foreigners from domestic production.

Indirect Tax: A tax you do not pay directly, but which is passed on to you by an increase in your expenses.

Q.35. What is total expenditure minus revenue receipts known as?

Q.36. Who prints and supplies currency notes in India?

Inflation: It is the percentage increase in the prices of goods and services.

Macroeconomics: The branch of economics that considers the relationships among broad economic aggregates such as national income, total volumes of saving, investment, consumption expenditure, employment, and money supply.

Microeconomics: The branch of economics concerned with individual decision units – firms and households and the way in which their decisions interact to determine relative prices of goods and factors of production and how much of these will be bought and sold.

Monetary Policy: The regulation of the money supply and interest rates by a central bank in order to control inflation and stabilise currency.

Open Economy: It is an economy that encourages foreign trade and has extensive financial and non-financial contacts with the rest of the world in areas such as education, culture and technology.

Opportunity Cost: The opportunity cost is the implied cost of not doing something that could have led to higher returns.

Recession: This is the situation, when there is excess production over demand.

Repo Rate: This is one of the credit management tools used by the Reserve Bank to regulate liquidity in South Africa (customer spending). The bank borrows money from the Reserve Bank to cover its shortfall. The Reserve Bank only makes a certain amount of money available and this determines the repo rate.

Statutory Liquidity Rate (SLR): It is the ratio of cash in hand, exclusive of cash balances maintained by banks to meet cash reserve.

Tax Base: The total property and resources subject to taxation.

Value Added Tax (VAT): A form of indirect sales tax paid on products and services at each stage of production or distribution, based on the value added at that stage and included in the cost to the ultimate customer.

ANSWERS

1. 29 per cent (approx.)
2. The Prime Minister
3. 1952
4. National Development Council
5. 25
6. Fifth
7. Janata Dal Government
8. Central Statistical Organization (CSO)
9. Annapurna
10. Twice
11. Hilton Young Commission
12. 27
13. 12 April 1992
14. Industrial Finance Corporation of India
15. 1956
16. Malhotra Committee
17. 23
18. Haryana
19. It is the gap between the value of exports and imports.
20. Gross Domestic Product per head in US dollar.
21. 12 per cent
22. The rate which banks lend to RBI
23. Monetary Policy
24. First Scheme of UTI, Unit Scheme 1964.
25. LIC
26. Thermal Power
27. Decreasing money supply.
28. The ratio of cash in hand, exclusive of cash balances maintained by banks to meet cash reserve.
29. Increase of interest rate on saving deposit.
30. 1978
31. Punjab National Bank
32. Presidency Bank, Kolkata
33. Secretary, Ministry of Finance
34. 1947
35. Fiscal deficit
36. Security Press, Nasik

6
INDIAN POLITY

CONSTITUTION OF INDIA

Drafting of Constitution

(i) The Constitution of India was framed by the Constituent Assembly of India, under Cabinet Mission Plan of 16 May 1946.
(ii) The first meeting of Constituent Assembly was summoned on 9 December 1946, under the presidentship of Sachidananda Sinha for undivided India.
(iii) Initially the Constituent Assembly was consisted of 389 members, of which 292 were elected by the elected members of the Provincial Legislative Assemblies, 93 were nominated by princely states and remaining four were from commissionaries.
(iv) With the creation of separate Constituent Assembly for Pakistan on 16 July 1947, the membership of Constituent Assembly of India was reduced to 299, of which 229 represented Provincial Legislative Assemblies and 70 were from princely states.
(v) With the demise of Sachidananda Sinha, Dr Rajendra Prasad was elected, as its President on 11 December 1946.
(vi) A Drafting Committee under the chairmanship of Dr B R Ambedkar was appointed by Constituent Assembly.

Members of the Drafting Committee

1. Dr B R Ambedkar, Chairman
2. N Gopalaswami Ayyangar
3. Alladi Krishnaswami Ayyar
4. K M Munshi
5. Syyed Mohd Saadulla
6. N Madhav Rao
7. D P Khaitan (T Krishnamachari, after Khaitan's death in 1948)
    (i) A draft Constitution was published in February 1948. 284 out of 299 members put their signature to the Constitution and adopted it on 26 November 1949.
    (ii) It came into effect on 26 January 1950.

(iii) It took 2 years 11 months 18 days to complete the Constitution.
(iv) Originally it had 395 articles and 8 schedules.

Parts of Indian Constitution

The Constitution of India consists of:
1. The Preamble
2. Parts (I to XXII – over 449 articles)
3. Schedules 1 to 12
4. An Appendix

The Preamble

> "**WE THE PEOPLE OF INDIA,** having solemnly resolved to constitute India into a **SOVEREIGN SOCIALIST SECULAR, DEMOCRATIC REPUBLIC** and to secure to all its citizens:
> **JUSTICE,** social, economic and political;
> **LIBERTY** of thought, expression, belief, faith and worship;
> **EQUALITY** of status and of opportunity;
> and to promote among them all;
> **FRATERNITY** assuring the dignity of the individual and the unity and integrity of the Nation;
> **IN OUR CONSTITUENT ASSEMBLY** this twenty-sixth day of November, 1949, do **HEREBY ADOPT, ENACT AND GIVE TO OURSELVES THIS CONSTITUTION.**

- It is the preface to the Constitution. The idea of Preamble was borrowed from the Constitution of USA.
- The words Socialist, Secular, Unity and Integrity were added Forty-second Amendment in 1976.
- The Supreme Court in 1973 gave the verdict on Keshavanand Bharati versus State of Kerala case that the Preamble is a part of the Constitution. In this case Supreme Court held that the basic features of the Preamble cannot be amended under Article 368.

Significance of Preamble

(i) It reflects the source from which the Constitution derives its authority, viz., the people of India.
(ii) It indicates the objectives of the Constitution.
(iii) It aids the legal interpretation of the Constitution.

Parts and the Articles

Part I (Article 1 to 4) deals with territory of India, formation of new states, alternation of names of existing states.

Part II (Article 5 to 11) deals with the Rights of Citizenship.

Part III (Article 12 to 35) states the Fundamental Rights.

Part IV (Article 36 to 51) deals with Directive Principle of State Policy.

Q. 1. From which country the idea of Preamble was borrowed?

Part IV-A (Article 51A) was added by the Forty-second Amendment in 1976 and this deals with duties of the Citizens.

Part V (Article 51 to 151) deals with the government at the Union Level.

Part VI (Article 152 to 237) deals with the government at state level.

Part VII (Article 238) was replaced by Seventh Amendment in 1956.

Part VIII (Article 239 to 241) deals with Union Territory.

Part IX (Article 242 to 243O) was added by Seventy-third Amendment in 1992 and this deals with Panchaytiraj.

Part IX-A (Article 243P to 243ZG) was added by Seventy-fourth amendment in 1992 and it deals with municipality.

Part X (Article 244 to 244A) deals with scheduled and tribal areas.

Part XI (Article 245 to 263) deals with relation between the Union and states.

Part XII (Article 264 to 300A) deals with distribution of revenue between Union and states, appointment of Finance Commission (Article 280), contracts, liabilities, etc.

Part XIII (Article 301 to 307) deals with trade, commerce and travel within the territory of India.

Part XIV (Article 308 to 323) deals with UPSC and State Public Service Commissions.

Part XIV-A (Article 323A to 323B) was added by Forty-second amendment in 1976 and it deals with administrative tribunals set up by the Parliament.

Part XV (Article 324 to 329) deals with elections and the Election Commission.

Part XVI (Article 330 to 342) deals with special provisions for SCs and STs, OBC and anglo-Indian.

Part XVII (Article 343 to 351) deals with official languages.

Part XVIII (Article 352 to 360) states the Emergency Provisions.

Part XIX (Article 361 to 367) deals with exemption of criminal proceedings against President and Governors.

Part XX (Article 368) deals with amendment of Constitution.

Part XXI (Article 369 to 392) deals with temporary, transitional and special provision of Parliament: (Article 370 contains temporary provisions for the state of Jammu and Kashmir).

Part XXII (Article 393 to 395) deals with short titles, commencement and repeal of the Constitution.

The Schedules

Schedules are lists in the Constitution that categorizes and tabulates bureaucratic activity and policy of the Government. The Schedules are added to the Constitution by amendment. The Original Constitution had only eight schedules. By the first amendment in 1951, the ninth Schedule was added and by Forty-fourth amendment, the latest Twelfth schedule was added to the Constitution.

First Schedule

It deals with territories of 28 States and seven Union Territories.

Second Schedule

It deals with salaries, allowances of President, Governors, Chief Justice of India, Judges of the Supreme Courts, High Courts and Comptroller and Auditor General of India.

Q.2. When the constitution of India was adopted by the Constituent Assembly?

Third Schedule

It deals with Forms of Oaths and affirmations for elected officials and judges.

Fourth Schedule

It deals with allocation of the number of seats in the Rajya Sabha per State or Union Territory.

Fifth Schedule

It deals with provisions for the administration and control of Scheduled Areas and Scheduled Tribes.

Sixth Schedule

It deals with provisions for the administration of tribal areas in Assam, Meghalaya, Tripura, Arunachal Pradesh and Mizoram.

Seventh Schedule

It deals with allocation of powers and functions between Union and States, which contains three lists: (i) Union List: 100 subjects, (ii) State List: 66 subjects and (iii) Concurrent List: 47 subjects.

Eighth Schedule

There are 22 official languages recognised by the Constitution of India. Originally there were only 14 languages. 'Sindhi' was added by Twenty-first Amendment in 1967 and three languages: Konkoni, Manipuri and Nepali were added by Seventy-first Amendment in 1992. In 2003, by Ninety-second Amendment another four languages were added to the list: Bodo, Dogri, Maithili and Santhali.

The languages are as follows:

1. Assamese
2. Bengali
3. Bodo
4. Dogri
5. Gujarati
6. Hindi
7. Kannada
8. Kashmiri
9. Malayalam
10. Maithili
11. Marathi
12. Oriya
13. Punjabi
14. Sanskrit
15. Sindhi
16. Tamil
17. Telugu
18. Santhali
19. Urdu
20. Konkani
21. Manipuri
22. Nepali

Ninth Schedule

It was added to the Constitution by first Amendment in 1951, which contains acts and orders related to land reforms and abolition of Zamindari system. It contains 257 Acts.

Tenth Schedule

It was added by Fifty-second Amendment in 1985, which contains provision of disqualification on the grounds of defection.

Q.3. Prohibition of discrimination on the grounds of religions, etc., (Article 15) is a fundamental right classifiable under:

Eleventh Schedule

It was added by Seventy-third Amendment on 20 April 1992, which contains provisions of Panchayati Raj. It lists 29 subjects.

Twelfth Schedule

On 20 April 1992, by Seventy-fourth Amendment of the Constitution this schedule was added, which contains provisions of municipality and lists 18 subjects.

Amendments of the Constitution

Methods of Amendment

The concept was borrowed from South Africa. There are three methods through which the Constitution is amended.

(i) *Method of Simple Majority*: In this method both houses of the Parliament should pass the proposal by a majority of the total membership. It applies to subjects pertaining to citizenship, abolishing or creating second chambers in the states, provisions relating to SCs and STs, etc.

(ii) *Special Majority of the Parliament and Ratification*: The proposal should be passed by two-third majority of the members of the both houses of the Parliament and also it must be ratified by not less than half of the state legislatures. It applies to the subjects pertaining to the election of the President and Vice-President, executive powers of the Union and states, division of legislative powers between the Union and states, matters related to Supreme Court and High Court, representation of states and the Parliament, Amendment of Article 368, etc.

(iii) *Special Majority of the Parliament*: The proposal should be passed by two-third majority of the total number of members present, which should not be less than half of the total membership of the house. After this, it is sent to the President for his assent.

Major Amendments of the Constitution

1. *First Amendment, 1950*: Ninth Schedule was added by this amendment.
2. *Seventh Amendment, 1956*: Reorganisation of states on linguistic basis was brought about by this amendment.
3. *Eighth Amendment, 1960*: Special provisions for reservation of seats for SCs, STs and Anglo-Indian in Lok Sabha and Legislative assemblies for a period of ten years from 1960 to 1970 was made through this amendment.
4. *Ninth Amendment, 1960*: Through this amendment certain territories were handed over to Pakistan in accordance with the 1958 Indo-Pak agreement.
5. *Tenth Amendment, 1961*: With this amendment, Dadra and Nagar Haveli was recognised as a UT.
6. *Twelfth Amendment, 1962*: With this amendment, Goa, Daman and Diu were recognised as UTs.
7. *Thirteenth Amendment, 1962*: This amendment resulted in the creation of Nagaland as a state in Union of India.
8. *Fourteenth Amendment, 1963*: With this amendment, Pondicherry, Koraikal,

Q.4. Under which section or under what name economic justice has been incorporated in the Constitution of India?

Mahe and Yanam, the former French territories were incorporated as Union Territory of Pondicherry in the Union of India.
9. *Eighteenth Amendment, 1966*: This amendment led to the recognition of Punjab into Punjab and Haryana as states, and Chandigarh as UT in the Union of India.
10. *Twenty-first Amendment, 1967*: With this Sindhi was added as fifteenth official language in the Eighth Schedule.
11. *Twenty-second Amendment, 1969*: A sub-state of Meghalaya within Assam was created with this amendment.
12. *Twenty-third Amendment, 1969*: This amendment extended the provisions for reservation of seats for SCs, STs and anglo-Indians in Lok Sabha and Legislative Assemblies for a further period of 10 years from 1970 to 1980.
13. *Twenty-sixth Amendment, 1971*: With this amendment, the titles and special privileges of former rulers of princely states were abolished.
14. *Twenty-seventh Amendment, 1971*: Manipur and Tripura were incorporated as states and Mizoram and Arunachal Pradesh as Union Territories in the Union of India with this amendment.
15. *Thirty-first Amendment, 1973*: This amendment increased the elective strength of Lok Sabha from 525 to 545. Upper limit of representative of state became 525 from 500.
16. *Thirty-sixth Amendment, 1975*: It created Sikkim as state in the Union of India.
17. *Thirty-eighth Amendment, 1975*: It provided that the President can make a declaration of Emergency and the promulgation of ordinances by the President, Governors and the Administrative Heads of the Union Territories would be final and could not be challenged under any court.
18. *Thirty-ninth Amendment, 1975*: With this amendment, the election to the Parliament of a person holding the office of Prime Minister or Speaker and election of the President and Vice-President was placed beyond challenge in courts.
19. *Fourty-second Amendment, 1976*: It provided supremacy of Parliament and gave primacy to Directive Principles over Fundamental Rights. It also added 10 fundamental duties. New words Socialist, Secular, Unity and Integrity were added to the Preamble of the Constitution.
20. *Fourty-fourth Amendment, 1978*: This amendment restored the duration of Lok Sabha and Legislative assemblies to five years. Right to Property was deleted from Part III. It limited the power of Government to declare the internal emergency.
21. *Fourty-fifth Amendment, 1980*: This amendment extended the provisions for reservation of seats for SCs, STs and Anglo-Indians in Lok Sabha and Legislative assemblies for a further period of 10 years till 1990.
22. *Fifty-second Amendment, 1985*: Provision of disqualification on the grounds of defection was added to the Tenth schedule of the Constitution with this amendment.
23. *Fifty-third Amendment, 1986*: With this amendment, Mizoram as a state in the Union of India was created.
24. *Fifty-fourth Amendment, 1986*: This enhanced the salaries of judges Supreme Court and High Courts.
25. *Fifty-fifth Amendment, 1986*: This amendment conferred statehood to Arunachal Pradesh.

Q.5. Who was the first speaker of Lok Sabha?
Q.6. Which part of the Indian Constitution deals with Panchayati Raj?

26. *Fifty-sixth Amendment, 1987*: After this amendment, the Hindi version of the Constitution of India was accepted for all purposes and it also conferred statehood to Goa.
27. *Fifty-eighth Amendment, 1987*: This amendment made provision for reservation of seats in legislatures for the four North-eastern states of Meghalaya, Mizoram, Arunachal Pradesh and Nagaland.
28. *Sixty first Amendment, 1989*: With this amendment, voting age was reduced from 21 to 18 for Lok Sabha and Assemblies.
29. *Sixty-second Amendment, 1989*: It extended the provisions for reservation of seats for SCs, STs and Anglo-Indians in Lok Sabha and Legislative assemblies for a further period of 10 years till 2000.
30. *Sixty-third Amendment, 1990*: This repealed the fifty-ninth amendment, which empowered the government to impose emergency in Punjab.
31. *Seventy-first Amendment, 1992*: Three languages: Konkoni, Manipuri and Nepali were added in the Eighth Schedule through this amendment.
32. *Seventy-second Amendment, 1992 (Panchayati Raj Bill)*: This made provision for the Gram Sabha in villages, Constitution of Panchayats at village and other levels, district elections for all the seats in Panchayats and reservation of seats for SCs and STs, women and backward classes.
33. *Seventy-third Amendment, 1992 (Nagarpalika Bill)*: It made provision for the Constitution of municipalities, reservation of seats in every municipality for SCs and STs, women and backward classes.
34. *Seventy-fourth Amendment, 1993*: It included a new part IX-A pertaining to the municipalities, which proposed the Constitution of three types of municipalities: Nagar Panchayats for areas in transition from a rural area to urban area; Municipal Councils for smaller urban areas; Municipal Corporations for larger urban areas.
35. *Seventy-ninth Amendment, 2000*: It extended the provisions for reservation of seats for SCs, STs and Anglo-Indians in Lok Sabha and Legislative assemblies for a further period of 10 years till 2010.
36. *Eightieth Amendment, 2000*: With this amendment, certain changes were made in tax distribution system provided under Articles 269, 270, 272 of the Constitution.
37. *Eighty-first Amendment, 2000*: The unfilled vacancies of a year, which are reserved for being filled up in that year in accordance with any provision for reservation made under Article 16 (Clause 4/4A) of the Constitution, shall be considered as a separate class of vacancies to be filled up in any succeeding year or years and such class of vacancies shall not be considered together with the vacancies of the year in which they are being filled up for determining the ceiling of 50 per cent reservation on total number of vacancies of that year.
38. *Eighty-fourth Amendment, 2001*: It made the provision to freeze the number of seats allotted to each State in Lok Sabha and Legislative Assemblies of the States, including the STs and SCs, on the basis of the population ascertained at the census of 1991 up to the year 2026.
39. *Eighty-Fifth Amendment, 2001*: It provided for the Promotion of SC/ST; in matters of promotion, with consequential seniority. (It came into force from seventeenth day of June 1995).

Q.7. Which schedule of the Indian Constitution deals with Allocation of Powers and functions between the Union and States?

40. *Eighty-sixth Amendment, 2002*: It deals with the insertion of a new Article 21A, after Article 21 of the Constitution. Article 21A provides free and compulsory education to all children from the age of six to fourteen years in such manner as the State may, by law, determine.
41. *Eighty-eighth Amendment, 2003*: This deals with insertion of a new Article 268A, after Article 268 of the Constitution, namely service taxes shall be levied by the Government of India and such tax shall be collected and appropriated by the Government of India and the States in accordance with such principles of collection and appropriation as may be formulated by Parliament by law.
    It also made the Amendment of Article 270 of the Constitution and Amendment of Seventh Schedule in the Union list to insert an entry 92C (Taxes on services) after the entry 92B.
42. *Eighty-ninth Amendment, 2003*: It made provisions for the Amendment of Article 338 of the Constitution, namely: National Commission for Scheduled Castes.
43. *Ninetieth Amendment, 2003*: Article 332 of the Constitution was amended, which provided that for elections to the Legislative Assembly of the State of Assam, the representation of the ST and non-ST in the constituencies included in the Bodoland Territorial Areas District, so notified, and existing prior to the Constitution of the Bodoland Territorial Areas District, shall be maintained.
44. *Ninety-first Amendment, 2003*: It made the provision that the total number of ministers, including the Prime Minister, in the council of ministers shall not exceed 15 per cent of the total number of members of the House of the People.
45. *Ninety-second Amendment, 2003*: Four languages: Bodo, Dogri, Maithili and Santhali were added to the Eighth Schedule of the Constitution with this Amendment.
46. *Ninety-fourth Amendment, 2006*: This provides that clause (1) of Article 164, in the proviso, for the word Bihar, the words Chhattisgarh and Jharkhand shall be substituted.

Citizenship in the Constitution

Part II (Article 5 to 11); deals with the Rights of Citizenship. The Constitution provides single citizenship. Citizenship can be acquired (as per Act of 1955) by birth, descent, registration, naturalisation or when India acquires new territories.

Dual Citizenship

(i) *Eligibility*: According to Citizenship Act 2003, those who were eligible to become citizens of India as on 26 January 1950 could apply for Dual Indian Citizenship. Government can also extend Dual Citizenship to those who were holding Persons of Indian Origin Card (PIOC) and who had migrated from India after the formation of Indian Republic.

(ii) *Applicable for*: It is applicable for persons of Indian Origin (PIO), who are citizens of Australia, Canada, Finland, France, Greece, Ireland, Israel, Italy, the Netherlands, New Zealand, Portugal, Cyprus, Sweden, Switzerland, the UK and USA.

Q.8. Which Article of the Indian Constitution provides for election to State Assembly?

Q.9. Which Article deals with Amendment of Constitution?

(iii) *Not Applicable for*: Persons, who have been citizen of Pakistan, Bangladesh or any other country that the government of India may notify in future.

1. Fundamental Rights (Articles 12 to 35): This concept was borrowed from the Constitution of the USA. Originally there were seven fundamental rights in the Constitution. After 44th Amendment of the Constitution in 1978, which abolished the Right to property, now there are only six fundamental rights.

(i) Right to Equality (Articles 14 to 18):
- Article 14: Equality before law and equal protection of law.
- Article 15: Prohibition of discrimination on grounds of religion, race, caste, sex or place of birth.
- Article 16: Equality of opportunity in case of public employment.
- Article 17: End of untouchability.
- Article 18: Abolition of titles.

(ii) Right to Freedom (Article 19): It guarantees:
- Freedom of speech and expression.
- Freedom of assembly.
- Freedom to form associations.
- Freedom of movements.
- Freedom of residents and settlement.
- Freedom of profession, occupation, trade or business.

(iii) Right to freedom of Religion (Articles 25 to 28):
- Article 25: Freedom of conscience and free profession, practice and propagation of religion.
- Article 26: Freedom to manage religious affairs.
- Article 27: Prohibits taxes on religious grounds.
- Article 28: Freedom to attend religious ceremonies in certain educational institutions.

(iv) Cultural and Educational Rights (Articles 29 to 30):
- Article 29: Protection of interests of the minorities.
- Article 30: Rights of minorities to establish and administer educational institutions.
- Article 31: *(*Right to Property*)* Omitted by Forty-fourth Amendment of the constitution.

(v) Right against Exploitation (Articles 23 to 24):
- Article 23: Human trafficking is prohibited.
- Article 24: Child, below 14 years cannot be employed.

(vi) Right to Constitutional Remedies (Article 32 to 35):
- Article 32: Right to move to Supreme Court in case of Constitutional violation.

2. Directive Principles of State Policy:
Under Part IV (Articles 36 to 51): This concept was borrowed from the Constitution of Ireland. The main Directive Principles of State Policy are:
- Provision of adequate means of livelihood for all.

Q.10. In which amendment of the Indian Constitution four languages Bodo, Dogri, Maithili and Santhali were added to the Eighth schedule of the Constitution?

- Free legal aid to the weaker sections of the society.
- Equal distribution of wealth among all.
- Equal pay for equal work irrespective of sex.
- Right to work, to education, to public assistance in case of unemployment, old age, sickness or disability.
- Protection of child and youth.
- Free and compulsory education for children up to 14 years.
- Prevention of cow slaughter.
- Prohibition of liquor.
- Organise agriculture and animal husbandry.
- Establishment of village Panchayats.
- Protection of Historical and Nationals monuments.
- State to protect natural environment, forests and wild life.
- Promotion of International cooperation and security of world.

3. Fundamental Duties: This concept was borrowed from the Constitution of USSR. It was added by the Forty-second Amendment of the Constitution in 1976. It contains 10 Fundamental duties for the Citizens under Article 51A.

Functionaries of Government

1. The President
2. The Vice-President
3. The Prime minister
4. Council of Ministers
5. The Parliament
6. Supreme Court
7. State Executive
8. The Governor
9. State Council of Ministers
10. High Court

The President

The President of India is the Constitutional head of Parliamentary system of government. This concept was borrowed from the Constitution of USA.

A. Qualification
B. Election
C. Terms and Emoluments
D. Powers
E. Impeachment
F. In case of vacancy

A. Qualification:

- He must be a citizen of India.
- He must not be less than 35 years of age.
- He must be eligible to be a member of Lok Sabha but shall not be a sitting member.
- He must not hold any government post in India or any other governments except Vice-President and Governor.

B. Election:

The President is elected indirectly by the Electoral College, which comprises:

(i) Elected members of the both Houses of the Parliament.
(ii) Elected members of the State legislature.

Calculation of the value of votes of each MLA and MP are as follows:

Q.11. In which amendment the words Socialist, Secular, Unity and Integrity were added to the Preamble?

Indian Polity 149

Value of vote of an MLA = State Population/1000 × Total number of elected MLAs.
Value of vote of an MP = Total value of votes of MLAs of all states/Total number of elected MPs (LS + RS)

- Supreme Court has the authority to address all disputes regarding presidential election.
- Takes oath in presence of Chief Justice of India (CJI) or the senior-most Judge in Supreme Court.

C. Terms and Emoluments:
- The President is elected for a period of five years.
- There is no upper limit on the number of times a person can become the President as per Article 57.
- The President can submit his/her resignation to the Vice-President.
- An emolument of Rs 1,50,000 per month is received by the President. He/she will also be entitled to a pension of 50 per cent of their salary.

D. Powers:
(a) Executive and Administrative Powers: The President appoints the senior officials of the State, including Prime Minister, CAG, Attorney General, CEC, members of UPSC, members of Finance Commission, Ambassadors. All Union Territories come directly under the President of India.

(b) Legislative Powers:
- Can summon sessions of the two houses of the Parliament.
- Can dissolve Lok Sabha.
- Addresses the first session after general elections and at the commencement of the first session of the year.
- Nominates 12 members to Rajya Sabha and two Anglo-Indian members to Lok Sabha.
- Passes only non-money bills to become laws or send them back (only once) to the Parliament for reconsideration.
- Can enact laws through Ordinance (must be passed in the Parliament within six weeks)

(c) Financial Powers:
- Appoints Finance Commission that distributes revenues between the Union and State governments.
- Sanctions the introduction of monetary bills.
- Budget to be presented before him.

(d) Judicial Powers:
- Appoints judges in Supreme Court and High Courts.
- Can pardon, reprieve, remit or suspend the sentences from the accused.

(e) Emergency Powers:
- Under Article 352, can proclaim national emergency due to external aggression or internal rebellion.

Q.12. Who presided over the inaugural session of the Constituent Assembly?
Q.13. Ninth Schedule of the Indian Constitution was included under which constitutional amendment?

- Under Article 356, can declare emergency due to failure of constitutional machinery in any state.
- Under Article 360, can declare emergency due to threat to financial stability or credit of the country.

The President cannot be questioned under any Court of Law or no criminal proceedings can be initiated against him.

E. Impeachment (Article 61):

- Can be impeached on the ground of violation of the Constitution.
- The impeachment process can be initiated in either house of the Parliament.
- If the house passes the resolution by not less than two-thirds majority, the matter will be referred to the other House.
- The charges are framed by one House and the other House investigates. At this time the President has the right to defend either in person or through lawyer.
- If after investigation the other House passes the resolution by not less than two-thirds majority, the President stands impeached.

F. In Case of Vacancy: In case of death, resignation or removal, the Vice-President acts as the President. In absence of VP, the CJI or the senior-most Judge of the Supreme Court acts as the President.

Presidents of India

Name	Tenure From	Tenure To
Dr Rajendra Prasad	26 Jan 1950	13 May 1962
Dr S Radhakrishnan	13 May 1962	13 May 1967
Dr Zakir Hussain	13 May 1967	3 May 1969
V V Giri (Vice President)*	3 May 1969	20 July 1969
Justice M Hidayatullah**	20 July 1969	24 Aug 1969
V V Giri	24 Aug 1969	24 Aug 1974
F Ali Ahmed	24 Aug 1974	11 Feb 1977
B D Jutti	11 Feb 1977	25 July 1977
N Sanjiva Reddy	25 July 1977	25 July 1982
Gaini Gail Singh	25 July 1982	25 July 1987
R Venkatraman	25 July 1987	25 July 1992
Dr S D Sharma	25 July 1992	25 July 1997
K R Narayanan	25 July 1997	25 July 2002
Dr A P J Abdul Kalam	25 July 2002	25 July 2007
Ms Pratibha Devisingh Patil	25 July 2007	till date

* Acting; ** M Hidayatullah, is the First Chief Justice to be appointed the President.

The Vice-President

A. Qualifications

- He must be a citizen of India.
- He must not be less than 35 years of age.

Q.14. In which part of the Indian Constitution is the Directive Principles of State Policy included?

Indian Polity

- He must be eligible to be a member of Rajya Sabha but shall not be a sitting member.
- He must not hold any government post in India or any other governments.

B. Election: The Vice-President is elected directly by the Electoral College, which consists of members of the both the Houses of the Parliament. However State legislatures are not part of it.

C. Terms and Emoluments

- He holds the office for five years and can be re-elected.
- He receives emoluments of Rs 1,25,000 per month and other benefits as the capacity of Chairman of Rajya Sabha. And will also be entitled to a pension of 50 per cent of their salary.

D. Functions

- The Vice-President acts as ex-officio chairman of Rajya Sabha.
- He acts as the President in case of death, resignation or removal of the President.

Vice-Presidents of India

Name	Tenure	
	From	To
Dr S Radhakrishnan	1952	1962
Dr Zakir Hussain	1962	1967
V V Giri	1967	1969
Bal Swaroop Pathak	1969	1974
Dr M Jatti	1974	1979
Justice M Hidayatullah	1979	1984
S Venkatraman	1984	1987
Dr Shankar Dayal Sharma	1987	1992
K R Narayanan	1992	1997
Krishan Kant	1997	2002
Bhairon Singh Sekhawat	2002	2007
Mohammad Hamid Ansari	2007	till date

The Prime Minister

The Prime Minister is the head of executive authority. He is the leader of the political party that wins the majority of seats in Lok Sabha. He also heads the council of ministers. He is appointed by the President of India.

His tenure is five years and continues in office till he enjoys the majority in Lok Sabha. If his party loses the majority in Lok Sabha, he along with cabinet has to resign.

Emoluments: He also draws same salary as other members of Parliament (MPs). In addition he gets some other allowances, free residence, free travel and medical amenities.

Council of Ministers

Council of ministers is appointed by the President, on the advice of the Prime Minster. Any

Q.15. Which article deals with the end of untouchability?

Q.16. According to which article of the Indian Constitution the state of Jammu and Kashmir has been accorded a special status?

General Knowledge Manual

person who wants to become a minister needs to be member of the legislature or he has to secure a seat in either House of the Parliament within six months.

Three types of ministers are there:

- *Ministers of Cabinet*: They are the real policy makers. Cabinet meeting is not attended by any other minister.
- *Minister of State*: They may hold independent charges or work with cabinet minister.
- *Deputy Ministers*: They do not hold separate charges. They play collective responsibility in Lok Sabha (Article 75).

Prime Ministers of India

Name	Tenure From	Tenure To
Jawahar Lal Nehru	15 Aug 1947	27 May 1964
Gulzari Lal Nanda	27 May 1964	9 Jun 1964
Lal Bahadur Shastri	9 June 1964	11 Jan 1966
Gulzari Lal Nanda	11 Jan 1966	24 Jan 1966
Indira Gandhi	24 Jan 1966	24 Mar 1977
Moraji Desai	24 Mar 1977	28 July 1979
Charan Singh	28 July 1979	14 Jan 1980
Indira Gandhi	14 Jan 1980	31 Oct 1984
Rajiv Gandhi	31 Oct 1984	2 Dec 1989
V P Singh	2 Dec 1989	10 Nov 1990
Chandra Sekhar	10 Nov 1990	21 Jun 1991
P V Narsimha Rao	21 Jun 1991	16 May 1996
Atal Bihari Vajpayee	16 May 1996	1 Jun 1996
H D Deva Gowda	1 June 1996	21 Apr 1997
I K Gujral	21 Apr 1997	19 Mar 1998
Atal Bihari Vajpayee	19 Mar 1998	13 Oct 1999
Atal Bihari Vajpayee	13 Oct 1999	22 May 2004
Dr Manmohan Singh	22 May 2004	22 May 2009
Dr Manmohan Singh	22 May 2009	till date

The Parliament

The Parliamentary type of Government was borrowed from the Constitution of UK. The Parliament consists of:

1. The President of India
2. The Council of states (also known as Rajya Sabha)
3. The House of People (also known as Lok Sabha)

Rajya Sabha

It is also known as the Upper House of the Parliament. The Vice-President is the ex-officio Chairman and the Deputy Chairman is elected among the members of Rajya Sabha.

Q.17. How many times can the President of India return a Non-Money Bill, passed by Parliament?

Q.18. Who decides if a particular bill is a Money Bill or not?

Indian Polity 153

Eligibility of the Members
- He must be a citizen of India.
- He must not be less than 30 years of age.
- He must be an elector from the state, from which he is representing.

Strength: It consists of 250 members, out of which 238 are representative of states and Union Territories, and 12 are nominated by the President amongst persons having significant knowledge or experience in the field of literature, science, art or social science.

Tenure: Unlike Lok Sabha it is not dissolved. The tenure is six years. One-third of the total members retire after every two years.

Functions
- Has the power in Constitutional Amendment.
- Can originate any bill except monetary bill.
- Can investigate in Presidential Impeachment.

Representatives from States and Union Territories

State/UTs	Lok Sabha	Rajya Sabha
Andhra Pradesh	42	18
Arunachal Pradesh	2	1
Assam	14	7
Bihar	40	16
Chhattisgarh	11	5
Goa	2	1
Gujarat	26	11
Haryana	10	5
Himachal Pradesh	4	3
Jammu & Kashmir	6	4
Jharkhand	14	6
Karnataka	28	12
Kerala	20	9
Madhya Pradesh	29	11
Maharashtra	48	19
Manipur	2	1
Meghalaya	2	1
Mizoram	1	1
Nagaland	1	1
Orissa	21	10
Punjab	13	7
Rajasthan	25	10
Sikkim	1	1
Tamil Nadu	39	18
Tripura	2	1
Uttar Pradesh	80	31
Uttarakhand	5	3
West Bengal	42	16
Andaman & Nicobar	1	–
Chandigarh	1	–
Dadra & Nagar Haveli	1	–

Daman & Diu	1	–
Delhi	7	3
Lakshadweep	1	–
Pondicherry	1	1

Lok Sabha

It is also known as the House of People or the Lower House in the Parliament.

It consists of 545 members, out of which 543 are directly elected from states and Union Territories (*Refer above Table*) and two are nominated by the President of India from Anglo-Indian community. To conduct the business in the House, Speaker is elected among members. And the Speaker of the House elects a Deputy Speaker to discharge the functions in his absence.

Eligibility of the Members

- He must be a citizen of India.
- He must not be less than 25 years of age.
- He must not hold any government office of profit.
- He must not be of unsound mind or insolvent.
- He must be an elector from any Parliamentary Constituency.

A member can be disqualified if the following cases are found true:

- He overrules the 'Whip'.
- Remains absent for 60 days without intimation.
- Can voluntarily give up membership.

Speakers of Lok Sabha

Name	Tenure From	Tenure To
G V Mavalankar	1952	1956
M A Ayyanger	1956	1957
M A Ayyanger	1957	1962
Hukam Singh	1962	1967
N Sanjiva Reddy	1967	1969
Dr G S Dhilon	1969	1971
Dr G S Dhilon	1971	1975
Baliram Bhagat	1976	1977
N Sanjiva Reddy	1977	1977
K D Hegde	1977	1980
Dr Balaram Jhakar	1980	1985
Dr Balaram Jhakar	1985	1989
Rabi Ray	1989	1991
Shivraj Patil	1991	1996
P A Sangma	1996	1998
G M C Balyogi	1998	1999
G MC Balyogi	1999	2002
Manohar Joshi	2002	2004
Somnath Chatterjee	2004	2009
Ms Meira Kumar	2009	till date

Indian Polity

Sessions of the Parliament

There are normally three sessions in the Parliament.
(i) Budget session: February to May.
(ii) Monsoon Session: July to August.
(iii) Winter Session: November to December.

There should not be gap of six months between two sessions.

Joint Session of Parliament

It can be ordered by the President, in one of the case:
- A bill passed by one House and rejected by another House.
- The amendment passed in one House is not acceptable to another House.
- A bill remains pending (unpassed) for more than six months.

The bill is passed with the majority of the total members of the both the Houses present.

Conduct of Business in Parliament

Ordinary Bills

All bills, except money bills, are introduced in either house of the Parliament.
- The Speaker of Lok Sabha has the prerogative to decide whether a bill is Money bill or not.
- After debate, a bill is passed by majority vote and passed to the other House. There some rectifications may be suggested and sent back to the House, where the bill originated.
- When the bill is passed in both the Houses, it is sent to the President for his assent.
- If the President gives his assent, it becomes an Act.
- If he withholds his assent, the bill is nullified.
- If he returns (only once) to the Parliament for reconsideration, then he is bound to give his assent.

Money Bills

It deals with subjects pertaining to taxes (imposition or abolition), regulation of the borrowing of money or the giving of any guarantee by the Country, declaring of any expenditure, etc.

Procedure for a Money Bill
- The Money bills are introduced only in Lok Sabha.
- Money bills passed by the Lok Sabha are sent to the Rajya Sabha. The Rajya Sabha may not amend them but can recommend amendments.
- A Money bill must be returned to the Lok Sabha within 14 days or the bill is deemed to have passed both houses in the form it was originally passed by the Lok Sabha.
- When a Money Bill is returned to the Lok Sabha with the recommended amendments of the Rajya Sabha it is open to Lok Sabha to accept or reject any or all of the recommendations.

Q.19. For a maximum of how many years is the Finance Commission appointed by the President of India?

The Supreme Court

Supreme Court stands at the apex of the judicial system of India. This concept was borrowed from USA.

On 28 January 1950, two days after India became a sovereign democratic republic, the Supreme Court came into being.

After its inauguration, the Supreme Court commenced its sittings in the Chamber of Princes in the Parliament House. The Court moved into the present building in 1958.

Features of Supreme Court

(i) Composition
(ii) Seat
(iii) Qualification
(iv) Tenure and Remuneration
(v) Retirement
(vi) Removal
(vii) Jurisdiction

Composition: The Supreme Court of India comprises the Chief Justice of India and not more than 30 other judges appointed by the President of India. However, the President must appoint judges in consultation with the Supreme Court, and appointments are generally made on the basis of seniority and not political preference.

Seat: The Supreme Court normally sits in New Delhi; however it can hold its meetings anywhere in India. The decisions are taken by CJI in consultation with the President.

Qualification

- He must be a citizen of India.
- He must have been a judge of any High Court for five years, or eminent jurist or an advocate of High Court for minimum 10 years.

Tenure and Remuneration: The judges can hold office till 65 years of age. Chief Justice of India receives a remuneration of Rs 33,000 per month, whereas other judges get Rs 30,000 per month.

Retirement: After retirement the CJI and other judges receive pension of Rs 60,000 and Rs 54,000 per annum respectively. After retirement a judge cannot plead or act in any Court, before any authority.

Removal: A judge can be removed only on the grounds of proven misconduct, incapacity to act {Article-124 (4)}.

Procedure for Removal: A Supreme Court Judge can only be removed by the order of the President, after being addressed by both House of the Parliament, supported by two-third majority of the total number of members of the both the Houses.

Jurisdictions

- It settles the disputes between the Union Government and states as well as between the states.
- The President can ask for the advice on any legal matter to the Supreme Court.
- Individual can move to Supreme Court

Q.20. Name the Article under which the President can declare emergency due to failure of constitutional machinery in any of the states.

directly for the enforcement of any of the Fundamental Rights referred in the Constitution.
- Supreme Court under Article 137 can review any judgement made by it, in order to clarify any mistakes that might be there in earlier judgements.
- It can review certain appeals in civil and criminal cases from High Courts.
- It ensures that laws passed by Legislatures, do not contravene any provisions of the Constitution.
- It decides the dispute regarding the election of the President and Vice-President.

Chief Justice of India

S. No.	Name	Tenure From	Tenure To
1	H J Kania	1950	1951
2	M P Shastri	1951	1954
3	Mehr Chand Mahajan	1954	1954
4	B K Mukherjee	1954	1956
5	Sudhi Ranjan Das	1956	1959
6	Bhuvaneshwar Prasad Sinha	1959	1964
7	P B Gajendragadkar	1964	1966
8	A K Sarkar	1966	1966
9	K Subba Rao	1966	1967
10	K N Wanchoo	1967	1968
11	M Hidayatullah	1968	1970
12	J C Shah	1970	1971
13	S M Sikri	1971	1973
14	A N Ray	1973	1977
15	Mirza Hameedullah Beg	1977	1978
16	Y V Chandrachud	1978	1985
17	P N Bhagwati	1985	1986
18	R S Pathak	1986	1989
19	E S Venkataramiah	1989	1989
20	Sabyasachi Mukharji	1989	1990
21	Ranganath Misra	1990	1991
22	K N Singh	1991	1991
23	M H Kania	1991	1992
24	L M Sharma	1992	1993
25	M N Venkatachaliah	1993	1994
26	Aziz Mushabbar Ahmadi	1994	1997
27	J S Verma	1997	1998
28	M M Punchhi	1998	1998
29	A S Anand	Oct-98	Oct-01
30	S P Bharucha	Nov-01	May-02
31	Bhupinder Nath Kirpal	May-02	Nov-02
32	G B Pattanaik	9 Nov 2002	18 Dec 2002
33	V N Khare	19 Dec 2002	1 May 2004
34	Rajendra Babu	2 May 2004	31 May 2004
35	R C Lahoti	1 June 2004	31 Oct 2005
36	Y K Sabharwal	2 Nov 2005	14 Jan 2007
37	K G Balakrishnan	15 Jan 2007	till date

STATE EXECUTIVE

The State Executive consists of:
1. The Governor
2. The Chief Minister
3. The Council of Ministers

The Governor

The Governor is the Executive Head of the State and is appointed by the President for a period of five years.

Qualification or Eligibility

- He must be a citizen of India.
- He must not be less than 35 years of age.
- He must be eligible to be a member of State Legislature.
- He should not be a member of the Parliament or any State Legislature.
- He must not hold any office of profit.

Remuneration: He receives a remuneration of Rs 1,10,000 per month and he is also entitled for free resident, medical facilities and other allowances.

Power

Executive Power: He appoints Chief Minister, other ministers, Chairman and members of the State Public Service Commission and Advocate General of the State.

Legislative Power

- He appoints one-sixth members of the Legislative Council.
- He nominates one member from Anglo-Indian community.
- He appoints the Vice-Chancellors of the State Universities.
- He addresses first session of the State Legislature after election and at the beginning of the new session.
- He can summon, prorogue and dissolve the State Legislature.

Financial Power: All Money Bill are introduced by his recommendations only.

Judicial Power: The President in consultation with the Governor appoints Chief Justice and other judges of the High Court. He appoints the judges of the lower courts.

Other Powers: He acts as the Chancellor of the state universities. He tables the reports of the State Public Service Commission.

The Chief Minister

- He is the real executive authority of State.
- The leader of the party that enjoys the majority in the State Assembly is appointed as the Chief Minister by the Governor.
- He may not be a member of the Assembly at the time of appointment as Chief Minister; however he is required to be elected within six months from his date of appointment.

Q.21. Who is the ex-officio chairman of Rajya Sabha?
Q.22. Who elects the members of the Rajya Sabha?

- The Governor appoints other ministers with proposed portfolio on the advice of the Chief Minister.
- He is appointed for the period of five years.
- He can be removed from his office, if his party loses majority in State Assembly or he fails to get elected within six months of his appointment or due to proclamation of emergency in the state by the President because of constitutional failure.

The Council of Ministers

- The council of ministers is the executive arm of the State Legislature.
- Once the Chief Minister is appointed, he recommends the list of Minister to be appointed by the Governor, so as to form the Council of Ministers.
- All the ministers have to be members of either house of the State Legislature as per the Constitution.
- If any minister remains absent in State legislature for more than six months, he ceases to be a minister.

THE STATE LEGISLATURE

It consists of:

(i) The Governor
(ii) The Legislative Assembly or/and the Legislative Council

It can be:

- Unicameral (one House, i.e. The Legislative Assembly)
- or Bi-cameral (Both the Houses)

Bicameral States: At present only five states have a bicameral legislative which are Bihar, Jammu and Kashmir, Karnataka, Maharashtra and Uttar Pradesh.

The Legislative Council (Vidhan Parishad)

It is also known as Upper House. It is a permanent House and cannot be dissolved.

Strength: The total strength does not exceed one-third of the strength of the State Assembly, subject to minimum of 40 members. The strength varies as per the population of the State.

Qualification: The person should possess same qualifications as it is required of a Member of Lok Sabha, except the age which is 30 years.

Tenure: Six years, with one-third of the members retiring every two years.

Election

- One-third of the members are elected by local bodies.
- One-third by Legislative Assembly.
- One-twelfth by university graduates of at least three years standing.

Q.23. When did the Supreme Court of India come into being?
Q.24. Who appoints members of the State Public Service Commission?
Q.25. With the consent of who does the President appoints the Judges of a High Court?

- One-twelfth by teachers (not less than Secondary School) of at least three years standing.
- One-sixth of the members are nominated by the Governor.

The Chairman and Vice-Chairman are elected among its members.

The Legislative Assembly (Vidhan Sabha)

It is also known as Lower House.

Strength: It consists of not more than 525 members and not less than 60 members. However, Legislative Assembly of Sikkim has 32 members.

Election and Tenure: The members are elected directly from State Constituencies for five years.

Qualification: The person should possess same qualifications as required of a member of Lok Sabha. The Assembly Speaker and Deputy Speakers are elected from among its members. They can be removed by Council of Ministers.

The Legislative Assembly can be dissolved by the Governor and can be extended by one year during National emergency. The Council of Ministers is collectively responsible to the Assembly.

THE HIGH COURT

It is the highest judicial body of the State.

At present there are 21 High Courts in India, though each State has one High Court, there can be common High Court between States, like Punjab, Haryana and Chandigarh (UT).

Strength of High Court depends on the Judicial Power of the State, viz., Allahabad High Court has 37 Judges, while Jammu and Kashmir High Court has five judges.

Appointment of Judges: High Court consists of Chief Justice and other judges, who are appointed by the President on consultation with CJI and the Governor of the concerned states.

Qualification of Judges

- He must be a citizen of India.
- He must have been an advocate of a High Court or two such courts in succession for minimum 10 years, or he should have held judicial office in India for minimum 10 years.

Tenure: A judge holds office till 62 years of age. He can tender his resignation to the President or he can be removed by the President only on the grounds of proven misconduct, incapacity to act {Article-124 (4)}.

Procedure for Removal: He can only be removed by the order of the President, after an address by the each House of the Parliament.

The Judge of High Court is not permitted to practice law before the authority of the same court, except the Supreme Court and any other High Courts.

Q.26. When was the first General Elections held in India?
Q.27. Which Indian State has the largest electorate?

Seats and Jurisdiction of High Court

High Court	Estd. in Year	Seat	Jurisdiction
Chennai	1862	Chennai	Tamil Nadu and Pondicherry
Kolkata	1862	Kolkata (Circuit bench at Port Blair)	West Bengal and Andaman and Nicobar
Mumbai	1862	Mumbai (bench at Nagpur, Panaji and Aurangabad)	Maharashtra, Dadra and Nagar Haveli, Goa, and Daman and Diu
Allahabad	1866	Allahabad (bench at Lucknow)	Uttar Pradesh
Karnataka	1884	Bangalore	Karnataka
Patna	1916	Patna	Bihar
Guwahati	1948	Guwahati (Bench at Kohima, Circuit benches at Imphal, Agartala and Shillong)	Assam, Manipur, Tripura, Mizoram and Arunachal Pradesh
Orissa	1948	Cuttack	Orissa
Rajasthan	1950	Jodhpur (bench at Jaipur)	Rajasthan
Andhra Pradesh	1954	Hyderabad	Andhra Pradesh
Kerala	1956	Ernakulum	Kerala and Lakshadweep
Madhya Pradesh	1956	Jabalpur (Bench at Gwalior and Indore)	Madhya Pradesh
Jammu and Kashmir	1957	Srinagar and Jammu	Jammu and Kashmir
Gujarat	1960	Ahmedabad	Gujarat
Delhi	1966	New Delhi	Delhi
Punjab and Haryana	1966	Chandigarh	Punjab, Haryana and Chandigarh
Himachal Pradesh	1971	Shimla	Himachal Pradesh
Sikkim	1975	Gangtok	Sikkim
Bilaspur	2000	Bilaspur	Chhattisgarh
Nainital	2000	Nainital	Uttarakhand
Ranchi	2000	Ranchi	Jharkhand

UNION STATE RELATIONS

This is divided into three categories as per the Constitution;
  (i) Union list (100 subjects)
  (ii) State list (66 subjects)
  (iii) Concurrent list (47 subjects)

Union List: It contains subjects like defence, foreign affairs, currency, communication, interstate trade and commerce, atomic energy, space research, postal, telecom sector, etc. The Parliament has exclusive power on these lists.

State List: State has exclusive power on these lists. It contains the subjects like public order, police administration, prison, local governments, agriculture, etc. On the proclamation of emergency, the Parliament has legislative power over the entire state list.

Q.28. What is the maximum gap that two sessions of the Parliament can have in between?

Q.29. By which Constitutional Amendment, the voting age was reduced from 21 years to 18 years?

Concurrent List: Both the Parliament and the State Legislature can legislate on these lists. It contains the subjects like criminal and civil law, forest, education, marriage and divorce, drugs, trade union, labour welfare, newspaper, books and printing press, population and family planning, etc.

Union Public Service Commission (UPSC)
- Composition is determined by the President.
- The members are appointed by the President for a period of six years or till they attain 65 years of age.
- The President can remove them by issuing orders only on the recommendation of the Supreme Court after an inquiry.
- The members cannot occupy any government office after retirement.
- It conducts various examinations for appointment to the posts under Union list.

Comptroller and Auditor General (CAG)
- He is appointed by the President.
- He holds office for a period of six years or till he attains 65 years of age.
- The President can remove him only on the recommendation of the Parliament, supported by two-thirds majority of the total number of members of both the Houses.
- He audits the accounts of the Union and States, to ensure that nothing extra expenditure occurs to the consolidated funds of India or of States without the sanctions of the Parliament or the State Legislatures.

Attorney General of India
He is the highest legal officer of the Union Government. He is appointed by the President.

Qualification: He must possess the qualification to be a judge of Supreme Court.

Duties and Responsibilities
- He advises on all legal matters of the Union Government.
- He also advises on the legal issues, referred or assigned to him by the President.
- He is entitled to audience in all courts of the Country.
- He can take part in the proceedings of the Parliament or its any committees.
- He is not permitted to take up private practices, for which he is not paid any remuneration, however, a retainer is paid, to be decided by the President.

Anti-Defection Law
It was inserted in tenth Schedule in the Constitution in 1985, to curb the political defection. And it says:
- If any member of any political party abstains from voting according to the party 'whip', he/she can be disqualified.
- If any independent candidate joins in any political party after election, he/she can be disqualified.

Q.30. At present how many Indian states have Bicameral Legislature?
Q.31. Where is the High Court of Andaman and Nicobar located?

- If any nominated member joins any political party before six months from his date of joining, he/she can be disqualified.

This law does not apply in case of:
- a division, where at least one-third of the members of a party are involved.
- a merger, where at least two-thirds of the members of a party are involved.
- a person resigns his party to become the presiding officer and rejoins the party, after leaving his office.

POLITICAL PROCESS IN INDIA

The political system in India is a constitutional democracy. The Parliamentary system of the Government holds free and fair elections to determine the:
- composition of the Government,
- the membership of the two Houses of the Parliament,
- the State and Union Territory Legislative Assemblies,
- local bodies composition at Panchayat and District level,
- the President and
- the Vice-President.

In India there is no Bi-Party system like in the US or UK. There are six national parties and several regional parties that take part in the various elections.

General Elections in India
- General Election held once in every five year, unless the Central Government is dissolved beforehand.
- The election Commission supervises the most complex task in the world's largest democracy.
- The first general elections were conducted in India in 1951, for 489 constituencies representing 26 Indian states.
- India follows a bicameral legislative structure. The members to the House of the People or the Lok Sabha are elected through the General elections.

Political Parties in India

With the decline of the Congress (I) in late 1980s, other political parties came up strongly in general elections. Though Congress (I) regained power in 1991, however it was not as dominant as it was earlier.

The coalition government became a strategy of political parties. The other political parties, viz., BJP, Janta Dal, BSP, etc., became popular among voters.

THE ELECTION COMMISSION

- Elections in India are conducted by the Election Commission of India, the authority created under the Constitution.

Q.32. Who is the non-elected person who can take part in the proceedings of the Parliament or any of its committees?

- The Election Commission consists of Chief Election Commissioner and other two Election Commissioners.
- The Chief Election Commissioner is appointed by the President of India for a period of six years or up to the age of 65 years, whichever is earlier.
- Other two Election Commissioners are appointed by the President in consultation with the Chief Election Commissioner.
- The Chief Election Commissioner can resign or can be removed from office by the President only through impeachment by Parliament.

Functions

- The announcement of various important dates and deadlines related to the election, including the dates for voter registration, the filing of nominations, vote counting and declaration of results.
- EC lays down the lines for the common code of conduct to be followed by all the political parties.
- Examining the election expenditure of the candidates.
- Recognisation of political parties and assigning electoral symbol.

Chief Election Commissioners of India

Name	Tenure	
	From	To
Sukumar Sen, ICS	21 Mar 1950	19 Dec 1958
K V K Sundaram	20 Dec 1958	30 Sep 1967
S P Sen Verma	1 Oct 1967	30 Sep 1972
Dr Nagendra Singh	1 Oct 1972	6 Feb 1973
T Swaminathan	7 Feb 1973	17 Jun 1977
S L Shakdhar	18 Jun 1977	17 Jun 1982
R K Trivedi	18 Jun 1982	31 Dec 1985
R V S Peri Sastri	01 Jan 1986	25 Nov 1990
V S Ramadevi	26 Nov 1990	11 Dec 1990
T N Seshan	12 Dec 1990	11 Dec 1996
M S Gill	12 Dec 1996	13 Jun 2001
J M Lyngdoh	14 Jun 2001	7 Feb 2004
T S Krishnamurthy	8 Feb 2004	15 May 2005
B B Tandon	16 May 2005	29 Jun 2006
N Gopalaswami	30 Jun 2006	20 Apr 2009
Navin Chawla	21 Apr 2009	till date

PANCHAYATI RAJ SYSTEM

Objective: The objective is to involve the people in village in self-governance, at the grass root level in the democratic process.

Development: The National Development Council in 1956 appointed a committee under Balwant Rai Mehta that submitted its reports in 1957. Its recommendations are:

Q.33. Which constitutional body recognises political parties and assign them electoral symbol?

Indian Polity 165

- A three-level structure of Panchati Raj – village level, intermediate level and district level was created.
- The three level structure was adopted for the first time in Nagaur District in Rajasthan on 22 Oct 1959.
- This was followed by Andhra Pradesh, Bihar, Gujarat, Himachal Pradesh, Maharashtra, Punjab, Tamil Nadu, Uttar Pradesh and West Bengal.
- In 1977, Ashok Mehta Committee was set up to review the working of Panchayats, that submitted its reports in 1978, which recommended a two level structure instead of three level structure, and it consists of Mandal Panchayats and Zila Parishads.

In 1992, in Seventy-third Amendment of the Constitution, the Panchayati Raj Bill was passed to ensure decentralisation of power and to involve the people in democratic process, which came into effect from 20 April 1993.

Some Facts About Elections in India

- Highest number of candidates contested for a single seat which is 1033 in Modaurichi Assembly Constituency in Tamil Nadu in 1996.
- In the General Election of 1988, Congress party did not win a single seat in Uttar Pradesh.
- Bahujan Samajwadi Party (BSP) and Republican Party of USA shares the same electoral symbol – the Elephant.
- The lowest voting turnover is three, happened in Bomdila district in Arunachal Pradesh.
- In 1950 General Election, different colour ballot boxes were used for each candidate, instead of ballot papers. The colour represents different political party.
- Atal Bihari Vajpayee is the politician who has won from six different constituencies, in four different states: UP, Gujarat, MP and Delhi; 1957, 1967: Balarampur; 1971: Gwalior; 1977, 1980: New Delhi; 1991: Vidisha; 1956: Gandhi Nagar; 1991, 1996, 1998, 2004: Lucknow.
- In 1998, BJP won for the first time in Tamil Nadu and West Bengal.
- The highest voting percentage in General Election has been 62.2 per cent in 1957 and lowest was 33 per cent in 1967.

Top five Constituencies (Area-wise)	Bottom Five Constituencies (Area-wise)
Ladakh (J&K)	Delhi Sadar (NCT)
Barmer (Rajasthan)	Mumbai South-Central (Maharashtra)
Kutch (Gujarat)	Mumbai South (Maharashtra)
Arunachal West (AP)	Kolkata North-West (West Bengal)
Arunachal East (AP)	Chandni Chowk (NCT)

GENERAL ELECTION 2004

The General Election was held in India in four phases between 20 April 2004 and 10 May, 2004. And result was announced on 13 May 2004.

The summary of the Election is:

Total number of States and UTs: 35

Q.34. When was Anti-Defection Law inserted in Tenth Schedule of the Constitution to curb the political defection?

Total number of Parliamentary Constituencies (PCs): 543 (two are appointed by the President of India)
Total Electors: 671524934
Electors where votes counted: 662210045
Voter Turnout: 56 per cent
Results available: 539
Following are few of the facts and figures:

- Total number of Political Parties: 220
- Total number of candidates: 5398
- Total votes polled: 378453223
- Average votes per candidates: 70665
- Number of registered voters: 675 millions
- Numbers of polling stations: 7,00,000
- Highest number of votes: (855543) for Sajjan Kumar from Outer Delhi
- Lowest number of candidates: 2 from Cuttack, Godhra and Tura
- Highest number of Candidates: 35 from Madras south
- Largest Parliamentary Constituencies (*area-wise*): Ladakh
- Total cost of election: Rs 1357.5 million

Electronic Voting Machine (EVM)

- EVMs are designed by Electronics Corporation of India Ltd. and Bharat Electronics Ltd.
- EVMs are first used in Kerala in 1989–90.
- Total EVMs used: 10.25 lakhs
- Operational speed of EVM: five votes per minute
- Number of votes one EVM can register: 3840
- Number of candidates an EVM can hold: 64

ORDER OF PRECEDENCE

Rank   Person
1. President of India.
2. Vice-President of India.
3. Prime Minister of India.
4. Governors of States (within their respective states).
5. Former Presidents of India, Deputy Prime Minister.
6. Chief Justice of India, Speaker of Lok Sabha.
7. Former Prime Ministers of India, Cabinet Ministers of the Union, leaders of Opposition in the Rajya Sabha and Lok Sabha, Deputy Chairman of Planning Commission of India, Chief Ministers of States (within their respective states), holders of the Bharat Ratna decoration.
8. Ambassadors Extraordinary and Plenipotentiary, and High Commissioners of the Commonwealth of Nations accredited to India,

Q.35. In which state Panchayati Raj was introduced for the first time in 1959?

Q.36. Which Indian political party shares the same electoral symbol as that of Republican Party of USA?

Indian Polity 167

Governors of states (outside their respective states), Chief Ministers of states (outside their respective states).
9. Judges of the Supreme Court of India, Comptroller and Auditor General of India, Chief Election Commissioner of India.
10. Deputy Chairman of Rajya Sabha, Deputy Speaker of Lok Sabha, Members of the Planning Commission, Deputy Chief Ministers of States, Ministers of State of the Union (and any other Minister in the Ministry of Defence for defence matters).
11. Attorney General of India, Cabinet Secretary, Lieutenant Governors (within their respective Union Territories).
12. Chiefs of Staff holding the rank of full General or equivalent rank.
13. Envoys Extraordinary and Ministers Plenipotentiary accredited to India.
14. Chairman and Speakers of State Legislatures within their respective States, Chief Justices of High Courts within their respective jurisdictions.
15. Cabinet Ministers in States within their respective States, Chief Ministers of Union Territories and Chief Executive Councilors of Delhi, within their respective Union Territories, Deputy Ministers of the Union.
16. Officiating Chiefs of Staff holding the rank of Lieutenant General or equivalent rank.
17. Chairman of Central Administrative Tribunal, Chairman of Minorities Commission, Chairman of Scheduled Castes and Scheduled Tribes Commission, Chairman of Union Public Service Commission, Chief Justice of High Courts outside their respective jurisdictions, Puisne Judges of High Courts within their respective jurisdictions.
18. Cabinet Ministers in States outside their respective States, Chairmen and Speakers of State Legislatures outside their respective States, Chairmen of Monopolies and Restrictive Trade Practices Commission, Deputy Chairmen and Deputy Speakers of State Legislatures within their respective States, Ministers of State in States within their respective States, Ministers of Union Territories and Executive Councilors of Delhi within their respective Union Territories, Speakers of Legislative assemblies in Union Territories and Chairman of Delhi Metropolitan Council within their respective Union Territories.
19. Chief Commissioners of Union Territories not having Councils of Ministers, within their respective Union Territories, Deputy Ministers in States within their respective States, Deputy Speakers of Legislative assemblies in Union Territories and Deputy Chairman of Metropolitan Council Delhi within their respective Union Territories.
20. Deputy Chairman and Deputy Speakers of State Legislatures, outside their respective States, Ministers of State in States outside their respective States, Puisne Judges of High Courts outside their respective jurisdiction.
21. Members of Parliament.
22. Deputy Ministers in States outside their respective States.
23. Army Commanders/Vice Chief of the Army Staff or equivalent in other Services, Chief Secretaries to State Governments within their respective States, Commissioner for Linguistic Minorities, Commissioner for Scheduled Castes and Scheduled

Q.37. In which state Electronic Voting Machines (EVMs) were used for the first time in 1989–90?
Q.38. Who was the first Chief Election Commissioner of India?

Tribes, Members of Minorities Commission, Members of Scheduled Castes and Scheduled Tribes Commission, Officers of the rank of full General or equivalent rank, Secretaries to the Government of India (including officers holding this office ex-officio), Secretary of Minorities Commission, Secretary of Scheduled Castes and Scheduled Tribes Commission, Secretary to the President, Secretary to the Prime Minister, Secretary to Rajya Sabha/Lok Sabha, Solicitor General of India, Vice-Chairman, Central Administrative Tribunal.

24. Officers of the rank of Lieutenant General or equivalent rank.
25. Additional Secretaries to the Government of India, Additional Solicitor General, Advocate Generals of States, Chairman of Tariff Commission, Charge Affairs and Acting High Commissioners a pied and ad interim, Chief Ministers of Union Territories and Chief Executive Councilors of Delhi outside their respective Union Territories, Chief Secretaries of State Governments outside their respective States, Deputy Comptroller and Auditor General, Deputy Speakers of Legislative assemblies in Union Territories and Deputy Chairman of Delhi Metropolitan Council outside their respective Union Territories, Director of CBI, Director General of BSF, Director General of CRPF, Director of Intelligence Bureau, Lieutenant Governors outside their respective Union Territories, Members of Central Administrative Tribunal, Members of Monopolies and Restrictive Trade Practices Commission, Members of Union Public Service Commission, Ministers of Union Territories and Executives Councilors of Delhi outside their respective rank, Principal Staff Officers of the Armed Forces of the rank of Major General or equivalent rank, Speakers of Legislative assemblies in Union Territories and Chairman of Delhi Metropolitan Council outside their respective Union Territories.
26. Joint Secretaries to the Government of India and Officers of equivalent rank, Officers of the rank of Major-General or equivalent rank.

ANSWERS

1. USA
2. 26 November 1949
3. The right to equality
4. Direct Principle of State Policy
5. GV Mavalankar
6. Part IX
7. Seventh Schedule
8. Article 170
9. Article 368
10. Ninety-second amendment
11. Forty-second Amendment
12. Sachidanand Sinha
13. First Amendment
14. Part IV
15. Article 17
16. Article 370
17. Once
18. Speaker of Lok Sabha
19. Five years
20. Article 356
21. The Vice-President
22. Elected members of the Legislative Assembly
23. 28 January 1950
24. The Governor
25. The Governor, the Chief Justice of the High Court concerned and CJI.
26. 1951
27. Uttar Pradesh
28. Six months
29. The sixty-first Amendment
30. Five
31. Kolkata
32. Attorney General
33. The Election Commission
34. 1985
35. Rajasthan
36. Bahujan Samajwadi Party (BSP)
37. Kerala
38. Sukumar Sen

7

INTERNATIONAL ORGANISATIONS

UNITED NATIONS ORGANISATION (UN)

Origin

United Nations originated during the World War II, on 1 January 1942, when representatives of 26 nations pledged their governments to continue fighting together against the Axis Powers.

UN Charter

- It is the constitution of UN, drawn by 50 countries at United Nations Conference on International Organsations in San Francisco from 25 April to 26 June 1945.
- The proposals were worked out by representative of China, the Soviet Union, the United Kingdom, and the United States at Dumbarton Oaks (Washington DC) from 21 August to 28 September 1944.
- The Charter was signed by 50 countries on 26 June 1945.
- Poland signed later; hence the number of original member states went up to 51.

United Nations Day

United Nations came into force on 24 October 1945, which is celebrated each year as United Nations Day.

Headquarter of UN

It is located at First Avenue, UN Plaza, New York City, USA.

Flag of the UN

It was adopted on 20 October 1947 by the General Assembly. The UN emblem is superimposed on the Flag in white centred on a light blue background.

The UN flag is not to be subordinated to any other flag in the world.

Emblem of the UN

The current United Nations emblem was approved by the General Assembly on 7

General Knowledge Manual

December 1946. The official emblem of the United Nations consists of two bent olive branches open at the top and the map of the world in between.

First regular session was held in London in January 1946 and Trygve Le was elected as the first Secretary General of the UN.

The UN has a post office, which has its own stamps. Recently it released a stamp to mark 140th birth anniversary of Mahatma Gandhi.

Some 52100 people work in the UN system.

Official Languages of the UN: Arabic, Chinese, English, French, Russian, Spanish.

Objectives of UN

- To maintain peace and security for all of its member states.
- It aims to protect human rights and provide humanitarian assistance when needed.
- It provides food, drinking water, shelter, and other humanitarian services to people displaced by famine, war and natural disaster.
- It plays an integral part in social and economic development through its various programmes.
- The UN also annually publishes the Human Development Index (HDI) to rank countries in terms of poverty, literacy, education and life expectancy.
- To facilitate cooperation in international law, economic development.

Membership

New member states are admitted by the General Assembly, on the recommendation of the Security Council. Two-thirds of the majority should vote in favour and also expel or suspend in the same way.

Permanent Members (5): China, France, Russia, UK and US.

- Each permanent members of the Security Council enjoys the power to Veto (negative vote).
- 50 members signed the UN Charter with Poland signing later; so there were originally 51 member states.
- In 1994, membership rose to 185.
- In September 2000, Tuvalu was admitted as one hundred and eighty-ninth Member state.
- In September 2002, East Timor was admitted as a member of the UN.
- On 28 June 2006, Montenegro became a member of the UN (the last one so far).
- Vatican City/Holy See and Palestine has been given the permanent Observer status in the UN.
- Presently there are 192 member states in the UN.

UN at Glance:
- Established: 24 October 1945
- Headquarters: New York City
- Membership: 192 Member States
- Current UN peacekeeping operations: 16
- Budget for 2008–09: USD 4.171 billion (peacekeeping operations not included).
- Official languages: Arabic, Chinese, English, French, Russian, Spanish.

Non-Members of the United Nations: Three countries are not members of the United Nations; they are: Kosovo, Taiwan and Vatican City.

Q.1. What portion of world economy is represented by G-20, which is a group of world's most powerful countries?

International Organisations

Principal Organs of the UN

1. The General Assembly (the main deliberative assembly)
2. The Security Council (decides certain resolutions for peace and security)
3. The Economic and Social Council (assists in promoting international economic and social cooperation and development)
4. The International Court of Justice (the primary judicial organ)
5. The Trusteeship Council (provides international supervision for self-government and independence)
6. The Secretariat (provides studies, information and facilities needed by the UN)

The General Assembly

- The General Assembly is located in New York City.
- It consists of the representatives of the all member states of the UN.
- Each member state has one vote however it may send five delegates.
- The General Assembly meets at least once in a year.
- It elects its President and Vice-President every year.
- It appoints the Secretary General, High Commission of Refugees, Managing Director of Fund, Executive Director and Director General of other oganisations, working under the UN.
- It discusses and makes recommendation on any subject, under UN Charter, except the subjects dealt by UN Security Council.

The Security Council

- The Security Council is located in New York City.
- Security Council has 15 members; out of which there are five permanent members – China, France, Russia, UK and the US.
- There are 10 Non-Permanent members – Austria (2010), Japan (2010), Uganda (2010), Burkino Faso (2009), Libya Arab Jamahiriya (2009), Vietnam (2009), Costa Rica (2009), Mexico (2010), Croatia (2009) and Turkey (2010).
- Non-Permanent members are elected for two years by two-thirds majority of the General Assembly.
- Retiring members are not eligible to immediate re-election.
- Each of the 15 members has one vote each; however permanent members have the power of veto to stop discussion on any subject or action.
- The Presidency of the Security Council is held for one month in rotation by member states in English alphabetical order of their names.
- The Security Council is the concerned body in International Peace and Security.
- It can use diplomatic channel or use of force to restore peace in any place in the World, irrespective of the membership of the Country.

The Economic and Social Council

- The Economic and Social Council is located in New York City.
- It has 54 members, one-third of its members are elected each year for three years by two-thirds majority of the General Assembly.

Q.2. Where is the headquarters of WHO located?

Q.3. How many member states were originally there in the United Nations?

- Seats on the Council are based on geographical representation with 14 allocated to African States, 11 to Asian States, 6 to Eastern European States, 10 to Latin American and Caribbean States, and 13 to Western European and other States.
- The president is elected for a one-year term and chosen among the small or middle powers represented on ECOSOC. The current president is Ambassador Sylvie Lucas, Luxembourg.
- It meets once a year in July for a four-week session.
- Its functions include taking action with regard to International economic, social and cultural, educational, health matters.

The International Court of Justice (ICJ)

- The International Court of Justice is located in the Peace Place in Hague (Netherlands).
- The International Court of Justice has 15 Judges, elected by both the General Assembly and the Security Council for nine-year term.
- Elections take place every three years, with one-third of the judges retiring each time, in order to ensure continuity within the court.
- Its official languages are English and French.
- The Court's role is to settle, in accordance with international law, legal disputes submitted to it by member States and to give advisory opinions on legal questions referred to it by authorised United Nations organs and specialised agencies.

The Trusteeship Council

- The Trusteeship Council is located at New York City.
- The Trusteeship Council is made up of the five permanent members of the Security Council – China, France, Russian Federation, the United Kingdom and the United States.
- Under the Charter, the Trusteeship Council is authorised to examine and discuss reports from the Administering Authority on the political, economic social and educational advancement of the people of Trust Territories and, in consultation with the Administering Authority, to examine petitions from and undertake periodic and other special missions to Trust Territories.
- Its objective is to promote the advancement of the inhabitants of Trust Territories and their progressive development towards self-government or independence, either as separate States or by joining neighbouring independent countries.

The Secretariat

- The Secretariat is composed of the Secretary General, who is the head of the organisation and an international staff is appointed by him under regulations established by the General Assembly.
- The Secretary-General is appointed by the General Assembly on the recommendation of the Security Council for a term of five years and can be reappointed when his term expires.
- He coordinates and supervises the various activities of the UN.

Q.4. When was the UN flag adopted by the General Assembly?

Q.5. How many permanent members are there in the UN Security Council?

International Organisations

Secretary Generals of the UN

Name	Tenure	Country
Trygve Lie	1946–1952	Norway
Dag Hammarskjöld	1953–1961	Sweden
U Thant	1961–1971	Myanmar
Kurt Waldheim	1972–1981	Austria
Javier Perez de Cuellar	1982–1991	Peru
Boutros Boutros-Ghali	1992–1996	Egypt
Kofi A. Annan	1997–2006	Ghana
Ban Ki-moon	1 Jan 2007–Till date	South Korea

Current Deputy Secretary General is Dr Asha Rose Mirigo of Tanzania, who took office from 1 February 2007. She is the third Deputy Secretary General to be appointed, since the post was created in 1997. In addition to 18 independent specialised agencies, there are 14 major UN Programmes and funds aimed to achieve economic and social development in the member states.

OTHER WORLD ORGANISATIONS

Apart from United Nations Organisation (UN), there are some other important International organisations which are discussed in the following sections.

European Union (EU)

- The European Union (EU) is an economic and political union of 27 member states, located in Europe.
- It was known as European Community until 1994.
- It was established by the Treaty of Maastricht on 7 February 1992 and came to being on 1 November 1993.
- The name covers three organisations with common membership – the European Economic Community, the European Coal and Steel Community and the European Atomic Energy Community.
- With a population of almost 500 million, the EU generates an estimated 30 per cent share (US$18.4 trillion in 2008) of the nominal gross world product.
- Between the years 1973 and 2007, it has enlarged six times to bring up current membership to 27.
- The founding members of the community were Belgium, the Netherland and Luxembourg (BeNeLux union), Italy, France and West Germany.
- Euro is the currency of 16 EU countries: Belgium, the Netherland, Luxembourg, Italy, France, Germany, Greece, Spain, Ireland, Portugal, Slovenia, Austria, Finland, Cyprus, Malta and Slovakia.
- Headquarters is located at Brussels, Belgium.
- President of EU is Mr Jerzy Buzek (Poland) and Secretary General is Javier Solana of Spain.

Q.6. Where is the headquarters of the International Court of Justice located?

Q.7. How many EU countries have adopted Euro as their currency?

The European Economic Community (EEC)

- The European Economic Community (EEC), also referred as the European Common Market, was created in March 1957.
- EEC comprises 12 members.
- The founding members were Belgium, France, Germany, Italy, Luxembourg and the Netherlands.
- Its objective is to promote a common market for free export and import and to bring about economic integration among member states.
- It was enlarged later to include six additional states and, from 1967, its institutions also governed the European Coal and Steel Community (ECSC) and European Atomic Energy Community (EAEC or Euratom) under the term European Communities.
- When the European Union (EU) was created in 1993, the EEC was transformed into the European Community, one of the EU's three pillars, with EEC institutions continuing as those of the EU.
- The headquarters of EEC is located at Brussels in Belgium.

Association of South-East Asian Nations (ASEAN)

- ASEAN was formed on 8 August 1967 (in Bangkok declaration).
- Original members were Indonesia, Malaysia, the Philippines, Singapore and Thailand.
- It has 10 members: Brunei Darussalam, Cambodia, Indonesia, Lao PDR, Malaysia, Myanmar, the Philippines, Singapore, Thailand and Vietnam.
- Its objective is to accelerate economic growth, social progress and cultural development and maintain economic stability of South-East Asia.
- Its Headquarter is located at Jakarta in Indonesia.
- The Secretary General is elected for three years term on rotation of English alphabetical order.
- Present Secretary General is Dr Surin Pitswan of Thailand (is elected for five years term).

South Asian Association of Regional Cooperation (SAARC)

- The South Asian Association for Regional Cooperation (SAARC) is an economic and political organisation of eight countries in Southern Asia.
- It was established on 8 December 1985.
- The SAARC Secretariat was set up in Kathmandu on 16 January 1987 and was inaugurated by King Birendra Bir Bikram Shah of Nepal.
- It is headed by a Secretary General appointed by the Council of Ministers from Member Countries in alphabetical order for a three-year term.
- Original member states are India, Pakistan, Bangladesh, Sri Lanka, Nepal, Maldives and Bhutan.
- In April 2007, Afghanistan became its eighth member, at its fourteenth summit.
- Its headquarters is at Kathmandu, Nepal.

Q.8. Where is the headquarters of EU located?

Q.9. What is the total number of members of ASEAN?

International Organisations 175

Secretary Generals of SAARC

Name	Tenure From	Tenure To	Country
Abul Ahsan	16 Jan 1987	15 Oct 1989	Bangladesh
Kant Kishore Bhargava	17 Oct 1989	31 Dec 1991	India
Ibrahim Hussain Zaki	1 Jan 1992	31 Dec 1993	Maldives
Yadav Kant Silwal	1 Jan 1994	31 Dec 1995	Nepal
Naeem U Hasan	1 Jan 1996	31 Dec 1998	Pakistan
Nihal Rodrigo	1 Jan 1999	10 Jan 2002	Sri Lanka
Q A M A Rahim	11 Jan 2002	28 Feb 2005	Bangladesh
Lyonpo Chenkyab Dorji	1 Mar 2005	29 Feb 2008	Bhutan
Sheel Kant Sharma	1 Mar 2008	Till date	India

Asia Pacific Economic Cooperation (APEC)

- APEC was formed on November 1989.
- It consists of 21 members.
- Its objective is to promote trade and investment among its member states and with rest of the world.
- Its headquarters is located at Singapore.
- Its Executive Director is Ambassador Michael Tay.

The Asian Development Bank (ADB)

- ADB was created on December 1966.
- It consists of 59 members: 43 regional and 16 non-regional members.
- Its objective is to provide fund and enhance economic cooperation among member countries.
- Its headquarters is located at Manila, Philippines.
- Presently Haruhiko Kuroda of Japan is the President of ADB.

The Arab League

- The Arab League, officially called the League of Arab States, is a regional organisation of Arab states in South-west Asia, and North and North-east Africa.
- It was formed in Tunisia on 22 March 1945 with six members: Egypt, Iraq, Transjordan (renamed Jordan after 1946), Lebanon, Saudi Arabia and Syria.
- After Iraq invaded Kuwait in August 1990, its headquarters was shifted to: Al Tahir Square, Cairo in Egypt.
- The Arab League currently has 22 members.
- The main goal of the league is to promote close relations between member States and coordinate between them, to safeguard their independence and sovereignty and to consider in a general way the affairs and interests of the Arab countries.
- Current Secretary General is Amr Mousa of Egypt.

Q.10. Where the SAARC Secretariat was set up?
Q.11. Where is the headquarters of Asian Development Bank (ADB) located?

Organisation of African Unity (OAU)

- OAU came into existence on 25 May 1963.
- It was disbanded on 9 July 2002 by its last chairperson, South African President Thabo Mbeki, and replaced by the African Union (AU).
- It comprises 53 members.
- Its objective is to promote unity and solidarity among African countries, defend the sovereignty of independent nations; ensure human rights and raise the living standards of all Africans and promote economic and social development among member states.
- Official languages are Arabic, French, Portuguese and English.
- Its headquarters is located at Addis Ababa, Ethiopia.
- Its Chairman is Muammar al-Gaddafi of Libya.

The Non-Aligned Movement (NAM)

- It was instituted in April 1955.
- The first Conference of Non-Aligned Heads of State, at which 25 countries were represented, was convened at Belgrade on September 1961.
- The founding members of the NAM were Pt Jawaharlal Nehru, first Prime Minister of India; Dr Sukarno, President of Indonesia; Marshal Tito, President of former Yugoslavia and G A Nasser, President of Egypt.
- The principles of NAM were defined in Bandung (Indonesia) declaration of 1955 and Broni (Yugoslavia) declaration of 1956, which are popularly known as 'Panchsheel Declaration'.
- It has 118 members as of 2007.
- The basic objective of the association was in favour of peace, disarmament, economic and social development, eradication of poverty and illiteracy; and to distance NAM from Soviet Union and Western Block and prevent its members from becoming pawns in the Cold War.
- The existing practice is to hold the Summit Conference every three years.
- Its current Chairman is Raul Castro of Cuba.

The Commonwealth

- Originally known as British Common Wealth of Nations, it is an association of independent states; most of them were formerly parts of the British Empire.
- It is an inter governmental organisation which has 53 independent member states, across all six inhabited continents.
- It was established in 1931.
- Flags of the members of the Commonwealth in Horse Guards Road, next to the Foreign and Commonwealth Office, London.
- Its headquarter is at Marlborough House, Pall Mall in London, UK.
- The members have a combined population of 2.1 billion people, almost one-third of the world population, of which 1.17 billion live in India and 94 per cent live in Asia and Africa combined.

Q.12. Who was the founder of International Committee of Red Cross?

Q.13. In which year Amnesty International was established?

International Organisations

- The land area of the Commonwealth nations is about 31,500,000 sq km or about 21 per cent of the total land area of the world.
- The Commonwealth members have a combined GDP (in terms of PPP) of $10.6 trn, 65 per cent of which is accounted for by the three largest economies: India ($3.3 trn), the United Kingdom ($2.3trn), and Canada ($1.3trn).
- The Commonwealth has no Constitution or Charter; however the member states have common constitutional features.
- The head of the Governments of member states hold Commonwealth Heads of Government Meetings (CHOGM) every two years to discuss issues of common interests.
- They cooperate within a framework of common values and goals, as outlined in the Singapore Declaration.
- These include the promotion of democracy, human rights, good governance and the rule of law, individual liberty, free trade, multilateralism and world peace.
- Its current Secretary General is Donald C McKinnon of New Zealand.

Commonwealth of Independent States (CIS)

- CIS was established in December 1991.
- It comprises 12 from 15 former Soviet Union republics.
- Members are: Armenia, Azerbaijan, Belarus, Georgia, Kazakhstan, Kyrgyzstan, Moldova, Russia, Tajikistan, Turkmenistan, Ukraine and Uzbekistan.
- Its objective is to provide a mechanism for orderly dissolution of Soviet Union.
- Its headquarter is located at Minsk, Belarus.
- Sergei Lebedev of Russia is the Executive Secretary.

Amnesty International (AI)

- Amnesty International was initiated in London in July 1961 by English labour lawyer Peter Benenson.
- Amnesty International (AI) is an International non-governmental organisation (NGO).
- There are five key areas which AI deals with:
  ☐ Women's Rights,
  ☐ Children's Rights,
  ☐ Ending Torture and Execution,
  ☐ Rights of Refugees and
  ☐ Rights of Prisoners of Conscience.

General Secretaries of the AI:

Name	Year
Peter Benenson	1961–66
Eric Baker	1966–68
Martin Ennals	1968–80
Thomas Hammarberg	1980–86
Ian Martin	1986–92
Pierre Sane	1992–2001
Irene Khan	2001–till date

- Its objective is to generate action to prevent abuses of human rights and to demand justice for those whose rights have been violated.
- It has more than 2.2 million members in 150 countries.
- Its headquarters is in London, UK.
- AI was awarded the 1977 Nobel Peace Prize for its campaign against torture.

International Red Cross Society

- International Committee of Red Cross was founded by Jean Henri Durrant in 1863.

Q.14. Where is the Head-quarter of INTERPOL?
Q.15. When was G-20 established?

General Knowledge Manual

- Delegates from 26 nations adopted the Geneva (Switzerland) Convention in 1864 and as a result Red Cross came into existence.
- 8 May is celebrated as World Red Cross Day and Red Crescent Day (in Muslim countries), which is the birthday of its founder JH Durrant.
- It has about 200 million members from 131 countries of the World.
- Its objective is to provide worldwide humanitarian aid and prevent or alleviate human suffering, without any discrimination based on nationality, race, religious beliefs, class or political opinions.
- The Red Cross was awarded Noble Prize in 1917, 1944 and 1963.
- Its headquarter is at Geneva in Switzerland.
- Its current President is Zakob Kellenberger.

Interpol

- Established in 1923, Interpol is the largest police organisation in the World.
- It has 186 member states.
- It facilitates cross border police cooperation; supports and assists all organisations, authorities and services whose aim is to prevent or combat international crime.
- Headquarter is at Lyon, France (earlier its headquarter was Paris).
- Its current Secretary General is Ronel K Noble.

Carribean Community and Common Market (CARICOM)

- CARICOM was established on August 1973.
- It comprises 13 members: Anguilla, Antigua, Barbados, Belize, Dominica, Grenada, Guyana, Jamaica, Montserrat, St Kitts-Nevis, St Lucia, St Vincent and Trinidad.
- Its objective is to increase cooperation in economic, health, education, culture, science and technology, tax administration and foreign policy among member states.
- Its headquarter is located at Georgetown (Guyana).
- Its Chairman is Dean Oliver Barrow of Belize, Secretary General Edwin W Carrington of Trinidad and Tobago.

Organisation of Petroleum Exporting Countries (OPEC)

- The Organisation of the Petroleum Exporting Countries (OPEC), a permanent intergovernmental organisation, was created on September 1960 (at the Baghdad Conference).
- The five Founding Members were Iran, Iraq, Kuwait, Saudi Arabia and Venezuela.
- Later joined by nine other Members: Qatar (1961); Indonesia (1962) – suspended its membership from January 2009; Socialist People's Libyan Arab Jamahiriya (1962); United Arab Emirates (1967); Algeria (1969); Nigeria (1971); Ecuador (1973) – suspended its membership from December 1992 – October 2007; Angola (2007); and Gabon (1975–94). Hence it has 12 members now.
- Its objective is to coordinate and unify petroleum policies among member countries, in order to secure fair and stable prices for petroleum producers;

Q.16. Name the place and the country, where the headquarters of WTO is located?

an efficient, economic and regular supply of petroleum to consuming nations; and a fair return on capital to those investing in the industry.
- The Headquarter is located at Vienna (Austria).
- Secretary General is Abdallah Salem el-Badri of Libya from 1 Jan 2007.

North Atlantic Treaty Organisation (NATO)

- It was formed on 4 April 1949 at Brussels in Belgium.
- It has 26 member states.
- Originally formed by 12 members – USA, UK, Canada, France, Denmark, Italy, Iceland, Norway, Portugal, Belgium, the Netherlands and Luxembourg.
- In 1952, Greece and Turkey were included.
- West Germany and Spain joined in 1955 and 1982 respectively.
- The fundamental role of NATO is to safeguard the sovereignty of its member states by military and political means.
- It also plays a key role in peace keeping and crisis resolution.
- Its current Secretary General is Jaap De Hoop Scheffer of Netherlands.

International Air Transport Association (IATA)

- It was formed in 1945.
- Its members are International and domestic airlines.
- Its objective is to promote safe, regular and economical air transport and forum for collaboration among members.
- Main offices are in: Geneva (Switzerland), Montreal, Quebec (Canada) and Singapore.
- Its Director General and CEO is Giovanni Bisignani.

Group of Eight (G8)

- It was created on September 1975.
- It consists of seven Industrialised countries and Russia.
- Original members were France, Germany, Italy, Japan, UK and US.
- Canada joined in 1976 summit of San Juan in Puerto Rico.
- Russia joined in 1998 summit of Birmingham in UK.
- Its objective is to tackle global challenges thorough discussion and taking required steps.
- It has no headquarter, budget or permanent staff.

Group of Fifteen (G-15)

- It was established in 1989.
- It consists of 17 developing countries from Asia, Africa and Latin America.
- The member states are Algeria, Argentina, Brazil, Chile, Egypt, India, Indonesia, Jamaica, Kenya, Nigeria, Malaysia, Mexico, Peru, Senegal, Sri Lanka, Venezuela and Zimbabwe.
- The membership of the G-15 has expanded to 17 countries, but the name has remained unchanged.

Q.17. Where was the treaty to form NATO signed?
Q.18. The principles of NAM are known as 'Panchsheel Declaration' When was it defined?

- Its objective is to promote economic cooperation among developing countries.

Group of Twenty (G20)

- It was established in 1999.
- As the name suggests, it has 20 members.
- The twentieth member is the European Union, which is represented by the rotating Council Presidency and the European Central Bank.
- In addition to these 20 members, the following institutions, represented by their respective heads, participate in meetings of the G-20, viz., International Monetary Fund, World Bank, International Monetary and Financial Committee and Development Committee of the IMF and World Bank.
- Its objective is to strengthen the international financial architecture and to foster sustainable economic growth and development.

Group of Seventy-Seven (G-77)

- It was established on 15 June 1964 by 77 developing countries.
- This group consists of 130 members.
- Its objective is to promote economic cooperation, trade interests and greater influence in world affairs among developing countries.

World Wide Fund for Nature (WWF)

- WWF was established on September 1961.
- All the countries of the world are its members.
- Its objective is to save the wildlife from possible dangers.
- Its headquarter is located at Gland, Switzerland.

Organisation for Economic Cooperation and Development (OECD)

- OCED was formed on September 1961.
- There are 30 members in this group.
- OCED replaced the Organisation for European Economic Cooperation (OEEC), which was formed after Second World War for reconstruction in war ravaged European countries.
- Its headquarter is located in Paris, France.
- Its Secretary General is Angel Gurria of Mexico.

World Trade Organisation (WTO)

- WTO was established on 1 January 1995, replacing General Agreement on Tariffs and Trade (GATT).
- It was founded by 85 members, including India. It has membership of 153 countries (on 23 July 2008).
- Its functions include:

Administering WTO trade agreements; forum for trade negotiations; handling trade disputes; monitoring national trade policies; technical assistance and training for developing countries; cooperation with other international organisations.

Q.19. In which year India became a member of the UN?
Q.20. Where is the headquarters of Commonwealth of Independent States (CIS)?

- It headquarter is in Geneva, Switzerland.
- Its Director-General is Pascal Lamy.

ANSWERS

1. 85 per cent
2. Geneva
3. 51
4. On 20 October 1947
5. 5
6. Hague
7. 16
8. Brussels, Belgium
9. 10
10. Kathmandu
11. Manila in Philippines
12. Jean Henri Durrant
13. 1961
14. Lyon, France
15. 1999
16. Geneva in Switzerland
17. Washington
18. It was defined in the Bandung Conference.
19. 1945
20. Minsk in Belarus

Agencies of the United Nations

Sl. No.	Name of the Agency & Chief Administrator	Year of Formation	Head-quarters	Purpose
1.	International Labour Organisation (ILO) *Director General*: Juan Somavia (Chile)	1919	Geneva	Promoting social justice, improve conditions and living standards of workers.
2.	International Telecommunication Union (ITU) *Secretary General*: Dr Hamadoun Toure (Turkey)	1947	Geneva	Regulating telecommunication, radio spectrum, international cooperation in assigning satellite orbits.
3.	World Health Organisation (WHO) *Director General*: Dr Margaret Chan (South Korea)	1948	Geneva	Promoting global health matter, provide technical support and monitor health trends.
4.	General Agreement on Tariffs Trade (GATT) (World Trade Organisation w.e.f. 1 January 1995) *Director General*: Pascal Lamy (France)	1948	Geneva	Administers, monitor international trade policies and handling trade disputes.
5.	World Meteorological Organisation (WMO) *Secretary General*: Michel Jarraud (France)	1950	Geneva	Promoting international exchange of weather reports and other weather related aspects.
6.	United Nations High Commissioner for Refugees (UNHCR) *High Commissioner*: Antonio Guterres (Portugal)	1950	Geneva	Providing protection to refugees.
7.	United Nations Conference on Trade and Development (UNCTAD) *Secretary General*: Dr Supachai Panitchpakdi (Thailand)	1964	Geneva	Accelerating economic growth of developing countries through international trade.
8.	World Intellectual Property Organization (WIPO) *Director General*: Mr Francis Gurry (Australia)	1974	Geneva	Promoting and protecting the intellectual property through cooperation among member states.
9.	United Nations Development Programme (UNDP) *Administrator*: Helen Clark (New Zealand)	–	New York	Helping developing countries for effective use of funds for various developmental programmes.

10.	United Nations Children's Fund (UNICEF) *Executive Director*: Ms Ann N Veneman (USA)	1946	New York	Promoting children's welfare in the world.
11.	United Nations Relief and Work Agency for Palestine Refugees (UNRWA) *Commissioner General*: Mr Karen Koning AbuZayd (USA)	1949	New York	For settlement of those displaced in Arab-Israel war.
12.	United Nations Institute For Training and Research (UNITAR) *Executive Director*: Mr Carlos Lopes	1965	New York	Providing training and research projects for peace, security and socio-economic progress.
13.	United Nations Fund for Population Activities (UNFPA) *Executive Director*: Ms Thoraya Ahmed Obaid (Saudi Arabia)	1969	New York	Promoting population related aspects.
14.	International Monetary Fund (IMF) *Managing Director*: Dominique Strauss-Kahn (France)	1945	Washington	Preserving economic stability and to manage financial crisis in the World.
15.	International Bank for Reconstruction and Development (IBRD) (known as World Bank) *President*: Robert B Zoellick (USA)	1945	Washington	Providing financial and technical assistance to member states.
16.	International Finance Corporation (IFC) *Chief Executive Officer*: Lars H Thunell (Sweden)	1956	Washington	Promoting economic development through private enterprise among its member states.
17.	International Development Association (IDA) (Lending arm of IBRD)	1960	Washington	Helping and serving middle-income countries with capital investment and advisory services.
18.	International Atomic Energy Agency (IAEA) *Director General*: Mr Yukiya Amano (Japan)	1957	Vienna	Advocating peaceful use of atomic energy.
19.	United Nations Industrial Development Organisation (UNIDO) *Director General*: Kandeh K Yumkella (Sierra Leone)	1966	Vienna	Advising developing and under-developed nations on all aspects of Industrial all aspects of industrial policies.

20.	Food and Agriculture Organisation (FAO) *Director General*: Dr Jacques Diouf (Senegal)	1945	Rome	Raising levels of nutrition, improving agricultural productivity, improving the lives of rural populations and contributing in the growth of the world economy.
21.	International Fund for Agricultural Development (IFAD) *President*: Kanayo Nwanze (Nigeria)	1977	Rome	Financing agricultural projects to improve food production.
22.	United Nations Educational, Scientific and Cultural Organisation (UNESCO) *Director General*: Koïchiro Matsuura (Japan)	1946	Paris	Promoting collaboration among nations through education, science and culture.
23.	International Civil Aviation Organisation (ICAO) *Secretary General*: Taieb Cherif (Algeria) (2003-Present)	1947	Montreal	Promoting safety, international aviation and establishing international standards and regulations.
24.	Universal Postal Union (UPU) *Director General*: Edouard Dayan (France)	1874	Berne	Developing social, cultural and commercial communication between people through the efficient operation of the postal service.
25.	Inter-Governmental Maritime Consultative Organisation (IMCO) *Secretary General*: Efthimios Mitropoulos (Greece)	1958	London	Promoting cooperation on maritime safety navigation and encouraging anti pollution measures.
26.	United Nations Environment Programme (UNEP) *Executive director*: Achmi Steiner (Germany)	1972	Nairobi	Promoting international cooperation regarding matters related to environment.

8
GENERAL SCIENCE AND TECHNOLOGY

BRANCHES OF SCIENCE

Acoustics: The study of sound and sound waves.
Aeronautics: Study of flight of air planes.
Agronomy: Study of soil management and production of crops.
Angiology: Study of blood vascular system.
Anthropology: Study of apes and man.
Anatomy: Study of structure of the animal and plants.
Astronautics: Study of space (travels and vehicles).
Astronomy: The study of celestial objects in the universe.
Astrophysics: The study of the physics of the universe.
Bacteriology: Study of bacteria in relation to disease.
Biochemistry: The study of the organic chemistry of compounds and processes occurring in organisms.
Biophysics: The application of theories and methods of the physical sciences to solve questions of biology.
Biology: The science that studies living organisms.
Botany: The scientific study of plant life.
Cardiology: It deals with study, diagnosis and treatment of various disorders of heart and major blood vessels.
Climatology: the study of climates and investigations of its phenomena and causes.
Cosmology: It is a branch of physical science that is associated with the nature of universe, its origin and overall structure.
Cytology: It is a branch of biological science that is associated with the study of structure, origin, function and pathology of cells.
Dermatology: It is a branch of medicine that deals with the skin disorders.
Dynamics: It is a branch of mechanics that includes the study of various forces, their action on bodies and changes in motion they produce.
Ecology: The study of how organisms interact with each other and their environment.
Electronics: Science and technology of electronic phenomena.
Engineering: The practical application of science to commerce or industry.

Entomology: The study of insects.
Etiology: It is the study of causes or origins of disease/abnormal condition.
Eugenics: It deals with the study of hereditary improvement of human race by controlled selective breeding.
Forestry: The science of studying and managing forests and plantations, and related natural resources.
Genetics: The science of genes, heredity and the variation of organisms.
Geology: The science of the earth, its structure and history.
Meteorology: Study of the atmosphere that focuses on weather processes and forecasting.
Microbiology: The study of microorganisms, including viruses, prokaryotes and simple eukaryotes.
Mineralogy: The study of the chemistry, crystal structure, and physical (including optical) properties of minerals.
Neurology: The branch of medicine dealing with the nervous system and its disorders.
Oceanography: Study of the earth's oceans and their interlinked ecosystems and chemical and physical processes.
Organic Chemistry: The branch of chemistry dedicated to the study of the structures, synthesis and reactions of carbon-containing elements.
Paleontology: The study of life-forms existing in former geological time periods.
Physics: The study of the behaviour and properties of matter.
Physiology: The study of the mechanical, physical, and biochemical functions of living organisms.
Radiology: The branch of medicine dealing with the applications of radiant energy, including x-rays and radio-isotopes.
Seismology: The study of earthquakes and the movement of waves through the earth.
Taxonomy: The science of classification of animals and plants.
Thermodynamics: The physics of energy, heat, work, entropy and the spontaneity of processes.
Zoology: The study of animals.

PHYSICS

Physical science is broadly divided into: (1) Physics (2) Chemistry

The branch of science that deals with the basic laws that nature follows in its functioning is called **physics**.

Major branches of physics are: (i) mechanics, (ii) heat and thermodynamics, (iii) optics (iv) electricity and magnetism.

Mechanics

- **Mechanics** is the branch of physics that deals with the behaviour of physical bodies when they are subjected to forces or displacements, and the subsequent effect of the bodies on their environment.
- Length, mass, time, electric current, temperature, luminous intensity and amount of mass are the fundamental quantities.

Q.1. What is the approximate value of escape velocity for the earth?
Q.2. Who was the scientist to recognise and name the nucleus?

General Science and Technology

- Astronomical Unit (AU) is the average distance between earth and the Sun (which is equal to 1.496×10^{11} m).
- The light year is the distance covered by light in one year (which is equal to 9.46×10^{15} m).
- Angstrom is used to express the small length (which is equal to 10^{-10} m).
- **Kinematics** is the branch of mechanics which describes the motion of objects without considering the causes leading to the motion.
- **Acceleration** is the rate of change of velocity of an object and is expressed in metre per square second (m/s^2).
- Negative acceleration is known as **retardation**, i.e. the velocity of the object decreases with respect to time.
- **Velocity** is the rate of change of displacement of an object and is expressed in metre per second (m/s).
- **Displacement** is the shortest distance between the initial position and the final position of an object.
- Displacement can be zero but distance cannot be zero.
- Tendency of an object is to remain in a state called **inertia**. It is of three types: inertia of rest, inertia of motion and inertia of direction.
- **Friction** is the force resisting the relative motion of solid surfaces, fluid layers, or material elements in contact.
- The phenomenon by which the molecules of one kind penetrate through the spaces between the molecules of another kind is called **diffusion**.
- The force of attraction between like molecules is known as **cohesion** and force of attraction between unlike molecules is known as **adhesion**.
- **Newton's First Law of Motion** states that a body remains at rest or remains in motion unless it is acted on by an external force.
- **Newton's Second Law of Motion** states that force equals mass times acceleration, i.e. the net force on an object is equal to the mass of the object multiplied by its acceleration.
- **Newton's Third Law of Motion** states that to every action there is an equal and opposite reaction.
- **Acceleration due to Gravity (g)** is the acceleration due to the gravitational force on an object, in particular due to the Earth's gravity. At sea level, it is 9.806 metres per second.
- **Pascal's Law** states that pressure in a fluid at rest is same at all points, if gravity is ignored.
- A **vector** is a quantity having both magnitude and dimension; **scalar** is a quantity that only have magnitude.
- All physical quantities can be divided into vector and scalars.
- **Centre of mass** of a body is defined as the point where the total mass of the body appears to be concentrated.

Sound

- The average range of audible frequency to which the human ear responds is usually between 20 Hz to 20,000 Hz. Frequency beyond 20,000 Hz is called

Q.3. At what temperature does the water has maximum density?
Q.4. Bronze is an alloy of which metals?

ultrasonic vibrations and below 20 Hz is known as **infrasonic vibration** (usually produced during earthquakes).
- The speed of aircraft is measured in terms of Mach number. Speed below 1.0 Mach is called **subsonic**, speed above Mach 1.0 called **supersonic** and very high speed upto Mach 5.0 is called **hypersonic**.
- Safe range of Audible sound is 0 to 120 dB (Decibel).
- Velocity of sound is 331m/s at 0 degree Celsius.
- An **echo** is heard when it reaches the human ear at least after 0.15 second of the original sound, and the minimum distance to create echo is 17m from the surface from where the original sound is created.
- **Doppler effect** is the change in frequency of wave due to a motion of source or observer.

Work, Power and Energy
- **Work** is said to be done when a force causes displacement in its own direction. In SI system, unit of work is Joule.
- The rate of doing work is called **power**; the unit of power is joule/second or Watt.
- **Energy** is the total amount of work done by a body; unit is same as work, viz., Joule.
- When a body works by virtue of its motion, it is called **kinetic energy**.
- If work is done by virtue of position or configuration of the body, it is called **potential energy**.
- **Law of conservation of energy** states that energy can neither be created nor destroyed. It may be transformed from one form to another, but total energy of the universe remains constant.
- **Pressure** is defined as thrust acting per unit area of the surface of contact, i.e. P = F/A, where P is the pressure, F is the force and A is the surface area. In SI unit system, the unit of pressure is Pascal.
- When a body is partly or wholly immersed in a fluid, it experiences certain force called **buoyant force** and the phenomenon called **buoyancy**.
- 1 Kilo watt hr = 36×10^5 watts
- 1 HP (Horse Power) = 746 watts.

Some devices can convert one form of energy to another:

Devices	From Energy	To Energy
Steam Engine	Heat	Electrical
Dynamo	Mechanical	Electrical
Microphone	Sound	Electrical
Loud Speaker	Electrical	Sound
Photo Electric Cell	Light	Electrical
Electric Motor	Electrical	Mechanical

Heat and Thermodynamics
- Heat is a form of energy that flows from one body to another due to difference of temperature.
- Unit of heat in SI system is Kelvin.
- At −40° both Celsius and Fahrenheit Scale give same reading.

Q.5. Which is the main atmospheric gas responsible for Greenhouse Effect?
Q.6. Which instrument is used to measure relative humidity in the atmosphere?

General Science and Technology

- A **black body** is a substance which absorbs perfectly 100 per cent of the radiation falling on it.
- **Thermodynamics** is the branch of physics that deals with the concept of the heat and temperature and their interconversion of heat and other forms of energy.
- **Zeroth law of thermodynamics** states that two systems in thermal equilibrium with third system separately, are in thermal equilibrium with each other.
- For the conversion of Celsius and Fahrenheit scale, this formula is used: $T_C = (5/9) \times (T_F - 32)$, where T_C and T_F are Celsius and Fahrenheit temperature.
- One calorie is defined as the amount of heat required to raise the temperature of one gram of water from 14.5° C to 15.5° C.
- Heat transfer can take place in either of three processes: Conduction, Convection and Radiation.
- **Convection** is the process by which heat is transmitted from one place to another due to motion of particles in the medium.
- **Radiation** is the process by which heat is transmitted from one place to another without action of intervening medium.
- Heat is measured in three scales: Celsius or Centigrade, Fahrenheit scale and Reaumur scale.
- The range of alcohol thermometer is –13° C to 75° C, of Mercury thermometer is –30° C to 330° C and standard hydrogen thermometer is –60° C to 1600° C.
- With the change of temperature of the substance, volume of the substance also changes. So density is changed as the mass remains constant, since density = mass/volume.
- Water has its minimum volume at 4° C. So volume of water increases either in heating or cooling.
- Substance which conducts heat easily is called good conductor, e.g. metal. Earth is also a good conductor.
- Substances that don't allow much heat to pass through are bad conductor of heat, e.g. all non-metals and water.

Optics and Wave Motion

- **Lunar eclipse** occurs when earth lies between sun and moon, i.e. sun, earth and moon are in a straight line, so that the shadow of the earth falls on moon.
- **Total lunar eclipse** occurs when earth totally covers the moon from sunlight, so that moon does not reflect any light, hence not visible at all.
- The portion of mirror from where the reflection actually takes place called **aperture**.
- In **concave mirror**, the image is always real and erect, except when the object is placed within focal length where image is virtual.
- In case of **convex mirror** irrespective of the position of the object, the image is always virtual and inverted.
- **Refraction** is a phenomenon due to which a ray of light always deviates from its original path while travelling from one optical medium to another medium.
- The power of lens is the convergence or divergence produced by it and measured in Diapters (D). In SI system, $1 D = 1 m^{-1}$.

Q.7. What is the chemical formula of baking soda?

Q.8. Which circuit element is used to block DC in an electric circuit?

- In human eye, function of retina is to receive the optical image of an object and convert it into optical pulses, which is sent to brain through optical nerves.
- The power of concave lens is +ve and convex lens is −ve.
- **Myopia** or short-sightedness is the condition in which a person can see the nearby objects and unable to see the distant objects; it can be rectified by use of concave lens.
- **Hypermetropia** or long-sightedness is the condition in which a person can see the distant objects but unable to see the nearby objects; it can be rectified by use of convex lens.
- **Presbiopia** is an old-age problem, in which the power of the eye decreases with ageing. Most of the people cannot see near object, so they cannot read and write comfortably without corrective eye glass.
- The crystalline lens of the eye focuses images of object, at different distances clearly on the retina.
- Cornea acts as the window that allows lights to enter eye.
- **Yellow spots** is responsible for forming a clear image, when we need to examine an object in detail, the image is focused at this point.
- **Cilliary muscle** is responsible for adjusting the focal length of the crystalline lens so that image of the object at various distances is clearly focused on retina.
- **Iris** of the eye controls the amount of light entering into eye.
- The electro-magnetic radiations which can affect our retina have wavelength between 8000-4000 A° (Angstrom unit).
- Wave length of visible light is 4×10^{-7} m to 8×10^{-7} m.
- **Dispersion** is the phenomenon due to which a polychromatic light splits into its components colours, when passed through prism.
- **Diffraction** is the spreading of light waves when it passes through a small hole.
- There are three types of emission spectra: line spectra, bond spectra and continuous spectra.
- Speed of light is 3×10^8 m/s. While traveling in air the speed is marginally less, where as in water and glass, it is reduced considerably.

Electricity and Magnetism

- When electric charge is in motion, it is called **electric current**. The unit is Ampere and measured with the help of Ammeter.
- **Resistance** is the obstruction offered by conductor in the passage of electron in the electric current. The unit of electric resistance is Ohm.
- Resistance is directly proportional to the length of the conductor and inversely proportional to its cross-sectional area. It increases with the rise of temperature.
- **Fuse** is the safety device in an electrical device. It is the weakest points of the circuit which melts down in case of overload, short circuit, etc.
- Fuse wire has low melting point and high resistance.
- Materials whose properties are in midway between conductors and insulators are called **semiconductor**.
- Pure-form of semiconductor is called **intrinsic semiconductor**.
- **Generator** converts mechanical energy to electrical energy, so does alternator

Q.9. What do the spectacles used for viewing 3D films have?
Q.10. What is mineral constituent of chlorophyll?

and dynamo. The reverse process is done by motor.
- **Null or neutral point** in a magnetic field is the point where the resultant intensity is zero.
- When a magnet is cut into two pieces, each piece acts like a magnet with north and south poles.
- A current which changes direction after equal interval of time is called **alternating current** (AC).

Gravitational Force

- Masses of bodies can be measured by different methods: Masses of heavenly bodies, such as, sun, earth, etc., can be measured by using Newton's universal law of gravitation and/or Kepler's third law of planetary motion.
- Masses of small bodies on earth can be measured by physical balance.
- Masses of atomic particles can be measured by application of electric and magnetic fields.
- The weight of body at the centre of earth is zero.
- **Escape velocity** is the velocity required by an object to move out of the gravitational field of earth. It is 11.2 km/sec on the surface of earth. It is independent of mass of the object.

SI system (*International System of Units*) is the modern metric system of measurement and the dominant system of international commerce and trade. SI units are gradually replacing Imperial and USCS units.

The SI is maintained by a small agency in Paris, the International Bureau of Weights and Measures (BIPM, for Bureau International des Poids et Mesures).

UNITS OF MEASUREMENT IN SI SYSTEM

Quantity	Units	Quantity	Units
Absolute temperature	Kelvin	Length	Metre
Acceleration	Metre/second square	Luminous flux	Candela
Area	Square metre	Mass	Kilogram
Angular velocity	Radian/second	Magnetic intensity	Orsted
Charge	Coulomb	Momentum	Kilogram metre/second
Density	Kilogram/metre cube	Pressure	Pascal
Depth of sea	Falhom	Power	Watt
Energy	Joule	Power of lens	Dioptre
Electric current	Ampere	Resistance	Ohm
Electromotive force	Volt	Surface tension	Newton/square metre
Electric energy	Kilowatt hour	Temperature	Kelvin
Electric power	Watt	Time	Second
Electrical conductivity	Ohm/metre	Volume	Cubic metre
Force	Newton	Velocity	Metre/second
Intensity of sound	Decibel	Viscosity	Poise
Electrical	Ohm/metre	Weight	Newton or kilogram
Heat	Joule	Work	Joule
Impulse	Newton-second		

CHEMISTRY

The branch of science which deals with study of elements and their properties is called **chemistry**.

Chemistry can be broadly divided into: (i) **Physical Chemistry** that deals with the study of physical phenomenon, (ii) Inorganic Chemistry – which deals with elements, their compound and their properties, (iii) **Organic Chemistry** deals with the carbon, its compound and their properties.

States of Matter

- **Matter** is a substance having mass and it occupies space.
- Matter can be either of five states: solid, liquid, gaseous, plasma and Bose-Einstein condensate.
- When temperature is applied to solid state, the kinetic energy of the particles increase and the particles vibrate, hence it becomes liquid.
- Similarly when temperature is applied on liquid they change into gaseous state.
- The temperature at which solid melts to become liquid at atmospheric pressure is called **melting point** (MP); however when solid melts the temperature remains same.
- The temperature at which liquid starts boiling at atmospheric pressure is called **boiling point**, at this point liquid changes into vapour state.
- The boiling point of water is 100° Celsius (= 373° K).
- In SI system unit of temperature is Kelvin (K). O° Celsius = 273.16° Kelvin.
- **Sublimation** is the process in which solid directly changes into gas without changing into liquid or vice-versa.
- Pressure exerted by gas is measured by atmosphere (atm). 1 atm = 1.05 Pa. Pa or Pascal is the unit of pressure.
- The pressure of air in the atmosphere is called **atmospheric pressure**. At sea level the atmospheric pressure is considered as normal, which is 1 atm.
- **Humidity** is the amount of water vapour present in air.
- A **solution** is the homogenous mixture of two or more substances. It has two components, **solvent** (present in larger quantity) and **solute** (present is smaller quantity).
- **Suspensions** are a heterogenous mixture in which the solute particles do not dissolve but remain suspended throughout the bulk in the medium.
- **Alloys** are homogenous mixtures of metals and cannot be separated into its components by physical methods, e.g. Brass (70 per cent copper + 30 per cent zinc).
- **Viscosity** in fluid is due to the frictional forces existing between different layers when the fluid is in motion. In liquid, viscosity is indirectly proportional to temperature and in gases it is directly proportional to temperature.

Q.11. What does the colour of a star indicate?
Q.12. What is the process called in which solid directly changes into gas without changing into liquid?

Classification of Matter

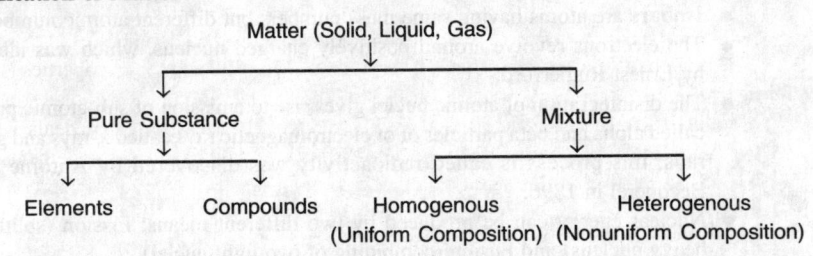

```
                    Matter (Solid, Liquid, Gas)
                              ↓
            ┌─────────────────┴─────────────────┐
            ↓                                   ↓
      Pure Substance                         Mixture
            ↓                                   ↓
      ┌─────┴─────┐                    ┌────────┴────────┐
      ↓           ↓                    ↓                 ↓
   Elements   Compounds           Homogenous        Heterogenous
                                (Uniform Composition) (Nonuniform Composition)
```

- **Element** is the basic form of matter that cannot be divided further into smaller substance by physical or chemical means, e.g. oxygen, hydrogen, mercury, etc.
- Robert Boyle was the first to use the term 'element' in 1661.
- There are more than 100 elements known at present out of which 92 are naturally occurring and rest are man-made.
- 11 elements are at gaseous state including oxygen, hydrogen, nitrogen, etc., two elements are in liquid state, i.e. mercury and bromine at room temperature.
- Majority of the elements are in solid state at room temperature.
- A **compound** is a substance made up of two or more elements combined with one another in fixed proportion by chemical means, i.e. salts, water, sugar, etc.
- **Homogenous mixtures** are procured when different compounds are mixed in known proportion, i.e. sugar in water, water and alcohol, etc.
- **Heterogenous mixture** is the mixture when two or more compounds are not mixed in definite proportion, i.e. sugar and salt, sand and salt, etc.
- Postulates of **Dalton's atomic theory**:
  (i) All matters are made up of atoms;
  (ii) Atoms are invisible particles that cannot be created or destroyed in chemical reactions;
  (iii) Atom of a given element have identical mass and chemical properties;
  (iv) Atoms combined in definite ratio of small whole numbers to form compounds;
  (v) Atoms of different elements have different masses and chemical properties.
- Radius of atoms is measured in nanometer (1 nanometer = 10^{-9}m).
- A **molecule** is the smallest particle of a substance which shows all the properties of the substance, capable of independent existence.
- Atoms of same elements or of different elements can form the molecule, e.g. H_2O is formed by combination of two atoms of hydrogen and one atom of oxygen.
- **Atomic Mass Unit** (AMU) is a mass unit equal to exactly 1/12 of mass of one atom of carbon-12.
- All relative atomic masses of all elements are measured with respect to an atom of carbon-12.
- Electron is the sub-atomic particle identified by JJ Thomson in 1900.
- Proton is another sub-atomic particle, the charge opposite to electron having mass 2000 times as that of electron, identified by E. Goldstein in 1886.

Q.13. What is chemical formula of heavy water?
Q.14. What is the scientific name of the atoms having same mass numbers but different atomic number?

194 General Knowledge Manual

- **Isotopes** are atoms of same elements which have different mass number.
- **Isobars** are atoms having same mass numbers but different atomic number.
- The electrons revolve around positively charged nucleus, which was identified by Ernest Rutherford.
- The disintegration of atomic nuclei gives rise to emission of sub-atomic particles called alpha and beta particles or of electromagnetic rays called x-rays and gamma rays; this process is called radioactivity was discovered by Antoine Henry Becquerel in 1896.
- Nuclear energy can be produced by two different means: Fission (splitting of heavy nucleus) and Fusion (combining of two light nuclei).
- All the elements are put in a systematic way as per their atomic number in the Periodic Table.

[Periodic Table of the Elements]

- The Periodic table is divided into four main blocks: s, p, d and f.
- The division is made on the basis of the sub-shelling to which valence electron enters.
- s-block includes the elements of group number 1 and 2 are known as alkaline metals; p-block consists of elements of group 13, 14, 15, 16, 17 and 18; d-block consists of elements of group 3, 4, 5, 6, 7, 8, 9, 10, 11 and 12; f-block includes two series Lanthanides and Actinides, each having 14 elements.
- Group 15 known as Pictogens, Group 16 as Chalcogens, Group 17 as Halogens, Group 18 as Inert gases or Noble gases.
- With the donation or sharing of one or more electrons the following types of bonds get formed: (i) Ionic Bond (e.g. Nacl, CaO), (ii) Covalent Bond (e.g. H_2O, HCl), (iii) Coordinate Bond (e.g. $NH_3H_2SO_4$).

Reactions and Compounds

- Chemical reactions are broadly classified as: **exothermic reaction** (chemical reactions which release heat) and **endothermic reaction** (chemical reactions which absorb heat).
- The **rate of reaction** is defined as the rate of decrease of concentration of reactants or increase in the concentration of the product.
- Mass and energy are equivalent and

Q.15. What is the name of the organ which is both endocrine and exocrine gland?

Q.16. What kind of an image is formed on the retina of a human eye?

- convertible as explained by Albert Einstein in the equation, $E = mc^2$, where E is the energy generated, m is the mass of the substance and c is the velocity of light ($= 3 \times 10^8$ m/s).
- Sodium thiosulphate (known as hypo) is used in photography as fixing agent.
- Potassium bromide (KBr) is used in photography as sensitive emulsion; it is also used as sedative (a drug for reliving anxiety and tension).
- Oxidation reaction is process in which oxygen combines with another element and forms an oxide; reactant loses an electron in the reaction.
- **Reduction** reaction is a process in which an oxide loses its oxygen; the reactant gains an electron.
- **P^H scale** is used to measure the strength of an acid: P^H =7, solution is neutral (e.g. water); P^H >7, solution is alkaline and P^H < 7, the solution is acidic.
- **Chain reaction** is a process in which neutrons released during fission process, leads to another fission and large amount of energy is generated.
- Half life period is the time after which the amount of the radioactive element becomes half of its initial. It is expressed as $t_{1/2}$.
- Producer gas is formed when air passes over red hot coke and oxygen combines with carbon to form carbon monoxide.

Metals and Metallurgy

- Most of the elements in the periodic table are metals.
- Some elements act as both metal and non-metal, e.g. Si, Ge, As, Sb, Te, etc.
- Some metals can be beaten into thin sheets; this property of metal is called **malleability,** e.g. gold, silver, copper, etc.
- Some metals can be drawn into very thin wires; this property of metal is called **ductility**. Silver and gold are most ductile metals.
- Inorganic elements or compounds which occur naturally in earth's crust are known as minerals.
- An **ore** is a type of rock that contains minerals that can be profitably extracted through mining and refined for use; For example, bauxite is the main ore of Aluminium.
- **Metallurgy** is the process of extraction of metals from their ores and refining them to make them usable.
- In an alloy if one of the metals is Mercury, it is called **amalgam**.
- Pure aluminium oxide is known as **alumina**, which is extracted from bauxite by Bayer's Process.

SCIENTIFIC INSTRUMENTS AND THEIR USES

Instruments	Uses
Altimeter	Measures altitudes and used in Aircraft
Ammeter	Measures strength of electric current
Anemometre	Measures force and velocity of wind and determines its direction
Audiometre	Measures intensity of sound
Barometre	Measures atmospheric pressure
Balometre	Measures heat radiation
Calorimetre	Measures quantities of heat

Cardiogram (EGG)	Traces movements of the heart recorded on a cardiograph
Cryometre	Measures very low temperatures, usually below zero degree centigrade
Dynamo	Converts mechanical energy into electrical energy
Electroencephalograph (EEC)	Records and interprets the electrical waves of the brain recorded on electroencephalograms
Electrometre	Measures very small, potential difference in electric current
Electroscope	Detects presence of an electric current
Fathometre	Measures depth of the ocean
Galvanometre	Measures the electric current
Hydrometre	Measures the relative density of liquids
Hygrometre	Measures level of humidity
Lactometre	Measures the relative density of milk to determine purity (fat content)
Microphone	Converts sound waves into electrical vibrations
Microscope	Used to obtain a magnified view of small objects
Pyrometre	Measures very high temperature
Radar	Detects the direction and range of an approaching aeroplane by means of radio waves (Radio, Angle, Detection and Range)
Refractometre	Measures refractive indices
Sphygmomanometre	Measures blood pressure
Stethoscope	Used by doctors to hear and analyse heart and lung sounds
Tachometre	Used to determine speed, especially the rotational speed of a shaft (used in aeroplanes and motor-boats)
Telescope	To view distance objects in space
Udometre	Rain gauge
Viscometre	Measures the viscosity of liquids
Voltmetre	Used to measure potential difference between two points
Wattmetre	Measures the power of an electric circuit

FATHER OF IMPORTANT BRANCHES OF SCIENCE

Father of Branches	Name
Father of Biology	
Father of Zoology	Aristotle
Father of Nature's History	
Father of Blood Circulation	William Harvey
Father of Blood Groups	Karl Landsteiner
Father of Bacteriology	Robert Koch
Father of Cytology	Robert Hooks
Father of Ecology	Reiter
Father of Eugenics	Francois Galton
Father of Genetics	Gregor John Mendel
Father of Genetic Engineering	Paul Berg
Father of Immunology	Edward Jenner
Father of Microbiology	Louis Pasteur
Father of Modern Embryology	Karl Ernestvon Baer
Father of Medicine	Hippocrates
Father of Mutation Theory	Hugo de Vries

General Science and Technology

Father of Palaentology	Leonardo da Vinci
Father of Pathology	Rudolf Virchow
Father of Taxonomy	Linneus
Father of Virology	WM Stanley

SCIENTIFIC INVENTIONS

Inventor	*Inventions*
J Guttenberg	Printing Press (1450)
Z Janssen	Compound Microscope (1590)
Galileo Galilei	Thermometer (1593)
Hans Lippershey	Telescope (1608)
J C Perier	Steam Ship (1775)
D Bushnell	Submarine (1776)
Louis Lenormand	Parachute (1783)
Charles Wheatstone	Microphone (1827)
Michel Faraday	Dynamo (1831)
Sir Isaac Pitman	Modern Shorthand (1837)
Samuel F B Morse	Telegragh Code (1837)
W H Foxtalbot	Photography (1841)
J Harrison and A Catlin	Refrigerator (1851)
Richard Gatling	Machine Gun (1861)
Thomas Alva Edison	Cinematograph (1891)/Electric Lamp (1879)/Gramophone (1878)
Karl Benz	Motor Car (Petrol) (1885)
Rudulf Diesel	Diesel Engine (1892)
Sir Charles Parsons	Turbine Ship (1894)
Wilhelm Roentgen	X-ray (1895)
John Ambrose Fleming	Diode – a vital part of radios and televisions (1904)
Orville and Wilbur Wright	Aeroplane (1903)
Christian Hulsmeyer	Radar system used in shipping (1904)
Leo Baekeland	Plastic (1905)
Reginald Fessenden	Radio Broadcasting (1906)
G Claude	Neon Lamp (1910)
Harry Brearley	Stainless Steel (1913)
Gidoen Sundback	Zip (1913)
John Thompson	Sub-machine gun (1920)
Karel Capek	Robot (1921)
Clarence Birdseye	Idea of Frozen Food (1924)
Robert Goddard	Liquid Fuel Rocket (1926)
Frank Whittle	Jet engine (1930)
Laszlo Jose Biro	Ballpoint Pen (1938)
Igor Sikorsky	Modern Helicopter (1939)
K Macmillan	Bicycle (1939)
Enrico Fermi	Nuclear Reactor at the University of Chicago (1942)
Percy LeBaron Spencer	Microwave Oven (1946)
Sir Christopher Cockerell	Hovercraft (1955)

General Knowledge Manual

Jack Kilby	Microchip (1958)
Douglas Engelbart	Computer Mouse (1964)
Stephanie Kwolek	Kevlar, the Synthetic Fibres (1966)
Jack Kilby, Jerry Merryman and James Von Tassel	Portable Calculator (1967)
Alfred Nobel	Dynamite (1967)
George Gray	LCD and LED (1970)
Herbert Boyer	Genetic Engineering (1973)
Akio Morita	Personal Stereo (1979)
Tim Berners-Lee	World Wide Web (1989)
Ian Wilmut	Headed the Team that Produced the First Cloned Sheep-Dolly (1997)

IMPORTANT LAWS AND PRINCIPLES

***Archimedes Principle*:** This principle states that, any object, wholly or partly immersed in a fluid, is buoyed up by a force equal to the weight of the fluid displaced by the object. Archimedes' principle does not consider the surface tension acting on the body.

***Avogadro's Law*:** The principle states that equal volumes of all gases under identical conditions of pressure and temperature contain the same number of molecules.

***Boyle's Law*:** If the temperature remains constant, the volume of a given mass of gas is inversely proportional to pressure.

***Charle's Law*:** As the temperature of a gas increases, the volume increases proportionally, provided that the pressure and amount of gas remain constant.

***Coulomb's Law*:** The magnitude of the electrostatic force between two points electric charges is directly proportional to the product of the magnitudes of each of the charges and inversely proportional to the square of the total distance between the two charges.

***Dalton's Law*:** Dalton's Law explains that the total pressure is equal to the sum of all of the pressures of the parts. This only is absolutely true for ideal gases, but the error is small for real gases. Mathematically, this can be represented as: $Pressure_{Total} = Pressure_1 + Pressure_2 ... Pressure_n$.

***Doppler's Principles*:** When the distance between the source of the wave and the observer increases due to their relative motion, the frequency of the wave appears to decrease. The inverse condition is also true.

Faraday's Laws of Electrolysis

***Faraday's First Law of Electrolysis*:** The mass of a substance is altered at an electrode during electrolysis is directly proportional to the quantity of electricity transferred at that electrode. Quantity of electricity refers to electrical charge, typically measured in coulombs, and not to electrical current.

***Faraday's Second Law of Electrolysis*:** For a given quantity of electricity (electric charge), the mass of an elemental material altered at an electrode is directly proportional to the element's equivalent weight.

The equivalent weight of a substance is its molar mass divided by an integer that depends on the reaction undergone by the material.

***Heisenberg Uncertainty Principle*:** It states that certain pairs of physical properties, like position and momentum, cannot both be known

Q.17. What is used in photography as fixing agent?

Q.18. What is the property of metals by virtue of which it can be beaten into thin sheets?

to arbitrary precision. That is, the more precisely one property is known, the less precisely the other can be known. It is impossible to measure simultaneously both position and velocity of a microscopic particle with any degree of accuracy or certainty.

Law of Conservation of Energy: It states that the total amount of energy in an isolated system remains constant.

Newton's Law of Cooling: It states that the rate of change of the temperature of an object is proportional to the difference between its own temperature and the ambient temperature (i.e. the temperature of its surroundings).

Newton's Laws of Motion: The three laws are:

First Law: A body at rest remains at rest, and a body in motion remain in motion, unless an external force is acted on it.

Second Law: Rate of change of momentum of a moving body is proportional to the applied force and takes place in the direction of the force i.e. $\mathbf{F = ma}$.

Third Law: To every action there is an equal and opposite reaction.

Newton's Law of Universal Gravitation: Every point mass attracts every other point mass in the universe, and it is directly proportional to the product of the two masses and inversely proportional to the square of the distance between them.

Kepler's three laws of planetary motion are:

First Law: The orbit of every planet is an ellipse with the sun at a focus.

Second Law: A line joining a planet and the sun sweeps out equal areas during equal intervals of time.

Third Law: The square of the orbital period of a planet is directly proportional to the cube of the semi-major axis of its orbit.

Laws of Thermodynamics: Generally, it is considered there are four principles:

The **Zeroth Law** of thermodynamics underlies the definition of temperature, which states that a system is said to be in thermal equilibrium when its temperature does not change over time.

The **First Law** of thermodynamics, states that energy can be transformed (changed from one form to another), but it can neither be created nor destroyed.

The **Second Law** of thermodynamics, states that the entropy of an isolated system which is not in equilibrium will tend to increase over time, approaching a maximum value at equilibrium.

The **Third Law** of thermodynamics, which concerns the entropy of an object at absolute zero temperature, implies that it is impossible to cool a system all the way to exactly absolute zero.

Ohm's Law: It states that the current through a conductor between two points is directly proportional to the potential difference or voltage across the two points, and inversely proportional to the resistance between them. The mathematical equation that describes this relationship is $I = V/R$.

Pascal's Laws: It states that a change in the pressure of an enclosed incompressible fluid is conveyed undiminished to every part of the fluid and to the surfaces of its container.

BIOLOGY

The branch of science that deals with the living beings is called **biology**. It is further divided into: (i) Zoology (ii) Botany.

Q.19. What is the study of hereditary improvement of human race by controlled selective breeding called?

Botany: The branch of science which deals with the plants is called **botany**.
Zoology: The branch of science which deals with the animals is called **zoology**.
Also there are other branches of biology, viz., microbiology, biotechnology, space biology.

Botany

- The basic unit of plant is called cell, which was first coined by Robert Hooke in 1665.
- In the course of time various developments happened: Cell Theory was developed by Schleiden in 1838 and Schwann in 1839, which states that all plants and animals are composed of cells, and cell is the basic unit of life.

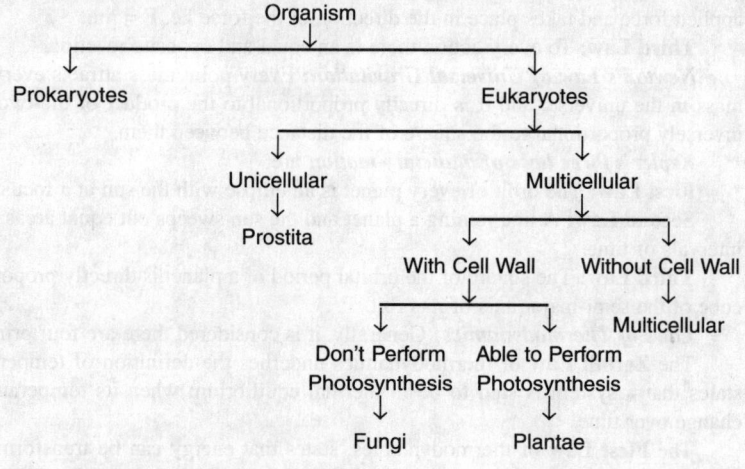

```
                         Organism
                            │
              ┌─────────────┴─────────────┐
              ↓                           ↓
         Prokaryotes                  Eukaryotes
                                          │
                              ┌───────────┴───────────┐
                              ↓                       ↓
                         Unicellular             Multicellular
                              ↓                       │
                          Prostita       ┌────────────┴────────────┐
                                         ↓                         ↓
                                   With Cell Wall            Without Cell Wall
                                         │                         ↓
                              ┌──────────┴──────────┐         Multicellular
                              ↓                     ↓
                         Don't Perform         Able to Perform
                         Photosynthesis        Photosynthesis
                              ↓                     ↓
                            Fungi                Plantae
```

- Nucleus was discovered by Robert Brown in 1831.
- Purkinji (1839) coined the term **protoplasm**, which is the fluid substance of the cell.
- **Cell wall** lies outside the plasma membrane, composed of cellulose in plant cell.
- Nucleus contains chromosomes; it contains hereditary traits in the form of Deoxy Ribose Nucleic Acid (DNA).
- The functional parts of DNA are called **genes**.
- **Prokaryotes** are the organisms, which lack nuclear membrane; organisms having nuclear membrane in the cell are called **eukaryotes**.
- **Cytoplasm** is the fluid which is contained inside the plasma membrane; it also contains many specialised structures like mitochondria, ribosome, golgi bodies, etc.
- **Golgi bodies** are described by Camillo Golgi; they are responsible for storage, modification and packaging and also for formation of lysosomes.
- **Lysosomes** help in digestion of foreign materials in the cell, since it contains digestive enzymes. It is also known as 'Suicide bag' of the cell.
- **Mitochondria** are the 'power house'

Q.20. For what purpose Hygrometer is used?
Q.21. Who invented nuclear reactor?

General Science and Technology

of the cell; the energy required by various activities is provided by it in the form of Adenosine Triphosphate (ATP).
- **Plastids** are only present in the plant cells. These are of two types: Leucoplasts (white or colourless plastids) and chloroplasts (contains Chlorophyll pigment).
- **Chloroplasts** are responsible for photosynthesis in plants.
- Mitosis and Meiosis are the two modes of cell division, responsible for the growth and development of organism.

Zoology

- The cell is the basic unit of animal.
- The animal kingdom has various levels: Kingdom – Phylum (for animals)/ Division (for plants) → Order → Family → Genus → Species
- Animals are broadly divided into following two categories of their food habits: **herbivorous** (who live on eating grass and green leaves etc.), for example rabbit, deer and grasshopper, etc., and **carnivorous** (who live on eating other animals), e.g. tiger, hawk, lion, etc.

HUMAN BODY

Anatomy and Physiology

The important parts of the human body are as follows:
1. Head
2. Neck
3. Four Extremities (Limbs): Two upper or superior and two lower or inferior
4. Trunk (Torso): Divided into two chambers by a flexible muscle partition, called the **diaphragm**. The upper chamber is called **chest** or **thorax** and the lower one is the **abdomen**. The lowest part of the abdomen is called **pelvic cavity**.

Elementary Constituents of the Human Body:
Cells → Tissue → Organs → Systems

Cell

- The structural and functional unit of the body.
- It consists of nucleus, cytoplasm and cell membrane.
- There are various types of cells: **epithelial cell** (found on the surface of the body), **connective tissue cell** (connects the other tissue and provides support).

Tissue: It is a collection of cells of similar structure and functions, e.g. muscle tissue, nerve tissue, etc.

Organ: It is a special part of system, e.g. liver (part of digestive system), lung (part of respiratory system), etc.

Organ System: It is composed of various types of tissues, serving a definite function in the body, e.g. digestive system (for digestion), respiratory system (for respiration), etc. The small intestine in human body is about 6.096 metres long and the large intestine 6 metres. The rate of

Q.22. What does the cell wall in the plant cell made of?
Q.23. Which component is considered as the 'power house' of the cell?

intestine process is about 2.54 cm per minute and it absorbs 40.64 metric tonnes of food over the course of 70 years.

Skin: 2.72 kg of skin covers 1.85 sq. metres of the surface area of the body of an average adult.

Blood

Blood is a fluid connective tissue.

On an average a healthy man has about 5-6 litres of blood in the body, while a woman has 500 ml less. It is about 6-8 per cent of the body weight and P^H of 7.4 (slightly alkaline).

Composition of Blood

1. Plasma (about 65 per cent):
It contains 90 per cent water, 7 per cent proteins and others like nutrients, salts, nitrogen waste, carbon dioxide and hormones.
2. Blood Cells (about 35 per cent)
   A. Red Blood Corpuscle (RBC) or Erythrocyte
   B. White Blood Corpuscles (WBC) or Leucocyte
      I. Granulocytes
         (i) Neutrophil
         (ii) Esonophil
         (iii) Basophil
      II. Agranulocytes
         (a) Lymphocyte
         (b) Monocyte
   C. Platelets or Thrombocyte

Red Blood Corpuscles (RBC) or Erythrocyte

- Main function is to carry oxygen.
- Total number in blood 4.5-5 millions per cubic millimetres.
- Average size of RBC is 7.4 cubic microns.
- It contains hemoglobin (iron content), which carries oxygen.
- It is produced in bone marrow (8 million per second).
- Deficiency of RBCs in the body is known as **anemia**.
- Excessive formation of RBCs is a condition called **Poly cythemia Vera**.

White Blood Corpuscles (WBC) or Leucocyte

- Leucocytes actively participate in the defence mechanism of the body.
- The total numbers of WBC found in blood is 6000-8000 per cubic millimetres.
- There are two types of WBC: Granulocytes and Agranulocytes
- Functions of WBC: **phagocytosis** (destruction of foreign bodies like bacteria), production of immunoglobulin (concerned with inherent resistance mechanism of the body) and some helpful role in cases of hypersentivity or allergic reactions.
- The condition of erratic formation of excessive and abnormal WBC is called **leukaemia** or **blood cancer**.

Q.24. What is the main function of Erythrocyte?
Q.25. What is the P^H of blood?
Q.26. Which bacteria are found in curd?

Platelets or Thrombocyte

- Total number of platelets in blood is 1,50,000–3,50,000 per cubic millimetre.
- Thrombocytes help in blood clotting.
- Deficiency of platelet or **thrombopenia** is found in certain type of haemorrhagic disorders like 'Thrombocytopenic Purpura'.

Blood Grouping

- This is based on the presence or absence of certain inherited antigens on the surface of red blood cells or RBCs.
- There are more than 30 blood group systems found in human beings, one of the most important of which is ABO system.
- This system was first classified by Karl Landsteiner (called as Father of Blood grouping) in 1901.
- This system is based on the presence or absence of antigens A and B.
- Blood group A and B contains antigens A and B respectively; blood group AB contains both A and B antigens; and blood group O contains neither of the antigens.

The table illustrates which blood groups can be used in transfusion (blood transfer) for each of the four groups:

Donors Blood Group	Antigen	Antibody	Blood Group of People Donor can Receive Blood from	Blood Group of People Donor can Give Blood to
A	A	B	A, O	A, AB
B	B	A	B, O	B, AB
AB	A & B	–	A, B, AB & O	AB
O	–	A & B	O	A, B, AB & O

- Blood group O is called 'Universal Donor' and blood group AB is known as 'Universal recipient'.
- A suitable person in the age group of 18–61 can donate blood every 4 months and at one sitting 250ml of blood is collected.

Rhesus Factor (Rh): A group of antigens that may be or may not be present on the surface of the red blood cells or RBCs; it forms the basis of Rh blood group system.

- Those are having Rh factor are called Rh positive and who lacks the Rh factor are known as Rh negative; 85 per cent of the World population is Rh positive and rest is Rh negative.
- Incompatibility between Rh positive and Rh negative blood cause 'hemolytic' (destruction of RBCs) in newborn.
- Rh positive can receive the blood from both Rh positive and Rh negative but Rh negative can receive blood only from Rh negative.

Blood Coagulation (Blood Clotting): This is the process whereby blood is converted from liquid to solid state. The process involves the interaction of a variety of substances and lead to production of enzyme 'thromboplastin', which converts the soluble blood protein 'fibrogen' into insoluble protein 'fibrin'.

It is an essential mechanism for the stopping of bleeding.

Q.27. The vessels which carry blood away from heart are called?

Q.28. Where is the seat of memory in the human brain located?

Blood Pressure (BP): It is lateral pressure exerted on the wall of the blood vessels.
- When heart contracts to send the blood to different parts, it is called **systolic pressure** and when heart relaxes or refill of blood takes place, it is called as **diastolic pressure**.
- The average normal BP in an adult is (Systolic/Diastolic) 120/80 mm of Hg (Mercury). However the BP varies from person to person (in different physical and mental conditions).
- The range of normal BP is 140–100/90–60 mm of Hg.
- BP is measured (millimetres of mercury) by Sphygmomanometer.

VARIOUS SYSTEMS OF THE BODY

There are seven major systems in our body:
- Circulatory System
- Respiratory System
- Digestive System
- Urinary System
- Reproductive System
- Nervous System
- Musculo-Skeletal System

Circulatory System (Cardiovascular System)

Cardiovascular system effects the circulation of blood around the body, which brings about transport of nutrients and oxygen to the tissues and the removal of waste products.

The system consists of the heart and two sets of networks of the vessels: the **systemic circulation** (through which heart pumps the oxygenated or pure blood through arteries to different parts of the body except the lungs) and **pulmonary circulation** (the transport of blood between heart and lungs happens through arteries).

The deoxygenated blood (blood bearing carbon dioxide, hence impure) is carried by pulmonary artery to the lungs and after processing oxygenated blood pumps into the heart, through pulmonary veins.

The Heart

- Heart is a hollow muscular cone-shaped organ. It is the central pumping station of the circulatory system.
- It is situated in the left side of the central part of the chest cavity.
- It is divided by partitions into four chambers; the upper two are called **atrium** and the lower two are called **ventricles**.
- The blood vessels which carry blood from heart to other parts of the body are called **arteries** and those carry blood to heart called **veins**.
- Pulmonary veins carry oxygenated blood from the lungs to heart and the pulmonary artery carry deoxygenated blood from heart to the lungs to be purified through gaseous exchange

Q.29. Which gland in the human body is called Master Gland?
Q.30. Which gland controls blood pressure?

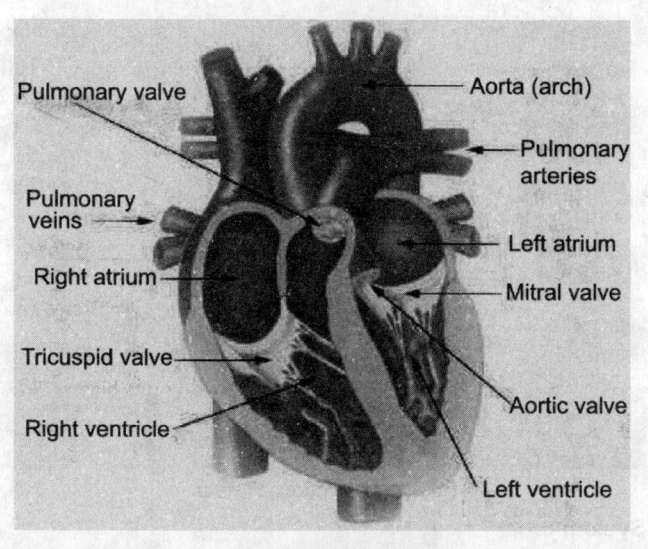

Internal View of the Heart

process (carbon dioxide leaving the circulation and oxygen entering).
- Average weight of the heart is 340 gms in men and 225 gms in women.
- Normal heart beat is 70–72 per minute.

Respiratory System

It is the combination of organs and tissues associated with breathing.
- It includes nostril (the nose), trachea (wind pipe), larynx (upper part of the wind pipe), bronchi (right and left), lung alveolus (called unit of respiratory system).
- Respiratory system involves two movements – **inspiration** (drawing in fresh air containing oxygen from outside) and **expiration** (expulsion of impure air containing carbon dioxide from within to outside).
- The main organ involved in the respiratory system is the lungs.

The Lungs

- There are two lungs – situated on either side of the heart in the chest cavity.
- The right lung is larger than the left one.
- Lungs are covered by serous membrane called **vascular pleura**.
- Lungs are fibrous elastic sacs that are expanded and compressed by movements of rib cage and diaphragm during breathing.
- Air enters through nasal cavity and passes through wind pipe (trachea), pharynx, bronchi which branch into bronchioles and ends at alveoli (air sac).
- The total capacity of the lungs in an adult male is about 5.5 litres, but during normal breathing only about 500 ml of air is exchanged.
- Along with blood purification, other functions of lungs include water evaporation, heat regulation of the body.
- Lungs weight between 1.18–1.19 kg in a healthy adult.

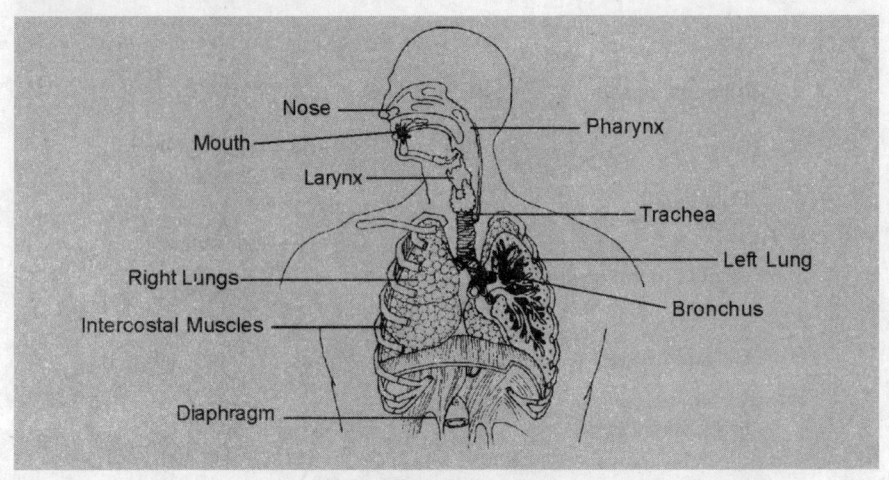

Human Respiratory System

Digestive System

This system involves the movement of food, the digestion and excretion.
- It starts with mouth cavity and ends at anus.
- Digestion involves the process in which the food is broken down in the alimentary canal into a form that can be absorbed and assimilated by the tissues of the body.
- It includes several mechanical processes such as chewing, churning and grinding foods as well as chemical action of digestive enzymes and other substances.
- Normally digestion starts at mouth with the action of saliva on food, but most part of the digestion occurs in stomach and small intestines, where the food is subjected to gastric juice, pancreatic juice.

Parts of Digestive System: Mouth, Pharynx (Food pipe), Oesophagus, Stomach, Small Intestine (Duodenum, Jejunum and Ileum) and Large intestine (Caecum, Colon – Ascending, transverse and descending, Rectum, Anal canal and Anus).

- Stomach is the centre of digestion, where food subjected to hydrochloric acid (HCl) and Pepsin enzyme.
- Small intestine performs the residual digestion and absorption with the help of various enzymes secreted in it and pancreatic juice (secreted from Pancreas), and bile juice (secreted from Liver).
- Large intestine functions being residual absorption and excretion of the residual or waste as formed faeces.

Organs Associated with Digestive System

Liver

It is the metabolic headquarter of the body.
- It is situated in the upper part of the right side of the abdominal cavity, just below the diaphragm.
- Liver is the largest gland; it weighs around 8.812 kg in a healthy adult.
- Gall bladder is attached to liver, which produces and stores bile.

General Science and Technology

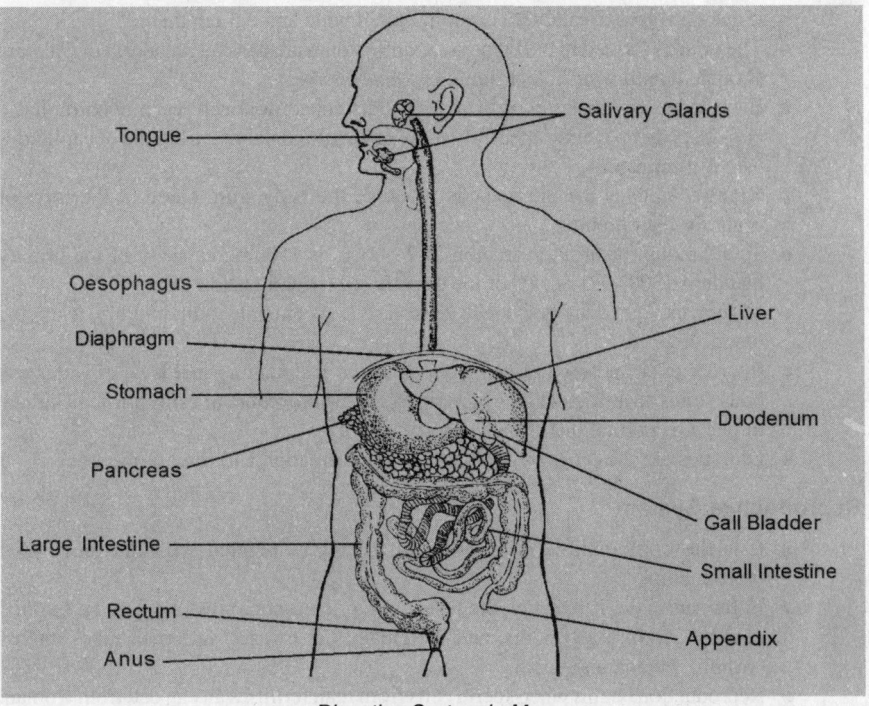

Digestive System in Man

- Other functions of the liver include maintaining of blood glucose level in the blood.

Pancreas

- Pancreas is situated behind the stomach.
- Secretions come via pancreatic duct and along with bile duct and opens in the duodenum through the Ampulla of vatir, a spincture (a valve).
- Pancreas also secretes the hormone 'insulin'.

Urinary System

- It constitutes the excretory mechanism for elimination of waste products from the body.
- The system consists of following parts: Kidney, Ureter (Urinary Tract), Urinary Bladder and Urethra.
- Excretion is the removal of waste products of metabolism from the body. It includes the loss of water, salts and urea through the sweat glands and carbon dioxide and water vapour from lungs and also ejection of faeces.
- There are two kidneys: one on either side of the abdominal cavity. Each

Q.31. 'Sub mucous Fibrosis' is a diseases related with which organ?

Q.32. Which hormone is secreted by the Pancreas?

kidney is approximately 10 cm long, 5 cm wide and 2.5 cm thick.
- The urine is formed in the kidneys. Kidney stones are basically made up of Calcium Oxalate due to insufficient liquid or water intake.
- Each kidney is made up of excretory units called **nephron**; each nephron has a cup-shaped upper end called **Bowman's capsule** containing a bundle of capillaries called **glumerulus**.
- Kidney removes the nitrogenous waste of the body from blood in the form of urine through urethra.
- Total amount of urine formation in 24 hours is 1500ml; capacity of the urinary bladder is 300–400 ml, P^H of the urine is six (slightly acidic).
- Kidney may get damaged due to several reasons like infection or injury, restricted blood flow, etc.
- In order to clean blood of metabolic waste to maintain normal level of water and body fluids an artificial kidney is employed; the procedure of using artificial kidney in place of normal one is called **dialysis**.
- Diuretics are the drugs which increase the formation and flow of the urine.

Reproductive System

- It is the combination of organs and tissues associated with the process of reproduction.
- In human male, it includes the testes, vasa deferentia, prostrate glands, seminal vesicles, urethra and penis, and in female, the ovaries, fallopian tubes, uterus (womb), vagina and vulva.
- Reproduction begins when sperm cells from man fertilises an egg cell from woman.
- A man's testes produce more sperm per second (about 2000) than a woman's ovary produce eggs in a lifetime (about 400).
- Seminal analysis is conducted in laboratory to examine the sperm count in the semens; sperm count is responsible to impregnate the woman (about 40 million or more per ml), semen should be adequate in quantity (approximately 4 ml).

Nervous System

- It is the vast network of cells specialised to carry out information in the form of impulses to and from all parts of the body in order to bring about bodily activities.

Nervous System

- Cerebro-spinal Nervous System or Voluntary Nervous System
  - ❒ Central Nervous System
  - ❒ Peripheral Nervous System
- Autonomic or Involuntary Nervous System
  - ❒ Sympathetic Nervous System
  - ❒ Para-sympathetic Nervous System
- Brain and Spinal Cord together form the Central Nervous System.
- Functions of the Nervous System: Coordination in the body, reception and reaction to external stimuli.
- Brain is located in skull and the Spinal

Q.33. In which vertebrate, oxygenated and deoxygenated blood get mixed?
Q.34. How many chromosomes does the human cell contains?

cord is located in vertebral column. The whole of the Central Nervous System is further protected by three successive layers of fibres covering called 'meninges'.
- The three layers of meninges from outer to inward are Piameter, Arachnoid meter and Durameter.
- In between these layers of meninges, is a fluid substance called Cerebro Spinal Fluid (CSF).

The Brain

- It consists of Cerebrum, the Cerebellum and the Medulla Oblongata.
- The average weight of brain of an adult male is 1.4 kg and 1.3 kg in case of female, which is about 3 per cent of the total body weight.
- Brain stores information equal to 5,00,000 sets of encyclopedia Britannica.
- Brain uses 20 per cent of oxygen, 20 per cent of total calorie intake and 15 per cent of blood of a person.
- *Cerebrum*: The largest part of the brain, which controls the thinking, speech and vision.
- It consists of two hemispheres or semi-circular parts joined together.
- *Cerebellum*: Mass of grey matter, lying above and behind medulla and connected to the brain stem, responsible for physical coordination and muscular movement and locomotion.
- It also has two hemispheres.
- *Medulla Oblongata*: The lowermost part of the brain; it controls involuntary functions, such as, circulatory system, digestive system, etc.
- The Neurons are the structural and functional unit of the nervous system. It is largest cell found in the body. It has three components: cell body, dendrites and axon.
- The brain consists of 100 billion neurons; 72.41 km of nerves send impulses as rapidly as 360 km/hr and the fastest nerve impulse travels at the rate of 532 km/hr.

Musculo-Skeletal System: (Bone, Joints and Muscles)

- Muscles are made up of elastic fibres. There are three types of muscles: Skeletal, Smooth and Cardiac Muscle.
- The skeletal muscles help in the movement of the body, while smooth muscles are found in the digestive system, blood vessels and in respiratory system.
- Cardiac muscles are found in the heart and help in the contraction and relaxation of the heart; these are involuntary in nature (not controlled by will).
- There are 639 muscles in human body, constituting 40 per cent of the total body weight.
- The largest muscle is Gluteus maximus or buttock muscle and smallest one is stapadius muscle in ear.
- The skeletal system consists of bones and joints.

Bones

- **Bones** are the hardest connective tissue and form the framework of the body.
- **Joints** are the meeting place between two or more bones.

Q.35. 'Bowman's capsule' is present in which organ of the body?

- New borne babies have about 300 bones and many of them fuse together as we grow up and an adult has about 206 bones.
- The largest bone of the body: 'femur' or the thigh bone (about ¼ of the total body height).
- The smallest bone is 'the stapes' or the stirrup-bone in the middle ear is only few millimeters.
- The strongest bone of the human body is the 'shin' bone (which connects the knee and the ankle, can support 1600 kg weight).
- More than half of the total number of bones found in hands and feet (about 106 bones): about 27 bones in each hand and 26 bones in each foot.
- Bone consists of inorganic part, e.g. Calcium and Phosphorous and inorganic part: matrix (inter-cellular substance) and bone cells (osteoblasts and osteocytes).

GLANDS OF HUMAN BODY

Glands are the specialised parts of the body that can secrete. There are two types of glands: Exocrine glands and Endocrine glands

Exocrine Glands: Those glands having ducts carry their secretions to the site of utilisation are called exocrine gland. For example, liver produces bile, salivary glands secretes saliva in mouth.

Endocrine Glands: These are ductless glands; their secretions are directly absorbed in blood. These secretions are called **hormones**, which are concerned with various metabolic functions of the body.

Following are some major endocrine glands:

(A) Pituitary Gland: It is located at the lower surface of the brain. It controls all other endocrine glands, hence called the **master gland**. It has two distinct parts: Anterior Pituitary, which secretes six hormones discussed below:

Growth Hormones: It is concerned with skeletal growth.

Adreno-Cortico Tropic Hormone (ACTH): It stimulates the Adrenal cortex to secrete adrenal cortical hormones.

Thyrotrophic Hormone or Thyroid Stimulating Hormone (TSH).

Gonad Tropic Hormones or Gonadotrophins: There are two distinct Gonadotrophins: Follicle Stimulating Hormones (FSH) and Luetinizing Hormones (LH).

Lactogenic Hormone or Prolactin: It stimulates milk secretion by fully developed mammary glands after child birth.

(B) Posterior Pituitary Glands: It secretes three hormones: (i) Vassopressin (ii) Oxytocin (iii) Anti Diuretic Hormones (ADH).

Thyroid Glands: It is located in the front of neck (butterfly shaped), having two lobes. It secretes the hormone called **thyroxine** – a metabolic hormone.

Enlargement of thyroid gland is generally called **goitre**. Excessive secretion of thyroxine causes the disease called **thyrotoxicosis** or Graves Disease.

Para-Thyroid Glands: These are four in numbers, situated at the beck of thyroid glands. This secretes the hormone 'parathormone', which controls the calcium and potassium metabolism.

Adrenal Glands: These are two in numbers,

Q.36. Which is the largest part of the brain?
Q.37. Which is the largest muscle in human body?

General Science and Technology 211

situated in abdomen. It has two parts: Adrenal Medulla (secretes Adrenaline) and Adrenal Cortex (secretes chemical steroids).

Adrenal cortex secretes cortisone, hydrocortisone (concerned with carbohydrate metabolism), aldosteron (concerned with water and electrolyte metabolism), testosterone and adrenosterone (masculine hormone), oestrogen and progesterone (feminine hormone).

Testes Glands (Male Sex Glands): These are two in number, situated within the scrotal sac. These secrete male sex hormone, testosterone.

Ovaries (Female Sex Glands): These are two in number, situated in each side of the abdomen. These secrete the hormone oestrogen and progesterone.

Pancreas: Situated at the posterior wall of the abdominal cavity. It secretes the hormone Insulin from the Beta cells of the Islands of Langerhans, which is the Anti-Diabetic Hormone (essential in carbohydrate metabolism). Deficiency of Insulin in the body causes Diabetes Mellitus.

HUMAN DIET

Body needs the food in appropriate quantity for overall growth. Essential materials in the food are called **nutrients**.

Balanced Diet: It means a diet that will supply all the nutrients necessary for the growth and development of the body. It should be able to provide 3000 calories per day for a normal adult.

Classification of Nutrients: Nutrients can be broadly classified on the basis of food stuffs as follows: (a) Carbohydrates, (b) Fats, (c) Proteins, (d) Minerals, (e) Vitamins, (f) Water Carbohydrates, fats and proteins are called **Macronutrients** since these are required in larger quantity.

Carbohydrates: Daily requirement is 500 gm (1gm provides 17 kilo joule of energy).

- *Sources*: Cereals (wheat, rice and maize), sugar, milk, fruit, honey, etc.
- Carbohydrates are of three types: Cellulose, Starch and Sugar.
- It is digested in stomach, alimentary canal and liver; it is supplied to the tissues in the form of glucose.
- Excess carbohydrate is stored in liver in the form of glycogen.

Fats: Daily requirement is 50 gm (1 gm provides 37 KJ of energy). These are concentrated source of energy and excess of fats are stored in liver as adipose tissues.

- Fats that circulate in the blood are of many types: Triglycerides, Phospholipids, etc.
- An enzyme called **lipase** digests fats and breaks it down to fatty acid and glycerol.
- *Sources*: Groundnut oil, sesame oil, sunflower oil, fishes and meats, etc.
- Higher quantity of fats increase the cholesterol level in the blood, causes blood pressure.

Proteins: Proteins comprises the chief substance of the muscles and tissues. These are essential for growth and repair of body.

- Amino acids are the Units of Protein. There are 20 amino acid normally found in the dietary proteins, out of which 10

Q.38. How many amino acids are synthesised in the body?
Q.39. Name the bacterium that causes Meningitis.

amino acid are synthesised in the body and rest to be supplied from external sources (called essential amino acids).
- A human adult requires eight essential amino acids while children require 9 or 10.

Minerals: Minerals accounts for about 4 per cent of the total body weight. Calcium and phosphorous form about ¾ of the total minerals; potassium, sulphur, chlorine, sodium and magnesium constitutes a bigger mass and rest in minute quantities are called **trace elements**.

- *Iron*: Hemoglobin of blood cells, which contains iron, carries oxygen in blood. Iron is found in green vegetables;
- Iodine helps in preparation of hormone Thyroxine is found in sea food and iodised salts;
- Calcium and phosphorous helps in bone and teeth formation; Sodium and potassium help in the contraction of heart muscles.
- *Water*: It is the vital constituent of the human diet which constitutes 70 per cent of the body weight. An average man contains 45 litres of water.
- Water is responsible for digestion and absorption of foods. It helps in transporting nutrients and body substances. It regulates body temperature and acts as purifying agent in the body and removes waste materials. Body gets water by drinking it and from other fluids.

Vitamins: Vitamins comprises **micronutrients**, since these are required in minute quantities. These are necessary for normal growth, good health, good vision, proper digestion of body, etc.

Vitamins are classified as **water soluble** vitamins – Vitamin B & B Complex and Vitamin C and **Fat soluble** vitamins – Vitamin A, Vitamin D, Vitamin E and Vitamin K.

Vitamins and Their Sources

Vitamins	Chemical Name	Sources	Deficiency Causes
Vitamin A	Retinol	Animal Fat, Eggs, Carrot Mangoes, Milk, Papayas	Night blindness, Dermatitis and Xerophthalmia
Vitamin B1	Thiamine	Cereals, Eggs	Beriberi
Vitamin B2	Riboflavin	Fish, Cereals	Ariboflavinosis
Vitamin B6	Pyridoxine	Cereals, Eggs	Convulsions in child
Vitamin B12	Cyanocabalamin	Eggs and cereals	Pernicious Anaemia
Vitamin C	Ascorbic Acid	Fruit, Orange, Lenons, Milk	Scurvey
Vitamin D	Calciferol	Fish, Eggs, Milk, Butter	Ricketts and Osteomalacia
Vitamin E	Tocopherol	Wheat germ, Milk, Eggs, Yolk	Sterility
Vitamin K	Phylloquinione	Wheat germ, Milk, cereals, Eggs	Hemophilia

HUMAN DISEASES

Diseases can be classified on the basis of their occurrence, which are as follows:

Epidemic: When a disease strikes many persons in a community, it is called epidemic. For example, cholera, smallpox, measles, etc.

Q.40. Who is affected by 'Foot and Mouth Disease?'
Q.41. Which disease is caused by the deficiency of vitamin B1?

General Science and Technology

Endemic Diseases: When the diseases strike the same region year after year, it is called endemic disease, e.g. Malaria.

Broadly all human diseases can be divided into the following main group:

1. Infective Diseases
2. Allergic Diseases
3. Traumatic Diseases
4. Degenerative Diseases
5. Metabolic and Endocrine Disorders
6. Deficiency Diseases
7. Neoplastic Diseases
8. Congenital Diseases

Infective Diseases

Diseases caused by infection of virus, bacteria, fungi and parasite, e.g. common cold, infective hepatitis (viral infection).

Insect borne Diseases

Disease	Spread by
Malaria	Female Anopheles Mosquitoes
Plague	Rat Flea
Leishmaniasis (Kalazar)	Sand Fly
Dengue fever	Aedes Mosquitoes

Diseases Caused by Virus: Chicken pox, Measles, Polio, Rabies, Mumps, Influenza, Hepatitis, Herpes, AIDS, Smallpox, Yellow Fever, etc.

Diseases Caused by Bacteria: Cholera, Diphtheria, Tuberculosis, Leprosy, Tetanus, Typhoid, Plauge, Whooping Cough, Sore throat, Pneumonia, Gonorrhea, Syphilis, Botulism, Meningitis, etc.

Diseases Caused by Fungi: Ringworm, Athlete's foot, Dhobie itch.

Diseases Caused by Parasite: Amobiasis, Malaria, Sleeping sickness, Kalazar (Leishmaniasis), Diarrhea, etc.

Diseases Caused by Worm: Filaria, Tapeworm, Hook worm, etc.

Diseases and Their Causative Organism:

Virus Borne Diseases	*Causative Organism*
Chickenpox	Varicella herpes
Influenza	Orthomyxo
Measles (Rubeola)	Paramyxovirus or togavirus
Poliomyelitis	Enterovirus
Rabies	Rabdo virus

Bacterium Borne Diseases	*Causative Organism*
Typhoid	Salmonella typhi
Tetanus	Clotridium titani
Cholera	Vibrio Cholera
Syphilis	Treponema pallidum
Pneumonia	Streptococcus pneumoniae
Gonorrhea	Neisseria gonorrhoeae
Leprosy	Mycobacterium leprae
Plague	Mycobacterium tuberculosis
Whooping cough	Berdetella pertusis

Meningitis	Meningococcus (bacterial meningitis or viral meningitis)
Diphtheria	Cornebacterium diptheriae

Allergic Diseases: Diseases caused by allergic or immune-allergic reaction in the body are urticaria, eczema, bronchial asthma, etc.

Traumatic Diseases: Diseases caused by trauma or injury like fracture of bone, burns, etc.

Degenerative Diseases: Diseases caused due to malfunction of some organ or organ system of the body, e.g. atherosclerosis (hardening of blood vessels with narrowing of its lumen), arthritis, diabetes mellitus, etc.

Metabolic and Endocrine Disorders: Diseases caused due to alteration of normal blood biochemistry and its effects on body.

Some of the metabolic disorders originate from generic disorders, e.g. Hypoglycemia (unusual low level of blood sugar).

Endocrine disorders caused by excessive or deficient hormonal secretion from specific endocrine glands, e.g. Thyrotoxicosis or Grave's disease (due to excessive secretion of Thyroxine).

Deficiency Diseases: Diseases caused by deficiency of nutrients or vitamins in the body.

Deficiency of	*Diseases caused*
(Diseases caused by Vitamin Deficiency have already been enlisted in the section on vitamins.)	*(Mineral Deficiency)*
Iron	Anemia
Iodine	Goitre
Sodium	Hyponatremia
Potassium	Hypokalemia

Neoplastic Diseases: Diseases caused due to neoplastic changes in the tissue (by some known or unknown causes), e.g. tumour (abnormal growth of tissue): may be benign tumour (do not readily spread from their original site) or malignant tumour (spread to distant tissues trough tissue connectivity or blood stream), e.g. leukaemia or blood cancer.

Congenital Diseases: Diseases caused due to single or multiple physical defects present from birth, e.g. harelip, cleft-palate, congenital heart diseases (defects in valves of the heart). Congenital defects may be corrected by timely surgical measures.

Diseases of Eye:

Astigmatism: Visual power is decreased, causes headache; it can be corrected by using cylindrical lens.

Cataract: Capacity of the lens in the eyes is decreased, may cause blindness. Artificial lens is used to correct it.

Glaucoma: Caused by defect in drainage and circulation of aqueous humour, may cause blindness.

Hypermetropia: Defect in short sight; corrected by using convex lens (or plus power lens).

Myopia: Defect in long sight; corrected by using concave lens (or minus power lens).

Presbiopia: Defect in close vision with difficulty in reading, corrected by appropriate glasses with plus power lens.

Q.42. Name the bacterium that causes Tetanus.

Q.43. Malaria affects which part of the body?

General Science and Technology

Diseases Affecting Different Parts of the Body

Disease	Affected Body Parts
AIDS	Immune System of the Body (Defensive Mechanism of Body)
Arthritis	Joints
Asthma	Bronchial Muscles (Lungs)
Cataract, Conjunctivitis	Eyes
Glaucoma, Trachoma	Eyes
Diabetes	Pancreas, Blood, Kidneys
Dermatitis	Skin
Diphtheria	Throat
Eczema	Skin
Goitre	Thyroid
Gout	Joints
Hepatitis, Jaundice	Liver
Malaria	Spleen, Liver
Meningitis	Brain
Ottis	Ear
Paralysis	Nerves, Limbs
Polio	Legs
Pyrrhoea	Teeth and Gums
Pleurisy	Lungs
Rheuhmatism	Joints
Pneumonia	Lungs
Sinusitis	Facial Bones
Typhoid	Intestines, Whole Body
Tuberculosis	Lungs
Tonsillitis	Glands in Throat (Tonsils)

PRINCIPLES OF MEDICAL TREATMENT

The basic treatment can be put under following three categories:

Specific Treatment: When exact nature and cause of the disease is well-known and the specific remedy is available, e.g. antibiotic used for the treatment of infectious diseases.

Symptomatic Treatment: Where the various distressful symptoms of a disease are treated with suitable drugs, e.g. analgesic drugs (pain killer) used for relief of pain, cough syrup for relief of coughs.

Supportive Treatment: It includes measures like rest, nutritive diets, etc., for general improvement of health, for enhancing early recovery.

Common Routes and Forms of Drug Administration

(i) By **oral route** as tablets, powders, mixtures (solutions, syrup suspensions).
(ii) By **Parenteral Injection:** Intravenous (IV), Intra muscular (IM), Sub-Cutaneous (SC), Intra dermal.

Q.44. With which part of the body is affected by Myopia ?
Q.45. Which part of the body is affected by Pyorrhea?

(iii) By **Inhalation:** Intra-nasal inhalation (oxygen, anaesthetics like chloroform, nitrous oxide, ether), Intra oral inhalation (medicated steam).
(iv) By **Rectal Route:** Suppository, enema.
(v) By **Topical Application:** (to the point of infection)
Skin – Powder, Cream, Ointment, Lotion, Adhesive, Plaster or Paste
Eye – Drop, Ointment, Lotion
Ear – Drop, Ointment
Gum – Paint
Throat – Paint, Lozenges
Intra-vaginal – Soluble Tablet, Vaginal Suppository

COMMON DRUGS

Analgesics: Analgesics are a class of drugs used to provide relieve from pain. The pain relief induced by analgesics occurs either by blocking pain signals going to the brain or by interfering with the brain's interpretation of the signals, without producing anaesthesia or loss of consciousness. There are basically two kinds of analgesics: local analgesics and general analgesics.

Antipyretics: These drugs are used to reduce body temperature.

Anaesthetics: Anaesthetics are the drugs that block sensory nerves that makes patient unconscious, so abolish the pain. Local anaesthetics are applied in particular area for making that area senseless.

Antibiotics: This kind of drug is used to treat infections caused by bacteria and other microorganisms. Antibiotic is a substance produced by one microorganism that selectively inhibits the growth of another.

Antihistamines: These are the drugs that combat the histamine released during an allergic reaction by blocking the action of the histamine on the tissue.

Enema: A quantity of fluid infused into the rectum through tune passed through the anus for desired action.

Lotion: A medical solution for washing or bathing the external parts of the body; usually it has cooling, soothing or antiseptic effect.

Narcotics: An addictive drug, that reduces pain, alters mood and behaviour, and usually induces sleep. Natural and synthetic narcotics are used in medicine to control pain.

Ointment: Greasy material, containing a medicament applied to skin or mucous membranes.

Paste: Medicinal preparation of a soft sticky consistency, which is applied externally for desired effect or action.

Sedatives: Drugs that are used to induce sleep.

Suppository: Medicinal preparation in solid form suitable for insertion into rectum or vagina, intended to act in the area of application.

Tranquillisers: These are medications that have calming effect on nervous system and prevent patients from stress, anxiety, etc.

Vaccines: Microbial preparations of killed or modified microorganisms that can stimulate an immune response in the body to prevent future infection by similar microorganisms.

General Science and Technology 217

MEDICAL INVENTIONS

Inventor	Inventions
Jean-Baptoste Denys	Blood Transfusion (1625)
William Harvey	Blood Circulation (1628)
Rene Laennec	Stethoscope (1819)
Samuel Guthrie	Chloroform (1831)
Alexander Wood	Hypodermic Syringe (1853)
Joseph Lister	Antiseptics (1867)
Sir Thomas Alllbutt	Clinical Thermometer (1867)
Robert Koch	Cholera and TB germs (1883)
Klebs N Loffler	Diphtheria Germs (1884)
Scipione Riva-Rocci	Sphygmomanometer (1896)
Dr Felix Hoffman	Aspirin (1899)
K Landsteiner	Blood Group (1902)
William Einstoven	Electrocardiogram (ECG) (1903)
Frederick Banting/Charles Best	Isolated Insulin (1921)
Alexander Fleming	Penicillin; it paved the way for antibiotics (1928)
Willem Kolff	Kidney Dialysis Machine (1944)
Ian Donald	Ultrasound (1950)
Carl Djerassi	Contraceptive Pill (1951)
John P. Merril	Organ Transplant (1953)
Wilson Greatbatch	Heart Pacemaker (1960)
Christian Barnard	Heart Transplant (1967)
Godfrey Hounsfield	CAT Scanner (1973)
Vaccines	
Edward Jenner	Vaccine for Small Pox (1796)
Louis Pasteur	Vaccine for Cholera (1880)/Rabbies (1885)
Emil Adolf Von Behring & Shibasaburo Kitasato	Vaccine for Diphtheria and Tetanus
Charles Nicolle	Vaccine for Typhus (1909)
Albert Calmette & Camille Guerin	Vaccine for TB (1922)
John F Enders & Thomas Peeble	Vaccine for Measles (1953)
Albert Buce Sabin	Oral Polio Vaccine (1955)
Jonas Salk	Vaccine for Polio (1955)

MEDICAL TECHNOLOGY

1. Diagnostic Instruments
2. Imaging Instruments
3. Therapeutic Instruments

Diagnostic Instruments

Electro Cardiography (*ECG*): Detects changes in 'electrical potentials' generated by contraction of heart muscles, which are recorded

Q.46. What is the name of the instrument that is used to measure the pulse rate?

by placing two special electrodes over particular point of the body. It helps in diagnosis of heart diseases, including myocardial infarction (or coronary thrombosis), myocardial ischaemia, cardiac arrhythmia.

Electro Encephalograph (EEG): Records the electrical activity of the brain on suitable paper, with the help of two special electrodes placed on the scalp. It helps in diagnosis of epilepsy, intracranial tumours (or brain tumours).

Electromyography (EMG): Involves graphic recording of muscle 'action potentials', which helps in diagnosis of various neuromuscular or muscular diseases and disorders.

Autoanalysers: These are computerised instruments that estimate accurate biochemicals present in the body fluids like urea, cholesterols, glucose, proteins, etc.

Sphygmomanometer: An instrument used to measure the blood pressure.

Shygmometer: An instrument used to measure the pulse rate.

Bronchioscope: An instrument with a lighted tube, which is passed down the trachea (wind pipe) for examination of air tubes of the lungs.

Cystoscope: An instrument used to examine the inside of the urinary bladder.

Laproscope: An instrument used to examine the abdominal cavity.

Imaging Instruments

Tomography: Used to create 3D-image of internal parts of the body, at any depth. It helps in diagnosis of cysts, calculi, cancer, etc.

CT Scanning: Technique used to scan the internal body parts through use of radioactive isotopes, having specific affinity for tissues of the organ to be scanned (e.g. I^{131} for thyroid gland). It helps in diagnosis of disorder in abdomen, chest, spinal cord, etc.

Computerised Axial Tomography (CAT) Scanning: A development of diagnostic radiology for examination of soft tissues of the body, through use of X-ray. It helps to reveal normal anatomy of brain, distinguish pathological conditions, such as, tumors, abscess in ventricles, etc.

Magnetic Resonance Imaging (MRI) Scanning: Sophisticated method of scanning using natural safe forces, viz., magnetic fields and radio waves having greater preciseness.

Ultrasound Scan: Used to reveal structural anatomy or stone in Urinary tract or kidney.

Endoscope: An instrument used for internal examinations by direct vision through lighted tubes fitted with a system of lenses.

Therapeutic Instruments

Artificial Kidney: It is a device containing tubes of chambers of a special membranes immersed in bath dialysing solutions, used to remove waste material from the blood of the patient, whose kidney do not work properly.

Pacemaker: It is a device used to produce and maintain a normal heart rate in patients, who have 'heart block'. It may be used as temporary measure with external battery or it may be permanent, when whole apparatus is surgically implanted under skin.

Angioplasty: Used to open blocked coronary artery vessel through ballooning.

Angiography: It is X-ray examination of blood. An X-ray opaque dye in injected into artery and a series of X-ray films are taken. It helps in diagnosis of health of heart wall, valves, ventricles, coronary arteries, etc.

Q.47. What are the anti-bodies that participate in the defence mechanism of our body made up of?

General Science and Technology

SCIENTIFIC EXPLANATIONS OF SOME FACTS

1. When a pendulum clock is taken to poles from equator, the time period will decrease because the value of acceleration due to gravity (g) decreases with latitude.
2. When a pendulum clock is taken to moon, its period of oscillation increases and hence it loses time.
3. Rain drops are spherical in shape due to surface tension, as they tend to have minimum surface area.
4. The shape of water molecules in a capillary tube is concave because the adhesive force between water and glass molecules is higher than the cohesive force between water molecules. The reverse is the case with mercury.
5. Soap reduces surface tension of water; hence it helps dirt particles get detached from cloths.
6. Water sticks to the finger because the adhesive force between water and particles and fingers is higher than the cohesive forces between water particles. The case is reverse when the finger is dipped into mercury.
7. Milk van is painted white because white absorbs minimum heat and hence keeps the milk fresh.
8. The coins of gold, silver and copper are not cast, i.e. not made from molten metal, because on solidification their designs get distorted. To avoid such distortions, the coins are stamped in heavy duty press.
9. When a man with a load jumps from a high building, the load experienced by him is zero. Because while falling, both the man and the load are falling with the same acceleration, i.e. acceleration due to gravity.
10. Steel is more elastic than the rubber for the same stress produced as compared with rubber.
11. The weight of a person on the surface on the moon will be 1/6 of his actual weight on earth as the gravity of the moon is 1/6 that of the earth.
12. A liquid burns if its molecules can combine with oxygen in the air with the production of heat; hence oil burns but water does not.
13. A solid chunk of iron sinks in water but floats in mercury because the density of iron is more than that of water but less than that of mercury.
14. Stars twinkle because when the light from stars passes through the earth's atmosphere it gets flickered by the hot and cold ripples of air and it appears as if the star is twinkling.
15. Magnetic needle of a compass because of the influence of the earth's magnetic field lies in a north-south direction. Hence we can identify direction with the help of magnet.
16. Kerosene floats on water because the density of kerosene is less than that of water.
17. It is difficult to breathe at higher altitude because due to low air pressure the quantity of air is less.
18. It is easier to swim in the sea than in the river because the density of sea water is higher than river water; hence up thrust is more.

Q.48. What is the genome of AIDS virus made up of?
Q.49. For treating which organ, dialysis is used?

19. Milk turns sour because the microbes react with milk and convert lactose to lactic acid, which is sour in taste.
20. Two eyes gives better vision than one because two eyes do not form exactly similar images and fusion of these two dissimilar images in the brain gives three dimensions of the stereoscopic vision.
21. The mass of an iron rod increases on rusting because on rusting hydrogen and oxygen get added and form ferric oxide, which adds to the mass of iron rod.

COMPUTER

A computer can be defined as an electronic data processing device, capable of reading, writing, computing, storing and processing large volume of data with speed and accuracy with reliability.

Computer Applications

Health and Medicine: Computers are helping to monitor patents and provide cross-sectional views of the body. Doctors use computers to assist them in diagnosing certain diseases.

Agriculture: Farmers use computers to help with billing, crop information and cost per acre, feed combinations and market price checks, for information about livestock breeding, etc.

Banking: Computer is used to maintain the account of the customers. Internet banking is another use of computer.

Traffic control: Computer helps police in traffic control, to regulate the traffic light.

Sports: In sports computers are used wildly in conjunction with video cameras. These are used to record the motion of all the sports men.

Schools and Colleges: There are many uses of computer in schools and colleges, e.g. student data is stored in computer. Multimedia, animations, graphics and charts could be used to teach the students.

Classification

Computers can be classified by size and power as follows:

Mainframe Computer: These are expensive, large and centralised computer facilities, where a super computer (e.g. PARAM or CYBER) is connected to several terminals. These are capable of supporting many hundreds or thousands of users simultaneously and have large memory and perform the assigned tasks (several billions per second).

Mini Computer: A multi-user computer capable of supporting from 10 to hundreds of users simultaneously.

Personal Computer: A small, single-user computer. These are used in education, entertainment, information sharing, emailing, online banking operations, etc.

Workstation: A powerful, single-user computer. A workstation is like a personal computer, but it has a more powerful microprocessor and a higher-quality monitor.

Q.50. What does the Central Processing Unit (CPU) consists of?
Q.51. What are the two kinds of main memory?

Measurements of Memory

a bit = one binary digit (1 or 0)
'Bit' is derived from the contraction bit (binary digit)
8 bits = one byte
One kilobyte = 1024 bytes
One megabyte = 1024 kilobytes.
One gigabyte = 1024 megabytes
bps = bits per second
K = kilobyte
Kb = kilobit
B = megabyte
Mb = megabit
MB/s = megabytes per second
Mb/s = megabits per second

Parts of a Computer

A computer consists of following parts: (i) An Input Device, (ii) An Output Device, (iii) The CPU.

Input Device: This is the conduit through which data and instructions are entered into a computer, e.g. keyboard and mouse, Optical Mark Reader (OMR), Optical Character Reader (OCR) and Magnetic Ink Character Recognition (MICR).

Keyboard: It is the device used to put data into computer. The speed of performance depends on the speed of the typing.

Optical Mark Reader (OMR)

- The Optical Mark Reader is a device that recognises the marks and characters. OMR can scan forms such as surveys or test answer forms written in either pen or pencils.
- The computer test forms designed for the OMR are known as NCS compatible scan forms. Tests and surveys completed on these forms are read by the scanner, checked, and the results are saved to a file.

Magnetic Ink Character Recognition (MICR)

- MICR is a character recognition technology; the characters are first magnetised in the plane of the paper with a North Pole on the right of each MICR character.
- It employs character styles designed specifically for Magnetic Ink Character Recognition, so that character can be formed accurately.
- Since it requires magnetic ink, the printing is expensive.
- Mainly adopted by the banking industry to facilitate the processing of cheques, but the amount issued, signature, date of issue, etc., are verified manually.

Optical Character Reader (OCR)

- OCR is a type of mail sorting machine that uses Optical Character Recognition technology to determine how to route mail through the postal system.

Q.52. Which input device is used in the banking industry to facilitate the processing of cheques?

- It works by capturing images of the front of letter-sized mail pieces and extracting the entire address from each piece.
- It looks up the postal code within each address in a master database, prints a barcode representing this information on the mail piece, and performs an initial sort.
- All of this occurs in a fraction of a second as the mail piece passes through the machine. The United States Postal Service is the largest user of these machines.

Output Device: It is a display screen, printer, or other device that lets you see what the computer has accomplished.

Printer: It is used to take the hard copy on the content in the computer.

Plotters: A line drawing device, which moves a pen in such a way that continuous lines and curves can be dawn. This device is used to draw maps, graphs, engineering drawing, etc., where precision of line drawing is much necessary.

Video Display Unit (VDU)

- A computer output device that uses a cathode ray tube or other technology to present visual images.
- The typical VDU creates images in a large evacuated cathode-ray tube (CRT) by directing a beam of high-energy electrons from the cathode onto a special glass screen.
- This coating emits light when struck by the fast-moving electrons. The electron beam creates the image from computer signals that control coils, at the back of the CRT, that sweep the electrons in the vertical and horizontal directions.
- These coils are called vertical and horizontal deflection coils. The electronic circuit used to create the image gives rise to static electric and magnetic fields, as well as low and high frequency electromagnetic fields.

Central Processing Unit (CPU)

- The CPU is the brain of the computer, where most calculations take place. In terms of computing power, the CPU is the most important element of a computer system.
- The CPU itself is an internal component of the computer. Modern CPUs are small and square and contain multiple metallic connectors or pins on the underside.
- The CPU is inserted directly into a CPU socket, pin side down, on the motherboard. Each motherboard will support only a specific type or range of CPU, so you must check the motherboard manufacturer's specifications before attempting to replace or upgrade a CPU.

CPU has the following two components:

- The *arithmetic logic unit (ALU)* is the part of a computer that performs all arithmetic computations, such as addition and multiplication, and all comparison operations.
- *Control unit (CU)* is the part that implements the microprocessor instruction set. It extracts instructions from memory and decodes and executes them, and sends the necessary signals

Q.53. What does one kilobyte equals to?

Q.54. What does the secondary storage device that follows the sequential mode of access called?

to the ALU to perform the operation needed. Control Units are either *hardwired* (instruction register is hardwired to rest of the microprocessor) or *micro-programmed*.

Opearting System

Operating systems perform basic tasks, such as recognising input from the keyboard, sending output to the display screen, keeping track of files and directories on the disk, and controlling peripheral devices such as disk drives and printers, e.g. DOS, UNIX, etc.

Components of computer are Hardware, Software and OS.

Operating systems can be classified as follows:

Multi-user: It allows two or more users to run programs at the same time. Some operating systems permit hundreds or even thousands of concurrent users.

Multi-processing: Supports running a program on more than one CPU.

Multi-tasking: Allows more than one program to run concurrently.

Multi-threading: Allows different parts of a single program to run concurrently.

Languages

There are two kinds of languages – Low level Language and High level Language – that are used in computers.

Low Level Language is again of two types: Machine Language and Assembly language;

Machine Language

- This is the lowest-level programming language (except for computers that utilize programmable microcode). Machine language is the only language understood by the computers.
- The language is in the form of binary codes – zeroes and ones.
- While easily understood by computers, machine language is almost impossible for humans to use because they consist entirely of the numbers.

Assembly Language

- Since machine language can only be executed by computer, it is difficult to remember the instructions in the form of binary codes; this resulted into development of a simpler language called assembly language.
- Assembly languages have the same structure and set of commands as machine languages, but they enable a programmer to use names instead of numbers.
- An assembly language contains the same instructions as a machine language, but the instructions and variables have names instead of being just numbers.
- Each type of CPU has its own machine language and assembly language.

High-Level Language

- It enables a programmer to write programs that are more or less independent of a particular type of computer. Such languages are considered high-level because they are closer to human languages and further from machine languages.

Q.55. In MSWord, which combination of keys is pressed to delete immediately without putting the file in Recycle Bin?

224 General Knowledge Manual

- The main advantage of high-level language over low-level language is that it is easier to read, write and maintain, however these languages are not understood by computer, which require a compiler or interpreter.
- The first high-level programming languages were designed in the 1950s. Now there are dozens of different languages, including Ada, Algol, BASIC, COBOL, C, C++, FORTRAN, LISP, Pascal and Prolog.
- Now, most programs are written in a high-level language such as FORTRAN or C.

Networking

It is a system to connect two or more computers together with the ability to communicate with each other.

Computers on a network are sometimes called *nodes*. Computers and devices that allocate resources for a network are called *servers*.

There are many types of computer networks, including:

(1) Local Area Networks (LAN)

- The computers are in geographically small area like in the same building, office, campus, etc.
- However, one LAN can be connected to other LANs over any distance via telephone lines and radio waves.
- Most LANs connect workstations and personal computers. Each *node* (individual computer) in a LAN has its own CPU with which it executes programs, but it is also able to access data and devices anywhere on the LAN.
- This means that many users can share expensive devices, such as laser printers, as well as data. Users can also use the LAN to communicate with each other, by sending e-mail or engaging in chat sessions.
- Data transfer takes place through this medium. It can be a telephone line or a coaxial cable or a fibre optical cable. Some networks do communicate without connecting media altogether, instead they communicate via radio waves.
- Network Interface Unit provides the base for LAN medium and computer hardware.
- Network software runs in each of the computers connected to LAN and provides the means to user software.

Common LAN Configurations

Star Configuration: In this case all the nodes are connected to server to form a star like picture.

Bus Configuration: Here all the nodes on LAN share the same cable in a back to back position.

Ring Configuration: In this scheme, the nodes are connected in a series and form a ring. Data flow from one terminal to another and is picked up by appropriate server.

Wide Area Networks (WAN)

- A computer network that spans a relatively large geographical area.
- The computers are farther apart and are connected by telephone lines or radio waves.

Q.56. What is the unit that performs the arithmetic and logical operation on the stored numbers known as?

- Computers connected to a wide area network are often connected through public networks, such as the telephone system. They can also be connected through leased lines or satellites. The largest WAN in existence is the Internet.

Campus Area Networks (CAN): The computers are within a limited geographic area, such as a campus or military base.

Metropolitan Area Networks (MAN): A data network designed for a town or city.

Networks can be broadly classified as using either a *peer-to-peer* or *client/server* architecture.

INTERNET

The internet, sometimes called 'the net', is a worldwide system of computer networks. It is a vast network of computers, in which one user can, get information from any other computer (if have permission).

Internet penetration in India has witnessed a dramatic growth in last few years. Now India has an online internet community of 32.1 million and total in the world is 1007.7 million.

India is in the seventh position worldwide in terms of unique visitors. China, United States, Japan, Germany, the UK and France are in the first six positions respectively; Russia, Brazil and South Korea stand next to India. (*Source: comScore World Metrix, released on 23 January 2009*). Internet is accessible in more than 150 countries.

Internet is not governed by any government or institution, however directed by Internet Society (ISOC), composed of volunteers. Internet is composed of people, hardware and software.

Origin of Internet: It was conceived by the Advanced Research Projects Agency (ARPA) of the US government in 1969 and was first known as the ARPANET. The original aim was to create a network that would allow users of a research computer at one university to be able to 'talk to' research computers at other universities.

A side benefit of ARPANet's design was that, because messages could be routed or rerouted in more than one direction, the network could continue to function even if parts of it were destroyed in the event of a military attack or other disaster.

World Wide Web (WWW): A system of internet servers that support specially formatted documents. The documents are formatted in a markup language called HTML (Hyper Text Markup Language) that supports links to other documents, as well as graphics, audio and video files. Not all internet servers are part of the World Wide Web.

There are several applications called web browsers that make it easy to access the World Wide Web; two of the most popular being Netscape Navigator and Microsoft's Internet Explorer.

There are a variety of ways to access the Internet. Most online services, such as America Online (AOL), MSN, etc., offer access to some Internet services. It is also possible to access through a commercial Internet Service Provider (ISP). Satyam, Dish Net, etc., are some of the ISPs in India.

An email is the address that helps to make contact with any person in the world. It has three

Q.57. What is meant by Boot (ing)?

Q.58. Which UPS is used in banking technology?

parts: user name, service provider and domain name. For example, info@yahoo.com, where info is the user name, Yahoo is the service provider and .com is the domain name.

A consortium between AT&T and Network Solutions called InterNIC (Internet Information System) manages the task of registering address or domain names.

Commonly Used Domain Names: .com (a commercial organisation, business or company), edu (an educational institution), gov (a non-military government entity), mil (a military organisation), int (an international organisation), net (a network administration). Also domains indicate the country of origin like in (for India), jp (for Japan) and uk (for UK) etc.

COMPUTER TERMINOLOGY

Access Time: The performance of a hard drive or other storage device – how long it takes to locate a file.

Application: A program in which you do your work.

ASCII (American Standard Code for Information Interchange): A commonly used data format for exchanging information between computers or programs.

Bit: The smallest piece of information used by the computer; derived from 'binary digit'; in computer language, either a one (1) or a zero (0).

Boot: To start up a computer.

Bug: A programming error that causes a program to behave in an unexpected way.

Bus: An electronic pathway through which data is transmitted between components in a computer.

Byte: A piece of computer information made up of eight bits.

Card: A printed circuit board that adds some feature to a computer.

Clipboard: A portion of memory where the Mac temporarily stores information, called a Copy Buffer in many PC applications because it is used to hold information which is to be moved, as in word processing where text is 'cut' and then 'pasted'.

Clock Rate (MHz): The instruction processing speed of a computer measured in millions of cycles per second (i.e. 200 MHz).

Command: The act of giving an instruction to your Mac either by menu choice or keystroke.

Compiler: A program the converts programming code into a form that can be used by a computer.

Compression: A technique that reduces the size of a saved file by elimination or encoding redundancies (i.e. JPEG, MPEG, LZW, etc.)

Control Panel: A program that allows you to change settings in a program or change the way a Mac looks and/or behaves.

Central Processing Unit or CPU: It is the processing chip that is called the 'brain' of a computer.

Crash: A system malfunction in which the computer stops working and has to be restarted.

Desktop File: An invisible file in which the Finder stores a database of information about files and icons.

DOS: Acronym for Disk Operating System – used in IBM PCs.

Q.59. What does WAIS stands for?
Q.60. Who/what is known as the precursor to internet?

DPI: Acronym for Dots per Inch – a gauge of visual clarity on the printed page or on the computer screen.

Driver: A file on a computer which tells it how to communicate with an add-on piece of equipment (like a printer).

EDP: Electronic Data Processing is the processing of data with electronic equipment.

Ethernet: A protocol for fast communication and file transfer across a network.

File: The generic word for an application, document, control panel or other computer data.

Folder: An electronic subdirectory which contains files.

Freeze: A system error which causes the cursor to lock in place.

Flow Chart: A graphic representation of the definition analysis or solution to a problem in which symbols are used to represent operation, data flow or equipment.

Hard Drive: A large capacity storage device made of multiple disks housed in a rigid case.

Hard Ware: Physical equipment such as mechanical, magnetic, electrical or electronic devices.

Interrupt Button: A tool used by programmers to enter the debugging mode. The button is usually next to the reset button.

Memory: The temporary holding area where data is stored while it is being used or changed; the amount of RAM a computer has installed.

Multi-tasking: Running more than one application in memory at the same time.

Nanosecond: One billionth of a second. (Or, the time between the theatrical release of a Dudley Moore film and the moment it begins to play on airplanes).

Operating System: The system software that controls the computer.

PCI: Acronym for Peripheral Component Interchange – the newer, faster bus architecture.

Print Spooler: A program that stores documents to be printed on the hard drive, thereby freeing the memory up and allowing other functions to be performed while printing goes on in the background.

Processor: A general term for any device capable of carrying our operation on data; sometime used as a synonym for central processor.

QuickTime: The Apple system extension that gives one the ability to compress, edit and play animation, movies and sound on the Mac.

Real Time: Method of operations where data is absorbed by the computer at the actual time of its occurrence.

Server: A central computer dedicated to sending and receiving data from other computers (on a network).

Software: Files on disk that contain instructions for a computer.

Source Language: A language used by the programmer to write a computer program.

String: A line of symbols of indefinite length treated as a single i=unit.

Start up Disk: The disk containing system software and is designated to be used to start the computer.

System File: A file in the system folder that allows your Mac to start and run.

System Folder: An all-important folder that contains at least the system file and the finder.

Time Sharing: A mode of operation in which several users through numerous terminal devices, share access to a central computer concurrently and interrupt with the programs during execution.

Time Slicing: A mode of operation in which the computer performs on one program for a short while, then goes to work on another programme for another short time and so forth.

Uninterruptible Power Source (UPS): Acronym for Uninterruptible Power Source; a constantly charging battery pack which powers the computer. An UPS should have enough charge to power your computer for several hours in the event of a total power failure, giving you time to save your work and safely shut down.

Virtual Memory: Using part of your hard drive as though it were 'RAM'.

WORM: Acronym for Write Once-Read Many; an optical disk that can only be written to once (like a CD-ROM).

Zero Suppression: Deleting leading zeros from number in order to make results more readable.

Zoom Box: A small square in the upper right corner of a window which, when clicked, will expand the window to fill the whole screen.

KEYBOARD SHORTCUTS

Keys	Functions
MS Natural Keyboard	
Win+E	Explorer
Win+M	Minimise All
Shift-Win+M	Undo Minimise All
Win+F/F3/Ctrl+F	Find Files or Folders
HOME	To beginning of line or far left of field or screen
Ctrl+Home	To the top
Ctrl+END	to the bottom
General control over folders/Windows Explorer	
F1	Help
F2	Rename
F5	Refresh
F11	Toggle Full Screen
Editing	
Ctrl+Z	Undo
Ctrl+Y	Redo
Ctrl+A	Select All
Ctrl+X	Cut
Ctrl +C	Copy
Ctrl +V	Paste
Ctrl+P	Print
Ctrl+S	Save
Ctrl+Alt+Del	Reboot the computer
Alt+F4	Shuts down the selected program
Ctrl+W	Close Tab
Shift+Delete	Delete immediately without putting the file in Recycle Bin
Ctrl+O	Open File
Ctrl+N	Open New Window

ANSWERS

1. 11 km/s
2. Robert Brown
3. 4°C
4. Copper and Tin
5. Carbon dioxide
6. Hygrometer
7. $NaHCO_3$
8. Capacitance
9. Polaroids
10. Magnesium
11. Temperature
12. Sublimation
13. D_2O
14. Isobars
15. Pancreas
16. Real and inverted
17. Sodium thiosulphate
18. Malleability
19. Eugenics
20. For measuring relative humidity in the atmosphere.
21. Enrico Fermi
22. Cellulose
23. Mitochondria
24. To carry oxygen
25. 7.4
26. Lactobacillus
27. Arteries
28. Cortex
29. Pituitary Gland
30. Adrenal glands
31. Oral cavity
32. Insulin
33. Amphibian
34. 46
35. Kidney
36. Cerebrum
37. Gluteus maximus or buttock muscle
38. 10
39. Meningococcus
40. Cattle
41. Beriberi
42. Clostridium
43. Spleen
44. Eyes
45. Gums
46. Shygmometer
47. Proteins
48. RNA
49. Kidney
50. Control unit, arithmetic- logic unit and primary storage
51. ROM and RAM
52. Magnetic Ink Character Recognition (MICR)
53. 1024 bytes
54. Magnetic Tape
55. Shift + Delete
56. Arithmetic Logic Unit (ALU)
57. To start up a computer.
58. On-line
59. Wide Area Information System
60. ARPANET

9
ENVIRONMENTAL SCIENCE

ENVIRONMENT

It is defined as the natural world in which people, animals and plants live.

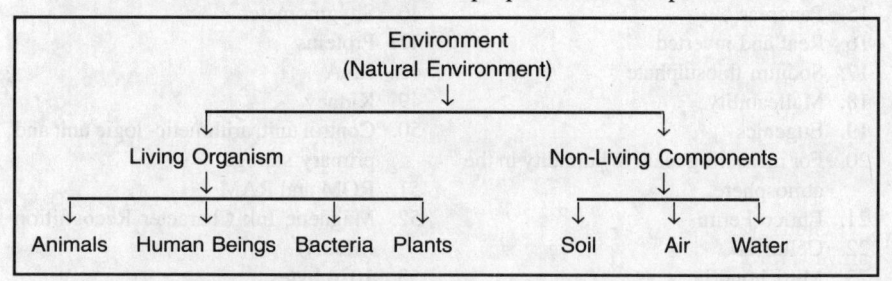

```
                    Environment
                (Natural Environment)
                          ↓
            ↓                           ↓
      Living Organism            Non-Living Components
            ↓                           ↓
  ↓      ↓       ↓       ↓        ↓      ↓      ↓
Animals  Human  Bacteria Plants  Soil   Air   Water
         Beings
```

- The environment provides resources which support life on the earth and which also help in the growth of a relationship between living organisms and the environment in which they live.
- For better environment, all its components should be protected from pollution and the surroundings should be clean. We need to take care of our land, water resources, forests and atmosphere.
- It is also necessary to ensure a balance between these resources and living organisms, to meet our needs.

Ecology: Study of plants and animals in relation to one another and to their surroundings is ecology. Different plants and animals are found in different environments, suitable to them. Any change in that environment may affect their living.

Ecological Balance: It is an ideal condition where we can live together with plants and animals, without disturbing each other.

Environmental Science: The systematic and scientific study of our environment and our role in it. It integrates knowledge from pure sciences, ecology, engineering, management and social science.

Environmental Pollution: Environmental pollution is caused due to overuse of natural resources, presence of a large number of people and livestock in congested areas, use of agro-chemicals, setting up of factories, running of automobiles, burning of fuel, etc. Environmental pollution is caused both in rural and urban areas.

Environmental Science 231

A change in the environment due to pollution also affects the ecological balance.
Biodiversity: It is a mixture of two words – biological and diversity, which means diversity of life forms.

- Biodiversity is defined as the number and variability of all the life forms pertaining to plants, animals and micro-organisms and the ecological complex they live.
- It also covers the entire range of life forms, the relationship between plants and animal and with other living organisms.
- Biodiversity has been an important aspect of human existence, since it meets the basic survival needs of a vast number of people.
- Even today there are a significant number of traditional communities which depend, wholly or partially, on the surrounding natural resources for their daily needs of food and shelter, clothing, household goods, medicines, etc.
- Other benefits of biodiversity are the preservation and continuance of the food chain. It is established that each species in a food web is dependent on the other.
- The extinction of any one species therefore, may let loose a chain reaction where many known and unknown life forms would perish altogether.
- Some instances of biodiversity loss in India include cheetah and the pink-headed duck. The adverse effects of biotic pressures on fisheries can be easily noticed in the Damodar and Hoogly rivers in West Bengal, Choliyar river near Calicut and Kalu river near Kalyan, Mumbai.

GLOBAL WARMING

Global warming is an average increase in the temperature of the atmosphere near the earth's surface and in the troposphere, which can contribute to changes in global climate patterns.

Global warming can occur from a variety of causes, both natural and human induced.

Also 'global warming' often refers to the warming that can occur as a result of increased emissions of greenhouse gases from human activities.

Global surface temperature has increased $0.74 \pm 0.18°$ C during the last century.

The Intergovernmental Panel on Climate Change (IPCC) concludes that increasing greenhouse gas concentrations resulting from human activity such as fossil fuel burning and deforestation caused most of the observed temperature increase since the middle of the twentieth century.

Causes of Global Warming: These are several causes of global warming:

(i) *Carbon dioxide Increasing in Atmosphere:* The atmospheric levels of the greenhouse gas carbon dioxide have increased 34 per cent, since pre-industrial times. Carbon dioxide is a by-product of the burning of fossil fuel to generate electricity, burning of gasoline in automobiles, etc.

(ii) *Increase of Methane* (a powerful greenhouse gas): Levels of atmospheric methane have risen 145 per cent in the last 100 years. Methane is derived from sources, such as, rice paddies, bovine flatulence, bacteria in bogs and fossil fuel production.

(iii) *Increasing of Water Vapour in the*

Q.1. When is the National Wildlife Week observed?
Q.2. Which is the major greenhouse gas which is responsible for maximum effect?

Atmosphere: Water vapour is the most prevalent and powerful greenhouse gas, but its increasing presence is the result of warming caused by carbon dioxide, methane and other greenhouse gases.

(iv) *Nitrous Oxide*: Nitrous oxide is naturally produced by oceans and rainforests. Also man-made sources of nitrous oxide include nylon and nitric acid production, the use of fertilisers in agriculture, cars with catalytic converters and the burning of organic matter.

(v) *Deforestation*: Deforestation accounts for about 20–25 per cent of all carbon emissions entering the atmosphere, by cutting of million acres of trees each year.

(vi) *Carbon in Atmosphere and Ocean*: The atmosphere contains about 750 billion tonnes of carbon, while 1020 billion tonnes are dissolved in the surface layers of the world's ocean and also soils contain 1580 billion tons of carbon and Deep Ocean contains 38100 billion tonnes of carbon. (*Source: US Global Change Research Information Office*)

Global Warming Effects: Since greenhouse gases stay in the atmosphere for years so global warming is going to have some effect on earth. These are few of them:

(i) *Greenhouse Effect*: Earth is warmed by radiant energy from the sun that reaches the surface through the atmosphere. As the surface warms, heat energy reflect back toward space; meanwhile, gases in the atmosphere absorb some of this energy and reradiate it near the surface. This is called the greenhouse effect.

(ii) *Spreading of Tropical Disease*: Global warming significantly increases the range of the transmission of both dengue and yellow fever. As northern countries become warm, disease carrying insects will migrate there, bringing plague and disease with them.

(iii) *Warmer Waters and More Hurricanes*: As the temperature of oceans rises, so will the probability of more frequent and stronger hurricanes.

(iv) *Increased Probability and Intensity of Droughts and Heat Waves*: Some areas of Earth will become wetter due to global warming; other areas will suffer serious droughts and heat waves.

(v) *Economic Consequences*: Most of the effects of global warming won't be good. Like hurricanes cause damage in the tune of billions of dollars, spread of diseases cost money to treat and control; effecting economic situation.

(vi) *Melting of Polar Ice Caps*: The melting of ice caps has several effects:

- It will raise sea levels. There are 5.7 million cubic miles of water in ice caps, glaciers, and permanent snow. If all glaciers get melted the seas would rise about 230 feet. (*Source: National Snow and Ice Data Centre*)
- Temperature rises and landscapes in the Arctic Circle will change which will endanger several species of animals.
- As ice caps melts down, the only reflector of sunlight is the ocean surface, but darker colours absorb light and hence causes warming of the Earth.

El Nino: It is an abnormal warming of the surface ocean water in the eastern tropical Pacific Ocean, every 4-12 years.

- There is no clear cause of El Nino. However it occurs and affects temperature and weather patterns.

Q.3. What does IPCC stands for?
Q.4. In which layer of earth's atmosphere, ozone is found?

Environmental Science 233

- Droughts in Africa, floods in California and forest fires in Indonesia are the results of El Nino.
- It is not clear if El Nino is related to global warming, but both involve changes in climate with potential human damage.

Kyoto Protocol

The Kyoto Protocol is a protocol to the United Nations Framework Convention on Climate Change (UNFCCC or FCCC), an international environmental treaty with the goal of achieving stabilisation of greenhouse gas concentrations in the atmosphere.

- The protocol emphasised on the reduction of four greenhouse gases, i.e. carbon dioxide, methane, nitrous oxide, sulphur hexafluoride and two groups of gases, i.e. hydrofluorocarbons and perfluorocarbons produced by industrialised nations, as well as general commitments for all member countries.
- The protocol was initially adopted on 11 December 1997 in Kyoto, Japan but came into force on 16 February 2005.
- As of February 2009, 183 states have signed and ratified the Kyoto Protocol.
- Under the Kyoto Protocol, industrialised countries agreed to reduce their collective greenhouse gases (GHGs) emissions by 5.2 per cent from the level in 1990. National limitations range from the reduction of 8 per cent for the European Union, 7 per cent for the United States, 6 per cent for Japan and zero per cent for Russia. The treaty permitted the emission increases of 8 per cent for Australia and 10 per cent for Iceland.
- While all countries should cut emissions, no targets have been set for the developing countries, since these countries have been responsible for only a small portion of global greenhouse gas emissions.

POLLUTION

Pollution is the introduction of contaminants into an environment that causes instability, disorder, harm or discomfort to the ecosystem, i.e. physical systems or living organisms. Pollution can be in the form of chemical substances, or energy, such as, noise, heat, or light.

Pollution can cause sickness and discomfort. It also affects the productivity of natural resources, such as land, water, forests and livestock.

The Blacksmith Institute publishes annually a list of the world's worst polluted places. The ten top nominees are located in Azerbaijan, China, India, Peru, Russia, Ukraine and Zambia (as in the 2007 publication).

Pollutants: A pollutant is a waste material that pollutes air, water or soil. These can be foreign substances or energies, or naturally occurring. When naturally occurring, they are called contaminants, as they exceed natural levels.

Three factors determine the severity of a pollutant: its chemical nature, the concentration and the persistence.

Forms of Pollution

The major forms of pollution are listed below along with the particular pollutants relevant to each of them:

Q.5. When was Kyoto Protocol adopted by the United Nations Framework Convention on Climate Change (UNFCCC or FCCC)?

Air Pollution: Air pollution occurs due to the rise in the levels of gases, solids or liquids present in the atmosphere which are harmful for the living organism.

There are two main types of air pollutants:

Primary Air Pollutants: These are harmful chemicals like oxides of carbon and nitrogen, sulphur dioxide, chlorofluoro-carbons (CFCs); hydrocarbons like methane and benzene; matters like asbestos, lead, sulphuric acids, etc., that are released directly from a source to the atmosphere.

Secondary Air Pollutants: These are harmful chemicals produced from chemical reactions of the primary pollutants. Examples: Ozone, a form of oxygen and Sulphuric trioxide, formed when sulphur dioxide reacts with oxygen.

Impact of Air Pollution: Air pollution causes respiratory, skin illness, cancer and lowers the immune system.

Increase of air pollution leads to global warming, greenhouse effect, acid rain and depletion of ozone layer.

Control of Air Pollution: Setting of emission standards and regulations for industries and automobiles, adopting cleaner technologies like incineration, electrostatic precipitation, etc.

The Indian government introduced Bharat Emission Norms for vehicular emission in 2000 following the Euro norms of the European Unions.

Water Pollution

It occurs because of release of waste products and contaminants into river drainage systems, wastes percolating into groundwater, wastewater discharges, etc.

Important Water Pollutants

- Soil sediments carried by flowing waters;
- Organic wastes from sewage, paper mills and food processing;
- Infectious microorganisms like worms, viruses and bacteria form infected organism as well as human and animal wastes;
- Organic compounds like synthetic chemicals containing carbon industrial effluents;
- Inorganic nutrients-substance like nitrogen and phosphorous from animal wastes, plant residue and fertiliser;
- Inorganic chemicals like acids, salts and heavy metals like lead and mercury;
- Radioactive substance like wastes from nuclear power plants, nuclear weapons production, mining and refining uranium and other ores.

Contamination of Groundwaters

- Excessive extraction is the natural pollutant of groundwater. It leads to the arsenic contamination of groundwater. As arsenics are present below and with the decrease in the level of groundwater, arsenic is released. It causes skin diseases, cancers, etc.
- Groundwater also gets contaminated from the underground tanks containing petrol, oils, chemicals, etc.
- Another reason of freshwater pollution is the pesticides contaminations.

Q.6. What is the emission norm introduced by the Government of India?

Effects of Water Pollution

Sediments reduce photosynthesis, destroy coral reefs and disrupt aquatic food webs. Infectious microorganism causes waterborne diseases. Inorganic chemicals make water unfit for drinking and irrigation.

- *Purification and Conservation of Water*: To purify water, chemicals are used to settle down suspended particles, and then water is filtered and disinfected. Various methods are used for water purification.
- *Reverse Osmosis or RO Method*: Water is forced through semi-permeable membrane and it filtered unwanted particles.
- *UV Method*: Ultraviolate radiation is directed through pre-filtered water as it helps in killing bacteria, viruses, fungi, etc.
- *Distillation*: Water is boiled to steam and further steams cools and gets condensed into pure water.

Water conservation is an important aspect to keep the groundwater level intact. For this, the recycling of water and rainwater harvest is quite essential.

Soil Contamination

It occurs when chemicals are released by spill or underground leakage. Major soil contaminants are hydrocarbons, heavy metals, herbicides, pesticides, etc.

Any physical and chemical changes in the soil condition lead to soil pollution.

Different factors of soil pollution are soil erosion, salinisation of soil, excessive use of chemical fertilisers and pesticides.

Soil Conservation: Soil erosion can be reduced by adopting better farming methods like crop rotation, terracing, contour farming, etc.

Another protective measure of soil erosion is the afforestation of hills and slopes.

Instead of using chemical fertilisers and pesticides, compost, bio-fertilisers and bio-pesticides can be used to prevent soil contaminations.

Marine Pollution

The main sources of marine pollution are:

- Dumping of hazardous waste including nuclear material, heavy discharges from industry and urban sewage system and inflow of fertilisers and pesticides from agricultural fields;
- Ships cause pollution through regular cleaning process, accidental oil spills, transfer of oil between ships at sea, emission from engines etc;
- Off-shore drilling for oil and gas causes pollution through the dumping of waste from oil rigs, accidental oil spills;
- Marine debris like sunken ships, lost fishing boats, etc., pollute seawaters.

Conservation of the Ocean and its Resources: A number of international agreements and programmes have focused on controlling marine and coastal pollution like London Dumping Convention, Global Programme of Action for the Protection of the Marine Environment from Land-based Activities (GPALBA) etc.

Q.7. What are the types of electromagnetic radiation that cause pollution?
Q.8. What is agro-forestry?

Marine Protected Areas (MPA) is set up by countries to protect marine ecosystems, natural habitats and species.

Some of India's important MPA's are in the Gulf of Kutch, the Gulf of Mannar and the Andamans.

Electromagnetic Radiation

It is of two types.

(*i*) *Ionising Radiation*: It is the radiation which produces ions while interacting with matters, having a short wavelengths and high energy.

Examples: X-rays used in medicine and gamma rays from resulting from nuclear power generation and nuclear weapons research, manufacture and deployment.

(*ii*) *Non-Ionising Radiation*: It does not produce ions while coming in contact with matters. It has a long wave length and short energy.

Examples: Personal computers, monitors, TV sets, microwaves, mobile phones, cordless phones, etc.

Effects of Electromagnetic Radiation

- Exposure to non-ionised radiation seems to increase the risk of developing cancers and other diseases.
- Ionised radiation causes health problems for those who are exposed to it and sometimes cause genetic defects in their descendants.
- *Protective Measures*: Strict enforcement of safety measures in nuclear plants, safe storage of nuclear wastes, reprocessing of spent fuels.

Noise Pollution

It encompasses roadway noise, aircraft noise, industrial noise as well as noise produced by high-intensity sonar. Other sources of noise pollution are, like transport sector, construction sectors, events using loud speakers like pop music shows, religious festivals, public meetings, etc.

Sonic boom is a thunder-like noise produced by an aircraft moving faster than the speed of sound. It can also be caused by high-speed trains passing through tunnels. These are also creating noise pollution.

Effects of Noise Pollution

Loud high-pitched noise damages the fine hair cell in the cochlea of the ear. Prolonged exposure to such noise may cause permanent loss of hearing.

It has other adverse effects like heart palpitation, migraine, nausea, dizziness, etc.

Control of Noise Pollution

Producing less noise is the best method of reducing noise pollution.

Indian government in the year 2000 notified the Noise Regulation Rules under the Environment Protection Act of 1986.

According to the rules, a regulated noise level in industrial area is 75 db, commercial area is 65 db and residential zone is 55 db.

There are also zones of silence of 100 m near schools, courts and hospitals.

Q.9. What are the major Marine Protected Areas (MPAs) of India?

Light pollution includes light trespass, over-illumination and astronomical interference.
Thermal pollution is a temperature change in natural water bodies caused by human influence, such as use of water as coolant in a power plant. Thermal pollution is usually associated with increase in water temperatures in a stream, lake, or ocean due to the discharge of heated water from industrial processes, such as the generation of electricity.

A common cause of thermal pollution is the use of water as a coolant by power plants and industrial manufacturers. When water is used as a coolant it is returned to the natural environment at a higher temperature, the change in temperature affects the organisms by decreasing oxygen supply and affecting ecosystem composition.

ACID RAIN

Rain, mist or snow formed when combines with a range of man-made chemical air pollutants.

- The main pollutants involved are oxides of nitrogen and sulphur.
- Automobiles coal and oil-fired power stations are major sources of such acid-forming compounds. Also burning of coal, oil and natural gas produce them.
- The acid rain ultimately falls on the ground, sometimes hundreds of kilometers from the area in which it is formed and generally one to four days later.

Effects of Acid Rain

- When soil is acidified, it leads to loss of productivity. The acidification damages plant and they will not be able to draw in enough nutrients to survive and grow.
- When trees, particularly conifers are exposed to acid rain, they lose their leaves and die.
- Acid rains falling on lakes and rivers leave them lifeless. Thousands of lakes in Sweden, Canada have been permanently affected by acid rain.
- Acid rain harms people when they breathe in the acidic air.

Ozone Layer Depletion: Ozone is a poisonous gas made up of three oxygen atoms (O_3). It is present in air in traces, representing three out of every 10 million of molecules.

- It exists in Stratosphere (Upper atmosphere), 10 to 50 km above the earth.
- It absorbs harmful ultraviolet – B (UV-B) radiation from the sun and also screens out deadly UV-C radiation. This is how ozone layer protects life.
- Depleting ozone layer allows more UV-B to reach earth, which results into skin cancers, cataracts, weakened immune systems, reduced plant yields, reducing fishing yields and also adverse effects on animals.
- It is found that Chlorofluorocarbons (CFCs) which are used as refrigerants and aerosol propellants cause Ozone layer depletion.
- Bromine atoms released by halons (used in fire extinguishers) also cause depletion in ozone layer.

Steps Taken Against Ozone Layer Depletion

- In 1985, several countries adopted Vienna Convention for the protection

Q. 10. Which is the largest area under mangrove cover in India?

of the ozone layer. The main aim was to phase out the use of ozone-depleting substance.
- Montreal Protocol was adopted in September 1987, to replace 96 Ozone-depleting substances with safer ones.
- This agreement bore positive results. The total CFCs consumption worldwide was reduced to 110000 tonnes in 2001 from 1.1 million tonnes in 1986.

WASTE

Anything which does not add value to a product or service in any activity, whether manufacturing or non-manufacturing is considered a waste.

Classification of Waste

General Waste: 'A General Waste is produced within the domain of local authorities and comprises rubble, domestic, commercial and non-hazardous industrial waste. It may contain small quantities of hazardous substances dispersed within it, e.g. batteries, insecticide and other pesticide residues in containers and medical waste discarded on domestic and commercial premises.'

Domestic Waste: Domestic waste is a waste from householders which cannot be recycled, composted, reused or disposed of by other means.

- This waste is generated as consequences of household activities such as the cleaning, cooking, repairing empty containers, packaging, huge use of plastic carry bags.
- There is no system of segregation of organic, inorganic and recyclable wastes at the household level.

Effects of Domestic Waste

- The improper handling and management of domestic waste from households causes adverse effect on the public health and deteriorates the environment.
- For example, the municipal workers are affected by the occupational hazards of waste handling; they suffer from illnesses like eye problems, respiratory problems, gastro and skin problems.
- The improper management and lack of disposal technique of the domestic waste pollutes the environment.
- It affects the water bodies; changes the physical, chemical and biological properties of the water bodies.
- Uncollected waste is scattered everywhere and reaches the water bodies through run-off water as well as it percolates down to underground water. The toxics contents in the waste contaminate the water.
- It also makes soil infertile and decrease the agricultural productivity.
- The Municipal Solid Waste (Management & Handling) Rules, which was framed by the Central Government and came into force in 2000 to deal with the domestic waste management and disposal techniques.

Q.11. Where was the Chipko movement started?
Q.12. What are the main pollutants that cause acid rain?

Environmental Science 239

Eradication of the Problem of Domestic Waste

- The government should take into account all the factors responsible for environment pollution and should give the priority to effective enforcement of Environmental Laws and Rules.
- There should be separate waste disposal policy through the Central Government and should separately allocate budget and work with the help of effective institutional arrangements at local level.
- Need to educate the people about storing waste at source in their own houses and dispose of the waste as per the directions of the local bodies.
- Domestic Waste should not be thrown in the neighbourhood, on the streets, roadsides, open spaces, vacant lands, into drains or water bodies.
- Stringent penalty must be imposed on people who throw away waste outside houses or on the street.
- Scientific and proper disposal techniques for safe disposal of domestic waste should be used by the local authorities.

Biodegradable wastes are environmentally friendly products that being can be broken down by natural processes into more basic components. The products are usually broken down by bacteria, fungi or other simple organisms.

Hence most chemicals are biodegradable; but the time taken to break down only varies. For example, a piece of bread will break down quickly, whereas a piece of plastic will take decades and beyond.

The final products of any complex product of Carbon, Hydrogen and Oxygen would be Carbon Dioxide (CO_2) and Water (H_2O). A majority of products are made mostly of these three elements.

Biodegradable plastics are plastics that will decompose in natural aerobic and anaerobic environments. Biodegradation of plastics can be achieved by enabling microorganisms in the environment to metabolise the molecular structure of plastic films to produce an inert humus-like material that is less harmful to the environment.

Biodegradable plastics typically are produced in two forms:

- injection molded (solid, 3D shapes), typically in the form of disposable food service items, and
- films, typically sold as collection bags for leaves and grass trimmings, and agricultural mulch.

HAZARDOUS WASTE

'A Hazardous Waste is a waste which because of its quantity, chemical or infectious characteristics may cause ill health, increased mortality, or adversely affect the environment, or pose an immediate threat, and exhibits the characteristics of corrosivity, toxicity, flammability, volatility, explosivity or radioactivity.'

Classification of Hazardous Waste

Explosive, e.g. Dynamite
Flammable, e.g. Acetone
Corrosive, e.g. Sulphuric acid
Radioactive, e.g. Nuclear fuel

Q.13. Which is the largest animal right organisation in the world?

Poisonous, e.g. Arsenic
Oxidizing, e.g. Hydrogen peroxide
Biologically active, e.g. Antibiotics

DISASTERS

Disaster as any occurrence, that causes damage, ecological disruption, loss of human life, deterioration of health and health services, on a scale sufficient to warrant an extraordinary response from outside the affected community or areas. (*Source*: WHO)

Classification of Disasters

Natural Disaster: A natural disaster is a consequence when a natural hazard (e.g. volcanic eruption or earthquake) affects humans.

Examples: Tsunami, Cyclones, Hurricanes, Tornado, Typhoons, Floods, Earthquakes, Avalanches, Landslides, Volcano eruptions, Forest fires, Droughts, etc.

Man-made Disaster: Disasters caused by human action, negligence, error, or involving the failure of a system are called man-made disasters.

Man-made disasters are in turn categorised as technological or sociological.

Technological disasters are the results of failure of technology, such as engineering failures, transport disasters, or environmental disasters.

Sociological disasters have a strong human motive, such as criminal acts, stampedes, riots and war.

Examples of man-made disaster are severe air pollution, building collapse, toxicological accidents, nuclear accidents, explosions, civil disturbances, water contamination and existing or anticipated food shortages, etc.

India's Disaster-Ridden History

- About 60 per cent of India's landmass is prone to earthquakes;
- Over forty million hectares of land are prone to floods;
- Nearly three lakh sq km are at risk of cyclones;
- The earthquake in Bhuj killed 14,000 people;
- The super cyclone in Orissa took away 10,000 lives;
- Between 1990 and 2000 on an average of about 3400 people lost their lives annually;
- About three crore people were affected by disasters every year;
- About 17,000 people perished by the Tsunami on 26 December 2004.

MAJOR DISASTERS

Earthquakes: An earthquake is a sudden motion or trembling of the ground produced by the abrupt displacement of rock masses. Most earthquakes result from the movement of one rock mass past another in response to tectonic forces.

The epicentre is the point on the earth's surface that is directly above the focus of the quake.

Earthquake magnitude is a measure of the strength of an earthquake as calculated from records of the event made on a calibrated seismograph.

In 1935, Charles Richter first defined local magnitude, and the richter scale is commonly used today to describe an earthquake's magnitude.

Earthquake intensity is a measure of the effects of an earthquake at a particular place. It is determined from observations of the earthquake's effects on people, structures and the earth's surface.

Hazards due to Earthquake: Hazards can be categorised as either direct hazards or indirect hazards:

Direct Hazards

- Ground shaking;
- Soil liquefaction;
- Immediate landslides or mud slides, ground lurching and avalanches;
- Floods from tidal waves, Sea Surges & Tsunamis

Indirect Hazards

- Dam failures;
- Pollution from damage to industrial plants;
- Delayed landslides.

Cyclone: The term 'cyclone' refers to all classes of storms, with low atmospheric pressure at the centre; they are formed when an organised system of revolving winds, clockwise in the Southern Hemisphere and anti-clockwise in the Northern Hemisphere, develops over tropical waters.

Cyclones are classified on the basis of the average speed of the wind near the centre of the system as follows:

Wind Speed	Classification
Up to 61 km/hr	Tropical Depression
61 km/hr – 115 km/hr	Tropical Storm
Greater than 115 km/hr	Hurricane

Hurricane: A hurricane is a low pressure, large-scale weather system which derives its energy from the latent heat of condensation of water vapour over warm tropical seas. A mature hurricane may have a diameter ranging from 150 to 1000 km with sustained wind speeds often exceeding 180 km/hr near the centre.

Tsunamis: (This is a Japanese word and means 'Harbour Waves') Tsunamis are Ocean Waves produced by earthquakes or underwater landslides.

Tsunami is actually a series of waves that can travel at a speed of 400–600 mph in the open ocean. As the waves approach the coast their speed decreases, but amplitude increases.

The unusual wave height of 10–20 ft is very destructive and causes many deaths and injuries.

Disaster Management

The fundamental aspects of Disaster Management Program:

Q.14. Name the programme of Government of India that deals with the domestic waste management, which came into force in 2000?

NATURAL HAZARDS

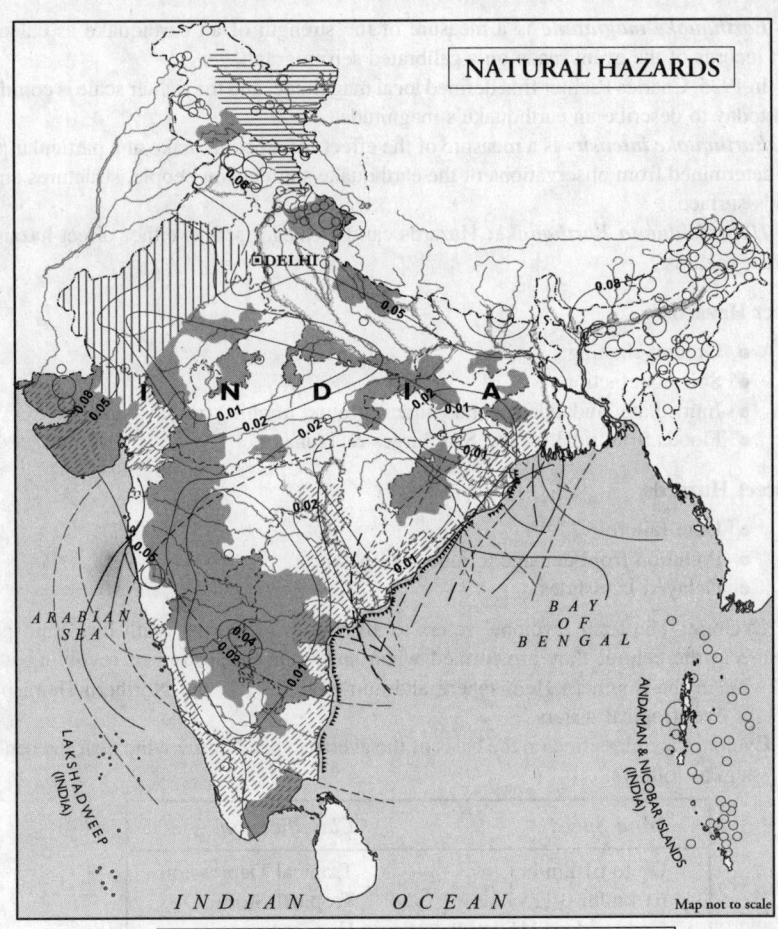

REFERENCES
EPICENTRES OF IMPORTANT EARTHQUAKES

Magnitude
5.0 - 6.5 ○   6.5 - 7.5 ○   7.5 and above ○

Horizontal Seismic Coefficient Isoline 0.01
Coast exposed to tsunamis ▲▲▲▲

PATHS OF CYCLONIC STORMS	
April, May	– – – –
July, September	– – – –
October, November	– – – –
December	– ·· – ·· –

Areas affected by cyclonic storms	
Cold desert	
Hot desert	
Drought prone areas	
Flood prone areas	

- Disaster prevention
- Disaster preparedness
- Disaster response
- Disaster mitigation
- Rehabilitation

Q. 15. What are the main sources of non-renewable energy?

- Reconstruction

Three fundamental aspects of Disaster Management are:
1. Disaster Response
2. Disaster Preparedness
3. Disaster Mitigation

1. Disaster Response

Objectives
- To prevent much of the death, injury and economic disruption resulting from disasters with the application of current technology;
- Prevent unnecessary morbidity, mortality and economic loss resulting from the disaster;
- In any disaster, prevention should be directed towards reducing;
- Curtail losses due to the disaster event itself.

2. Disaster Relief: An effective plan for public health during a disaster would minimise the effects of the catastrophe. These efforts can be summarised as closely situation analysis and response.

Following a disaster, the desire to provide immediate relief may lead to hasty decisions which are not based on the actual needs of the affected population.

Reliable information must be obtained on problems occurring in the disaster stricken area, relief resources made available and relief activities already in progress, for which surveillance systems must be set up immediately.

The objective of Surveillance in a disaster situation is to obtain information required for making relief decisions.

The specific information required would vary from disaster to disaster, but a basic, three-step processes includes:
1. Collect data,
2. Analyse data,
3. Respond to data.

3. Disaster Preparedness: The objectives of the disaster preparedness is to ensure that appropriate systems, procedures and resources are in place to provide prompt, effective assistance to disaster victims, thus facilitating relief measures and rehabilitation services.

Steps for Disaster Preparedness
- Evaluate the risk of the country or particular region to disasters;
- Adopt standards and regulations;
- Ensure coordination and response mechanisms;
- Adopt measures to ensure that financial and other resources are available for increased readiness and can be mobilised in disaster situations;
- Develop public education programmes;
- Organise disaster simulation exercises that test response mechanisms.

4. Disaster Mitigation: It is virtually impossible to prevent occurrence of most natural disasters, but it is possible to minimise or mitigate their damage effects.

Mitigation measures aim to reduce the vulnerability of the system. Disaster prevention

Q.16. Who coordinates relief operations for natural disasters in India?

implies complete elimination of damages from a hazard, but it is not realistic in most hazards. Medical Casualty could be drastically reduced by improving the structural quality of houses, schools, public or private buildings. The safety of health facilities, public health services, water supply, sewerage system, etc., must also be ensured.

India's National Disaster Management Policy

Disaster management is a multidisciplinary activity involving a number of departments and agencies spanning across all sectors of development.

The policy notes that state governments are primarily responsible for disaster management including prevention and mitigation, while the Government of India provides assistance where necessary as per the norms laid down from time to time.

National Disaster Framework covers institutional mechanisms, disaster prevention strategy, early warning system, disaster mitigation, preparedness and response and human resource development.

Main Features of the National Policy on Disaster Management

(i) A holistic and pro-active approach towards prevention, mitigation and preparedness will be adopted for disaster management.

(ii) Each Ministry/Department of the Central/State Government will set apart an appropriate quantum of funds under the plan for specific schemes/projects addressing vulnerability reduction and preparedness.

(iii) There will be close interaction with the corporate sector, non-governmental organisations and the media in the national efforts for disaster prevention/vulnerability reduction.

Authorities Accountable for Implementation of Policy

At the national level, the Ministry of Home Affairs is the nodal Ministry for all matters concerning disaster management.

The Central Relief Commissioner (CRC) in the Ministry of Home Affairs is the nodal officer to coordinate relief operations for natural disasters. The CRC receives information relating to forecasting/warning of a natural calamity from Indian Meteorological Department (IMD) or from Central Water Commission in Ministry of Water Resources on a continuous basis.

The Ministries/Departments/Organisations concerned with the primary and secondary functions relating to the management of disasters include are:

- Indian Meteorological Department,
- Central Water Commission,
- Ministry of Home Affairs,
- Ministry of Defence,
- Ministry of Finance,
- Ministry of Rural Development,
- Ministry of Urban Development,
- Ministry of Health,
- Ministry of Water Resources,
- Ministry of Power,
- Ministry of Railways,

Q.17. From which language the word Tsunami has originated?
Q.18. Which harmful radiations from the sun are absorbed by the ozone layer?

- Planning Commission, Cabinet Secretariat,
- Ministry of Environment and Forest.

Each Ministry/Department/Organisation nominates their nodal officer to the Crisis Management Group chaired by Central Relief Commissioner. The nodal officer is responsible for preparing sectoral Action Plan/Emergency Support Function Plan for managing disasters.

The states have also been advised to formulate State DM Policies with the broad objective to minimise the loss of lives and social, private and community assets and contribute to sustainable development.

Energy

Sources of Commercial Energy: World's commercial energy, i.e. the energy we pay for, comes from mostly fossils fuels like oil, coal and natural gases.

Share of different Sources of Total Energy Used

	Energy Source	Total Energy (%)
Non-Renewable Sources	Oil	32
	Coal	21
	Natural Gas	23
	Nuclear Power	6
Renewable Sources	Biomass	11
	Solar, Wind, Hydro and Geothermal Power	7

Global Energy Consumption Pattern

Industry	40%
Domestic and Commercial Purposes	30%
Transportation	24%
Agriculture and Others	6%

According to Food and Agriculture Organisation (FAO), 77 developing countries with 2.7 billion people uses only 30 per cent of the total energy, whole industrialised countries (about 255 of world's total, populations) consume 70 per cent of the commercial energy.

Non-Renewable Sources

Coal Reserves

Among the fossil fuels, coal is most harmful to environment. Coal has to be mined from underground or from surface. Underground mines besides being dangerous, also cause lung diseases.

- Coal is responsible for 36 per cent of CO_2 emission in the world. It also releases huge amount of radioactive particles into the atmosphere.
- Every year air pollution from coal kills thousands of people and causes respiratory diseases in thousands more.
- At current rate of use, world's coal reserves will probably last for 200 years.

Q.19. Which department of UN is responsible for mitigation and prevention aspects of disaster management?

Natural Gas

Natural gas is the composed of methane, ethane, butane and propane, and it is found above most oil reserves.

- About 40 per cent of the natural gas reserves are in Russia and Kazakhstan.
- The available reserves are expected to last for about 250 years.
- There are different types of fuels that are derived from oil and natural gases:
  (i) LPG (Liquefied Petroleum Gas)
  (ii) LNG (Liquefied Natural Gas)
  (iii) CNG (Compressed Natural Gas)
- These three gases are safer than petrol, since they release lesser amount of greenhouse gases.

Nuclear Power

In nuclear reactor neutrons split the nuclei of elements like uranium and plutonium and release energy in the form of heat. This heat is used to produce steam which runs the electric turbine. However costs of nuclear plants and its operating costs are high and sometimes complex technical problems arise. So nuclear power is not an alternative to fossil fuel.

Renewable Sources

Renewable energy sources are generally exhaustible and don't cause much environmental damage or environmental pollution.

Solar energy, Wind energy, hydropower, Hydrogen energy are the major renewable energy sources of energy.

Solar Energy

The earth receives enormous amount of solar energy. It is estimated that the amount of solar energy that the earth receives is more than all the energy stored in all fossil fuels.

This energy does not pollute the atmosphere.

However there are few problems to in using the solar energy:

(a) Difficult to collect it efficiently.
(b) Not easy to convert it into a useable form like electricity.
(c) No efficient way of storing the energy is available.
(d) Cost of production is still high.

Wind Energy

Windmills produce electricity at low cost and there is no emission. Wind farms can be quickly set up and easily expanded. However it requires steady wind with certain velocity, hence not suitable for every place. A backup is required during windless days. However windmills create some noise pollutions which could also interfere with flight of migratory birds.

Hydropower

Twenty percent of the world's electricity

Q.20. Name the agent which is used to metabolise the plastics to produce inert materials that is less harmful for the environment.

comes from hydropower. The potential energy of water falling from a height runs turbine and generates electricity.

Hydropower has several advantages:
(a) Cost of generation of energy is low and produces no emission.
(b) The reservoir can be used for multipurpose, like irrigation, fishing etc.
(c) The reservoir can provide the drinking water to towns and cities.

Hydrogen Power

When hydrogen burns it releases energy; it combines with oxygen to produce water vapour. So there is no pollution or emission of carbon dioxide.

However hydrogen is not available in free state; either it is in water or in other compounds like methane, petrol, etc.

So to get free hydrogen, energy is required. And it can be provided by fossil fuel or solar energy.

However storage of hydrogen is another problem. Since it is highly explosive, it requires being stored in compressed tanks or can be stored in the form of liquid, which requires energy.

So it is not a good alternative to fossil fuel due to the costs involved to make it useable.

Other Renewable Sources of Energy:

(a) **Biofuels:** Oil extracted from seeds of certain trees like *jatropha* and *pongamia* can be mixed with diesel, which reduces consumption of fossil fuels and produces less pollution.
(b) **Biomass:** In biogas plants, animal and human wastes are used to produce methane which can be used for lighting and cooking, and the slurry that remains can be used as fertilisers.
(c) **Geothermal Energy:** Below the earth's crust, there is a layer of hot liquid rock. When water reaches this layer it becomes hot. The energy in this water is called geothermal energy. This energy can be trapped in some places and can be used to generate electricity.

GLOBAL OIL SUPPLY AND DEMAND

The estimated oil reserves are 1.4 to 2.1 trillion barrels (one barrel is 159 litres). There are 1500 major oilfields that are in operation; of which 400 large ones accounts for about 60–70 per cent of production.

Total global demand per year is about 24 billion barrels, however current new discoveries amount to 12 billion barrel per year.

ANSWERS

1. 1–7 October
2. Water vapour (causes about 36–70 per cent of the greenhouse effect)
3. Intergovernmental Panel on Climate Change
4. Stratosphere
5. 11 December 1997
6. Bharat emission norm
7. Ionising and non-ionising radiation
8. It is the method that combines growing

crops along with trees.
9. Gulf of Kutch, the Gulf of Mannar and the Andamans.
10. Sunderbans
11. Tehri Garhwal
12. Oxides of nitrogen and sulphur
13. People for the Ethical Treat-ment of Animals (PETA)
14. The Municipal Solid Waste (Management & Handling) Rules
15. Coal, oil and natural gas
16. Central Relief Commissioner (CRC)
17. Japanese
18. UV-B and UV-C
19. United Nations Development Programme (UNDP)
20. Microorganisms

10

BASIC GENERAL KNOWLEDGE

ABBREVIATIONS

A

AAFI	Amateur Athletics Federation of India
ABC	Audit Bureau of Circulation; American (or Australian) Broadcasting Company
AD	Anno Domini (After Christ)
ADR	American Depositary Receipt
AEC	Atomic Energy Commission
AICC	All India Congress Committee
AICTE	All India Council of Technical Education
AIDS	Acquired Immune Deficiency Syndrome
AINEC	All India Newspaper Editors Conference
AIIMS	All India Institute of Medical Sciences
AILTA	All India Lawn Tennis Association
AIREC	All India Railway Employees Confederation
AITUC	All India Trade Union Congress
AM	Ante Meridian (Before Noon)
AMIE	Associate Member of Institution of Engineers
AOC	Air Officers Commanding
AP	Associates Press
APEC	Asia Pacific Economic Corporation
APL	Above Poverty Line
APPLE	Ariane Passenger Pay Load Experiment
APRSAF	Asia Pacific Regional Space Agency Forum
ARCIL	Asset Reconstruction Company of India Limited
ASC	Army Service Corps
ASEAN	Association of South East Asian Nations
ASI	Archaeological Survey of India
ASLV	Augmented Satellite Launch Vehicle
ASPAC	Asian and Pacific Council
ASSOCHAM	Associated Chambers of Commerce and Industry
ATM	Automated Teller Machine

AU	Astronomical Unit
AVSM	Ati Vishist Seva Medal
AWACS	Airborne Warning and Control System

B

BA	Baccalaureus Artium (Bachelor of Arts)
BAFTA	British Academy of Film and Television Arts
BAI	Badminton Association of India
BALCO	Bharat Aluminium Company Limited
BARC	Bhabha Atomic Research Centre
B2B	Business to Business
BC	Before Christ
BBC	British Broadcasting Corporation
BCCI	Board of Control for Cricket in India
BCG	Bacillus Calmette Guerin (Vaccine for Tuberculosis)
BEL	Bharat Electronics Limited
BENELUS	Belgium, the Netherland and Luxembourg
BHEL	Bharat Heavy Electrical Limited
BIMSTEC	Bangladesh, India, Myanmar, Sri Lanka, Thailand Economic Corporation
BIS	Bureau of Indian Standards
BIT	Binary Digit
BOSE	British Overseas Airways Corporation (Now British Airways)
BPCL	Bharat Petroleum Corporation Limited
BPL	Below Poverty Line
BPO	Business Process Outsourcing
BRO	Border Roads Organisation
BSE	Bombay Stock Exchange
BSF	Border Security Force
BSNL	Bharat Sanchar Nigam Limited

C

CAD	Computer Aided Design
CAG	Comptroller Auditor General
CAR	Capital Adequacy Ratio
CARE	Cooperative for American Relief Everywhere
CAS	Conditional Access System
CBDT	Central Board of Direct Taxes
CBFC	Central Board of Film Certification
CBI	Central Board of Investigation
CBR	Central Board of Revenue; Crude Birth Rate
CBSE	Central Board of Secondary Education
CBT	Children's Book Trust
C-DOT	Centre for Development of Telematics
CDM	Clean Development Mechanism

Q.1. On which date is World Forestry Day celebrated?
Q.2. Who is the author of **Broken Wings?**

Basic General Knowledge

CDMA	Code Division Multiple Access
CDRI	Central Drug Research Institute
CDSL	Central Depository Services (India) Limited
CEC	Chief Election Commission
CEO	Chief Executive Officer
CER	Certified Emission Reduction
CFC	Chlorofluoro Carbon
CFO	Chief Financial Officer
CFSI	Children's Film Society of India
CFTRI	Central Food Technological Research Institute
CHOGM	Commonwealth Heads of Government Meeting
CII	Confederation of Indian Industry
CIA	Central Intelligence Agency (of USA)
CIS	Commonwealth of Independent States
CISF	Central Industrial Security Force
CID	Criminal Investigation Department
CIF	Cost, Insurance and Freight
CIIL	Central Institute of Indian Languages
CITES	Convention of International Trade in Endangered Species
CITU	Centre of Indian Trade Union
CIWTC	Central Inland Water Transport Corporation
CLRC	Central Land Reform Committee
CMIE	Centre for Monitoring Indian Economy
CNN	Cable News Network
COAI	Cellular Operation Association of India
COFEPOSA	Conservation of Foreign Exchange and Prevention of Smuggling Act
CPC	Civil Procedure Code
CPF	Contributory Provident Fund
CPI	Communist Party of India
CPO	Central Paramilitary Organisation
CRIS	Central Railway Information System
CRISII	Credit Rating Information Services of India Limited
CRPF	Central Reserve Police Force
CRR	Cash Reserve Ratio
CRRI	Central Road Research Institute
CRY	Child Relief and You
CSE	Centre for Science and Environment
CSIR	Council of Scientific and Industrial Research
CSO	Central Statistical Organisation
CVR	Cockpit Voice Recorder

D

DA	Dearness Allowance
DAE	Department of Atomic Energy

Q.3. With which game is the name Surya Shekhar Ganguly related?
Q.4. What is FIEO?

General Knowledge Manual

DDT	DichloroDiphenyl Trichloro Ethane
DMRC	Delhi Metro Rail Corporation
DLO	Dead Letter Office
DMK	Dravida Munnetra Kazhagam
DMKP	Dalit Mazdoor Kisan Party
DPT	Diphtheria, Pertusis and Tetanus (a vaccine)
DNA	Deoxy Ribonucleic Acid
DOD	Department of Ocean Development
DRDL	Defence Research and Development Laboratory
DRDO	Defence Research and Development Organisation
DRI	Differential Rate of Interest
DTH	Direct to Home Service
DV	Deo Volente (God Willing)
DVDR	Digital Versatile Disc Recordable

E

ECA	Economic Commission for Asia
ECAFE	Economic Commission for Asia and Far East
ECG	Electrocardiogram
ECGC	Export Credit and Guarantee Corporation
ECM	European Common Market
ECOSOC	Economic and Social Council (of UNO)
ECS	Electronic Clearance Services
EFTA	European Free Trade Association
EG	Exampli Gratia (for Example)
ELSS	Equity Linked Saving Scheme
ENLF	Eelan National Liberation Front
EPABX	Electronic Private Automatic Branch Exchange
EPS	Earning Per Share
ESCAP	Electronic and Social Commission for Asia and Pacific
ESMA	Essential Services Maintenance Act
ESPN	Entertainment and Sports Programming Network

F

FAO	Food and Agriculture Organisation (of UNO)
FBI	Federal Bureau of Investigation
FCD	Fully Convertible Debenture
FCI	Food Corporation of India; Fertilizer Corporation of India
FDI	Foreign Direct Investment
FEMA	Foreign Exchange Management Act
FERA	Foreign Exchange Regulation Act
FII	Foreign Institutional Investor
FICCI	Federation of Indian Chambers of Commerce and Industry
FIFA	International Football Federation
FIPB	Foreign Investment Promotion Board
FIR	First Information Report
FLAG	Fiber Optic Link Around the Globe

Q.5. Who invented mobile phone?
Q.6. What is 'Mistral'?

Basic General Knowledge

FM	Frequency Modulation
FCMG	First Moving Consumer Court
FOB	Freight on Board
FTZ	Free Trade Zone

G

GAIL	Gas Authority of India Limited
GATS	General Agreement on Trade and Services
GATT	General Agreement on Tariffs and Trade
GDR	Global Depositary Receipt
GDP	Gross Domestic Product
GETF	Gold Exchange Traded Funds
GIC	General Insurance Corporation
GIS	Geo-Special Information System
GLOBE	General Learning and Observation to Benefit the Environment
GMO	Genetically Modified Organisms
GMT	Greenwich Mean Tim
GNLF	Gorkhaland National Liberation Front
GNP	Gross National Product
GPF	General Provident Fund
GPO	General Post Office
GSLV	Geo-Synchronous Satellite Launch Vehicle

H

HAL	Hindustan Aeronautics Limited
HE	His/Her Excellency
HEC	Heavy Engineering Company
HLC	Humanitarian Law Commission (of Red Cross)
HLL	Hindustan Lever Limited
HMI	Himalayan Mountaineering Institute
HSD	High Speed Diesel
HUDCO	Housing and Urban Development Corporation

I

IAA	International Airport Authority
IAEA	International Atomic Energy Commission
IAFC	Indian Agricultural Finance Corporation
IAMC	Indian Army Medical Corps
IARI	Indian Agricultural Research Institute
IATA	International Air Transport Association
IBEC	International Bank for Economic Cooperation
IBM	International Business Machines
IBRD	International Bank for Reconstruction and Development (of UNO)

Q.7. Which university was esta-blished by Rabindranath Tagore?
Q.8. With which sports is FA Cup related to?

ICAO	International Civil Aviation Organization
ICAR	Indian Council of Agricultural Research
ICBM	Inter Continental Ballistic Missile
ICC	International Cricket Council; International Crime Court; International Control Commission
ICICI	Industrial Credit and Investment Corporation of India
ICJ	International Court of Justice
ICRA	Investment and Credit Rating of India
ICRC	International Committee of Red Cross
ICSI	Institute of Company Secretaries of India
ICSW	Indian Council for Social Welfare
ICWAI	Institute of Cost and Works Accounts of India
IDA	International Development Agency
IDC	Industrial Development Corporation
IDBI	Industrial Development Bank of India
IDPL	Indian Drugs and Pharmaceuticals Limited
IDRC	International Development Research Centre
IFAD	International Fund for Agricultural Development
IFCI	Industrial Finance Corporation of India
IHF	Indian Hockey Federation
IIFT	Indian Institute of Foreign Trade
IIP	Index of Industrial Production
IIMA	Indian Military Academy
IMF	International Monetary Fund
INS	Indian Naval Ship
INSAT	Indian National Satellite
INTERPOL	International Policy
INTUC	Indian National Trade Union Committee
IOA	Indian Olympic Association
IOC	International Olympic Committee
IPC	Indian Penal Code
IPCC	Intergovernment Penal on Climate Change
IPI	International Press Institute
IPO	Initial Public Offering
IQ	Intelligence Quotient
IRBM	Intermediate Range Ballistic Missile
IRDA	Insurance Regulatory and Development Authority
IRDP	Integrated Rural Development Programme
IREDA	Indian Renewable Energy Development Agency
ARSS	Indian Remote Sensing Satellite
ISBN	International Standard Book Number

Q.9. 'Federal Investigation Agency' is a central investigative agency of which country?
Q.10. 'Sprinter's Cup' is related to which sports?

Basic General Knowledge 255

ISC	Indian Science Congress
ISO	International Standards Organisation
ISRO	Indian Space Research Organisation
ITBP	Indo-Tibetan Boarder Police
ITDC	Indian Tourism Development Corporation
IVF	In-Vitro Fertilization

J

JPC	Joint Parliamentary Committee
JRY	Jawahar Rozgar Yojana
JKLF	Jammu and Kashmir Liberation Front

K

KBE	Knight of British Empire
KG	Kindergarten
KGBVS	Kasturba Gandhi Balika Vidyalaya Scheme
KVIC	Khadi and Village Industries Commission

L

LASER	Light Amplification by Stimulated Emission of Radiation
LSD	Lysergic Diethylamide
LTTE	Liberation Tiger of Tamil Eelam
LCA	Light Combat Aircraft
LLB	Legum Baccalaureus (Bachelor of Law)
LNG	Liquefied Natural Gas
LOC	Line of Control
LSE	London School of Economics

M

MBT	Main Battle Tank
MCC	Marylebone Cricket Club
MBBS	Bachelor of Medicine and Bachelor of Surgery
MCI	Medical Council of India
MENA	Middle East News Agency
MFN	Most Favoured Nation
MISA	Maintenance of Internal Security Act
MMS	Multimedia Messaging Service
MODEM	Modulator Demodulator
MODVAT	Modified Value Added Tax
MRTPC	Monopolies and Restrictive Trade Practices Commission
MTCR	Missile Technology Control Regime
MVC	Maha Vir Chakra

Q.11. 'Sheru' is official mascot of which Games?
Q.12. With which game 'Radha Mohan Cup' is related to?

N

NAAI	National Airport Authority of India
NABARD	National Bank for Agricultural and Rural Development
NAFTA	North American Free Trade Agreement
NAM	Non-Aligned Movement
NASA	National Aeronautics and Space Administration (of USA)
NASDAQ	National Association of Securities Dealers Automated Quotation
NASSCOM	National Association of Software and Service Companies
NATO	North Atlantic Treaty Organisation
NAV	Net Asset Value
NB	Nota Bene (Not Well/Not Below)
NBFC	Non-Banking Finance Company
NBT	National Book Trust
NCD	Non-Convertible Debenture
NCERT	National Council of Educational Research and Training
NCM	National Commission for Minorities
NDDB	National Diary Development Board
NEERI	National Environmental Engineering Research Institute
NEFA	North-East Frontier Agency
NEPA	National Environment Protection Act
NFDC	National Film Development Corporation
NGRI	National Geographical Research Institute
NHAI	National Highway Authority of India
NHDP	National Highways Development Project
NHPC	National Hydro-Electric Power Corporation
NHRC	National Human Rights Commission
NID	National Institute of Design
NIEO	National Economic Order
NIIT	National Institute of Information Technology
NIO	National Institute of Oceanography
NITIE	National Institute for Training in Industrial Engineering
NMDC	National Mineral Development Corporation
NOC	No Objection Certificate
NPA	Non-Performing Assets
NPCIL	Nuclear Power Corporation of India Limited
NPT	Nuclear Non-Proliferation Treaty
NRE	Non-Resident External (Bank Account)
NRSA	National Remote Sensing Agency
NSE	National Stock Exchange
NTPC	National Thermal Power Corporation

Q.13. Where the Earth Hour was started?
Q.14. Accenture Match Play Championship is related to which sports?

O

OAPEC	Organisation of Arab Petroleum Exporting Countries
OAU	Organisation of African Unity
ONGC	Oil and Natural Gas Corporation
OPEC	Organisation Petroleum Exporting Countries

P

PAN	Permanent Account Number (for Income Tax)
PBX	Private Branch Exchange (for Telephone)
PDS	Public Distribution System
PEN	Poet, Editors and Novelists Association
PER	Price Earnings Ratio
PETA	People for the Ethical Treatment of Animals
PIN	Postal Index Number
PIO	Person of Indian Origin
PCC	Pradesh Congress Committee
PDA	Preventive Detention Act
PFA	Press Foundation of Asia, Prevention of Food Adulteration
PGCIL	Power Grid Corporation of India Limited
PHC	Primary Health Centre
PII	Press Institute of India
PIN	Public Interest Litigation
PLOTE	People's Liberation Organisation of Tamil Eelam
PLR	Primary Landing Rate
PM	Post Meridian, Prime Minister
PNR	Passenger Name Recorder
POTA	Prevention of Terrorist Activities Act
POW	Prisoner of Work
PPP	Purchasing Power Parity, Pakistan People's Party
PRO	Public Relations Officer
PS	Post Script
PSLV	Polar Satellite Launch Vehicle
PSP	Praja Socialist Party
PTI	Press Trust of India
PVC	Param Vir Chakra
PWD	Public Works Department

Q

QMT	Quantitative Management Technique
QR	Quarterly Report

Q.15. On what date is the World Hemophilia Day celebrated?
Q.16. Which bank launched Indo-Nepal Remittance Scheme?

R

RADAR	Radio Detecting and Ranging
RAW	Research and Analysis Wing
RBI	Reserve Bank of India
R&D/RND	Research and Development
RAF	Rapid Action Force
RDX	Research Developed Explosive
RLEGS	Rural Landless Employment Guarantee Scheme
RPM (rpm)	Revolution per Minute
RSVP	Repondez Sin Vous Plait (Reply if You Please)
RTC	Round Table Conference

S

SAARC	South Asian Association for Regional Cooperation
SAFMA	South Asian Free Media Association
SAFTA	South Asian Free Trade Agreement
SAIL	Steel Authority of India Limited
SARS	Severe Acute Respiratory Syndrome
SCI	Shipping Corporation of India
SDR	Special Drawing Rights
SEBI	Securities and Exchange Board of India
SENSEX	Sensitivity Index (of Bombay Stock Exchange)
SEZ	Special Economic Zone
SEATO	South-East Asia Treaty Organisation
SFF	Special Frontier Force
SFI	Student Federation of India
SHCIL	Stock Holding Corporation of India Limited
SGPC	Shiromani Gurudwara Prabandhak Committee
SIDBI	Small Industries Development Bank of India
SIDC	Small Industrial Development Corporation
SITA	Suppression of Immoral Traffic in Women and Girls Act
SLV	Satellite Launch Vehicle
SLR	Self Loading Rifle, Statutory Liquidity Ratio
SMS	Short Messenger Services
SPCA	Society for Prevention of Cruelty to Animals
SSC	Staff Selection Commission
SSI	Small Scale Industries
STD	Subscriber Trunk Dialing
SWAPA	South-West African People's Organisation

Q.17. 'Padma Vibhushan' is our country's.....highest civilian award.
Q.18. For achievements in which fields is Pulitzer Prize given?

Basic General Knowledge

T

TA	Travelling Allowance, Territorial Army
TADA	Terrorist and Disruptive Activities (Prevention) Act
TAX	Trunk Automatic Exchange
TDA	Trade Development Authority
TDP	Telugu Desam Party
TDS	Tax Deducted Source
TELCO	Tata Engineering and Locomotive Company
TELEX	Teleprinter Exchange
TERLS	Thumba Equatorial Rocket Launching Station
TIFR	Tata Institute of Fundamental Research
TMO	Telegraph Money Order
TMT	Technology Media Telecom
TNC	Trans National Corporation
TNT	Tri-Nitro toluene (Explosive Material)
TQM	Total Quality Management
TRAI	Telecom Regulatory Authority of India
TRIPS	Trade Related Intellectual Property Rights
TRP	Television Rating Points
TULF	Tamil United Liberation Front
TUC	Trade Union Congress
TWA	Trans World Airlines

U

UCTA	United Chamber of Trade Association
UDF	United Democratic Front
ULFA	United Liberation Front of Assam
UNCIP	United Nations Commission for India and Pakistan
UNCITRAL	United Nations Conference on International Trade Law
UNCNRSE	United Nations Conference for New and Renewable Sources of Energy
UNCTAD	United Nations Conference on Trade and Development
UNDC	United Nations Disarmament Commission
UNDP	United Nations Development Programme
UNEF	United Nations Emergency Force
UNEP	United Nations Environment Programme
UNESCO	United Nations Educational Scientific and Cultural Organization
UNFCC	United Nations Framework Convention on Climate Change
UNFPA	United Nations Fund for Population Activities
UNHCR	United Nations High Commissioner for Refugees
UNI	United News of India
UNICEF	United Nations Children's Education Fund

Q.19. Injaz is the name given to world's first cloned...
Q.20. What is the date on which World Red Cross Day is celebrated?

UNIDO	United Nations Industrial Development Organization
UNITAR	United Nations Institute for Training and Research
UFO	Unidentified Flying Object
UGC	University Grants Commission
ULFA	United Liberation Front of Assam
UPS	Uninterrupted Power Supply
USP	Unique Selling Proposition
UNRRA	United Nations Relief and Rehabilitation Administration
UPSC	Union Public Service Commission

V

VAT	Value Added Tax
VSNL	Videsh Sanchar Nigam Limited
VPP	Value Payable Post
VSSC	Vikram Sarabhai Space Centre
VRDE	Vehicle Research and Development Establishment

W

WEF	World Economic Forum
WII	Wild Life Institute of India
WLL	Wireless in Local Loop
WMD	Weapons of Mass Destruction
WPI	Wholesale Price Index
WWW	World Wide Web
WFC	World Food Council
WHO	World Health Organisation (of UNO)
WMO	World Metrological Organisation (of UNO)
WTO	World Trade Organisation

Y

YMCA	Young Men's Christian Association, Young Women's Christian Association
YMIA	Young Men's Indian Association

Z

ZBB	Zero Based Budgeting
ZS	Zoological Society
ZSI	Zoological Survey of India

Q.21. Saurav Ghosal is related to which sports?
Q.22. On which date International Day against Drug Abuse and Illicit Trafficking is celebrated?

FAMOUS BOOKS AND THEIR AUTHORS

A

A Bend in the River	V S Naipaul
A Brush with Life	Satish Gujral
A Case of Exploding Mangoes	Mohammed Hanif
A Secular Agenda	Arun Shourie
Adventures of Sherlock Holmes	Sir Arthur Conan Doyle
A Suitable Boy	Vikram Seth
Across Borders, Fifty-years of India's Foreign Policy	J N Dixit
Adhe Adhure	Mohan Rakesh
Adonis	P B Shelley
Adventures of Huckleberry Finn	Mark Twain
Adventures of Robinson Crusoe	Daniel Defoe
Adventures of Tom Sawyer	Mark Twain
Affluent Society	J K Galbraith
Agony and the Ecstasy	Irving Stone
Ain-i-Akbari	Abul Fazal
Airport	Arthur Hailey
Ajatashatru	Jai Shankar Prasad
Alice in Wonderland	Lewis Carroll
All is Well that Ends Well	William Shakespeare
All the King's Men	Robert Penn Warren
All the President's Men	Carl Bernstein and Bob Woodward
All Things Bright and Beautiful	James Herriot
An Idealist View of Life	Dr S Radhakrishnan
Androcles and the Lion	George Bernard Shaw
Animal Farm	George Orwell
Anna Karenina	Count Leo Tolstoy
Antony and Cleopatra	William Shakespeare
Apple Cart	George Bernad Shaw
Arabian Nights	Sir Richard Burton
Area of Darkness	V S Naipaul
Arms and the Man	George Bernard Shaw
As You Like It	William Shakespeare
Aspects of the Novel	E M Forster
Atonement	Ian McEwan
Autobiography of an Unknown Indian	Nirad C Chaudhuri

Q.23. Who has written the book My Presidential Year?
Q.24. Who is known as Bangabandhu?

B

Ben Hur	Lewis Wallace
Bend in the Ganges	Manohar Malgonkar
Brick Lane	Monica Ali
Bridge's Book of Beauty	Mulk Raj Anand
Broken Wings	Sarojini Naidu
By God's Decree	Kapil Dev

C

Caesar and Cleopatra	George Bernard Shaw
Canterbury Tales	G Chaucer
Chitra	Rabindranath Tagore
City of Joy	Dominique Lapierre
Comedy of Errors	William Shakespeare
Confessions of a Lover	Mulk Raj Anand
Coolie	Mulk Raj Anand
Culture in the Vanity Bag	Nirad C Chaudhuri

D

Dark Room	R K Narayan
Das Kapital	Karl Marx
Daughter of the East	Benazir Bhutto
David Copperfield	Charles Dickens
Days of his Grace	Eyvind Johnson
Death of a City	Amrita Pritam
Death of a Salesman	Arthur Miller
Decline and fall of the Roman Empire	Edward Gibbon
Decline of the West	O' Spengler
Descent of Man	Charles Darwin
Dilemma of Our Time	Harold Joseph Laski
Discovery of India	Jawaharlal Nehru
Distant Neighbours	Kuldip Nayar
Divine Comedy	A Dante
Divine Life	Swami Sivananda
Doll's House	Ibsen
Don Quixote	Cervantes
Dreams from my Father	Barack Obama
Dynamics of Social Change	Chandra Shekhar

E

East West	Salman Rushdie
Elegy Written in a Country Churchyard	Thomas Gray
Emma	Jane Austen

Q.25. Name the sacred text of Buddhism?
Q.26. What are the names of two sects of Buddhism?

Enchantress of Florence	Salman Rushdie
Ends and Means	Aldous Huxley
End of an Era	C S Pandit
English August	Upamanyu Chartterjee
Essays on Gita	Aurobindo Ghosh
Expanding Universe	Arthur Stanley Eddington
Eye of the Storm	Patrick White

F

Faces to Everest	Maj. H P S Ahluwalia
Family Matters	Rohinton Mistry
Far From the Madding Crowd	Thomas Hardy
Farewell to a Ghost	Manoj Das
Farewell to Arms	Ernest Hemingway
Farm House	George Orwell
Fine Balance	Rohinton Mistry
Freedom at Midnight	Larry Collins and Dominique Lapierre
Freedom from Fear	Aung San Suu Kyi
Friends and Foes	Sheikh Mujibur Rehman
Freedom in Exile	Dalai Lama
From Hero to Eternity	James Jones
Full Moon	P G Wodehouse

G

Gardener	Rabindra Nath Tagore
Gitanjali	Rabindra Nath Tagore
Glimpses of World History	Jawaharlal Nehru
Godaan	Munshi Prem Chand
Golden Gate	Vikram Seth
Golden Girl	P T Usha
Golden Threshold	Sarojini Naidu
Gone with the Wind	Margaret Mitchell
Gora	Rabindra Nath Tagore
Guide	R K Narayan
Gulliver's Travels	Jonathan Swift

H

Hamlet	William Shakespeare
Heat and Dust	Ruth Prawer Jhabwala
Hero of Our Times	Richard Hough
Heroes and Hero worship	Thomas Carlyle
Himalayan Blunder	Brig JP Dalvi
Hindu View of Life	Dr S Radhakrishnan
Hindu Civilisation	J M Barrie
House Divided	Pearl S Buck
Human Factor	Graham Greene
Humour	Ben Jonson
Hungry Stones	Rabindra Nath Tagore

I

I Am Not an Island	K A Abbas
I Follow the Mahatma	K M Munshi
Idiot	Fyodor Dostoevsky
Idols	Sunil Gavaskar
Importance of Being Earnest	Oscar Wilde
In Search of Gandhi	Richard Attenborough
India 2020: A Vision for the New Millennium	Dr A P J Abdul Kalam and Dr Y S Rajan
India – A Wounded Civilisation	V S Naipaul
India – From Curzon to Nehru and After	Durga Dass
Indian Home Rule	M K Gandhi
India's Economic Crisis	Dr Bimal Jalan
India Divided	Rajendra Prasad
India Wins Freedom	Maulana Abul Kalam Azad
Indian Muslims	Prof. Mohd Mujeeb
Invisible Man	H G Wells
Iron in the Soul	Jean Paul Sartre
Ivanhoe	Sir Walter Scott

J

Jai Somnath	K M Munshi
Jane Eyre	Charlotte Bronte
Julius Caesar	William Shakespeare
Jungle Book	Rudyard Kipling

K

Kadambari	Bana Bhatt
Kanthapura	Raja Rao
Kapal Kundala	Bankim Chandra Chatterjee
Kashmir-Behind the Vale	M J Akbar
Kayakalp	Munshi Prem Chand
King of Dark Chamber	Rabindra Nath Tagore
Kiratarjuniya	Bharavi
King Lear	Shakespeare

L

Lady of the Lake	Sir Walter Scott
Life Divine	Aurobindo Ghosh
Lipika	Rabindranath Tagore
Long Walk to Freedom	Nelson Mandela
Lost Child	Mulk Raj Anand
Lolita	V Nabokov
Lycidas	John Milton

Q.27. Who is known as the father of English Poetry?
Q.28. What does the words Citius, Altius and Fortius of the Olympic motto denote?

M

Macbeth	William Shakespeare
Mahabharata	Vyasa
Man and Superman	G B Shaw
Man Eaters of Kumaon	Jim Corbett
Man for All Seasons	Robert Bolt
Man of Destiny	George Bernard Shaw
Mansfield Park	Jane Austen
Many Worlds	K P S Menon
Mati Matal	Gopinath Mohanty
Mayor of Casterbridge	Thomas Hardy
Mein Kampf	Adolf Hitler
Memories of the Second World War	Churchill
Men Who Killed Gandhi	Manohar Malgonkar
Midnight's Children	Salman Rushdie
Midsummer Night's Dream	William Shakespeare
Mill on the Floss	George Eliot
Mistaken Identity	Nayantara Sehgal
Moor's Last Sigh	Salman Rushdie
Mother	Maxim Gorky
Mountbatten and Independent India	Larry Collins and Dominique Lapierre
Murder in the Cathedral	T S Eliot
My Country My Life	L K Advani
My Days	R K Narayan
My Early Life	M K Gandhi
My Experiment with Truth	M K Gandhi
My India	S Nihal Singh
My Music, My Love	Ravi Shankar
My Truth	Indira Gandhi
My Prison Diary	J P Narayan
My Reminiscences	R N Tagore

N

Nacked Face	Sydney Sheldon
Naked Triangle	Balwant Gargi
Nelson Mandela: A Biography	Martin Meredith
Netaji – Dead or Alive	Samar Guha
Nicholas Nickelby	Charles Dickens
Non-Violence in Peace and War	M K Gandhi
Northanger Abbey	Jane Austen

O

Odakkuzal	G Shankara Kurup
Odyssey	Homer

Q.29. Who has written the book 'Long Walk to Freedom'?
Q.30. In India, what is the highest honour given in sports?

Of Human Bondage	W Somerset Maugham
Old Man and the Sea	Ernest Hemingway
Oliver Twist	Charles Dickens
One Hundred Years of Solitude	Gabriel Garcia Marquez
One World and India	Arnold Toynbee

P

Painter of Signs	R K Narayan
Pair of Blue Eyes	Thomas Hardy
Pakistan in the Twentieth Century Political History	Lawrence Ziring
Pakistan – The Gathering Storm	Benazir Bhutto
Panchtantra	Vishnu Sharma
Paradise Lost	John Milton
Paradise Regained	John Milton
Passage to England	Nirad C Chaudhuri
Passage to India	E M Forster
Pather Panchali	Bibhuti Bhushan Bandyopadhyaya
Peter Pan	J M Barrie
Persuasion	Jane Austen
Pinjar	Amrita Pritam
Post Office	Rabindranath Tagore
Prem Pachisi	Prem Chand
Price of Partition	Rafiq Zakaria
Prisoner's Scrapbook	L K Advani
Prince	Machiavelli
Prithviraj Raso	Chand Bardai
Pride and Prejudice	Jane Austen
Pygmalion	G B Shaw

R

Ram Charit Manas	Tulsidas
Ramayana	Maharishi Valmiki (in Sanskrit)
Rangbhoomi	Prem Chand
Ratnavali	Harsha Vardhan
Republic	Plato
Resurrection	Leo Tolstoy
Return of the Native	Thomas Hardy

S

Saket	Maithili Sharan Gupta
Satyartha Prakash	Swami Dayanand
Satanic Verses	Salman Rushdie

Q.31. Who established the Magsaysay Award?
Q.32. What stands for ICBM?

Savitri | Aurobindo Ghosh
Sceptred Flute | Sarojini Naidu
Schindlr's List | Thomas Keneally
Sea of Poppies | Amitav Ghosh
Second World War | Winston Churchill
Seven Summers | Mulk Raj Anand
Shantaram | Gregory David Roberts
Story of My Life | Helen Keller

T

Tale of Two Cities | Charles Dickens
Talisman | Sir Walter Scott
Tess of D'Urbervilles | Thomas Hardy
The Age of Shiva | Manil Suri
The Agony and Ecstasy | Irving Stone
The Alchemist | Ben Johnson
The Blind Assassin | Margaret Atwood
The Da Vinci Code | Dan Brown
The Godfather | Mario Puzo
The Inheritance of Loss | Kiran Desai
The Insider | P V Narasimha Rao
The Kalam Effect-My years with the President | P M Nair
The Namesake | Jhumpa Lahiri
The Universe in a Single Atom | Dalai Lama

U

Ulysses | James Joyce
Unaccustomed Earth | Jhumpa Lahiri
Uncle Tom's Cabin | Mrs Hariet Stowe
Unhappy India | Lala Lajpat Rai
Utouchable | Mulk Raj Anand
Uttar Ramcharita | Bhava Bhuti
Utopia | Thomas More

V

Vanity Fair | William Makepeace Thackeray
Vendor of Sweets | R K Narayan
View from the UN | U Thant
Village by the Sea | Anita Desai
Village | Mulk Raj Anand
Vinay Patrika | Tulsidas
Virangana | Maithili Sharan Gupta
Voice of Conscience | V V Giri

Q.33. The term 'Gambit' is related to which sports?
Q.34. Who is known as the 'father of the white revolution' in India?

W

Waiting for Godot	Samuel Beckett
Waiting for the Mahatma	R K Narayan
War and Peace	Leo Tolstoy
War of Indian Independence	Vir Savarkar
War of the Worlds	H G Wells
Waste Land	T S Eliot
We, Indians	Khushwant Singh
Wealth of Nations	Adam Smith
Westward Ho	Charles Kingsley
Wings of fire, an Autobiography	Dr A P J Abdul Kalam & A Tiwari
Wuthering Heights	Emily Bronte

Y

Yajnaseni	Dr Pratibha Roy
Yama	Mahadevi Verma
Yashodhara	Maithili Sharan Gupta
Years of Pilgrimage	Dr Raja Ramanna

Z

Zool: The Final Odyssey	Arthur C Clarke

GREAT PERSONALITIES

A

Abraham Lincoln (1809–65): He was the sixteenth President of the USA. He formed Republican Party and abolished slavery. He was assassinated by John Wilkes Booth in 1865.

Abdul Gaffar Khan (1890–1988): He was popularly known as 'Frontier Gandhi' as he worked among the *pathans* of North-West Frontier Province. He started the *Khudai Khidmatgar* (Servants of God) Movement. He was awarded 'Bharat Ratna' in 1987.

Abhinav Bindra (b. 1983): Sharpshooter from Chandigarh who won India's first ever individual Olympic Gold Medal in the 10m Air Rifle event in Beijing Olympic. He is also the first Indian shooter to win a World Championship Gold in Zagreb. He was conferred the Rajiv Gandhi Khel Ratna Award (2001) and Padma Bhushan (2009).

Adolf Hitler (1889–1945): Austrian-born German Dictator who rose to power in Germany during early 1930s at a time of social, political and economic upheaval. He was the ruler of Germany from 1933 to 1945, serving as chancellor from 1933 to 1945 and as head of state from 1934 to 1945. He initiated the World War II by invading Poland in 1939 and Germany was defeated in 1945. During the final days of the war in 1945, Hitler married his mistress Eva Braun. Less than two days later, the two committed suicide.

Alexander the Great (356–323 BC): King of Macedonia, who conquered South-west Asia, Egypt and Greece. He founded Alexandria and invaded India in 327 BC. He died at Babylon (Modern Baghdad) in 323 BC.

Q.35. Who is Tania Sachdev?
Q.36. Who is the first Asian to win Nobel Prize?

Albert Einstein (1879–1955): German-born, physicist of the twentieth century who is best known for his theories of special relativity and general relativity. He was awarded the Nobel Prize in Physics in 1921.

Dr A P J Abdul Kalam (b. 1931): He is the eleventh President of India. One of the most distinguished scientists of the country, he is also known as the man behind India's missile programmes. He has the unique honour of receiving 30 honorary doctorates. He has been awarded Bharat Ratna (1997). He has written four books: *'Wings of Fire', 'India 2020 – A Vision for the New Millennium', 'My Journey'* and *'Ignited Minds – Unleashing the power within India'*.

A R Rahman (b. 1967): Hailed by *Times* magazine as the 'Mozart of Madras', A R Rahman has redefined contemporary Indian music. He has won thirteen Filmfare Awards, four National Film Awards, a BAFTA Award, one Golden Globe and two Academy Awards.

Archimedes (287–212 BC): Greek mathematician, known for his 'Archimedes Principle' and he invented Archimedean screw. He is called the 'father of integral calculus' and also the 'father of mathematical physics'.

Arundathi Roy (b. 1961): She is the first Indian writer to win the Booker Prize, for her novel – *The God of Small Things*. She is also the winner of Sydney Peace prize in 2004.

Aryabhata (AD 476–520): He was an Indian mathematician who wrote the *Aryabhatiya* which summarises Hindu mathematics and and *Arya-Siddhanta*. India's first satellite was named after him.

Ashapurna Devi (1909–95): She is a Bengali writer and the first woman Jnanpith Awardee of India. Her works include *Subarnolata, Bokulo Katha*, and *Prathama Pratishruti*, etc.

Aurobindo Ghosh (1872–1950): He was a freedom fighter, poet, scholar, yogi and philosopher. He worked towards the cause of India's freedom, and for further evolution of life on earth. His important writings include *The Life Divine, The Synthesis of Yoga, Secrets of the Vedas, Essays on the Gita*, etc., in prose and in poetry his principal work is *'Savitri – A Legend and a Symbol'* in blank verse.

Azim Hasham Premji (b. 1945): He is the founder of Wipro (Third largest IT Company in India). *Fortune* (August 2003) named him as one of the 25 most powerful business leaders outside the US; *Business Week* featured (October 2003) him on their cover with the sobriquet 'India's tech king'.

B

Bankim Chandra Chartterjee (1838–94): Poet, novelist and patriot from Bengal who wrote 'Vande Mataram', the National Song of India which is excerpted from his novel *'Anand Math'*.

Benjamin Franklin (1706–90): One of the founding fathers of the United States of America who was a scientist, inventor, statesman and economist. He served as a delegate to the Constitutional Convention and signed the Constitution.

Bhimrao Ramji Ambedkar (1891–1956): A well-known jurist, social worker, politician is considered as the emancipator of the untouchables. Also known as father of Indian Constitution awarded Bharat Ratna in 1990.

Bismillah Khan (1916–2006): Indian shehnai maestro, who was perhaps single handedly responsible for making the shehnai a

Q.37. For what kind of achievement is the Ashoka Chakra awarded?

Q.38. When is the National Wild-Life Week celebrated?

famous classical instrument. He was the third classical musician to be awarded the Bharat Ratna (2001).

C

Sir Charles Spencer Chaplin Jr (1889–1977): He was the most famous comic actor, notable filmmaker, composer and musician. Some of his well-known movies are *The Kid, Gold Rush, Lime Light, The Tramp,* etc. He won one Oscar in a competitive category, and was given two honorary Academy Awards.

Charles Dickens (1812–70): Most popular English novelist of the Victorian era. His works include *David Copperfield, Oliver Twist, Pickwick Papers* and *Great Expectations*.

Charles Darwin (1809–82): English naturalist who established *The Theory of Evolution* based on natural selection. His works include on *The Origin of Species* and *Descent of Man*.

Chhatrapati Shivaji (1627–80): The great Maratha leader was the last Hindu King, who fought against Mughal Emperor Aurangzeb. The kingdom established by Chhatrapati Shivaji known as 'Hindavi Swaraja' (Sovereign Hindu state).

D

Dalai Lama (b. 1935): Tenzin Gyatso, the fourteenth Dalai Lama, is the Spiritual leader of Tibet. He fled to India in 1959 after Tibetan uprising and established government-in-exile at Dharmashala. He was awarded the Nobel Peace Prize in 1989.

Dhyan Chand Singh (1905–79): Hockey Wizard, born at Prayag (Allahabad), won three Olympic Gold Medals in 1928, 1932 and 1936. India celebrates twenty-ninth of August as National Sports Day in memory of his birthday. He was honoured Padma Bhushan in 1956.

Dhirajlal Hirachand Ambani (1932–2002): Popularly known as Dhirubhai Ambani is the founder of the Reliance Industry (now India's Largest Private Company). He was conferred with The Economic Times Award for Corporate Excellence for Lifetime Achievement on August 2001.

E

Euclid (350–300 BC): Known as Father of Geometry, he was a Greek Mathematician. He used the Deductive Principle of Logic as the basis of geometry and he propounded many geometrical theorems.

F

Florence Nightingale (1820–1920): She was an English nurse and founder of Modern nursing. She is known as 'Lady with the Lamp'. She was the first woman to receive the 'Order of Merit'.

G

Galileo (1564–1642): Italian physicist, mathematician, astronomer and philosopher who improved the telescope, discovered four largest satellites of Jupiter, named the Galilean moons in his honour and observed and analysed the sunspots.

George Washington (1732–99): The first President of the United States, who led the revolt against British and declared American independence. He presided over the Philadelphia Convention that drafted the United States Constitution in 1787.

Q.39. Who wrote the book **Friends and Foes** *?*

Q.40. Term Cannon is related to which sports?

Ghanshyam Das Birla (1894–1983): He was the great architect of India's industrial growth, formed the Birla Brothers Limited in 1919. He set up an Aluminum Plant 'Hindalco', near Mirzapur. He was awarded, the Padma Vibhushan in 1957.

Govind Ballabh Pant (1887–1961): He was a statesman, an activist of Indian nationalist movement. He led the movement to establish Hindi as the national language of India. He was the Home Minister in Nehru's Cabinet. He was awarded Bharat Ratna in 1957.

H

Homer (9 BC): He is the legendary ancient Greek epic poet, known as author of two of ancient Greece's most important literary works: *The Iliad* and *The Odyssey*.

I

Sir Isaac Newton (1642–1727): He is mathematician and physicist. One of the foremost scientific intellects of all time, he described universal gravitation and the three laws of motion which dominated the scientific view of the physical universe. He is also known for his work on the composition of white light and calculus. Posthumously published writings include: *The System of the World* (1728), the first draft of Book III of the *Principia* and *Observations upon the Prophecies of Daniel and the Apocalypse of St John* (1733).

J

Jamshedji Tata (1839–1904): Regarded as the 'father of Indian industry', established the Indian Institute of Science Bangalore (IISc). He founded the Tata Group of companies.

Jayaprakash Narayan (1902–79): Widely known as JP, he was an Indian freedom fighter and political leader. He is remembered especially for leading the opposition against Indira Gandhi in the 1970s and for giving a call for peaceful *Total Revolution*. He was awarded Magsaysay award (1965) and the Bharat Ratna posthumously in 1998.

Jaya Dev (Twelfth Century): The twelfth-century poet, Jayadeva, born in Orissa, is known for his composition of the *Gita Govinda*, which describes the relationship between Krishna and the *gopis*. This work has been of great importance in the development of the Bhakti tradition of Hinduism.

John F Kennedy (1917–63): Referred to by his initials JFK, he was the youngest of all the presidents to be elected as the President of United States. His famous books are: *Why England Slept* and *Profile in Courage*. He was assassinated on 22 November 1963.

J K Rowling (b. 1965): She is a British author, best known as the author of the *Harry Potter* series. The 2008 *Sunday Times Rich List* enlisted her as the twelfth richest woman in Britain.

K

Karl Marx (1818–83): The German philosopher, socialist and revolutionary, Karl Marx, is regarded as the most influential socialist thinker in the nineteenth century and founder of modern communism. He has written *The Communist Manifesto* and *Das Kapital*.

Karnam Malleshwari (b. 1976): She is the first Indian woman to win an Olympic medal (Bronze) in weightlifting. She was awarded Rajiv Gandhi Khel Ratna Award in 1995-96 and Padma Shri in 1999.

Kiran Bedi (b. 1949): She became India's first woman Indian Police Service officer in 1972.

Q.41. Who was the founder of Judaism?

Q.42. How many players are there in each side in Water Polo?

She has worked with the United Nations in the Department of Peace Keeping Operations. She was awarded the Ramon Magsaysay Award in 1995 and UN medal for outstanding service in 2004.

L

Lakshmi Mittal (b. 1950): He is Indian born industrialist based in the United Kingdom. Chairman of Arcelor-Mittal Steel Company, he was named as world's fifteenth most admired CEO in 2005. As of 2009, Mittal is the world's eighth richest person and the richest person in the UK.

Lata Mangeshkar (b. 1929): An Institution of Indian Music in herself, she is known as the Melody Queen of India. She is honoured with the Dada Saheb Phalke Award, Rajiv Gandhi Sadbhavana award and Bharat Ratna (2001).

Leonardo Da Vinci (1452–1519): A great Italian genius who was at once a scientist, mathematician, engineer, inventor, painter, sculptor, architect, musician and writer. Leonardo has often been described as the archetype of the Renaissance man. Two of his works, the *Mona Lisa* and *The Last Supper*, are the most famous painting of all time.

Leo Tolstoy (1828–1910): Russian novelist and writer, known for his masterpieces *War and Peace, Resurrection* and *Anna Karenina*. He had profound impact on Gandhi and Martin Luther King, Jr.

M

Madam Marie Curie (1867–1934): Poland born scientist, who jointly with husband Pierre Curie discovered radium for which they shared the Nobel Prize in Physics in 1903. She won Nobel Prize again for Chemistry in 1911.

Mahesh Bhupati (b. 1974): He is the first Indian to win a Grand Slam tournament. He is among the best doubles tennis players in the world with 11 Grand Slam titles to his credit. He was awarded Padma Shri in 2001.

Martin Luther King Jr (1929–68): Prominent leader in the African-American civil rights movement, his main legacy was to secure progress on civil rights in the United States. In 1964, he became the youngest person to receive the Nobel Peace Prize. He was assassinated on 4 April 1968.

N

Nanak, Guru (1469–1539): The founder of Sikhism and the first of the ten Gurus of the Sikhs. He tried to put an end to religious strife through his message that 'God is one', whether he is Allah or Ram.

Neil Armstrong (b. 1930): American Astronaut Commander Armstrong was the first person to set foot on the Moon on 20 July 1969 (APOLLO XI).

Nelson Mandela (b. 1918): He is the former President of South Africa and the first black man to be elected in a fully representative democratic election in the country. Under his leadership South Africa became a non-racist democracy.

He received the Bharat Ratna Award in 1990 and the Nobel Peace Prize in 1993. He has written the book *Long Walk to Freedom*.

N R Narayana Murthy (b. 1946): He is the co-founder of Infosys Technology, retired in 2006. He is currently the non-executive Chairman and

Q.43. Who was the author of the **Kadambari,** *a great romantic play?*

Q.44. What does BMD stand for?

Chief Mentor of Infosys. Ranked eighth among the top 15 most admired global leaders in 2005 by *The Economist*. He was awarded the Padma Vibhushan and Légion d'honneur, the highest civilan award by France in 2008.

P

Pandit Ravi Shankar (b. 1920): This legendary sitarist and composer is India's most esteemed musical Ambassador of Indian classical music. He has received many awards and honours from all over the world, including fourteen doctorates, the Bharat Ratna in 1999, the Music Council UNESCO award in 1975, the Magsaysay Award, two Grammy's, the Fukuoka Grand Prize from Japan and the Crystal award from Davos are to name some.

Pankaj Advani (b. 1985): He is an Indian billiards and snooker player. He is the only player ever to have achieved a 'Grand Double' of winning both points and timed formats at the IBSF World Billiards Championship in both 2005 and 2008. He is the second Indian, after Geet Sethi to win World Professional Billiards in 2009. He was honoured with Arjun Award in 2004, Rajiv Gandhi Khel Ratna Award in 2006 and Padma Shri in 2009.

R

Rajiv Gandhi (1944–91): He was the youngest Prime Minister of India at the age of 40. As a Prime Minister, Rajiv Gandhi made a valuable contribution in modernising Indian administration. He had the vision and foresight that information technology will play a key role in the development of India and worked towards it. On 21 May 1991 Rajiv Gandhi was assassinated.

Ratan Naval Tata (b. 1937): He is the Chairman of the Tata Group, one of the largest group of industries. He was honoured with Padma Vibhushan and the NASSCOM Global Leadership Awards in 2008.

S

Sachin Tendulkar (b. 1973): He is regarded as one of the greatest batsmen in the history of cricket. Wisden ranked him the second greatest Test batsman of all time, next to Donald Bradman, and the second greatest one day international (ODI) batsman of all time, next to Sir Vivian Richards in 2002. He has been honoured with Rajiv Gandhi Khel Ratna Award (1998) and Padma Vibhushan (2008).

Saina Nehwal (b. 1990): Born in Hyderabad, he is the first Indian badminton ace to reach the quarter finals at the Olympic Games and the first Indian to win the World Junior Badminton Championships. She was honoured with Arjun Award in 2009.

Satyajit Ray (1921–92): He is one of the greatest film directors of India. He won special Academy Award and Bharat Ratna (1992). Some of his acclaimed films are *Pather Panchali, Aparajita,* and *Charulata,* etc.

Sigmund Freud (1856–1939): He is an Austrian psychiatrist who founded the psychoanalytic school of psychology. His works include *The Interpretation of Dreams* and *The Ego and the Id*.

Shanti Swarup Bhatnagar (1894–1955): Well-known Indian scientist, known as 'The Father of Research Laboratories'. The Council of Scientific and Industrial Research (CSIR) was set up under his chairmanship. After his death, CSIR established the Shanti Swarup Bhatnagar Award in his honour.

Q.45. Le Corbusier, the architect of Chandigarh, was a national of which country?

Q.46. National Sports Day is celebrated on 29 August in memory of what?

Sundarlal Bahuguna (b. 1927): Indian Environmentalist, Gandhian Peace worker, he is the founder of Chipko Movement. He was awarded Right Livelihood Award in 1987 and Padma Vibhushan in 2009.

Sunil Gavaskar (b. 1949): Regarded as one of the greatest opening batsmen in test cricket, set world records for the most runs and most centuries scored by any batsman during his career. The Border-Gavaskar Trophy has been instituted in his (co-) honour. He has written *Sunny Days* (autobiography) and *One Day Wonders*. He has been awarded the Padma Bhushan.

Swami Vivekanand (1863–1902): Disciple of Ramkrishna Paramahamsha, he founded Ramakrishna Mission. Swami Vivekananda is known as the greatest philosopher and spiritual leader of twentieth century. He represented India as a delegate in the 1893 Parliament of World religions at Chicago.

Swaraj Paul (b. 1931): Britain-based Indian Industrialist, he was appointed deputy speaker of House of Lords in UK in December 2008. He is the first person of Indian origin to hold the post. He was awarded the Padma Bhushan in 1983.

T

Thomas Alva Edison (1847–1931): American inventor who, singly or jointly, held a world record 1,093 patents. In addition, he created the world's first industrial research laboratory. Edison's first inventions were the transmitter and receiver for the automatic telegraph; his other inventions include incandescent lamp, gramophone, microphone, etc.

V

Ved Vyas: He is the profound author of one of the greatest epics *Mahabharata*, a marvel in the literature of the world. Besides he also classified the four *Vedas* and wrote eighteen *Puranas* and *Brahma sutras*.

Dr Verghese Kurien (b. 1921): He is called the 'father of the white revolution' in India. He is credited with architecting 'Operation Flood'. He was awarded Ramon Magsaysay Award for Community Leadership (1963), World Food Prize Award (1989) and Padma Vibhushan (1999).

Vijaylakshmi Pandit (1900–90): She was the sister of Jawaharlal Nehru; she was also the first women cabinet minister. She became first woman elected president of the UN General Assembly in 1953.

Vladimir Ilyich Lenin (1870–1924): He was a Russian revolutionary, Bolshevik leader, communist politician, principal leader of the October Revolution and the first head of the Soviet Union. His contributions to Marxist theory are commonly referred to as Leninism.

Vinoba Bhave (1895–1982): Often called *Acharya*, he was an advocate of non-violence and human rights. He started the Bhoodan Movement and Sarvodaya movement. In 1958 Vinoba was the first recipient of the international Ramon Magsaysay Award for Community Leadership. He was awarded the Bharat Ratna posthumously in 1983.

Viswanathan Anand (b. 1969): The chess whizkid who became the first Indian to win the World Junior Chess Championship in 1987 and is India's first Grandmaster (1988). He won the Chess Oscar in 1997, 1998, 2003, 2004 and 2007. He was first recipient of the Rajiv Gandhi Khel Ratna Award (1991–92) and the Padma Bhushan in 2000. He is the first Asian to win the World Chess Championship title. He

Q.47. Who wrote A Passage to India?

Q.48. For achievement in which field is the David Cohen prize given?

wrote a book *My Best Games of Chess* for which he got the British Chess Federation 'Book of the Year' Award in 1998.

W

Walt Disney (1901–66): American film producer, director, screenwriter, voice actor, animator, entrepreneur and philanthropist, who was also the creator of famous cartoon character 'Mickey Mouse' and 'Donald Duck'. The corporation he co-founded, now known as The Walt Disney Company. He won twenty-six Academy Awards, including a record four in one year, and received a further fifty-nine nominations, holds the individual record for the most awards and the most nominations.

Sir Winston Churchill (1874–1965): British statesman, soldier, politician known for his leadership of the United Kingdom during the World War II. He is the only British Prime Minister who has ever received the Nobel Prize in Literature (1953).

William Shakespeare (1564–1616): English poet, dramatist considered to be the greatest dramatist of all time, has written 37 plays and 154 sonnets. Shakespeare's plays include *Hamlet, Romeo and Juliet, Othello, Macbeth, The Tempest*, etc.

Y

Yuri Gagarin (1934–68): He is popularly called 'The Columbus of the Cosmos'. On 12 April 1961, he became the first human to orbit earth in spacecraft Vostok I.

IMPORTANT DATES

Important National Days

Date	Day
12 January	National Youth Day
15 January	Army Day
26 January	Republic Day
30 January	Martyrs' Day
24 February	Central Excise Day
28 February	National Science Day
5 April	National Maritime Day
1 May	National Technology Day
13 May	National Solidarity Day
9 August	Quit India Day
15 August	Independence Day
29 August	National Sports Day
5 September	Teachers' Day and Sanskrit Day
2 October	Gandhi Jayanti
8 October	Indian Air Force Day
10 October	National Postal Day
14 November	Children's Day

Q.49. Who is the first Indian woman to receive Borlaug award?
Q.50. In which year was the Nobel Prize instituted?

4 December	Navy Day
18 December	Minorities Rights Day
23 December	Farmers Day [Kisan Divas]

Important International Days

Date	Day
10 January	World Laughter Day
26 January	International Customs Day
30 January	World Leprosy Eradication Day
8 March	International Women's Day
15 March	World Disabled Day and World Consumer Rights Day
21 March	World Forestry Day and International Day for the Elimination of Racial Discrimination
22 March	World Day for Water
23 March	World Meteorological Day
4 March	World TB Day
7 April	World Health Day
17 April	World Hemophilia Day
18 April	World Heritage Day
22 April	Earth Day
23 April	World Book and Copyright Day
26 April	Intellectual Property Day
1 May	International Labour Day or May Day
3 May	Press Freedom Day
8 May	World Red Cross Day
9 May	Mothers' Day
12 May	International Nurses Day
15 May	International Day of the Family
17 May	World Telecommunication Day
24 May	Commonwealth Day
31 May	Anti-tobacco Day
5 June	World Environment Day
20 June*	Father's Day
*(3rd Sunday in June)	
27 June	World Diabetes Day
1 July	Doctors Day
11 July	World Population Day
1 August	World Breast Feeding Day
6 August	Hiroshima Day
9 August	Nagasaki Day
8 September	World Literary Day
16 September	World Ozone Day
26 September	Day of the Deaf
27 September	World Tourism Day
1 October	International Day for the Elderly
3 October	World Habitat Day

Basic General Knowledge

4 October	World Animal Welfare Day
12 October	World Sight Day
16 October	World Food Day
24 October	UN Day
30 October	World Thrift Day
14 November	Diabetes Day
29 November	International Day of Solidarity with Palestinian People
1 December	World AIDS Day
10 December	International Day of Broadcasting

National and International Week

India's Tourism Week	20–25 January
National Rail Week	10–16 April
World Breastfeeding Week	1–7 August
National Nutrition Week	1–7 September
National Post Week	9–15 October
National Wildlife Week	2–8 November
National Book Week	14–20 November
National Pharmacy Week	18–24 November
National Communal Integration Week	19–25 November

Nickname of Famous Personalities

Father of Comedy	Aristophanes
Father of Sunday Newspaper	John Bell
Father of Chemistry	Robert Boyle
Father of English Poetry	Geoffrey Chaucer
Father of Aviation	Sir George Cayley
Father of Immunology	Edward Jenner
Father of Modern Chemistry	Antoine Lavoisier
Father of Atom Bomb	Dr Robert Oppenheimer
Father of Nuclear Physics	Ernest Rutherford
Father of Economics	Adam Smith

RELIGIONS OF THE WORLD

Buddhism

Founded by	:	Gautam Buddha (563–483 BC)
Founded in	:	525 BC
Followed in	:	Sri Lanka, Tibet, Nepal, India, China, Japan, Myanmar, Bhutan, Vietnam, Taiwan, Indonesia, Korea, Mongolia, Laos, Thailand
Sacred Text	:	*Tripitaka* (Collection of Buddha's teaching) also called *sutras*
Sacred Places	:	Lumbini (Nepal), where Buddha was born; Bodha Gaya (Bihar), where he received enlightenment and Kushinagar (UP), where he attained *Nirvana*
Place of Worship	:	Vihar (temple) and Monastery (where monk resides)
Sects	:	*Mahayana* and *Hinayana*

Confucianism

Founded by	: King Fu Tsu, also known as Confucius (551–479 BC), born in the tate of Lu in China
Founded in	: 500 BC
Followed in	: China, Taiwan, South Korea, Nauru and Vietnam
Sacred Text	: *The Analects*
Sacred Places	: Beijing (China)
Place of Worship	: No particular place

Christianity

Founded by	: Jesus Christ (5 BC–AD 30), born in Judea
Founded in	: 2000 years ago
Followed in	: All over the world
Sacred Text	: Holy Bible consisting of Old Testament (before Christ) and New Testament (after Christ)
Sacred Places	: Jerusalem
Place of Worship	: Church
Sects	: Catholic and Protestants

Hinduism

Founded by	: Divine Origin
Founded in	: 1500 BC
Followed in	: Bhutan, India, Nepal, Fiji, Indonesia, Mauritius, Sri Lanka, South Africa, Surinam, Trinidad and Tobago, Guyana
Sacred Text	: *The Vedas*, *The Upanishads*, *The Bhagavat Gita*, *Mahabharata* and *Ramayana*
Place of Worship	: Temple

Islam

Founded by	: Prophet Muhammed (AD 570–632) born in Mecca
Founded in	: AD 622
Followed in	: Tanzania, Southern part of Russia, China, India, Pakistan, Bangladesh, Malaysia, Indonesia, Iraq, Iran, Afghanistan, UAE, Saudi Arabia
Sacred Text	: Quran, Hadis (Collection of Prophet's sayings)
Sacred Places	: Mecca in Saudi Arabia
Place of Worship	: Mosque
Sects	: Sunnis and Shias

Judaism

Founded by	: Moses, born in Egypt
Founded in	: 1300 BC
Followed in	: Israel and USA

Q.51. Who is known as the 'Father of Geometry'?
Q.52. Where the Right Livelihood Awards are presented annually?

Sacred Text : Hals, found in the five book of the Bible; Torah known as Talmud and Midrash
Sacred Places : Jerusalem
Place of Worship: Synagogue

Shintoism

Founded by : Began with Japanese culture and tradition
Followed in : Japan
Sacred Text : No specific text
Sacred Places : Central shrine of Ise (Central Japan) and the Yasukuni Shrine in Tokto

Sikhism

Founded by : Guru Nanak (1469–1539)
Founded in : AD 1500
Followed in : India
Sacred Text : Guru Granth Saheb
Sacred Places : Golden Temple of Amritsar (Punjab)
Place of Worship : Gurudwara

Taoism

Founded by : Lao-Tse, Chinese Philosopher
Founded in : Sixth Century BC
Followed in : China, Taiwan, Nauru, Brunei, Singapore and Vietnam
Sacred Text : Tao-Te-Ching

Zoroastrianism

Founded by : Zoroaster, born in Medea (Modern Iran) in about 660 BC.
Founded in : around 500 BC
Followed in : Iran, India
Sacred Text : *Zend A Vesta*
Place of Worship : Fire Temple

Official Books

An official report of the British Government	Blue Book
Official publication of Italy	Green Book
Official reports of the Government of Japan and Belgium	Grey Book
Official publication of the Government of the Netherlands	Orange Book
Official publication of the China, Germany and Portugal	White Book
Official paper of the Government of Britain and India on a particular issue	White paper
Official book the Government of France	Yellow Book

Q.53. Who was the first woman Prime Minister in the world?
Q.54. Who is the author of India Divided?

AWARDS, HONOUR AND PRIZES

International Awards

Nobel Prize

Nobel Prize is the most prestigious award in the world. This award is administered by the Nobel Foundation in Stockholm, Sweden. Each prize consists of a medal, personal diploma, and a cash award. The Nobel Prize amount for 2008 was Swedish kronor (SEK) 10 million for full Nobel Prize.

Every year since 1901 the Nobel Prize has been awarded for achievements in Physics, Chemistry, Physiology or Medicine, Literature and for Peace.

In 1968, Sveriges Riksbank (Sweden's central bank) established Prize in Economic Sciences in memory of Alfred Nobel, founder of the Nobel Prize.

The medals for Physics, Chemistry, Physiology or Medicine and Literature were modelled by the Swedish sculptor and engraver Erik Lindberg and the Peace medal by the Norwegian sculptor Gustav Vigeland. The medal for The Sveriges Riksbank Prize in Economic Sciences in Memory of Alfred Nobel was designed by Gunvor Svensson-Lundqvist.

The Nobel Peace Prize has been awarded to 109 individuals and 20 organisations since its inception (up to October 2009).

Other International Awards

Pulitzer Prize

The prizes, originally endowed with a gift of $500,000 from the newspaper magnate Joseph Pulitzer, were given in the month of May since 1917. The awardees are decided by Columbia University on the recommendation of The Pulitzer Prize Board, composed of judges appointed by the university.

The prizes have varied in number and category over the years but currently 14 prizes in the field of journalism, six prizes in letters, one prize in music and four fellowships are given away.

Magsaysay Award

The Award was established in April 1957 by the trustees of the Rockefeller Brothers Fund (RBF) based in New York City. The prize was created to commemorate Ramon Magsaysay, the late president of the Philippines, to perpetuate his example of integrity in government, courageous service to the people and pragmatic idealism within a democratic society.

Every year the Ramon Magsaysay Award Foundation gives away prizes to Asian individuals and organisations for achieving excellence in their respective fields. The awards are given in six categories:

- Government Service
- Public Service
- Community Leadership
- Journalism, Literature and Creative Communication Arts

Q.55. Which is the sacred text of the Confucianism?
Q.56. Which is India's largest Indoor Stadium?

- Peace and International Understanding
- Emergent Leadership

Templeton Prize

The prize was established by the late Sir John Templeton in 1972, the prize aims to identify 'entrepreneurs of the spirit' – outstanding individuals who have devoted their talents to expanding our vision of ultimate purpose and reality.

The prize is a monetary award in the amount of £1,000,000.

Booker Prize

The Man Booker Prize, also known as the Booker Prize was established in 1968.

It is a literary prize, awarded each year for the best original full-length novel, written in the English language, by a citizen of the Commonwealth of Nations. P H Newby was the first winner of the Booker Prize.

Oscar Award (Academy Award)

This award was instituted in 1929. It is conferred every year by Academy of Motion Pictures towards outstanding contribution in the field of motion pictures.

The British Academy of Film and Television Arts (BAFTA) Award

This award is organised annually by The British Academy of Film and Television Arts (BAFTA) for excellence in film, television and interactive media. It was founded in 1947.

Grammy Award

Established in 1958, the Grammy Awards (originally called the Gramophone Awards) or Grammys are presented annually by the National Academy of Recording Arts and Sciences of the USA for outstanding achievements in the music industry.

Jawaharlal Nehru Award

This is an international award presented by the Government of India founded in 1965. This award is being given away annually by Indian Council for Cultural Relations (ICCR) for 'outstanding contribution to the promotion of international understanding, goodwill and friendship among people of the world'. The money constituent of this award is 2.5 million rupees.

Right Livelihood Award

This award was established in 1980 by philatelist Jakob von Uexkull to honour and support those 'offering practical and exemplary answers to the most urgent challenges facing us today'. The Right Livelihood Awards are annually presented in the Swedish Parliament.

There are now 133 Laureates from 57 countries.

Monika Hauser received the Right Liveli-hood Award in 2008 for her work with women who have experienced sexualised violence.

National Awards

The National Awards can be broadly classified as:

1. Civilian Awards
2. Gallantry Awards

Q.57. Where is the headquarters of the International Olympic Committee located?

Q.58. In which year were the Winter Olympics held for the first time?

Civilian Awards

Bharat Ratna

- Bharat Ratna is the highest civilian honour, given for exceptional service towards advancement of art, literature and science and in recognition of public service of the highest order.
- The provision of Bharat Ratna was introduced in 1954.
- The original award was a circular gold medal, 35 mm in diameter; the radiating sun can be seen with the word *Bharat Ratna* inscribed beneath it. The reverse side carried the state emblem and motto. It was to be worn around the neck attached with a white ribbon. This design was altered after a year.
- There is no written provision that Bharat Ratna should be awarded to Indian citizens only or be awarded every year.
- The first recipients were:
  Dr Chandrasekhar Venkatraman (1888–1970);
  Dr Sarvepalli Radhakrishnan (1888–1975); and
  Chakravarthi Rajagopalachari (1878–1972).

Padma Vibhushan

- The Padma Vibhushan is India's second highest civilian honour, instituted in 1954, is awarded to recognise exceptional and distinguished service to the nation in any field, including government service.
- It consists of a medal and a citation; it is awarded by the President of India.
- As of March 2009, 242 people have received the award.

Padma Bhushan

- This is the third highest civilian award, given for exceptional and distinguished service in any field, including service rendered by government servants, was introduced on 2 January 1954.
- The recommendations for Padma Awards are received from the State Governments/ Union Territory Administrations, Central Ministries/Departments, Institutions of Excellence, etc., which are considered by an Awards Committee.
- As of February 2008, 1003 people have received the award. The Padma Bhushan award was received by 30 people in 2009.

Padma Shri

- This award is given by the Government of India generally to Indian citizens to recognise their distinguished contribution in various spheres of activity including the arts, education, industry, literature, science, sports, social service and public life.
- As of February 2008, 2095 people have received the award; ninety-three people received the Padma Shri award in 2009.

Other Civilian Awards are Given by the Government of India

- Gandhi Peace Prize
- Pravasi Bharatiya Samman
- Dadasaheb Phalke Award

Q.59. Which country hosted the first Asian Games?

Q.60. 'Bishop' is the term associated with which game?

Gallantry Awards
Param Vir Chakra

- This is the highest gallantry award for officers and other enlisted personnel of all military branches of India for the highest degree of valour in the presence of the enemy. It was introduced on 26 January 1950; this award may be given posthumously.
- Param Vir Chakra was designed by Mrs Savitri Khanolkar who was born in Russia on 20 July 1913.
- Till date India has fought four wars where 21 soldiers got this medal of which 14 are posthumous.

The awardees are:
1. Major Somnath Sharma, (4 Kumaon)
2. Company Havildar Major Piru Singh, (6 Rajputana Rifles)
3. Naik Jadunath Singh, (4 Guards)
4. Captain Gurbachan Singh Salaria, (3/1 Gorkha)
5. Subedar Joginder Singh, (1 Sikh, later 4 Merchanised Infantry)
6. Major Shaitan Singh, (13 Kumaon)
7. Company Havildar Major Abdul Hamid, (4 Grenadiers)
8. Lieutenant Colonel A B Tarapore, (17 Horse)
9. Lance Naik Albert Ekka, (14 Guards)
10. Flying Officer Nirmal Jit Singh Sekhon, (18 Sqadron IAF)
11. Second Lieutenant Arun Khetarpal, (17 House)
12. Major Ramaswamy Parameswaran, (8 Mahar)
13. Captain Vikram Batra (13 Jammu and Kashmir)
14. Lieutenant Major Pandey, (1/11 Gorkha Rifles)
15. Lance Naik Karam Singh, (1 Sikh, later 4 Merchanised Infantry)
16. Second Lieutenant Rama Raghoba Rane (Bombay Sappers Engineers)
17. Major Dhan Singh Thapa, (3 Merchanised Infantry)
18. Major Hoshiyar Singh, (13 Kumaon)
19. Naib Subedar Bana Singh, (8 Jammu and Kashmir)
20. Grenadier Yogender Singh Yadav, (18 Grenadiers)
21. Rifleman Sanjay Kumar (13 Jammu and Kashmir)

Maha Vir Chakra

- It is the second highest decoration and is awarded for acts of conspicuous gallantry in the presence of the enemy whether on land, at sea or in the air.
- It is made of standard silver and is circular in shape.

Vir Chakra

This is gallantry award for officers and other enlisted personnel of India for the act of gallantry in the presence of the enemy. The medal is made up of silver.

Other Civilian Gallantry Awards Given by the Government of India

- Ashoka Chakra
- Shaurya Chakra
- Kirti Chakra

Q.61. Who was the founder of Advaitic Philosophy?
Q.62. Where is Yuva Bharti Stadium located?

Military Distinguished Service Awards
- Param Vishisht Seva Medal
- Ati Vishisht Seva Medal
- Vishisht Seva Medal

Other National Awards

Rajiv Gandhi Khel Ratna Award: Instituted in the year 1991–92, it is the highest honour given in all sports disciplines for outstanding achievement. It carries a medal, a scroll of honour and a substantial cash component. Chess wizard Vishwanathan Anand was the first recipient.

Arjuna Award: This award was instituted in 1961 by the Government of India to recognise outstanding achievement in national sports. The award carries a cash prize of Rs 3,00,000, a bronze statuette of Arjun and a scroll.

Dronacharya Award: Instituted in 1985, Dronacharya Award is presented by the government of India for excellence in coaching in sports. The award comprises a statuette of Dronacharya intricately carved out in bronze, a cash component of Rs 3,00,000 and a scroll of honour.

Bharatiya Jnanpith Award: Instituted on 22 May 1961, it is given for the best creative literary writing by any Indian citizen in any of the languages included in the Eighth Schedule of the Indian Constitution. The award is presented by the Jnanpith Trust, publishers of *The Times of India*. The award presented every year, carries a cheque for Rs 500,000, a citation plaque and a bronze replica of Goddess Saraswati. The first recipient of the Jnanpith Award was Malayalam writer G. Sankara Kurup in 1965.

Dadasaheb Phalke Award: It was introduced in the National Award in 1969, the birth centenary year of the Father of Indian Cinema, Dadasaheb Phalke. It is given annually for distinguished contribution to the medium, its growth and promotion. Devika Rani was the first recipient.

THE WORLD OF SPORTS

Olympics

The Olympic Games are an international event that takes place every four years and comprise summer and winter games, in which thousands of athletes participate from across the world in a variety of events.

Winter Olympics were first time held in 1924. Originally both winter and summer games were held in same year but from 1994 these have been held with a gap of two years.

Ancient Olympics: Originally, the ancient Olympic Games were held in Olympia, Greece, from the 776 BC until AD 393 when it was banned by Roman Emperor Theodosius.

Modern Olympics

- They were revived by French nobleman, Pierre Fredy, Baron de Coubertin in 1894 and the first Olympic Games were started in 1896 in Athens.
- To organise the games, International Olympic Committee (IOC) was established with Greek Demetrius Vikelas as its first President. In second Olympic of 1900, women were allowed to participate for the first time.
- Summer Olympic have not been held in 1916, 1940 and 1944 due to World Wars.

Basic General Knowledge

- Currently there are 203 members in the Olympics and Marshall Islands being the latest, which joined on 9 February 2006.

Olympic Symbols

- The symbol is made up of five rings. These intertwined rings represent the unity of the five continents.
- These rings appear in five colours: red, blue, green, yellow and black. The Olympic flag is made up of white silk. Adopted in 1914, it was used for the first time in the Antwerp Olympics of 1920.
- The Olympic motto is *Citius, Altius, Fortius*, a Latin phrase meaning 'Swifter, Higher, Stronger.' It was introduced in 1920.
- The Olympic flame is lit in Olympia and brought to the host city by runners. This custom was introduced in the Berlin Olympics of 1936.

India in Olympics: India participated in the games for the first time in 1920 with four athletes and two wrestlers.

Locations of Olympic Summer Games

Year	Venue	Country
1896	Athens	Greece
1900	Paris	France
1904	St Louis	USA
1908	London	UK
1912	Stockholm	Sweden
1920	Antwerp	Belgium
1924	Paris	France
1928	Amsterdam	Netherlands
1932	Los Angeles	USA
1936	Berlin	Germany
1948	London	UK
1952	Helsinki	Finland
1956	Melbourne	Australia
1960	Rome	Italy
1964	Tokyo	Japan
1968	Mexico City	Mexico
1972	Munich	West Germany
1976	Montreal	Canada
1980	Moscow	USSR
1984	Los Angeles	USA
1988	Seoul	South Korea
1992	Barcelona	Spain
1996	Atlanta	USA
2000	Sydney	Australia
2004	Athens	Greece
2008	Beijing	China
2012	London	UK (Scheduled)
2016	Rio de Janeiro	Brazil (Scheduled)

*Games were not held in 1916 due to World War I and also in 1940 &1944 due to World War II.

Commonwealth Games

- Commonwealth Games held every four years, involves the athletes of the Commonwealth of Nations. First edition of this game was held in 1930 in Hamilton, Canada.
- The Commonwealth Games Federation (CGF) is the organisation that is responsible for the direction and control of the Commonwealth Games.
- Currently there are 53 members of the Commonwealth of Nations.
- Six teams have attended every Commonwealth Games: Australia, Canada, England, New Zealand, Scotland and Wales.

Location of Commonwealth Games

Year	Venue	Number of Countries Participated	Number of Disciplines
1930	Hamilton, Canada	11	6
1934	London, UK	16	6
1938	Sydney, Australia	15	7
1950	Auckland, New Zealand	12	9
1954	Vancouver, Canada	24	9
1958	Cardiff, UK	35	9
1962	Perth, Australia	35	9
1966	Kingston, Jamaica	34	9
1970	Edinburgh, UK	42	9
1974	Christchurch, New Zealand	39	9
1978	Edmonton, Canada	46	10
1982	Brisbane, Australia	46	10
1986	Edinburgh, UK	26	10
1990	Auckland, New Zealand	29	10
1994	Victoria, Canada	24	13
1998	Kuala Lumpur, Malaysia	70	16
2002	Manchester, UK	70	16
2006	Melbourne, Australia	71	16
2010	New Delhi, India (Scheduled)	72	17
2014	Glasgow, Scotland (Scheduled)		

Asian Games

- This is also known as Asiad, held in every four years among athletes across Asian continent. The games are regulated by the Olympic Council of Asia (OCA) under the supervision of the International Olympic Committee (IOC).
- The idea of holding the Asian Games was proposed by Guru Dutt Sondhi, the Indian IOC representative in 1948, London Olympics.
- The first games were held in 1951 at New Delhi. 489 athletes from 11 nations participated in the inaugural games, which featured six events: Football, athletics, basketball, cycling, swimming, and weightlifting.
- The Asiad motto is 'Ever Onward', given by Pt Jawahar Lal Nehru and the emblem is 'a bright full rising sun with interlinking rings'.

Location of Asian Games

Year	Asiad	Place	Country
1951	I	New Delhi	India
1954	II	Manila	Philippines
1958	III	Tokyo	Japan
1962	IV	Jakarta	Indonesia
1966	V	Bangkok	Thailand
1970 (Originally to be hosted by South Korea)	VI	Bangkok	Thailand
1974	VII	Tehran	Iran
1978 (Originally to be hosted by Pakistan)	VIII	Bangkok	Thailand
1982	IX	New Delhi	India
1986	X	Seoul	South Korea
1990	XI	Beijing	China
1994	XII	Hiroshima	Japan
1998	XIII	Bangkok	Thailand
2002	XIV	Busan	South Korea
2006	XV	Doha	Qatar
2010	XVI	Guangzhou	China

South Asian Federation (SAF) Games

- The South Asian Federation Games, popularly known as SAF games, were first time held from 17 September to 23 September in 1984 in Nepal. They are hosted in any of the South Asian countries by any of the SAARC members to foster greater unity.
- The motto of SAF Games is 'Peace, Prosperity and Progress'.

Location of South Asian Federation Games

Year	Edition	Venue
1984	First SAF Games	Kathmandu, Nepal
1985	Second SAF Games	Dhaka, Bangladesh
1987	Third SAF Games	Calcutta, India
1989	Fourth SAF Games	Islamabad, Pakistan
1991	Fifth SAF Games	Colombo, Sri Lanka
1993	Sixth SAF Games	Dhaka, Bangladesh
1995	Seventh SAF Games	Chennai, India
1999	Eighth SAF Games	Kathmandu, Nepal
2004	Ninth SAF Games	Islamabad, Pakistan
2006	Tenth SAF Games	Colombo, Sri Lanka
2008	Eleventh SAF Games	Dhaka, Bangladesh

National Sports of Some Countries

Country	National Sport	Country	National Sport
Australia	Cricket	Korea (Rep.)	Taekwondo
Bangladesh	Kabaddi	Malaysia	Badminton
Bhutan	Archery	New Zealand	Rugby
Canada	Ice Hockey and Lacrosse	Pakistan	Hockey
China	Table Tennis	Scotland	Rugby
Cuba	Baseball	Spain	Bull fighting
England	Cricket	Sri Lanka	Volleyball
India	Hockey	USA	Baseball
Japan	Judo		

Important Trophies and Cups

Trophy	Game	Trophy	Game
International		Guru Nanak Championship	Hockey (Women)
American Cup	Yatch racing	Lady Ratan Tata Trophy	Hockey (Women)
Ashes	Cricket (Australia and England)	Maharaja Ranjit Singh Gold Cup	Hockey
Canada Cup	Golf World Championship	Murugappa Gold Cup	Hockey
Colombo Cup	Football (India, Pakistan, Sri Lanka and Myanmar)	Scindia Gokd Cup	Hockey
		Nehru Trophy	Hockey
Corbillion Cup	Table Tennis (Women)	Rangaswami Cup	Hockey
Davis Cup	Tennis	Yadavindra Cup	Hockey
Derby	Horse Racing	Dr BC Roy Trophy	Football-(National Junior)
Holker	Bridge		
Jules Rimet Trophy	Football	Durand Cup	Football
Merdeka Cup	Football (Asia)	Nizam Gold Cup	Football
Ryder Cup	Golf	Rovers Cup	Football
Swaythling Cup	Table Tennis (Men)	Sanjay Gold Cup	Football
Todd Memorial Trophy	Basket Ball	Santosh Trophy	Football
		Subroto Mukherjee Cup	Football
Thomas Cup	Badminton (Men)	Todd Memorial Trophy	Football
Tunkku Abdul Rehman Cup	Badminton (Asia)	Vittal Trophy	Football
		IFA Shield	Football
U Thant Cup	Lawn Tennis	Duleep Trophy	Cricket
Uber Cup	Badminton (Women)	Irani Cup	Cricket
Yonex Cup	Badminton	Ranji Trophy	Cricket
Walker Cup	Golf	Sheesh Mahal Trophy	Cricket
William Cup	Basket Ball	Vizzy Trophy	Cricket
Wimbledon	Lawn Tennis	Barna Bellack Cup	Table Tennis (Men)
National		Ejar Cup	Polo
Aga Khan Cup	Hockey	Radhamohan Cup	Polo
Beighton Cup	Hockey	Wellington Trophy	Rowing
Dhyan Chand Cup	Hockey	Burdwan Trophy	Weightlifting

Sport Stadiums in India

Stadium	Location
Nehru Stadium (Chepauk)	Chennai
Wankhede Stadium	Mumbai
Brabourne Stadium	Mumbai
Ambedkar Stadium	New Delhi
National Stadium	New Delhi
Shivaji Stadium	New Delhi
Jawaharlal Nehru Stadium	New Delhi
Vallabhbhai Patel Stadium	Ahmedabad
Keenan Stadium	Jamshedpur
Yadvindra Stadium	Patiala
Barabati Stadium	Cuttack
Eden Gardens	Kolkata
Yuva Bharti Stadium (Salt Lake Stadium)	Kolkata
Ranjit Stadium	Kolkata
Netaji Indoor Stadium	Kolkata
Green Park Stadium	Kanpur
Sawai Mansingh Stadium	Jaipur

Dimensions of Sports Field

Sport	Field Dimension
Badminton	Court: 13.41 × 6.09 m
	Net line: 6.70 × 6.09 m
Basketball	Court or Diamond: 28 m × 15 m
Cricket	Pitch (L): 20.12 m
	Pitch (B): 3.05 m
Football	Field: 109.72 × 48.76 m
Hockey	Field: 123.82 × 24.76 m
Kabaddi	Field: 12.5m × 10m
Kho Kho	Field: 27m by 15m
Lawn Tennis	Court: 23.77 × 10.97 m
Table Tennis	Table: 2.74 × 1.525 m
Marathon Race	Length: 42.195 km
Volleyball	Court: 18 × 9 m

Terms Used in Games and Sports

Terms Associated with Games

Sports	Associated Terms
Badminton	Deuce, Double, Drop, Fault, Love, Let, Smash
Baseball	Bunting, Diamond, Home, Pitcher, Put Out, Strike
Basketball	Block, Dribble, Held Ball, Pivot, Basket
Billiard	Break, Cue, Cannon, Baulk, Long Jenny, Short Jenny, Spider, In-off, Jigger, Pot Scratch
Boxing	Knock out, Count down, fly weight, Welter Weight, Jab, Upper cut, Hook, Punch
Bridge	Dummy, Tricks, Trump, Ruff, Duplicate Bridge, Rubber
Chess	Check, Check mate, Stale Mate, Move, Gambit, Rook, Pawn
Cricket	Bouncer, Crease, Duck, Follow on, Gulley, Hit wicket, Leg break, Mid on, Yorker, Beamer, Flick, Hattrick, Slips, Silly
Football	Corner kick, throw-in, Foul, Off-side, Touchline, Trap, Forward, Defender, Free Kick
Hockey	Centre, Defender, Forward, Penalty stroke, Striking Circle, Pushing, Touch line, Off-side, Dribble, Carry, Half

Golf	Links, Tee, Hole, Caddie, Niblic, Bardie, Eagle, Threesome, Foursome
Horse Racing	Jockey, Punter, Bets, Steeplechase
Polo	Mallet, Bunker, Chucker, Sixty Yarder
Shooting	Bull's Eye, Plug, Skeet
Table Tennis	Smash, Drop, Deuce, Spin, Let, Service
Lawn Tennis	Volley, Deuce, Game, Set, Love, Ace, Top spin, Back-hand, Fore- hand
Valleyball	Blocking, Doubling, Book Store, Heave, Point, Volley

World Cup Hockey

Year	Venue	Runners up	Winner
1971	Barcelona, Spain	Spain	Pakistan
1973	Amsterdam, Holland	India	Holland
1975	Kuala Lampur, Malaysia	Pakistan	India
1978	Buenos Aires, Argentina	Holland	Pakistan
1982	Mumbai, India	Germany	Pakistan
1986	London, UK	Pakistan	Australia
1990	Lahore, Pakistan	Pakistan	Holland
1994	Sydney, Australia	Holland	Pakistan
1998	Utrecht, Netherlands	Spain	Holland
2002	Kuala Lampur, Malaysia	Australia	Germany
2006	Monchengladbach, Germany	Australia	Germany
2010	India (Scheduled)		

Soccer World Cup

Year	Venue	Runners up	Winner
1930	Uruguay	Argentina	Uruguay
1934	Italy	Czechoslovakia	Italy
1938	Brazil	Hungary	Italy
1950	Brazil	Brazil	Uruguay
1954	Switzerland	Hungary	West Germany
1958	Sweden	Sweden	Brazil
1962	Chile	Czechoslovakia	Brazil
1966	England	West Germany	England
1970	Mexico	Italy	Brazil
1974	West Germany	Holland	West Germany
1978	Argentina	Holland	Argentina
1982	Spain	West Germany	Italy
1986	Mexico	West Germany	Argentina
1990	Italy	Argentina	West Germany
1994	USA	Italy	Brazil
1998	France	Brazil	France
2002	Japan	Germany	Brazil
2006	Germany	France	Italy
2010	South Africa (Scheduled)		

World Cup Cricket

Year	Venue	Runners up	Winner
1975	Lord's, England	Australia	West Indies
1979	Lord's, England	England	West Indies
1983	Lord's, England	West Indies	India
1987	Kolkata, India	England	Australia
1992	Melbourne, Australia	England	Pakistan
1996	Lahore, Pakistan	Australia	Sri Lanka
1999	Lord's, England	Pakistan	Australia
2003	Johannesburg, South Africa	India	Australia
2007	Bridgetown, West Indies	Sri Lanka	Australia
2011	Mumbai, India		
2015	Melbourne, Australia	(Scheduled)	
2019	Lord's, England		

Popular Names of Famous Personalities

Name	Known as
Abdul Ghaffar Khan	Frontier Gandhi or Badshah Khan
Adolf Hitler	Fuehrer
Bal Gangadhar Tilak	Lokmanya
Baneto Mussolini	II Duce
Bismark	Man of Blood
C F Andrews	Deenabandhu
C N Annadurai	Anna
C Rajagopalachari	Rajaji or C R
C R Das	Deshbandhu
Dadabhai Naoroji	Grand Oldman of India
David Eisenhower	Ike
Duke of Wellington	Iron Duke
Earl of Warwick	King Maker
General Erwin Rommel	Desert Fox
Florence Nightingale	Lady with the Lamp
Francisco Franco	E I Caudillo
George Bernard Shaw	G B S
Jagjivan Ram	Babuji
Jawaharlal Nehru	Panditji or Chachaji
Jayaprakash Narayan	J P or Loknayak
Joan of Arc	Made of Orleans
Lalbahadur Shastri	Man of Peace
Lala Lajpat Rai	Sher-e-Punjab or Punjab Kesari
M K Gandhi	Bapu, Mahatma, Father of the Nation
M S Golwalaar	Guruji
Madan Mohan Malaviya	Mahamana
Napoleon Bonaparte	Little Corporal or Man of Destiny
Narendre Datta	Swami Vivekananda
Field Marshal K M Cariappa	Kipper
Queen Elizabeth I	Maiden Queen

Rabindranath Tagore	Gurudev
Rajendra Singh	Sparrow
Samuel Longhorn Clemens	Mark Taiwan
Sardar Vallabhbhai Patel	Man of Iron or Strongman of India
Sarojini Naidu	Nightingale of India
Sheikh Mohammad Abdullah	Sher-e-Kashmir
Sheikh Mujibur Rehman	Bangabandhu
Subhas Chandra Bose	Netaji
Tenzing Norgay	Tiger of Snows
T Prakasam	Andhra Kesari
Sir Walter Scott	Wizard of the North
William Ewart Gladstone	Grand Oldman of Britain
William Shakespeare	Bird of Avon

ANSWERS

1. 21 March
2. Sarojini Naidu
3. Chess
4. Federation of Indian Export Organisations
5. Nathan B Stubblefield
6. It is the famous high speed train of France.
7. Viswa Bharti University
8. Football
9. Pakistan
10. Horse races
11. Commonwealth Games to be held at Delhi in 2010
12. Polo
13. Sydney in 2007
14. Golf
15. 17 April
16. RBI
17. Second
18. Newspaper Journalism, Literature and Music Composition
19. Camel
20. 8 May
21. Squash
22. 26 June
23. R Venkataraman
24. Sheikh Mujibur Rehman
25. Tripitak
26. Mahayanists and Hinayanists
27. Geoffrey Chaucer
28. Swifter, Higher and Stronger
29. Nelson Mandela
30. Rajiv Gandhi Khel Ratna Award
31. Rockefeller Brothers Fund (RBF)
32. Inter Continental Ballistic Missile
33. Chess
34. Dr Verghese Kurien
35. Chess Player
36. Rabindranath Tagore
37. For bravery or self sacrifice on land, air or sea but not in the presence of enemy.
38. 2 to 8 November
39. Sheikh Mujibur Rehman
40. Billiards
41. Moses
42. Seven
43. Banabhatta
44. Ballistic Missile Defence
45. France
46. Dhyan Chand's birthday
47. EM Foster
48. Literature
49. Dr Amrita Patel
50. 1901
51. Euclid
52. Swedish Parliament
53. Smt Sirimavo Bandaranaike of Sri Lanka.
54. Rajendra Prasad
55. The Analects
56. Indira Gandhi Indoor Stadium in New Delhi
57. Lusanne
58. In 1924
59. India
60. Chess
61. Sankaracharya
62. Kolkata

11

NATIONAL INSIGNIA AND INDIAN MISCELLANEA

NATIONAL INSIGNIA

National Anthem

- The song 'Jana Gana Mana', composed by Rabindranath Tagore, was adopted as 'National Anthem' by the Constituent Assembly on 24 January 1950.
- It was first sung on 27 December 1911 at Calcutta Session of Indian National Congress.
- The first stanza (out of five stanzas) forms the national anthem.
- Playing time of the full version of the National Anthem is 52 seconds. A shorter version consisting of first and last lines of the stanza takes 20 seconds to play and played on certain occasions.

National Song

- The National Song 'Vande Mataram' is composed by Bankimchandra Chattopadhya. It is taken from his novel 'Anand Math' written in Sanskrit.
- It has an equal status with 'Jana Gana Mana'.
- It was first sung in 1896 Session of Indian National Congress.
- The English translation of the stanza was rendered by Sri Aurobindo (in Sri Aurobindo Birth Centenary Library popular edition, 1972, vol. 8).

National Flag

- National flag was adopted by the Constituent Assembly on 22 July 1947 and was presented to India on 14 August 1947 at the midnight session of the Assembly.
- The ratio of the width to the length is 2:3. All the three colours are of equal width, with deep saffron at the top, white in the middle and dark green at the bottom.
- The saffron stands for courage, sacrifice and spirit of renunciation; the white for purity and truth and the green for faith and fertility.
- In the centre of the white band, there is a wheel with 24 spokes in navy blue to indicate the 'Dharma Chakra', which is the wheel of law in the Lion Capital at Sarnath.

Flag Code of India

- Flag Code of India, 2002 has taken effect from 26 January 2002 by superseding the 'Flag Code – India' as it existed.
- As per the provision of the Flag code of India, 2002, display of National flag has no restrictions by the Indian Nationals, public or private organisations, educational institutions, etc., except the restrictions stipulated in the Emblems and Names (Prevention of Improper Use) Act, 1950, Prevention of Insult to National Honour Act 1971 and any other laws enacted there to the subject.

National Emblem

- National Emblem is the replica of the Lion Capital at Sarnath (Uttar Pradesh).
- The four lions standing back to back (one seems hidden while viewing) rest on a circular abacus (base plate). It symbolises power, courage and confidence.
- The abacus is girded by four animals, considered the guardians of the four directions; the Lion of the north, the Elephant of the east, The Horse of the south and the Bull of the west.
- The abacus lies on the full bloom lotus, which symbolises fountain lead of life and creative inspiration.
- The motto 'Satya meva Jayate' from Mundak Upanisad are inscribed below the emblem in Devnagari script, which means 'truth alone triumphs'.
- The National Emblem was adopted by Government of India on 26 January 1950, the day India became a republic.

National Calendar

- The National Calendar based on the Saka era with 'Chaitra' as the first month and a normal year of 365 days, was adopted from 22 March 1957.
- At the time of Independence, the Government of India followed the Gregorian calendar based on Christian era.
- The date of the Saka Calendar has the permanent correspondence with date of Gregorian calendar, Chaitra 1 being the March 22 of the Gregorian calendar in a normal year and March 21 in a leap year.

National Animal

- Tiger (*Panthera Tigris*) has been adopted as National Animal since November 1972.
- To safeguard the tiger population Government launched Tiger Project on 1 April 1973. Under this project more than 40 tiger reserves have been established throughout the country.

National Bird Peacock (Pavo cristatus);

Peacocks have been given full protection under the Indian Wildlife (Protection) Act, 1972.

National Flower

- Lotus (*Nelumbo nucifera*) is the national flower of India. The Lotus symbolises spirituality, fruitfulness, wealth, knowledge and illumination.

Q.1. When was 'Jana Gana Mana' adopted as 'National Anthem' by constituent assembly?

National Fruit

- Mango (*Mangifera Indica*) is the national fruit of India.

National Tree

- Banyan (*Ficus bengalensis*) is the National tree of India.
- The roots give rise to more trunks and branches symbolising longevity for which it is considered immortal and is an integral part of the myths and legends of India.

National Sport

Hockey is the national sport of India.

National Days

15 August	Independence Day	India achieved Independence on this day in 1947.
26 January	Republic day	India became republic on this day in 1950.
30 January	Martyr's day	Gandhiji was assassinated on this day in 1948.
5 September	Teacher's day	Birthday of Dr S Radhakrishnan
14 November	Children's day	Birthday of Pt Jawaharlal Nehru.
2 October	Gandhi Jayanti	Birthday of M K Gandhi.

INDIA'S DEFENCE SYSTEM

- The President of India is the Supreme Commander of the armed forces.
- This is discharged through the Ministry of Defence, which provides the policy framework to the armed forces to discharge their responsibilities in the context of the defence of the country.
- It is currently the third largest armed force in the world.
- India's defence system is divided into three services: the Army, the Navy and the Air Force.

The Indian Army

The Army Headquarters is in New Delhi.
The Army is headed by Chief of Army Staff.
Chief of Army staff is assisted by Vice-Chief of army staff and seven other Principal Staff Officers (PSOs):

(a) Two deputy chiefs
(b) Adjutant General
(c) Master General of Ordnance
(d) The Quartermaster General
(e) Military Secretary
(f) Engineer-in-Chief

It is organised into seven operational commands.

Each command is headed by general officer commander in chief of the rank of Lieutenant General. Commands are divided into areas and sub-areas.

Q.2. Our National Calendar is based on which era?

Q.3. The motto 'Satya meva Jayate' inscribed below the national emblem is taken from where?

Area is headed by Major General and sub-area is by a Brigadier.

Command	Headquarter
Western Command	Chandigarh
Eastern Command	Kolkata
Northern Command	Udampur
Southern Command	Pune
Central Command	Lucknow
Training Command (added in 1991)	Mhow
South-Western Command	Jaipur

Army Training Institutes

(a) Indian Military Academy, Dehradun
(b) Army Officers' Training School, Pune and Chennai
(c) The Armoured Corps Centre and School, Ahmednagar
(d) The College of Military Engineering, Kirkee
(e) The School of Signals, Mhow
(f) The School of Artillery, Deolali
(g) The Infantry School, Mhow
(h) The Army Ordnance Corps School, Jabalpur
(i) The Army Education Corps and Training Centre, Pachmathi
(j) The Service Corps School, Bareilly
(k) The Remount, Veterinary and Farms Corps Centre and School, Meerut
(l) The School of Physical Training, Pune
(m) The School of Mechanical Transport, Bangalore
(n) The Corps Military Police Centre and School, Faizabad
(o) The Military School of Music, Pachmarhi
(p) The Electrical and Mechanical Engineering School, Trimulghery and Secunderabad

India's Battle Tanks: Vijayanta, T-55, T-59, T-71, MI Ajeya, Arjun.

MI Ajeya acquired from erstwhile USSR and Arjun is the main battle tank, inducted in 1993.

Commanders-in-Chief

General Sir Roy Bucher	1948–49
General K M Cariappa	1949–53
General Maharaja Rajendra Singhji	1953–55

Q.4. In how many operational commands is the Indian Army divided into?
Q.5. Who is the first Indian Chief of Army Staff?

List of Chief of Army staff

Name	Tenure From	To
General Sir Robert Lockhart	15 Aug. 1947	31 Dec. 1947
General Sir Roy Bucher	1 Jan. 1948	15 Jan. 1949
Field Marshal K M Cariappa	16 Jan. 1949	14 Jan. 1953
General K S Rajendra Sinhiji	15 Jan. 1953	14 May 1955
General S M Shrinagesh	15 May 1955	07 May 1957
General K S Thimayya	8 May 1957	7 May 1961
General P N Thapar	8 May 1961	19 Nov. 1962
General J N Chaudhuri	20 Nov. 1962	7 Jun. 1966
General P P Kumaramangalam	8 Jun. 1966	7 Jun. 1969
Field Marshal S H F J Manekshaw	8 Jun. 1969	15 Jan. 1973
General G G Bewoor	16 Jan. 1973	31 May 1975
General T N Raina	1 Jun. 1975	31 May 1978
General O P Malhotra	1 Jun. 1978	31 May 1981
General K V Krishna Rao	1 Jun. 1981	31 Jul. 1983
General K Sundarji	1 Feb. 1985	31 May 1988
General V N Sharma	30 Jun. 1988	30 Jun. 1990
General S F Rodrigues	1 Jul. 1990	30 Jun. 1993
General B C Joshi	1 Jul. 1993	19 Nov. 1994
General S Roychowdhury	22 Nov. 1994	30 Sep. 1997
General V P Malik	1 Oct. 1997	30 Sep. 2000
General S Padmanabhan	1 Oct. 2000	30 Dec. 2002
General N C Vij	31 Dec. 2002	31 Jan. 2005
General J J Singh	1 Feb. 2005	30 Sep. 2007
General Deepak Kapoor	30 Sep. 2007	till date

The Indian Air Force

The Indian Air Force (IAF) is the world's fourth largest air force after those of the United States, Russia and China. The headquarter of Air Force is in New Delhi.

The Air Force is headed by Chief of Air Staff.

The Air Chief is assisted following staffs:

(a) Vice-Chief of Air staff
(b) Deputy Chief of Air Command
(c) Central Air Command
(d) Officer-in-Charge, Maintenance
(e) Inspector General of Flight Safety and Inspection

It is organised into five commands:

(i) Western Air Command
(ii) Central Air Command
(iii) Eastern Air Command
(iv) Southern Air Command
(v) South-Western Air Command

In addition other two functional commands: Maintenance Command and Training Command.

Q.6. What is Brahmos?
Q.7. Which style of Indian Classical Music Singing was developed by Tansen?

Aircraft of Indian Air Force: It operates more than 760 combat and 1200 non-combat aircraft (including UAV's).

Combat Aircraft: Su-30MKI/27, MiG-29SMT, Mirage 2000 H, Jaguar IS, Jaguar IM+IS, MiG-27UPG, MiG-21 Bison, MiG-21*bis,* MiG-21M/MF, MiG-23, MiG-25, Su-75.

MIG-29 were acquired from erstwhile USSR and renamed as *Baaz;* Mirage 2000 acquired from France, is renamed as *Vajra.*

Future Combat Aircraft: HAL Tejas (expected to be commissioned in 2010), MRCA (expected to be commissioned in 2012–14), FGFA (expected to be commissioned in 2015–16).

Helicopters Used in Air force: SA 315B Cheetah, SA 316B Chetak, Mi-17, Dhruv (to be inducted by 2012), HAL Light Combat Helicopter (to be inducted by 2011).

DRDO has developed a Pilotless Target Aircraft (PTA), called Lakshya.

Air Force Training Centres

(a) Air Force Academy, Hyderabad
(b) Air Force Administrative College, Coimbatore
(c) Air Force Technical College Jalahalli, Bangalore
(d) Flying Instructors School, Ambala
(e) Paratroopers Training School, Agra
(f) College of Air Warfare, Secunderabad
(g) Software Development Institute, Kempapura, Bangalore

List of Chief of Air Staffs

Name	Tenure From	To
Sir Thomas Walker Elmhirst	15 Aug. 1947	22 Feb. 1950
Ronald Ivelaw Chapman	22 Feb. 1950	9 Dec. 1951
Sir Gerald Ernest Gibbs	10 Dec. 1951	31 Mar. 1954
Subroto Mukerjee	1 Apr. 1954	8 Nov. 1960
Aspy Merwan Engineer	1 Dec. 1960	31 Jul. 1964
Arjan Singh	1 Aug. 1964	15 Jul. 1969
Pratap Chandra Lal	16 Jul. 1969	15 Jan. 1973
Om Prakash Mehra	16 Jan. 1973	31 Jan. 1976
Hrushikesh Moolgavkar	1 Feb. 1976	31 Aug. 1978
Idris Hassan Latif	1 Sep. 1978	31 Aug. 1981
Dilbagh Singh	1 Sep. 1981	4 Sep. 1984
Laxman Mohan Katre	4 Sep. 1984	1 Jul. 1985
Denis Anthony La Fontaine	3 Jul. 1985	31 Jul. 1988
Surinder Kumar Mehra	1 Aug. 1988	31 Jul. 1991
Nirmal Chandra Suri	31 Jul. 1991	31 Jul. 1993
Swaroop Krishna Kaul	1 Aug. 1993	31 Dec. 1995
Satish Kumar Sareen	31 Dec. 1995	31 Dec. 1998
A Y Tipnis	31 Dec. 1998	31 Dec. 2001
S Krishnaswamy	31 Dec. 2001	31 Dec. 2004
S P Tyagi	31 Dec. 2004	31 Mar. 2007
Fali H Major	31 Mar. 2007	31 May 2009
Pradeep Vasant Naik	31 May 2009	till date

The Indian Navy

Indian Navy is the world's fifth largest navy. It is headed by Chief of Naval Staff and it's headquarter is at New Delhi.

The Chief of Naval Staff is assisted by five principal staff officers:
  (a) Vice Chief of Naval Staff
  (b) Deputy Chief of Naval Staff
  (c) Chief of Personnel
  (d) Chief of Material
  (e) Controller of Logistic support

The Navy is organised into three commands:

Command	Headquarter
Eastern Command	Vishakhapatnam
Southern Command	Kochi
Western Command	Mumbai

It has two naval bases, at Mumbai and Vishakhapatnam.
Each command is headed by a Flag Officer Commanding in Chief.

Aircraft Carriers of Indian Navy

INS Vikrant: India's first aircraft carrier;
INS Viraat: India's largest aircraft carrier;
INS Vikramaditya: Inducted in 2008.

List of Some Submarines, Warships and Missile Boars

Submarines: INS Shankul, INS Sindhushastra, INS Sindhurakshak, INS Chakra
Warships: INS Savitri, INS Delhi, INS Mysore, INS Brahmaputra, INS Ghariyal, INS Kulish, INS Satpura, INS Talwar, INS Airavat (biggest warships, commissioned in May 2009)
Missile Boars: INS Bibhuti, INS Prahar, INS Prashant, INS Nashak, INS Vipul

Naval Training Institutes

  (i) Indian Naval Academy, Kochi
  (ii) Naval Air Station, Kochi
  (iii) INS Venduruthy, Kochi
  (iv) Torpedo/Anti Sub-marine School, Kochi
  (v) Navigation Direction School, Maormugoa
  (vi) INS Shivaji, Lonavala, Maharashtra
  (vii) INS Valsure, Jamnagar, Gujarat
  (viii) INS Angre, Mumbai
  (ix) INS Hamla, Mumbai
  (x) INS Circars, Vishakhapatnam
  (xi) INS Agrani, Coimbatore
  (xii) INS Chilika, Chilika, Orissa
  (xiii) INS Jarawa, Port Blair

Q.8. Mirage 2000 renamed as Vajra was acquired from which country?
Q.9. What is Lakshya?

Chief of Naval Staff

Name	Tenure	
	From	To
Rear Admiral John Talbot Savignac Hall	15 Aug. 1947	14 Aug. 1948
Sir William Edward Parry	14 Aug. 1948	13 Oct. 1951
Sir Charles Thomas Mark Pizey	13 Oct. 1951	21 Jul. 1955
Sir Stephen Hope Carlill	21 Jul. 1955	21 Apr. 1958
R D Katari	22 Apr. 1958	4 Jun. 1962
B S Soman	4 Jun. 1962	3 Mar. 1966
A K Chatterji	3 Mar. 1966	28 Feb. 1970
S M Nanda	28 Feb. 1970	28 Feb. 1973
S N Kohli	28 Feb. 1973	29 Feb. 1976
Jal Cursetji	29 Feb. 1976	28 Feb. 1979
R L Pereira	28 Feb. 1979	28 Feb. 1982
O S Dawson	28 Feb. 1982	30 Nov. 1984
R H Tahiliani	30 Nov. 1984	30 Nov. 1987
J G Nadkarni	30 Nov. 1987	30 Nov. 1990
Laxminarayan Ramdas	30 Nov. 1990	30 Sep. 1993
V S Shekhawat	30 Sep. 1993	30 Sep. 1996
Vishnu Baghwat	30 Sep. 1996	30 Dec. 1998
Sushil Kumar	30 Dec. 1998	29 Dec. 2001
Madhvendra Singh	29 Dec. 2001	31 Jul. 2004
Arun Prakash	31 Jul. 2004	31 Oct. 2006
Suresh Mehta	31 Oct. 2006	31 Aug. 2009
Nirmal Kumar Verma	31 Aug. 2009	till date

Rank of Officers in Three Services

Army	Air Force	Navy
General	Air Chief Marshal	Admiral
Lt General	Air Marshal	Vice Admiral
Major General	Air Vice Marshal	Rear Admiral
Brigadier	Air Commodore	Commodore
Colonel	Group Captain	Captain
Lt Colonel	Wing Commander	Commander
Major	Squadron Leader	Lt. Commander
Captain	Flight Lieutenant	Lieutenant
Lieutenant	Flying Officer	Sub- Lieutenant

Inter Services Establishments

1. National Defence Academy, Khadakvasla
2. National Defence College, New Delhi
3. Defence Service Staff College, Wellington, Kochi

Q.10. What is the playing time of the shorter version of National Anthem?

Q.11. Who started the first English newspaper in India?

4. Armed Forces Medical College, Pune
5. National Cadet Corps, New Delhi
6. College of Defence Management, Sainikpuri, Hyderabad
7. School of Land/Air Warfare, Secunderabad
8. School of Foreign Language, New Delhi
9. Himalayan Mountaineering Institute, Darjeeling

Defence Production Establishments

Hindustan Aeronautics Limited (HAL), Bangalore: HAL has seven factories which are in Nasik, Kanpur, Lucknow, Koraput, Karwa, Barrackpur and Hyderabad.

Bharat Electronics Limited (BEL): It is located at following places: Bangalore, Pune, Machilipatnam, Tajola, Ghaziabad, Panchkula, Kotwara, Hyderabad and Mysore.

Bharat Earth Movers Limited (BEML): It is located at Mysore, Bangalore, Kolar Golf Fields, Hyderabad.

Shipbuilding Factories

Mazgaon Dock Limited (MDL), Mumbai; Garden Reach Shipbuilders and Engineering Ltd (GRSE), Kolkata; Goa Shipyards Limited (GSl), Goa.

Women in Armed Forces: Women can join in Medical Services, Dental Services and Military Nursing Service of the Armed Forces.

Under the Army Act, 1950, Section 12, women are not allowed in Army and similar provisions also existed for the Air Force and Navy.

However Government has allowed women into non-combat branches in the three forces.

PARAMILITARY AND RESERVED FORCES

Central Reserve Police Force (CRPF): It was established in 1939 to assist the State and Union territory police in maintenance of law and order.

Eighty-eighth battalion of CRPF is the world's first paramilitary force which comprises women only. It was commissioned on 30 March 1986 known as Mahila Battalion.

Indo-Tibetan Border Police (ITBP): It was established in 1962. It is deployed mainly in Northern frontiers for monitoring the borders and to check smuggling and illegal immigration.

Central Industrial Security Force (CISF): It was setup in 1968, on the recommendation of Justice B Mukherjee. Its job is to monitor the industrial establishments of the central government.

Border Security Force (BSF): It was established in 1965. It was formed to keep vigil on the International Borders against the intrusion in the country.

National Security Guard (NSG): It was established in 1986. It has primarily been utilised for counter-terrorism activities. It works within the Central Paramilitary Force structure.

Assam Rifles: Established in 1835, it is the oldest paramilitary force in the country. It maintains internal security under the control of the army through the conduct of counter insurgency and border security operations.

Q.12. Which is the highest airfield in India?
Q.13. Name India's largest aircraft carrier?

Coast Guard: Coast Guard was created on 18 August 1978 as an independent entity as per the Coast Guard Act. Its primary objective is to guard India's vast coastline and operates under the control of the Ministry of Defense. Its responsibilities include:

- Assisting the Customs and other authorities in anti-smuggling operations;
- To preserve and protect the marine environment and control marine pollution;
- Measures for safety of life and property at sea including aid to mariners in distress;
- Ensuring the safety and protection of artificial islands, offshore terminals and other installations.

Rapid Action Force (RPF): RPF is a specialised wing of the CRPF (Central Reserve Police Force). It was established on 11 December 1991 and became operational in October 1992. Its objective is to deal with communal riots and related unrest. Currently it has 10 battalions.

Home Guard: It was organised in 1962. The main functions are to assist the police in maintaining security and to help defence forces in case of eventuality.

National Cadet Crops (NCC): It was established on 15 July 1948. Director General of NCC is located in New Delhi, which controls and oversees various activities through 16 NCC Directorates across the country.

The main objective is to motivate the youth to take up a career in the Armed Forces and to build up reserve forces for the expansion of Armed forces.

DEFENCE RESEARCH

- **Defence Research and Development Organisation** (DRDO) was formed in 1958 by the merger of Technical Development Establishment and the Directorate of Technical Development and Production with the Defence Science Organisation.
- DRDO formulates and executes various progresses of scientific research, design and development of new weapons as required by the Armed Forces.
- DRDO executes various research and development projects through a network of 51 laboratories spread across the country.
- The organisation includes more than 6,000 scientists and about 35,000 engineers, other scientific, technical and supporting personnel.
- **Integrated Guided Missile Development Programme** (IGMDP) was launched by DRDO in 1983, under the chairmanship of Dr A P J Abdul Kalam for the development of a comprehensive range of missiles.
- The following missiles are the part of the programme:

Prithvi

- Prithvi was the first missile developed as part of IGMDP.
- It is a surface-to-surface, short-range ballistic missile (SRBM).
- The Prithvi missile project has developed three variants for use by Armed Forces. These are: Prithvi I (SS-150) – Army Version (150 km range with a payload of 1,000kg), produced on 25 February 1988; Prithvi II (SS-250) – Air Force Version (250 km range with a payload of 500 kg), produced on 27

Q.14. Where is Defence Service Staff College located?
Q.15. Which is the oldest paramilitary force of India?

National Insignia and Indian Miscellanea 303

January 1996; Prithvi III (SS-350) – Naval Version (350 km range with a payload of 500 kg), produced on 23 January 2004;
- Dhanush: It is a naval version of Prithvi which can be launched from ships, produced on 11 April 2000.

Agni
- Agni is medium to intercontinental range ballistic missile.
- Agni missile comprises following variants:
  (i) Agni-I is short range ballistic missile; it has a range of 700–800 km with a payload of 1,000 kg; first tested at the Interim Test Range in Chandipur (Orissa) in 1989.
  (ii) Agni-II medium range ballistic missile (MRBM); it has a range of 2,500 km with a payload of 1,000 kg first tested at the Interim Test Range in Chandipur (Orissa) on 11 April 1999. (iii) Agni-III intermediate range ballistic missile; it has a range of 3,500 km with a payload of 2490 kg and was tested from Wheeler Island, off the coast of the eastern state of Orissa on 9 July 2006. There will not be an Agni-IV missile, with DRDO upgrading from intermediate range Agni-III to ICBM type. Agni-V intercontinental ballistic missile (ICBM) which has a range of 5,000–6,000 km is expected in 2010.

Akash
- Akash is a medium range surface to air missile with 60 kg Fragmentation or Nuclear Warhead.
- It was first tested in 1990 and development tests were carried out till 1997.
- It can target aircraft up to 30 km away, at altitudes up to 18,000 m.
- It is guided by phased array fire control radar called 'Rajendra'.

Trishul
- It is a short range surface to air missile, range of 9 km, with a 5.5 kg warhead to counter a low level (sea skimming) attack.
- It is developed for all three services.

Nag
- Nag is India's third generation 'Fire-and-forget' anti-tank missile.
- It is all weather, top attack missile, which has a range of 3 to 7 km with 8 kg warhead.

Astra
- It is air to air missile with a range of 60 to 100 km with 15 kg directional warhead which can be launched from fighter planes.
- It was first tested in May 2003.

Forthcoming Missiles: Surya (Intercontinental Ballistic Missile with a range of 500 km), Sagarika (first submarine – launched nuclear – capable cruise missile, can be launched from sea surface with a range of 750 km, can carry a payload up to 500 kg).

Q.16. When was Indo-Tibetan Border Police (ITBP) formed?
Q.17. What does IGMDP stands for?

Intercontinental Missile

BRAHMOS

- It is a supersonic cruise missile which can be launched from submarine, ship, aircraft and mobile autonomous launchers.
- It is anti-ship missile which has a range of about 300 km with a payload of 300 kg over the speed three times that of sound.
- It is a joint venture between India's Defense Research and Development Organisation (DRDO) and Russia's NPO Mashinostroeyenia.
- The name has been derived from Brahmaputra and Moskova, which is the river of Russia.
- It was first tested (BRAHMOS DO1) on 12 June 2001 from Interim Test Range in Chandipur (Orissa).
- BRAHMOS DO2 was tested on 28 April 2002 from Interim Test Range in Chandipur (Orissa).
- BRAHMOS DO3 was successfully tested from one of the warship off eastern coast on 12 February 2003.

Some of the Achievements in Defence Research

(a) MBT Arjun: India's main battle tank (MBT) is designed and developed by DRDO. It has global positioning system (GPS) to facilitate to find its position.
(b) Lakshya: Pilotless Target Aircraft.
(c) Nishant: Remotely piloted vehicle (RPV) for surveillance purpose.
(d) Tejas: Smallest light weight, single seat, multi-role Light Combat Aircraft (LCA).
(e) Warship Nilgiri: First indigenous stealth warship, built at Mazagaon Dock, Mumbai.
(f) Pinaka: It is a lethal ground-based multi-barrel rocket launcher. First successfully tested in July 2003. It has the capability of firing 12 rockets in less than 40 seconds with a range of 38 km.
(g) INS Prahar: It is the fastest missile ship in the world. It was commissioned in 1997.
(h) INS Mysore: Indian Navy's most advanced warship which was commissioned in 1999.

Space Research

- India's space research programme started with the set up of Indian National Committee for Space Research (INCOSPAR) in 1962.
- The first establishment for space research was Indian Space Research Organisation (ISRO), which was set up in 1969. Its headquarter is in Bangalore.
- Space Commission was set up in 1972.
- India's first satellite communication Earth Centre was set up at Arvi, near Pune.
- Aryabhata, India's first satellite which was launched on 19 April 1975 from Baikanur (Erstwhile USSR) to perform X-ray experiments in space and send data back to earth.
- India launched its second satellite 'Bhaskar' (436 kg) from Baikanur (Erstwhile USSR) on 7 June 1979 to collect information on land, water, forest and ocean resources of India.
- India's first remote sensing satellite (IRS-1A) was launched on 17 March 1988 for monitoring and management of natural resources.

Q.18. Where is India's first satellite communication Earth Centre located?

Q.19. Where is Space Application Centre (SAC) located?

- India launched its first communication satellite 'APPLE' (Ariane Passenger Payload Experiment) on 19 June 1981 from Kaurou in French Guyana (South America). It was first geo-stationary satellite weighing 673 kg.
- Squadron leader Rakesh Sharma, at the age of 35, was the first Indian and 138th person in the world, to have gone into space. He spent eight days in space abroad Salyut 7 along with two other Soviet Cosmonaut on 2 April 1984.

Principal Space Establishments

1. **Thumb Equatorial Rocket Launching Station** was set up in 1963 near Thiruvananthapuram for launching vehicles.
2. **Sriharikota Range (SHAR)** was set up in Sriharikota (Andhra Pradesh), which was later renamed as Satish Dhawan Space Centre. It is a satellite launching station and production centre for propellants.
3. **ISRO Satellite Centre, Bangalore:** It is spacecraft maintenance and development centre.
4. **Auxiliary Propulsion System Unit (APSU):** It is located in two places: Bangalore and Thiruvananthapuram. It develops propulsion control packages for launch vehicles and spacecrafts.
5. **National Remote Sensing Agency (NRSA):** It was set up in Hyderabad to utilise the potential of remote sensing satellites for monitoring of natural resources.
6. **Development and Educational Communication Unit**, Ahmedabad: It produces and develops educational television programs.
7. **Master Control Facility** for INSAT spacecraft is located in Hassan, Karnataka.
8. **Physical Research Laboratory (PRL), Ahmedabad:** It carries out research in outer space.
9. **Vikram Sarabhai Space Centre, Thiruvananthapuram:** It develops rocket launching vehicles.
10. **ISRO-Telemetry, Tracking and Command Network (ISTRAC):** It consists of ground stations at Sriharikota, Kuvalpur, Thiruvananthapuram, Car Nicobar and Ahmedabad with headquarter at Bangalore.
11. **Space Application Centre (SAC), Ahmedabad:** It is the main centre for space application and development of space aircraft's payload.

Milestones in Indian Space Programme

Satellite	Launch Vehicle	Date	Place	Type
Aryabhata	Cosmos	19 Apr. 1975	Baikanur	Scientific
Bhaskar-I	Cosmos	07 Jun. 1979	Baikanur	Geosurvey
Rohini	SLV-3	10 Aug. 1979	Sriharikota	Geosurvey
Rohini-D-I	SLV-3	18 Jul. 1980	Sriharikota	Geosurvey
Rohini	SLV-3	31 May 1981	Sriharikota	Communication
APPLE	Ariane	19 Jun. 1981	Kourou	Geosurvey
Bhaskar-II	Cosmos	20 Nov. 1981	Baikanur	Communication
INSAT-IA	Delta	10 Apr. 1982	America	Scientific
Rohini*	SLV-3 D2	17 Apr. 1983	Sriharikota	Communication
INSAT-IB	Space Shuttle	30 Aug. 1983	America	Technological
SROSS-I*	ASLV-D1	24 Mar. 1987	Sriharikota	Remote-sensing

General Knowledge Manual

IRS-IA	Vostok	17 Mar. 1988	Baikanur	Technological
SROSS-II	SLV-D2	13 Jul. 1988	Sriharikota	Communication
INSAT-IC*	Ariane-4	21 Jul. 1988	Kourou	Communication
INSAT-ID	Delta	12 Jun. 1990	America	Remote sensing
IRS-IB	Vostok	29 Aug. 1991	Baikanur	Multi-purpose
INSAT-2A	Ariane-4	10 Jul. 1992	Kourou	Multi-purpose
INSAT-2B	Ariane-4	23 Jul. 1993	Kourou	Remote sensing
IRS-PI*	PSLV-D1	20 Sept. 1993	Sriharikota	Scientific
SROSS-IV	ASLV-D3	04 May 1994	Sriharikota	Remote sensing
IRS-P$_2$	PSLV-D2	15 Oct. 1994	Sriharikota	Multi-purpose
INSAT-2C	Ariane-4	07 Dec. 1995	Kourou	Remote sensing
IRS-IC	Molenia	28 Dec. 1995	Baikanur	Remote sensing
IRC-P3	PSLV-D3	21 Mar. 1996	Sriharikota	Communication
INSAT-2D*	Ariane-4	04 Jun. 1997	Kourou	Remote sensing
IRS-ID	PSLV-C1	29 Sept. 1997	Sriharikota	Multi-purpose
INSAT-2E	Ariane-4	03 Apr. 1999	Kourou	Remote sensing
IRS-P$_4$	PSLV-C2	04 May 1999	Sriharikota	Communication
INSAT-3B	Ariane-5	22 Mar. 2000	Kourou	Communication
GSAT-I*	GSLV-D1	28 Mar. 2001	Sriharikota	Communication
GSAT-1	GSLV-D1	18 Apr. 2001	Sriharikota	Communication
INSAT-3C	Ariane-4	24 Jun. 2002	Kourou	Communication
METSAT	PSLV-C4	11 Sept. 2002	Sriharikota	Meteorology
INSAT-3A	Ariane-5	10 Apr. 2003	Kourou	Communication
GSAT-2	GSLV-D2	08 May 2003	Sriharikota	Communication
EDUSAT	GSLV-F1	20 Sept. 2004	Sriharikota	Education
CARTOSAT	PSLV-C6	05 May 2005	Sriharikota	Mapping
HANSAT	PSLV-c6	05 May 2005	Sriharikota	Communication
INSAT-4A	Ariane-5	22 Dec. 2005	Kourou	Communication
INSAT-4C*	GSLC-Fo2	10 Jul. 2006	Sriharikota	Communication
CARTOSAT-2 SRE LAPAN-TUBSAT PEHUENSAT-1	PSLV-C7	10 Jan. 2007	Sriharikota	Remote sensing
INSAT-4B CARTOSAT-2A	Ariane-5	12 Mar. 2007	Kourou	Communication
IMS-1	PSLV-C9	28 Apr. 2008	Sriharikota	Remote sensing

*Failed Satellites

CHANDRAYAAN – 1

- India launched its first mission to the Moon, Chandrayan-1, on 22 October 2008 from Satish Dhawan Space Centre, Sriharikota, Andhra Pradesh, weighing 1380 kg was put into transfer orbit around the earth by a modified version of the PSLV-C11.

Q.20. Who was the first Indian woman to become the President of UN General Assembly?

National Insignia and Indian Miscellanea

- The spacecraft is carrying 11 payloads, out of which five were entirely designed and developed in India, three were from European Space Agency, one from Bulgaria and two from the USA, to achieve scientific objectives.
- The vehicle was successfully inserted into lunar orbit on 8 November 2008.
- The Moon Impact Prove (MIP) is the first Indian built object to reach the surface of the moon.
- The Indian space programme achieved a unique feat on 14 November 2008, making India the fourth country in the world, with the placing of Indian tricolour on the Moon's surface.
- The point of MIP's impact was near the Moon's South Polar Region.
- The MIP hit rim of the Shackleton crater at the South Pole on 14 November 2008. This space was identified by US Space Agency, NASA for a possible lunar out spot.
- Over a two-year period, it is intended to survey the lunar surface to produce a complete map of its chemical characteristics and 3-dimensional topography.

The *primary objectives* of Chandrayaan-1 were:
(i) To place an unmanned spacecraft in an orbit around the moon;
(ii) To conduct mineralogical and chemical mapping of the lunar surface;
(iii) To upgrade the technological base in the country.

Principal Launch Vehicles of India

- The first-stage satellite Launch Vehicle (SLV-3), was developed to launch satellite Rohini on 10 August 1979.
- The second-launch vehicle was augmented satellite launch vehicle (ASLV), which was used to launch SROSS-1 satellite on 24 March 1987.
- The third-stage launch vehicle was Polar Satellite Launch Vehicle (PSLV), in which along with solid propellant the liquid propellant was used for the first time. It was used to launch IRS-P1 on 20 September 1993.
- PSLV-C9 successfully delivered the biggest satellite mission in the world, of 824 kg consisting of 10 satellites into orbit on 28 April 2008 from Satish Dhawan Space Centre (SDSC) SHAR, Sriharikota. Out of which two were India's latest Remote Sensing Satellite CARTOSAT-2A and Indian Mini Satellite (IMS-1) along with eight nanosatellites; from Canada, Japan, Denmark, Germany and the Netherlands.
- The fourth-stage launch vehicle was geosynchronous satellite launch vehicle (GSLV), in which second- and fourth-stage uses cryogenic engines, and liquid hydrogen and liquid oxygen were used as propellant.
- It was used to launch the communication satellite GSAT-1 on 28 March 2001. It is capable of launching 2000 kg class satellite into Geosynchronous Transfer Orbit (GTO).
- Some upcoming satellite Launch Vehicles are: GSLV Mk-I, GSLV Mk-II, GSLV Mk-III.
- Some of the upcoming Satellite: Agile, INSAT-3D, GSAT5/INSAT-4D, ANUSAT, GSAT-6, INSAT-4E, GSAT-8, INSAT-4G, GSAT-7/INSAT-4F.

ATOMIC RESEARCH

India's atomic research programme got a momentum with the set up of Atomic Energy

Q.21. Who is known as Indian Bismark?
Q.22. Who are popularly known as trinity of Carnatic music?

Commission (AEC) in 1948, under the chairmanship of Dr Homi Jahangir Bhabha.

Department of Atomic Energy (DAE) was setup in 1954, for implementation of atomic energy programmes,

DAE has five research centres:

(a) Bhabha Atomic Research Centre (BARC): Established in 1957, it is the largest atomic centre of India located in Trombay (Maharashtra).
(b) Indira Gandhi Center for Atomic Research (ISCAR): Established in 1971, it is located at Kalpakam (Tamil Nadu).
(c) Variable Energy Cyclotron Center (VECC): Established in 1977, located in Calcutta.
(d) Center for Advanced Technology (CAT): Established in 1971, is located at Indore (Madhya Pradesh).
(e) Atomic Minerals Directorate for Exploration Research (AMD): Established in 1949, it is located in Hyderabad.

The following Public Sector Undertakings are supported by DAE:

1. Nuclear Power Corporation of India Limited (NPCIL), Mumbai
2. Uranium Corporation of India Limited (UCIL), Jaduguda (Jharkhand)
3. Indian Rare Earth Limited (IRE), Mumbai
4. Electronic Corporation of India Limited (ECIL), Hyderabad

DAE supports following service organisations:

1. Directorate of Purchase and Stores (DPS), Mumbai
2. Construction Service and Estate Management Group (DCSEM), Mumbai
3. General Services Organisation (GSO), Kalpakkam (Tamil Nadu)
4. Atomic Energy Education Society (AEES), Mumbai

DAE financially supports the following institutes:

1. Tata Institute of Fundamental Research (TIFR), Mumbai
2. Tata Memorial Centre (TMC), Mumbai
3. Saha Institute of Nuclear Physics (SINP), Kolkata
4. Institute of Physics (IOP), Bhubaneswar
5. Harischandra Research Institute (HRI), Allahabad
6. Institute of Mathematical Studies (IMS), Chennai
7. Institute of Plasma Research (IPR), Ahmedabad

List of Nuclear Power Plants in Operation

Name	Location
I. Tarapur Atomic Power Station (Units: TAPS-1, TAPS-2, TAPS-3, TAPS-4)	Tarapur (Maharashtra)
II. Madras Atomic Power Station (Units: MAPS-1, MAPS-2)	Kalpakkam (Tamil Nadu)
III. Rajasthan Atomic Power Station (Units: RAPS-1, RAPS-2, RAPS-3, RAPS-4)	Rawatbhata (Rajasthan)
IV. Narora Atomic Power Station (Units: NAPS-1, NAPS-2)	Narora (Uttar Pradesh)
V. Kakrapar Atomic Power Station (Units: KAPS-1, KAPS-2)	Kakrapar (Gujarat)

National Insignia and Indian Miscellanea

VI. Kaiga Atomic Power Station (Units: Kaiga-1, Kaiga-2, Kaiga-3)	Kaiga (Karnataka)
VII. Kudan Kulam Nuclear Power Station	Kudan Kulam (Tamil Nadu)

Nuclear Explosion

On 18 May 1974, India conducted its first nuclear explosion at Pokhran, in Rajasthan (Thar Desert). The main objective was to use atomic energy for peaceful purposes. This made India the sixth nuclear nation in the world.

On 11 and 13 May 1998, India conducted five nuclear tests in Pokhran, which includes a thermonuclear device, a fission device and three sub-kiloton nuclear devices.

Media

Print Media

- It covers daily newspapers, weekly magazines, monthly and annually published magazines and books (periodicals).
- The first major newspaper in India – *The Bengal Gazette* – was started in 1780 by James Augustus Hickey during the British rule. Total number of newspapers and periodicals was 65,032 in the year 2007.
- *Dainik Jagran* (in Hindi) is the largest circulated daily news paper which is followed by *The Times of India* (in English) and *Malayala Manorama* (in Malayalam).
- *Malayala Manorama* (in Malayalam) is the largest selling weeklies, followed by *Anand Vikatan* (in Tamil).
- *Vanitha* (in Malayalam) is the highest circulated monthly magazine.
- *Kal Nirnay* (in Marathi) is the largest selling annual magazine.

Electronic Media

- Radio, television, internet, etc., comprise the electronic media. In today's world electronic media is an effective medium to inform and educate people besides providing healthy entertainment.
- All India Radio and Doordarshan functioned as departments under Ministry of Information and Broadcasting.

Radio Broadcasting

- Broadcasting started in India in 1927 with two privately-owned transmitters in Bombay (Mumbai) and Calcutta (Kolkata).
- The Government took over the transmitters in 1930 and started operating them under the name of Indian Broadcasting Service.
- It was changed to All India Radio (AIR) in 1936 and later it came to be known as Akashvani from 1957.
- Network: During Independence, AIR had a network of six stations and a complement of 18 transmitters.
- AIR today has a network of 232 broadcasting centres with 149 medium frequency (MW), 54 high frequency (SW) and 171 FM transmitters.
- The coverage is 91.79 per cent of the area,

Q.23. Mrinalini Sarabhai is an exponent of which classical dance?

Q.24. Who is the only Indian to win the Nobel Prize in Physics?

serving 99.14 per cent of the people in the largest democracy of the world.
- AIR covers 24 languages and 146 dialects in home services. In external services, it covers 27 languages, 17 national and 10 foreign languages.

Television

- The national television of India is one of the largest terrestrial networks in the world.
- On 15 September 1959, the first television transmission started from a makeshift studio in the Akashvani Bhavan, New Delhi.
- A transmitter of 500W power carried the signals within a radius of 25 km from Delhi.
- The regular service with a News bulletin was started in 1965. Television went to a second city Mumbai, only in 1972, and by 1975 Kolkata, Chennai, Srinagar, Amritsar and Lucknow also had television stations.
- Colour transmission was introduced in 1982, during Asian Games held in New Delhi.

Music and Dance of India

Music

- Music can be broadly classified into western classical, hindustani classical, carnatic classical, folk pop, jazz, fusion, etc.
- India's classical music tradition, including carnatic and hindustani music, has a history spanning millennia and, developed over several eras.
- Pivotal concept of Indian music is *'raga'* (melody). Ragas are made up of different combination of *Sapta* (seven) *swara*: *Sa* (*Sadjam*), *Re* (*RishaBam*), *Ga* (*Gandharam*), *Ma* (*Madhyamam*), *Pa* (*Panchamam*), *Dha* (*Dhaivadam*), *Ni* (*Nishadam*).
- Western classical contains Octaves, which consists of 12 notes, while Indian music contains Octaves consisting of 22 (*srutis*) notes.
- While *Swara* is a note, *sruti* is the macrotonal intervals between two *swaras*.
- *Taala* is defined as rhythm. Major *taalas* are: *Adi Taala* (a combination of eight *maatras* and beats), *Chautaala* or *Eaka Taala* (consists of 12 *maatras*), *Jhaptaala* (consists of 10 maatras).
- One of the new forms of Hindustani music, known as *'Khayal'*, emerged during thirteenth and fourteenth century. Amir Khusro is considered as Proponent of this music.
- Thygaraja, Muthuswami Deekshitar and Shyam Shastri are popularly known as trinity of Carnatic music.

Indian Musical Instruments and Their Masters

Musical Instruments	Prominent Personalities
Flute	Harprasad Chaurasia, Pannalal Ghose, T R Mahalingam
Mridungo	Thakur Bhikam Singh, Dr Jagdish Singh, Paldhar Raghu,
Rudra veena	Ustad Sadique Ali Khan, Asad Ali Khan
Sarod	Amjad Ali Khan, Ali Akbar Khan, Allaaudin Khan, Partho Sarathy
Santoor	Shivkumar Sharma
Sarangi	Ustad Bindu Khan
Shahnai	Ustad Bismillah Khan, Daya Shankar Jagannath
Sitar	Pt Ravi Shankar, Vilayat Khan, Nikhil Banarjee, Umashankar Mishra
Tabla	Ustad Zakir Hussain, Thirakwa Ustad Alla Rakha, Ustad Tari Khan

| Violin | Dr N Rajan, L. Subramanyum, Gajanan Rao Joshi, TN Krishnan |
| Veena | S Balachandran, K R Kumara Swamy Iyer, Pt Vishwamohan Bhatt, Dorrai Swamy Iyengar |

Dance of India

Two main divisions of the dances are: Classical and Folk.

The major schools of classical dance in India are Kathak, Manipuri, Odissi, Bharata Natyam, Kuchipudi, Kathakali and Mohiniattam, apart from the Folk and Tribal dances.

Classical Indian Dance

The criteria for being considered as classical is the style's adherence to the guidelines laid down in *Natyashastra* by the sage Bharata Muni (400 BC), which explains the Indian art of acting. Acting or *natya* is a broad concept which encompasses both drama and dance.

- The Sangeet Natak Akademi confers classical status on eight 'dance' forms:
  - (i) Bharatanatyam
  - (ii) Odissi
  - (iii) Kuchipudi
  - (iv) Manipuri
  - (v) Mohiniaattam
  - (vi) Sattriya
  - (vii) Kathak
  - (viii) Kathakali

Bharatnatyam: Bharatnatyam dance has its origins in Tamil Nadu.

- This dance uses the base of storytelling combined with pure dance movements.
- The origins of this dance go back to the *Natyashastra*. In the ancient days, this dance was performed only by the *Devdasis*.
- It is a solo dance and highly traditional.
- *Some Exponents*: Bala Saraswati, CV Chandrasekhar, Mrinalini Sarabhai, Padma Subramanyam, Rukmini Devi, Yamini Krisnhnamurthy.

Odissi: This classical dance has its origins in Orissa and can be distinguished from other styles of Indian dance due to the specific movements of the body.
Famous Dancers: Kalucharan Mahapatra, Sanyukta Panigrahi, Debaprasad Das, Dhirendra Nath Pattanaik, Priyambada Mohanty, Sonal Mansingh.

Kuchipudi: This classical Indian dance has its roots in Andhra Pradesh. It is performed on the accompaniment of Carnatic music.
It is a solo dance performed by men in attires of women.
Famous Dancers: Josyula Seetharamaiah, Venpathi Chinna Satyam.

Manipuri: It originates from North eastern part of India.
It is a highly lyrical and ritualistic dance.
Famous Dancers: Guru Bipin Sinha, Jhaveri sisters, Nirmala Mehta, Savita Mehta.

Mohiniattam: This dance has its origins in Kerala.
It is a solo dance and mainly performed by women. It originates from Devdasis dances similar to Bharatnatyam and Odissi.
Famous Dancers: Ms Kanaka Rele, Ms Bharati Shivaji, Guru Thankamani Kutti and Pratima Gouri.

Sattriya: This traditional style of dance originated from Assam. This style of dance was the creation of Sankardeva. It is performed only by males.

Q.25. Which Indian classical dance is a solo dance performed by men in attires of women?

Q.26. Yakshagana is a traditional dance of which state?

Kathak: This dance originated from the temples in the northern part of India in the form of Radha Krishna Lilas.

Kathak is also performed in various styles or Gharanas, such as the Lucknow Gharana, Jaipur Gharana, Rajgarh Gharana and the Banaras Gharana.

Famous Dancers: Bharti Gupta, Birju Mahaj, Damayanti Josjhi, Durga Das, Sambhu Maharaj, Sitara Devi.

Kathakali: This is a form of dance drama that originated in Kerala. It is condered to be the most scientific dance form. The body and the hand movement and eye ball movement comprises its languages.

Classical Dances of India

Dance	State
Bharat Nattyam	Tamil Nadu
Odissi	Orissa
Kuchipudi	Andhra Pradesh
Manipuri	Manipur
Mohiniattam	Kerala
Sattriya	Assam
Kathak	North India
Kathakali	Kerala
Ottam-Thullal	Kerala
Chhau	WB, Orissa, Bihar

Folk and Tribal Dances of India

States	Dances
1. Maharashtra	Tamasha/Lavani Dance, Dindi And Kala, Koli
2. Gujarat	Garba Dance, Dandiya Dance
3. Rajasthan	Kalbelia Dance, Chari Dance, Ghoomar Dance, Fire Dance, Kachhi Gori, Gangori, Tera Tali
4. Karnataka	Dollu Kunitha, Yakshagana
5. Goa	Ghode Modni, Tarangmel
6. Lakshadweep	Lava Dance of Minicoy
7. Kerala	Padayani, Kodiatam, Krishnavattam
8. Tamil Nadu	Kummi, Kolattam
9. Andhra Pradesh	Bathakamma, Kolattam, Perini, Thapetta Gullu
10. Orissa	Dalkhai, Goti Puas, Sambalpuri
11. Assam	Bihu Dance, Tubal choubi
12. Tripura	Hajgiri
13. Meghalaya	Nongkrem, Wangala Lahu
14. Manipur	Dhol-Cholom
15. West Bengal	Brita Dance, Chau

Q.27. Who is the first Indian to become President of International Court of Justice (ICJ)?
Q.28. Which dance's language comprises body gestures, hand movements and eye movements?

National Insignia and Indian Miscellanea

16.	Punjab	Bhangra, Gidda
17.	Jammu & Kashmir	Dumhal, Rauf
18.	Himachal Pradesh	Hikat, Namagen, Karyala
19.	Uttarakhand	Hurka Baul
20.	Haryana	Dhamyal, Swang
21.	Madhya Pradesh	Gaur Dance, Muria Dances, Kaksar Dance
22.	Chhattisgarh	Saila Dance, Karma Dance
23.	Bihar	Natanatini, Jatra, Lagui

First in India (Male)

1.	First President	Dr Rajendra Prasad
2.	First Vice-President	Dr S Radhakrishnan
3.	First Muslim President	Dr Zakir Hussain
4.	First President who died in office	Dr Zakir Hussain
5.	First Sikh President	Dr Giani Zail Singh
6.	First Prime minister	Pt Jawaharlal Nehru
7.	First Prime Minister who resigned without completing full-term	Moraji Desai
8.	First Prime Minister who didn't face the Parliament	Charan Singh
9.	First Indian to win Noble Prize	Rabindranath Tagore
10.	First President of INC	W C Banerjee
11.	First British Governor General of India	Warren Hastings
12.	First British Viceroy of India	Lord Canning
13.	First Governor General of free India	Lord Mountbatten
14.	First and the last Governor General of free India	C Rajgopalchari
15.	First man who introduced printing press	James Augutus Hicky
16.	First Indian to join the ICS	Satyendranath Tagore
17.	First Indian in Space	Rakesh Sharma
18.	First Indian commander in chief	General Chriappa
19.	First Indian chief of the Army staff	General Maharaja Rajendra Singhji
20.	First Indian Field Marshal	S H F J Manekshaw
21.	First Indian chief of the naval staff	Vice Admiral R D Katari
22.	First Indian chief of the Air Staff	Subroto Mukherjee
23.	First Indian Air Marshal	Arjan Singh
24.	First Indian in British Parliament	Dadabhai Nauroji
25.	First Indian to circumnavigate	Lt Col K S Rao
26.	First Indian to become member of Viceroy executive council	S P Sinha
27.	First Indian to become President of ICJ (UN)	Dr Nagendra Singh
28.	First Chief Justice of India	Justice H L Kania
29.	First Chief Election Commission	Sukumar Sen
30.	First Indian High Court Judge	Justice Syed Mehmood

Q.29. The dance drama, **Kajri** *belongs to which state?*
Q.30. Which Academy promotes and develops literature in all the 22 languages in India?

31.	First Speaker of Lok Sabha	G V Mavlankar
32.	First Indian to make a solo air flight	J R D Tata
33.	First Indian leader to visit England	Raja Rammohan Roy
34.	First Indian member of House of Lords (Britain)	Lord S P Sinha
35.	First Chairman of Rajya Sabha	Dr S Radhakrishnan
36.	First Indian to reach the South Pole	Col J K Bajaj
37.	First Indian recipient of Victoria Cross	Khudada Khan
38.	First Indian to swim across the English Channel	Mihir Sen
39.	First Indian to climb Mt. Everest	Tenzing Norgay
40.	First man to reach Mt. Everest without Oxygen	Phu Dorji
41.	First Indian to climb Mt Everest twice	Nwang Gombu
42.	First Indian test cricketer	Ranjit Singhji
43.	First Judge to face Impeachment in Lok Sabha	Justice V Ramaswamy
44.	First Indian to receive Jnanpith Award	Sri Shankar Puru
45.	First Education Minister	Abul Kalam Azad
46.	First Home Minister	Sardar Vallabhbhai Patel
47.	First to receive Paramvir Chakra	Major Somnath Sharma
48.	First Indian to receive Magsaysay Award	Acharya Vinoba Bhave
49.	First Indian to receive Stalin Prize	Saifuddin Kitchlu
50.	First Indian Tennis Player to win a Grand slam	Mahesh Bhupati

First in India (Female)

1.	First President	Pratibha S Patil
2.	First Prime Minister	Indira Gandhi
3.	First Chief Minister of State (UP)	Sucheta Kripalini
4.	First Cabinet Minister	Vijayalakshmi Pandit
5.	First Speaker of Lok Sabha	Meira Kumar
6.	First Governor	Sarojini Naidu
7.	First President of INC	Dr Annie Besant
8.	First Indian President of INC	Sarojini Naidu
9.	First President of UN General Assembly	Vijayalakshmi Pandit
10.	First to swim across English Channel	Arti Saha (Gupta)
11.	First to climb Mt Everest	Bachhendri Pal
12.	First to climb Mt Everest twice	Santosh Yadav
13.	Youngest to climb Mt Everest (19)	Dicky Dolma
14.	First to circumnavigate	Ujwala Rai
15.	First IAS Officer	Anna George Malhotra
16.	First IPS Officer	Kiran Bedi
17.	First Advocate	Camelia Sorabji
18.	First Judge of Supreme Court	M Fatima Beevi
19.	First Judge of High Court	Anna Chandi
20.	First Pilot in Indian Air Force	Harita Kaur Dayal
21.	First to receive Bharat Ratna	Indira Gandhi

Q.31. In which year tiger was adopted as the National Animal of India?
Q.32. When National Emblem of India was adopted?
Q.33. Which is India's first nuclear reactor?

National Insignia and Indian Miscellanea

22. First to receive Ashok Chakra — Nirja Bhanot
23. First to receive Sena Medal — Bimla Devi (CRPF)
24. First Jnanpith Award — Ashapurna Devi
25. First Magistrate — Omana Kunjamma
26. First Indian to be crowned Miss World — Reita Faria
27. First Indian to be crowned Miss Universe — Sushmita Sen
28. First Cosmonaut from India — Kalpana Chawla

World Records Held by Indian

Field	Name
1. Maximum number of Songs recording	Lata Mangeshkar
2. Women to Climb Mt Everest twice	Mrs Santosh Yadav
3. Youngest to climb Mt Everest (19 yrs)	Dicky Dolma
4. Long distance swimming	Mihir Sen
5. Women Air Pilot for logging maximum flying hours	Capt. Durga Bannerjee
6. Performing maximum eye operations (40 per hour)	Dr M C Modi
7. Fastest Computing (Faster than Computer)	Mrs Shakuntala Devi
8. Accurate and Fastest Typing	Dr Rajendra Singh
9. Marathon Typing (123 hours)	Sambhu Govind Anbhawane

Indian Nobel Laureates

Rabindranath Tagore (1861–1941)

- He became Asia's first Nobel Laureate when he won the Nobel Prize in 1913 in Literature for *Gitanjali*.
- He founded, Shantiniketan at Bolepur, West Bengal, which later came to be known as Visva-Bharati University.
- In protest against the 1919 Jallianwala Bagh massacre, he resigned the knighthood that had been conferred upon him in 1915.
- Tagore holds the unique distinction of being the composer of the national anthems of two different countries, India and Bangladesh.
- Some of his works includes novels like *Gora, Ghare Baire, Kabuliwallah*, etc., and poems like *Manasi, Sonar Tori (Golden Boat), Balaka* and *Purobi*.

C V Raman (7 November 1888–21 November 1970)

- He was an Indian Physicist, who won the Nobel Prize in 1930 in recognition of his work on the molecular scattering of light and for the discovery of the Raman Effect, which is named after him.
- He was also honoured with Knighthood (1929), Bharat Ratna (1954) and Lenin Peace Prize (1957).
- India celebrates National Science Day on 28 February of every year to commemorate the discovery of the Raman Effect in 1928.

Har Gobind Khorana (9 January 1922)

He was awarded the Nobel Prize in Physiology or Medicine in 1968 for his work on the interpretation of the genetic code and its function in protein synthesis.

Q.34. Name India's first communication satellite.
Q.35. Who is the first Indian to reach the South Pole?

Mother Teresa (26 August 1910–5 September 1997)
- Agnes Gonxha Bojaxhiu born in Skopje, Yugoslavia (now Macedonia), came to India in 1928 and became an Indian citizen.
- She founded the Missionaries of Charity in 1950 in Calcutta (Kolkata).
- She won the Nobel Peace Prize in 1979 for her humanitarian work.
- She was also honoured India's highest civilian honour, the Bharat Ratna, in 1980, Jawaharlal Nehru Award for International Understanding in 1969, Ram Magsaysay Award in 1962.

Subrahmanyan Chandrasekhar (19 October 1910–21August 1995)
- He was an Indian born American astrophysicist.
- In 1983 he was awarded the Nobel Prize in physics along with William Alfred Fowler for their work in the theoretical structure and evolution of stars.
- Chandrasekhar's most famous success was the astrophysical Chandrasekhar limit, which describes the maximum mass of a white dwarf star (~1.44 solar masses) or equivalently, the minimum mass, above which a star will ultimately collapse into a neutron star or black hole (following a supernova).
- He was the nephew of Indian Nobel Laureate Sir C V Raman.

Amartya Sen
- A distinguished economist-philosopher who won the Nobel Prize in Economic Sciences in the year 1998.
- He is known 'for his contributions to welfare economics' in his work on famine, human development theory, welfare economics, underlying mechanisms of poverty, gender inequality and political liberalism.

ANSWERS

1. 24 January 1950.
2. Saka Era
3. Mundak Upanisad
4. Seven
5. Field Marshal K M Cariappa
6. A Supersonic Cruise Missile
7. Dhrupad
8. France
9. Pilotless Target Aircraft (PTA)
10. 20 seconds
11. James Augustus Hickey
12. Chushul
13. INS Viraat
14. Wellington, Kochi
15. Assam Rifle
16. 1962
17. Integrated Guided Missile Development Programme
18. Arvi (Pune)
19. Ahmedabad
20. Smt. Vijayalaxmi Pandit
21. Sardar Patel
22. Thygaraja, Muthuswami Deekshitar and Shyam Shastri
23. Bharatnatyam
24. Sir C V Raman
25. Kuchipudi
26. Karnataka
27. Dr Nagendra Singh
28. Kathakali
29. Uttar Pradesh
30. Sahitya Academy
31. 1972
32. 26 January 1950
33. Apsara
34. APPLE (Ariane Passenger Payload Experiment)
35. Col J K Bajaj

12
CURRENT AFFAIRS

GENERAL ELECTIONS 2009

The general elections was held in all the States (28) and Union Territories (7), along with assembly elections were also held in three states, viz., Andhra Pradesh, Orissa and Sikkim, in five phases, from 16 April to 13 May. The result was announced on 16 May 2009.

Total number of states and UTs: 35
Total number of Parliamentary Constituencies (PCs): 543 (2 are appointed by the President of India)
Total Electors: 71,00,74,177
Electors where votes counted: 67,18,48,666
Voter Turnout: 58.43 per cent
Results available: 543
Nageswar Rao of Telugu Desam Party from Khammam (AP) Parliamentary constituency (PC) is the richest MP with net worth of Rs 173 crore.

Youngest Member of Parliament is Mumahhed Hamdulla, 26 years of age, of INC. He was elected from Lakshadweep Parliamentary Constituency (PC).

The oldest member of Lok Sabha is Ram Sundar, 83 years old, of JD (U) elected from Hajipur Parliamentary Constituency (PC).

Average age of the House is 53.03 years, which is the third oldest House so far, being thirteenth Lok Sabha was the Oldest House (55.5 years).

Following are few of the facts and figures:

- Total number of political parties: 369
- Total number of candidates: 8070
- Total votes polled: 414,913,023
- Average votes per candidates: 53038
- Numbers of polling stations: 8,28,804
- Number of polling personnel deployed : 46,90,575
- Highest number of votes: (5,85,016 votes) for Deepender Singh Hooda from Rohtak, Haryana
- Highest winning margin: (4,45,736 votes) by Deepender Singh Hooda from Rohtak, Haryana

- Lowest number of candidates: 3 from Nagaland
- Highest number of Candidates: 43 from Madras south
- Highest .... polling station: AuleyPhu, Leh AC (Ladakh)
- Largest Parliamentary Constituency (*area-wise*): Ladakh (173266.37 sq. km)
- Smallest Parliamentary Constituency (*area-wise*): Chandni Chowk (10.59 sq. km.)
- Total cost of election: Rs 1,120 Crores

STATE ASSEMBLY ELECTIONS 2009

Three State Assembly Elections were held along with the general elections: Andhra Pradesh, Orissa and Sikkim.

Andhra Pradesh

Andhra Pradesh assembly elections were held in two phases in April 2009 for 294 assembly seats. The first phase of election was held for 154 seats on 16 April 2009 in 10 districts including Hyderabad and second phase of polling was held for 140 seats on 23 April 2009 in remaining 13 districts. A voter turnout of 65 per cent was registered in first phase in Andhra Pradesh and in the second phase, the voting turnout was 68 per cent. The result was declared on 16 May 2009.

Party	Seats Won
INC	158
TDP	105
PRP	18
Others	13
Total	294

On 30 May 2009, Dr Y S Rajasekhar Reddy* was sworn in as the Chief Minister of Andhra Pradesh for second term. (*K Rosaiah sworn in as CM after the death of Y S R Reddy in September 2009.)

Orissa

Elections for the assembly of Orissa were held in two phases on April 2009 for 147 seats. The first phase of election was held for 70 seats on 16 April 2009 and second phase of polling was held for 77 seats on 23 April 2009. 52.6 per cent voting was recorded in the first phase assembly elections and 55 per cent in second phase of elections in Orissa. The result was declared on 16 May 2009.

Party	Seats Won
BJD	109
INC	26
BJP	7
Others	5
Total	147

On 21 May, Mr Naveen Patnaik was sworn in as the Chief Minister for the third consecutive term.

Q.1. Who was the India's chief guest at the sixtieth Republic Day?
Q.2. Who has been appointed as the First Director General of National Investigation Agency?

Sikkim

Sikkim assembly elections were held in one phase on 30 April 2009 for 32 assembly seats in all four districts. A record 83 per cent voter turnout was registered in assembly elections. The result was declared on 16 May 2009.

Party	Seats Won
SDF	32
Total	32

Mr Pawan Chamling was sworn in as the Chief Minister on 20 May 2009.

NATIONAL NEWS

Bill to Set Up a National Investigation Agency (NIA): Government on 16 December 2008 introduced in Lok Sabha a Bill to set up a National Investigation Agency (NIA) to strengthen law against terror. On 1 January 2009 the National Investigative Agency Bill became a law. The new anti-terror laws were enacted by Parliament following the 26/11 terror strikes in Mumbai. Radha Vinod Raju on 19 January 2009 took over as the first head of National Investigation Agency (NIA).

Project Snow Leopard Launched: The government on 20 January 2009 launched 'Project Snow Leopard' to safeguard and conserve India's unique natural heritage of high-altitude wildlife populations and their habitats by promoting conservation through participatory policies and actions. The Project Snow Leopard is an initiative for strengthening wildlife conservation in the Himalayan high altitudes, covering Jammu and Kashmir, Himachal Pradesh, Uttarakhand, Arunachal Pradesh and Sikkim. It aims at promoting a knowledge-based and adaptive conservation framework that fully involves the local communities, who share the snow leopard's range, in conservation efforts. It will be treated at par with other flagship species programmes of the country such as Project Tiger and Project Elephant.

India, the Third Largest Steel Producer: India has emerged as the third largest steel producer in the world, leaving behind Russia and the US, in the first quarter of 2009. As per the World Steel Association estimates for the January-March period of 2009, India reported 1 per cent increase in output at 13.17 million tonnes for three months ended against the year-ago period. China recorded a steel production of about 126 million tonnes, while Japan had 17.60 million tonnes in the three months. *The first five are:* China, Japan, India, Russia and the US.

Chief Guest at Republic Day Parade: Kazakhstan President Nursultan Nazarbayev was the Chief Guest at the sixtieth Republic Day parade at the Rashtrapati Bhavan. The annual Beating Retreat and Prime Ministers NCC Rally were cancelled following the death of former President Ramaswamy Venkataraman.

125 Years of PLI: A commemorative stamp was released on 11 February 2009 to celebrate 125 Years of Postal Life Insurance (PLI) Scheme.

Top Power Selling States: Central Electricity Regulatory Commission (CERC) released its market monitoring report on 24 April 2009. According to the report Chhattisgarh, Delhi, Gujarat, West Bengal and Punjab have emerged as the top five states selling electricity (71.19 per cent of total

Q.3. Which country has recently emerged as India's largest defence supplier?

volume). Rajasthan, Andhra Pradesh, Maharashtra, Karnataka and Tamil Nadu are top five electricity purchasing states (73.05 per cent of the total volume).

Haryana has become the first state in the country to set up a **2800 MW Nuclear Power Plant** in Kaumaharia Village in Fatehgarh district.

World Bank Grant for India's Power Plants: The World Bank on 18 June 2009 has approved a $180 million loan for the renovation and modernisation of old, polluting and inefficient coal-fired power plants in India. The project, which is expected to lower carbon emissions and boost power production at these plants, is co-financed with a $45.4-million grant from the Global Environment Facility (GEF). This has been done as a move to reduce carbon emissions. With the proposal, three coal-fired power plants with 200-220 MW capacity each at Bandel in West Bengal, Koradi in Maharashtra, and Panipat in Haryana will be modernised.

Appointment of Armed Force Tribunal: The Central Government finally on 22 June 2009 approved the appointment of eight judicial and 15 administrative members in the Armed Forces Tribunal (AFT) for a period of four years to dispense cost-effective and speedy justice to the armed forces personnel. AFT was inaugurated by the President Ms Pratibha Patil, following which over 9800 cases pending in different High Courts filed by serving or retired military personnel will be transferred to it. Former Supreme Court Justice Ashok Kumar Mathur was appointed as Chairperson of the AFT in 2008. The appointed members will serve for a period of four years or till the age of 65 years, whichever is earlier. AFT has the power of a High Court and its verdicts will be open to challenge in Supreme Court. It has one principal bench at New Delhi and eight regional benches at Chandigarh, Lucknow, Guwahati, Mumbai, Kochi, Chennai and Jaipur.

Apex Court Bench to Replace Environment Tribunal: The government has decided to replace the proposed National Environment Tribunal with a green bench to be formed by Supreme Court Judges. The national green bench will be the highest judicial body to deal with environment related court cases, especially those where industrial plans are often ranged against the concerns of civil society. All civil disputes relating to mandatory environmental and forest clearances required for new industrial projects will be settled by this bench. The bench would also replace the National Environment Appellate Authority.

Global Advisory Council for Government of India: Economist Amartya Sen, business tycoon L N Mittal and Pepsico CEO Indra Nooyi are among the members of a high-level panel headed by Prime Minister, Manmohan Singh, constituted to advise the government. The Global Advisory Council will develop an inclusive agenda for engagement between the country and the best Indian brains living abroad and the council will also consider ways and means for accessing the skills and knowledge of Indian diaspora for meeting the country's development goals and facilitating investments by overseas Indians into the country. Other panelists of the 23-member council includes External Affairs Minister S M Krishna, City group CEO Vikram Pandit, NRI entrepreneur Karan Bilimoria, economist Jagdish Bhagwati, educationists Sam Pitroda.

Tri-Service Landing Operation Exercise Tropex 2009: The armed forces on 9 February 2009 conducted the largest-ever amphibious exercise on the Madhavpur beach in Gujarat. Amphibious landing is considered the most complex of all military manoeuvres, involving coordination and synergy from conceptualisation to planning and final execution. The pre-assault manoeuvres were completed at the Karwar naval base in Karnataka and the

Q.4. Which bank launched Indo-Nepal Remittance Scheme?
Q.5. What is Tropex 2009?

amphibious task force sailed on 5 February 2009. They landed at Madhavpur four days later using the newly inducted Landing Platform Dock INS Jalashwa, several Landing Ship Tank Large, fleet ships with their integral helicopters, shore-based aircraft and submarines from the Navy and hovercraft of the Coast Guard. This was the first time the Joint Doctrine on Amphibious Warfare of the armed forces, formulated last year, was put into practice. As a precursor to the operation, a tri-Service landing operation, 'Triveni,' was conducted at the Lakshadweep islands in January.

Set up of the Unique Identification Authority of India (UIA): The government on 25 June 2009 appointed Infosys co-chairman Nandan Nilekani as the chairperson of Unique Identification Authority, formed to issue IDs to every citizen in the country. As Chairman of the body, Nilekani will have Cabinet minister rank and status, a three year deadline and corpus of Rs 100 crore. He has been provided with the flexibility to draw talent from private sector to build his core team for the implementation of the project. The UIA will help implement a scheme to assign a unique identification number to every Indian. It will also own and operate the database and maintain it. The move to set up the UID Authority of India (UIDAI), under the aegis of the Planning Commission, is aimed at providing a unique identity to the targeted population of the flagship schemes such as the National Rural Employment Guarantee Scheme, Sarva Shiksha Abhiyan, National Rural Health Mission and Bharat Nirman. Nilekani stepped down from the Infosys board on 9 July 2009. The 54-year-old has served Infosys as chief operating officer, chief executive officer and managing director, and most recently as the co-chairman of the board of directors.

Specifics of the Unique ID Card:
- Rs 1,50,000 crore unique Identification Card (UIC) project will catalogue personnel details of every Indian citizens on the smart cards.
- The card would include name, sex, address, marital status, photo, identification mark and finger biometrics.
- Will be based on sophisticated application called SCOSTA, a secured electronic device that is used for keeping data and other information in a way that only authorised persons can view it.
- UIC card will be used for many purposes ranging from being used as a proof to register to have voter I-card to open bank account. It can help to deter illegal immigration and curb terrorism.
- Scheme was launched in November 2003 and card has so far been given to only 31 lakh citizens.

More Judges for Apex Court: The central government has notified an increase in the number of Supreme Court Judges from 26 to 31, including the Chief Justice of India. This follows enactment of the Supreme Court (Number of Judges) Amendment Act, 2008. In 1986, the number of judges was increased from 18 to 25, excluding the CJI. At present there are two vacancies and there is no woman judge. In 2002, the court directed the Centre to increase the number of judges in the Supreme Court and the High Courts in a phased manner to tackle mounting arrears. There has been an increase in the number of cases being filed, causing an increase in the pendency, which is about 49,000 cases, including admission and regular matters.

NTPC-BHEL Power Plant Equipment: A Rs 6,000 crore project to manufacture power plant equipment will be established near

Q.6. Which committee has been constituted by Supreme Court to curb the menace of ragging?

Srikalahasti in Chittoor district of Andhra Pradesh as a joint venture of two public sector giants, NTPC and BHEL. This will be the highest public sector investment in a project in the State after Visakhapatnam Steel Plant and it will provide jobs to nearly 6,000 persons directly and to 35,000 indirectly.

MoU Between USEL and Government of Gujarat: Singapore based multibillion Dollar Universal Success Enterprises Ltd. (USEL) signed three MoUs with Government of Gujarat at the 'Vibrant Gujarat Global Investors' Summit 2009', committing to invest close to Rs 87,000 crore in the various infrastructure projects in the State over the next 10 years. As a part of the MoUs, USEL would be setting up a 10,000 MW Thermal Power Plant with an investment of about Rs 50,000 crore. The port project involves the development of Port Terminals and related infrastructure initially for bulk cargo for the power plants and gradually to be upgraded as a Commercial Port for all kinds of cargo. Besides the above, the other major investment includes the mixed use Industrial and Urban Infrastructure development, at Dholera SIR near Ahmedabad.

Joint Initiative of Microsoft and Government of India: Microsoft India has rolled out 'Project Vikas' for the pharmaceutical manufacturing cluster of Hyderabad. 'Project Vikas' is a joint initiative of Microsoft India and the National Manufacturing Competitiveness Council (NMCC), Government of India, that focuses not just on driving IT penetration, but also skill and capacity building, helping the clusters increase their efficiency and reliability, Rajiv Sodhi of Engineering Geographies, Microsoft India said in Hyderabad. Project Vikas brings to life Microsoft's vision of enabling a world of software plus services, where customers have a choice of how to consume and use software-based solutions.

Anti-Ragging Helpline Launched: The Centre launched round-the-clock anti-ragging helpline on 20 June 2009 based on the Raghavan Committee recommendations. The Supreme Court directed the University Grants Commission to fund a toll-free helpline for students in distress across the country. The helpline 1800-180-5522 was launched by Human Resource Development Minister Mr Kapil Sibal. Students, parents and guardians will now be able to file complaints via internet on this helpline. The call centre is located in New Delhi and the professionals managing it will respond to calls in English, Hindi and a selected regional language with a call recording system.

World Bank Loan for Power Plants: World Bank has sanctioned a loan of $225.5 million to India as assistance for renovation and modernisation of a number of coal-fired units with a combined capacity of 640 MW, as per the official statement released on 20 June 2009. The Global Environment Facility (GEF) assisted coal-fired generation rehabilitation project, which will help rehabilitate and modernise three coal-fired power plants at Bandel, in West Bengal, Karadi in Maharashtra and Panipat in Haryana. The assistance comprises an International Bank for Restructuring and Development (IBRD) loan $ 180 million and a GEF grant of $ 45.5 million. The aim of the project is to reduce carbon emission to improve water treatment and ash disposal at these three plants.

Eighth Indo-Gulf Conference Held in Chennai: The eighth edition of Indo-Gulf conference was held in Chennai on 24 June 2009. Representatives of various Arab nations organised the meet in collaboration with ASSPCHAM. The conference was named 'Indo-Gulf Conference on Current Economic Scenario'.

OVL Consortium to Invest $ 5 Billion in Iran: Oil and Natural Gas Corporation Videsh Limited (OVL) in partnership with Indian Oil

Q.7. With which country did India renew its Protocol on Inland Water Transit and Travel recently?

Corporation (IOC) and Oil India Limited (OIL), has outlined a plan to invest around $ 5 billion over next four years to produce gas from Farsi Block discovered in offshore Iran as per a report released on 25 June 2009. Iran's state-owned National Iranian Oil Company (NIOC) is the owner of the oil and gas found in that country. The discovery, which was subsequently named Farzad gas field, could possibly hold in reserves of up to 21.68 trillion cubic ft (tcf), of which recoverable reserves may be 12.8 tcf. Iranian authorities has not yet approved to the detailed investment and development plan.

Longest Total Solar Eclipse of the Century: The solar eclipse of 22 July 2009 was the longest total solar eclipse during the twenty-first century. It lasted a maximum of 6 minutes and 39 seconds off the coast of South-east Asia. Starting off in India just after dawn, the eclipse was visible across a wide swath of Asia before moving over southern Japan and then off into the Pacific Ocean. It was visible in eastern China, Japan, India and Nepal. In India the path of total eclipse passed over Bhavnagar, Surat, Ujjain, Indore, Bhopal, Sagar, Jabalpur, Varanasi, Allahabad, Gaya, Patna, Bhagalpur, Jalpaigudi, Guwahati, Dibrugarh and Itanagar. Next total eclipse will be visible on 13 June 2132.

Prime Minister Manmohan Singh, Chief Guest at French National Day: Prime Minister Manmohan Singh on 14 July watched Indian troops march down the stately Champ Elysees, alongside the French contingents during the French National day parade on Bastille Day. Dr Singh became the first Indian head of government to have the honour of being the Chief Guest at the parade that seemed like a scaled down version of the Republic Day parade. Though missing the rich diverse and vibrant cultural component, the French displayed, like India, their military might on the occasion. French fighters, bombers and other aircraft flew in various formations overhead as the tanks and armoured vehicles straddled the famous street.

World's Largest Solar Steam System at Shirdi: Union Minister for New and Renewable Energy, Mr Farooq Abdullah inaugurated the world's largest solar steam system, installed at Sri Sai Baba Sansthan, Shirdi on 30 July 2009.

Parliament Approves Right to Education Bill: The Union Parliament adopted the Right of Children to Free and Compulsory Education Bill, 2009, which envisages free and compulsory education for children between the age group of 6-14 years with the Lok Sabha approving it by voice vote on 4 August 2009. Earlier it was passed by the Rajya Sabha on 20 July 2009.

The Bill has made provision for 25 per cent seats to weaker sections in school and seeks to stop the practice of schools taking fees before admission and any kind of screening procedures for parents. The Bill also seeks to evolve standards of primary education and norms like minimum qualifications for teachers, student-teacher ratio and ban on private tuitions by teachers.

India's Largest Rail Bridge: A 4.62 km long rail bridge connecting the main land to the container trans-shipment terminal on Vallarpadam Island across Vembanad Lake in Ernakulam district of Kerala, will be commissioned in November 2009. This will be the longest rail bridge in India. Current record is held by Nehru Setu (3.065 km) near Dehri over river Sone.

Q.8. Which two European countries are redrawing the borders?

Q.9. Where did the finance ministers and central bankers of the G-20 meet on 14 March 2009?

INTERNATIONAL NEWS

Operation Cast Lead on Gaza by Israel: On 27 December 2008, Israeli forces launched a major air attack on Hamas political and military targets in Gaza. On 3 January 2009 Israeli troops launched the ground invasion of the Gaza Strip in what Israel calls the 'second stage of Operation Cast Lead'. On 17 January, Israel announced a unilateral ceasefire, deciding to halt operations without first securing an agreement with Hamas. The next day, 18 January, Hamas, Islamic Jihad and other Palestinian militia groups declared they would halt the launching of rockets into Israel for one week, while demanding that Israel withdraws from Gaza within the week. On 21 January, Israeli troops completed their pullout from the Gaza Strip. The Palestinian Ministry of Health put death toll at the total of 1,324 Gazans killed, of which most were civilians.

Planet-Hunting Spacecraft Kepler Sent to Space: NASA's planet-hunting spacecraft, Kepler, rocketed into space on 6 March 2009 on an historic voyage to track down other worlds in a faraway patch of the Milky Way Galaxy. The objective is to find any Earth-like planets circling stars in the so-called habitable zone orbits where liquid water could be present on the surface of the planets.

India and Israel Sign Biggest Defence Deal: India has signed its biggest defence deal with Israel for the purchase of a state-of-the-art air defence system at a whopping cost of USD 1.4 billion (Rs 7,042 crore). The defence deal between the two countries was signed on 27 February 2009 under which Israel will develop and manufacture seaborne and shore-based systems against missile attack on India. As per the agreement, Israel Aerospace Industries (IAI) has also undertaken to procure military or aviation products and services from India. It will invest in defence companies in India up to an amount equal to 30 per cent of the contract. India is currently Israel's largest arms buyer.

India-Spain Sign Trade Pact: India and Spain signed three key trade agreements in a bilateral meeting in Madrid, Spain. These three agreements will boost cooperation in six fields: Infrastructure development, Renewable Energy, Agriculture, Research and Development, Tourism and Cooperation in Latin America.

General Election of South Africa: The African National Congress (ANC), led by Jacob Zuma has won the Country's parliamentary elections held on April 2009. The win paved the way for Mr Zuma to become the next President.

Chang'e-1 Impacts Moon: Chang'e-1, China's first lunar probe, impacted the Moon on 4 March 2009 according to sources with the State Administration of Science, Technology and Industry for National Defence. This was the first phase of China's three-stage moon mission, which will lead to a landing and launch of a rover vehicle around 2012. 'Chang'e' is named after a legendary Chinese Moon goddess.

Cyclone Aila hit India and Bangladesh: Millions of people in India and Bangladesh remained marooned without food or water, four days after cyclone Aila hit on 25 May 2009. In Bangladesh, more than three million people have been hit by the cyclone and the death toll touched 175. In Indian state of West Bengal, at least 5.1 million people were displaced, with more than one million people stranded in Sundarban islands alone and the cyclone killed at least 275 people.

New Prime Minister of Nepal Sworn in: Mr Madhav Kumar Nepal took oath as Prime Minister of Nepal on 25 May 2009. He became the PM after Maoist Mr Pushpa Kamal Dahal Prachand resigned.

Q.10. Where did the Arab League Summit 2009 conclude in recently?

Q.11. Who developed the satellite ANUSAT?

China-Russia Military Ties: China and Russia announced their plan to boost military ties between two countries on 28 April 2009. They have planned 25 joint maneouver and war practices during 2009. Both the nations are slated to hold an anti-terror war exercises – Peaceful Mission 2009 – on their territories.

China Increases Aid to Nepal: Chinese Government on 19 April 2009 announced that it would increase annual aid package to Nepal by 50 per cent. It is aimed at facilitating the infrastructure development, science and technology, tourism and agriculture in Nepal.

Indo-Bangladesh Sign Protocol: India and Bangladesh have renewed the Protocol on Inland Water Transit and Travel for two more years. The bilateral agreement which was to expire on 31 March 2009, is for the use of waterways for commerce and keeping river routes navigable. The protocol, signed in 1972, is renewed every two years. Both countries allow each other four points as ports of call to ferry goods.

2009 as the International Year of Astronomy: UNESCO and the International Astronomical Union (IAU) declared 2009 as the International Year of Astronomy under the theme 'The Universe, Yours to Discover'. The IYA2009 is a global celebration of astronomy and its contributions to society and culture, with events at national, regional and global levels throughout the whole of 2009. With the aim of providing low-cost telescopes that offer views, the venture has picked up significant pace since the IYA2009 began. More than 4000 Galileoscopes have been donated by the IYA2009 and individuals to organisations and schools in developing countries.

India Tops in World Green Index (WGI): India tops among all the nations of the World in World Green Index, released on 14 May 2009. Brazil and China comes second and third respectively in the list and at bottom end of the ladder were Americans, Canadians and the Japanese. The WGI is the survey conducted by National Geographic Society of USA and the International Polling firm GlobeScan.

G20 Meet: On 2 April 2009, world leaders from the G-20 countries – which account for 85 per cent of the world's output – met in London.

The major outcomes:

- $1.1 trillion injection to boost global economy by IMF.
- To act against Tax Heavens for greater transparency in banking.
- IMF to sell gold reserves to help poor nations.
- Agreement to act urgently to conclude WTO Doha round.
- New rules on pay and bonuses for corporate chiefs.

On India's Front:

- India would now be a member of the Financial Stability Forum as well as the Basle Committee on Banking Supervision.
- The $1.1 trillion injection into global economy would help stimulate India's trade.
- India was accepted as a major player on world economic stage.

The United States will host the next G-20 Summit on 24 and 25 September in Pittsburgh, Pennsylvania.

LTTE's Demand for Independent State Came to an End: After two decades of fighting and three failed attempts of peace talks, including the unsuccessful deployment of the Indian Army as a peacekeeping force from 1987 to 1990, Liberation Tigers of Tamil Eelam (LTTE)

Q.12. Where did Bharti-Wal-Mart, the joint venture of the American retailer and India's Bharti Enterprises, open its first Indian store in?

announced an end to its armed struggle for an independent Tamil state in Sri Lanka on 17 May 2009.

2202 Import Items from Singapore Free from Import Duty: The Central Government has decided to abolish the import duty on 2202 items as part of its tariff elimination commitment under the Comprehensive Economic Cooperation Agreement (CECA) with Singapore. Ever since CECA came into effect in August 2005, the bilateral merchandised trade has seen near fivefold increase in three years for about $ 3.6 billion to $ 19.11 billion. Also tariffs on 2413 items have been reduced under CECA. The items on which tariff have been eliminated include sail boats, ships, trawlers and fishing vessels, dredgers, aircraft parts, optical fibres, helicopters, rail coaches, new aircraft tyres, fish, etc.

First BRIC Summit: Leaders of the four BRIC nations, Brazil, Russia, India and China, met in Yekaterinburg, Russia on 16 June 2009 for the first BRIC Summit. The acronym BRIC (for **B**razil, **R**ussia, **I**ndia, **C**hina) was first used in a Goldman Sachs thesis projecting that the economic potential of Brazil, Russia, India and China is such that they may become among the five most dominant economies by the year 2050. The summit ended with their agreeing on a collective agenda ranging from food security and financial reforms to the creation of a more diversified international monetary system and more democratic and multipolar world order. The 16-point statement issued in the Summit said that the BRIC countries were committed to advance the reform of International Financial Institutions so as to reflect changes in the World economy. It also endorsed the creation of a BRIC joint business forum which could cooperate in diverse areas as agriculture, aviation, energy, pharmaceuticals and services. The Summit also made the statement that International Financial Institutions like IMF and World Bank must have greater voice and representation from emerging and developing economies. Also the head and senior leaderships of these bodies should be appointed through an open, transparent and merit-based selection. Next year the summit is scheduled to take place in Brazil.

Agreement with Ukraine to Upgrade AN-32 Aircraft: India has signed a $ 400 million agreement with Ukraine to upgrade its fleet of transport AN-32 as per report released by Ministry of Defence on 17 June 2009. The upgradation plan is aimed at extending the aircraft's life and improving avionics. In the first phase the upgradation will be done in Ukraine and in the second half, at Kanpur in India. The accord envisaged the upgradation of over AN-32 aircraft over next five years. Antoner-32(AN-32) is the aircraft used for carrying cargo, supplies and troops to difficult terrains. This medium range transport aircraft has been in service of Air Force for over two decades.

Eighth Indo-Gulf Conference Held in Chennai: The eighth edition of the Indo-Gulf Conference was held in Chennai on 24 June 2009. Representative of various Arab nations organised the meet in collaboration with Assocham. The conference was named 'Indo-Gulf Conference on Current Economic Scenario'.

Zurich is the Most Livable City in the World: According to an International report released on 24 June 2009, Switzerland's financial capital Zurich takes the top place in the Annual Index of the World's 25 most livable cities. Copenhagen (Denmark), Tokyo (Japan) came second and third respectively in the third annual quality life index study. Munich (Germany), which topped in the first Index came fourth followed by Helsinki (Finland), Stockholm (Sweden), Vienna (Austria), Paris (France), Melbourne (Australia), and Berlin (Germany).

Q.13. Who has been conferred with Nikkei Asia Prize for year 2009?

Q.14. Where is the first BRIC Summit held?

Current Affairs 327

The Index is based on a number of measures including investment in public transport, public safety, health, education and the number of cinema screens in a city.

One-Sixth of the World Population is Hungry Now: As per United Nations reports released on 20 June 2009, one in six people in the world or more than one billion is now hungry. This historic high is due to global economic crisis and high food prices. The Food and Agricultural Organisation (FAO) said, as compared to last year, 100 million more people are hungry, which means they receive less than 1800 calories a day. The report said that there are 1.02 billion people are hungry, which is 11 per cent more than last year's 915 million. Asia-Pacific representing 642 million and sub-Saharan Africa representing 265 million has the highest hunger rate (32 per cent) of the region's total population.

G-8 Finance Ministers Meet: The Group of Eight (G-8) Finance Ministers held a crucial meeting in Leece, Italy on 13 June 2009, which underlined the rich nations' effort to bring back their economies on track. The drafted declaration of the meeting of the G8 – which comprises the US, Germany, Japan, Russia, Britain, France, Italy and Canada – highlighted the fact that how these nations will unveil emergency steps to bring back their economies on the path of recovery.

US Senate Okays $ 7.5 Billion Pak Aid for Five Years: US Senate passed a bill on 25 June 2009, tripling Pakistan's civilian aid to $ 7.5 billion for next five years. Also the Senate recommended another $ 7.5 billion for subsequent five years. The bill titled 'Enhanced Partnership with Pakistan Act of 2009' says, subject to improving political and economic climate in Pakistan an additional $ 1.5 billion should be provided for 2014–18.

Fifteenth NAM Summit: Two-day NAM Summit took place at Sharm-el-Sheikh, Egypt from 15–16 July 2009. The 118 members of NAM were unanimous in their view to unite and fight against terrorism as per the consensus of the UN Charter. Other issues like food and energy security and climate were also discussed.

Miss Universe 2009: Miss Venezuela, Stefania Fernandez, bagged the Miss Universe 2009 crown at Atlantis Paradise Island, in Nassau, Bahamas on 23 August 2009.

SCIENCE AND TECHNOLOGY

PSLV Puts RISAT-2 into Orbit: The Polar Satellite Launch Vehicle (PSLV C-12) of the Indian Space Research Organisation (ISRO) successfully placed two satellites: Radar Imaging Satellite (RISAT-2) and ANUSAT, in the orbit on 22 April 2009.

RISAT-2 is a surveillance satellite and ANUSAT is India's first university-built satellite, designed and developed by 37 aerospace engineering students of the Anna University, Chennai under the guidance of ISRO.

RISAT-2 has ability to take images of the earth precisely, while ANUSAT has been designed to store data and to relay messages from one station to another in the digital format.

DRDO Test-Fire Astra Missile: DRDO conducted the flight trial of Astra, Beyond Visual Range Air-to-Air Missile (BVRAM) on 7 May 2009 from Integrated Test Range at Chandipur, Orissa.

Astra is an indigenously built high-end tactical missile, which is capable of ducking Radar eyes and attacking enemy targets up to 110 km. It can intercept enemy aircraft at supersonic speed.

Q.15. Who has been recently appointed as ATS Chief of Maharashtra Police?

Artificial Brain Developed: Experts at Aston University in the Birmingham, England have created an artificial brain for the first time. The dreaded disease Alzheimer could be cured by it. This new development is viewed as crucial breakthrough for the treatment of conditions such as Dementia and Parkinson's disease.

Largest Ever Telescope Launched from French Guiana: Riding an Ariane 5 rocket, the world's largest telescope was launched on 15 May 2009 from the Kourou spaceport in French Guiana to investigate the origins of the universe. The Herschel telescope was developed by the European Space Agency (ESA) at a cost of 1.1 billion Euros ($ 1.49 billion). The main objective behing building and launching this telescope is to determine how the stars and galaxies are formed in the universe. The stars are made of gas and dust, a mix that makes it impossible to see into the star itself with light. Herschel's strength is to enable a look into the gas-dust clouds. The primary mirror of the Herschel telescope is 3.5 meters in diameter, more than four times larger than those of previous infrared space telescopes and almost one and a half times larger than the Hubble space telescope. Herschel will tap into previously unexplored wavelengths and examine phenomena that had been out of reach for other observatories.

New Mechanism Controlling Neuronal Migration Discovered: The molecular machinery that helps brain cells migrate to their correct place in the developing brain has been identified by scientists at St Jude Children's Research Hospital. The finding offers new insight into the forces that drive organisation of brain in developing foetuses and children during their first years. Disruption of this brain-patterning machinery can cause epilepsy and mental retardation and understanding its function could give new insight into such disorders.

NASA Blasts off Two Moon Probes: National Aeronautics and Space Administration (NASA), USA successfully blasted off two probes into space on 18 June 2009 for lunar exploration mission. The main aim of this mission is to scout for water sources and landing sites in anticipation of sending humans back to moon in the year 2020. The lift-off of the dual Lunar Reconnaissance Orbiter (LRO) and Lunar Crater Observation and Sensing Satellite (LCROSS) missions atop an Atlas V rocket took place from Florida's Cape Canaveral Air Force station. The LRO is to learn more about moon through a one year stay at an orbit of about 50 km, which is the closest continual lunar orbit of any spacecraft. The LRO's $ 500 million mission is designed to provide NASA with maps of unprecedented accuracy, which will be crucial for scoping out possible landing sites.

India Joins Elite Club with Nuclear Submarine Launch: India's first nuclear submarine INS Arihant, was launched by Prime Minister, Manmohan Singh and his wife Gursharan Kaur on 26 July 2009, for sea trials. It is expected to be ready for induction into the Navy by 2011 after a series of exhaustive trials. Once inducted, the 6,000 tonne Arihant – the name means destroyer of enemies – would be the vital third leg of India's nuclear policy that hinges around the 'second strike' theory. With this India made its entry into an elite club of six nations comprising the US, which has 74 nuclear submarines, Russia (44), the UK (13), France (10) and China (10) who also possess nuclear-powered submarines.

US Space Shuttle Endeavour Sent to International Space Station: US space shuttle Endeavour – the 4.5 million pound (2.04 million-kg) spaceship and its seven-member crew launched from NASA's Kennedy Space Center in Florida on 15 July 2009. The mission will deliver the final segment to the Japan Aerospace

Q.16. Who has been recently chosen for Mahatma Gandhi International Award for Peace and Justice 2009?

Exploration Agency's Kibo laboratory and a new crew member to the International Space Station. Endeavour's 16-day mission includes five spacewalks and the installation of two platforms outside the Japanese module. One platform is permanent and will allow experiments to be directly exposed to space. The other is an experiment storage pallet that will be detached and returned with the shuttle. During the mission, Kibo's robotic arm will transfer three experiments from the pallet to the exposed platform. Future experiments also can be moved to the platform from the inside of the station using the laboratory's airlock.

ECONOMIC AND BUSINESS

Launch of Tata Motors Much-Awaited 'People's Car' Nano: Tata Motors on 23 March 2009 commercially launched its people's car, Nano in Mumbai, promising to stick to the Rs 1,00,000 price tag for the base model. The four-door car, Nano has a 623 cc engine and a mileage of 23.6 km per litre. It is available in three different versions, including one with air-conditioning.

Indian Telecom Company Create World Record: Indian Telecom Industry created the world record of the highest subscriber addition in a month by adding 18.57 million subscribers in March 2009.

DAE Pact with Russian TVEL for Uranium: The Department of Atomic Energy on 11 February 2009 signed a contract with TVEL, a joint stock company of the Russian Federation, for long-term supply of 2000 tonnes of natural Uranium pellets to India. These natural Uranium pellets will be for India's Pressurised Heavy Water Reactors, to be placed under civil domain of the IAEA safeguards. The two have also signed another contract for about 60 tonnes of Low Enriched Uranium pellets for Boiling Water Reactors at Tarapur, operated by the Nuclear Power Corporation of India limited. The contract was signed by TVEL President Y. Olenin with DAE Director of Purchase and Stores H.C. Soni in Mumbai.

Government Approves BRPL Merger with IOC: The government has approved the merger of Bongaigaon Refinery and Petrochemicals Limited (BRPL) with Indian Oil Corporation (IOC). BRPL shareholders to get four shares of IOC for every 37 held. Currently, IOC holds 74.46 per cent equity in BRPL.

Tech Mahindra Wins the Satyam Bid: Ending the three-month ordeal of about 50,000 employees, Tech Mahindra on 13 April 2009 emerged as the top bidder with an offer of Rs 58 per share for a 31 per cent stake in beleaguered Satyam Computer, beating a strong rival Larsen and Toubro. The government-appointed board of Satyam Computer on 13 April 2009 announced that board of directors has selected Venturbay Consultants Private Limited, a subsidiary of Tech Mahindra Limited as the highest bidder to acquire a controlling stake in the company, subject to the approval of the Company Law Board.

Joint Venture Between Andhra Bank, Bank of Baroda and Indian Overseas Bank: Three Indian banks – Andhra Bank, Bank of Baroda and Indian Overseas Bank – have put up an initial investment of 86 million dollars into a joint venture to set up a subsidiary, the India BIA Bank (Malaysia) Bhd. in Malaysia. Under the joint venture, Bank of Baroda will have a 40 per cent stake, IOB 35 per cent and Andhra Bank 25 per cent.

Microsoft India Launches 'Online Services' for Indian Businesses: Microsoft India launched 'online services' for small and medium-sized businesses (SMBs) to provide them with

Q.17. Name the nation(s) with which India has struck a civil nuclear deal.

IT-related service by saving 50 per cent of their IT-related costs. It has also announced a free trial period of two-months for the range of services, which include e-mail, collaboration, conferencing and productivity capabilities. Online Services will allow businesses to stay in touch with customers, associates and teams across geographic boundaries round the clock and provide instant access to information, thereby enhancing efficiency and reducing costs.

UNION BUDGET

Union Finance Minister Pranab Minister on 6 July 2009 presented the General Budget 2009–10 in the Parliament. Its key features are:

Budget Estimates

- The Budget estimates a total expenditure of Rs 10, 20,838 crore for the financial year 2009–10.
- Out of it, Rs 6,95,689 crore is non-plan expenditure and Rs 3, 25,149 crore is plan expenditure.
- Thus, the total expenditure for this year has increased by 36 per cent over that of 2008–09. The increase in non-plan expenditure comes to 37 per cent whereas the increase in Plan expenditure is 34 per cent.
- The government has taken a conscious decision to enhance the gross budgetary support for the annual plan 2009-10 by Rs 40,000 crore over the Interim Budget.
- The state governments will be permitted to raise additional open market loans of about Rs 21,000 crore in the current year.
- The gross tax receipts are budgeted at Rs 6,41,079 crore, lower than last year; while the non-tax revenue receipts have been estimated at Rs 1,40,279 crore which higher as compared to last year.
- The revenue deficit as a percentage of GDP is projected at 4.8 per cent as compared to 1 per cent in budget estimate (BE) 2008–09 and 4.6 per cent as per provisional accounts of 2008–09.
- The fiscal deficit as a percentage of GDP is projected at 6.8 per cent as compared to 2.5 per cent in budget estimate (BE) 2008–09 and 6.2 per cent as per provisional accounts 2008-09.

Infrastructures

- Infrastructure Finance Company Limited (IIFCL) to refinance 60 per cent commercial bank loans for PPP projects in critical sectors over the next fifteen to eighteen months. IIFCL and Banks are now in a position to support projects involving total investment of Rs 1,00,000 crore.
- Allocation of funds to National Highways Authority of India (NHAI) for the National Highway Development Programme (NHDP) increased by 23 per cent over budget estimate (BE) 2008–09 in budget estimate (BE) 2009–10.
- Allocation of funds for railways increased from Rs 10,800 crore in Interim budget estimate 2008–09 to Rs 15,800 crore in budget estimate 2009–10.
- Allocation under Jawaharlal Nehru National

Q.18. Up to what fraction FDI in defense sector is allowed in India?
Q.19. Where is the headquarters of SAARC University located?

Urban Renewal Mission (JNNURM) stepped up by 87 per cent to Rs 12,887 crore in budget estimate 2009–10 over budget estimate 2008–09.
- A new scheme, Rajiv Gandhi Yojana, will be introduced with aim to make country slum-free in next five years.

Agriculture

- The target for agriculture credit flow has been increased from Rs 2,87,000 crore in 2008–09 to Rs 3,25,000 crore for 2009–10.
- The interest subvention available for short-term crop loans up to Rs 3 lakh per farmer will continue and an additional subvention of 1 per cent will be paid from this year to those farmers who repay such loans on schedule. Thus, the interest rate for these farmers will come down to 6 per cent per year.
- Under the farm loan waiver scheme of Rs 71,000 crore implemented in the last budget, the time for paying 75 per cent of overdues has been extended to 31 December 2009.
- The allocation for Rashtriya Krishi Vikas Yojna (RKVY) is being stepped up by 30 per cent and that for Accelerated Irrigation Benefit Programme by 75 per cent over the allocation last year.
- To ensure balanced application of fertilisers, the government intends to move towards a nutrient-based subsidy regime instead of the current product pricing regime.
- The proposed National Food Security Act will ensure that every family living below the poverty line in rural or urban areas will be entitled by law to 25 kilos of rice or wheat per month at Rs 3 a kilo.

Education

- Rs 2,113 crore allocated for IITs and NITs which includes a provision of Rs 450 crore for new IITs and NITs.
- The overall plan budget for higher education is to be increased by Rs 2,000 crore over interim budget estimate 2009–10.
- Allocation of Rs 50 crore to Chandigarh University.
- Rs 25 crore each for establishing campuses of Aligarh Muslim University at Murshidabad in West Bengal and Malappuram in Kerala.
- Full interest subsidy for students in approved institutions.

Exports

- The budget provides a special fund of Rs 4,000 crore to support the micro, small and medium enterprises. This fund will incentivise banks and State Finance Corporations to lend to micro and small enterprises by refinancing 50 per cent of incremental lending to them.
- The allocation for the Market Development Assistance Scheme, which provides support to exporters in developing new markets, has been enhanced by 148 per cent.
- The 2 per cent interest subvention on pre-shipment credit to employment-oriented export sector has been extended till 31 March 2010.

Improving Delivery of Services

- A massive programme of housing will be launched to create one lakh dwelling units for Central Para-Military Forces personnel.

Q.20. What is the name of the official mascot of Commonwealth Games to be held at Delhi in 2010?

- The government has accepted the recommendations of the Committee for one Rank one Pension for ex-servicemen.
- It has been decided to substantially improve the pension of pre-1.1.2006 defence pensioners below officer rank and bring pre-10.10.1997 pensioners at par with post-10.10.1997 pensioners. This will benefit more than 12 lakhs jawans and JCOs and would cost over Rs 2,100 crore per year.
- A sum of Rs 1,000 crore has been kept in the budget for rebuilding the infrastructure damaged by Cyclone Aila.
- Rs 100 crore has been earmarked to ensure provision of at least one centre/Point of Sales for banking services in each of the unbanked block in the country.
- The government to hike allocation to National Ganga Project to Rs 562 crore.
- Unique Identification ID project to tap private talent in 12–18 months.

Defence

- Defence outlay has been substantially increased.
- As against Rs 1,05,600 crore in 2008–09, Rs 1,41,703 crore has been alotted in the budget for 2009–10.
- Total provision for subsidies during 2009–10 has been raised to Rs 1,11,276 crore from Rs 71, 431 crore in the budget estimate 2008–09.

Tax Proposals

- New Direct Taxes Code within the next 45 days for structural changes.
- The share of Direct Taxes in Centre's Tax Revenues has increased to 56 per cent in 2008–09 from 41 per cent in 2003–04.
- *Increase in Tax Exemption Limit*: The exemption limit for Senior Citizens has been increased from Rs 2.25 lakh to Rs 2.40 lakh; for women tax payers the limit has been increased by Rs 10,000 to from Rs 1.80 lakh to Rs 1.90 lakh and from Rs 1.50 lakh to Rs 1.60 lakh for all other categories of individual taxpayers.
- *Elimination of Surcharge:* The 10 per cent surcharge on taxes for those earning annual income above Rs 10 lakh will no longer exist.
- *Abolishment of Fringe Benefit Tax (FBT):* FBT on the value of fringe benefits provided by employers to employees has been abolished. Reimbursements will be taxed as perquisites at the marginal tax rate.
- *Increase in Wealth Tax Exemption:* The exemption limit for wealth tax has been increased from Rs 15 lakh to Rs 30 lakh.
- *Minimum Alternate Tax (MAT):* It has been increased from 10 per cent to 15 per cent of book profit; however, it is proposed to extend the period allowed to carry forward the tax credit under MAT from seven years to 10 years.
- The Commodities Transaction Tax (CTT) has been abolished.
- *Corporate Tax Rates:* No changes has been made in corporate Tax; it continues to stand at 30 per cent plus surcharge of 10 per cent of the corporate tax (for companies with profits above Rs 10 million) along with an education cess that amounts to three percent of corporate tax, totalling to 33.9 per cent.
- *Goods and Services Tax (GST):* GST is to be implemented by 1 April 2010, cumulative incidence of GST expected to be around 18 per cent.

> *Q.21. Which team was the runner up of the second edition of IPL?*
> *Q.22. In which State of India did the cyclone 'Aila' cause heavy damage?*

- Income of the NPS Trust and any dividend paid to this Trust from Dividend Distribution Tax has been exempted from Income Tax.
- Donation to electoral trusts to get 100 per cent deduction in computation of income of donor.
- All purchase and sell of equity shares and derivatives will also be exempted from the Security Transaction Tax.
- The scope of Presumptive Taxation has been expanded to all small businesses with a turnover of Rs 40 lakh. All such tax payers will have the option to declare their income from business (at the rate 8 per cent of their turnover) and simultaneously enjoy exemption from the compliance burden of maintaining books of accounts.
- Tax holiday under Section 80–IB(9) will be extended in respect of profits derived from the commercial production of Mineral Oil and Natural gas from oil and gas blocks which are awarded under the new Exploration Licensing Policy-VIII round of bidding.
- 80E benefits for the interest on loan for higher education to cover all specified fields, including vocational studies.
- On the front of Indirect Tax, Excise Duty has been hiked on several items to 8 per cent, barring food items, drugs, pharmaceuticals, paper, paper board, pressure cookers, cheaper electric bulbs and low price footwear.
- The basic Customs Duty on bio-diesel has been brought down from 7.5 to 2.5 per cent.
- Set-top box for television will attract Customs Duty of 5 per cent while Customs Duty on LCD panels will be reduced from 10 to 5 per cent.
- Excise duty on petrol driven trucks has been brought down from 20 per cent to 8 per cent. Excise duty on man-made fibre and yarn has been increased from 4 to 8 per cent. It has also been increased on PTA, DMT and polyester chips from 4 to 8 per cent.
- Service tax will be imposed on service provided in relation to transport of goods by rail, coastal cargo and goods through inland water including National Waterways.
- To provide necessary fiscal support to the New Pension Scheme for establishment of the much needed social security system.
- Cosmetic and plastic surgery and advise, consultancy and technical assistance in the field of law will also attract service tax. This however, will not be applicable if the service provider or the service receiver is an individual.

Inclusive Development

- The provision for the Bharat Nirman Schemes has been raised by 45 per cent, National Rural Employment Guarantee Scheme (NREGS) gets 144 per cent more, Pradhan Mantri Gram Sadak Yojana (PMGSY) 59 per cent more, Rajiv Gandhi Grameen Viduytikaran Yojana (RGGVY) 27 per cent more and Indira Awas Yojana (IAY) 63 per cent more than last year.
- The Swarna Jayanti Gram Swarozgar Yojana (SGSY) is to be restructured as National Rural Livelihood Mission to make it universal in application, focused in approach and time bound, for poverty eradication by 2014–15.
- A new project is being launched for modernisation of the Employment Exchanges to enable job seekers to register online from anywhere and approach any employment exchange.

Q.23. With which country did India sign a $ 397 million deal recently to modernise its aging transportaircraft fleet?

Highlights of Central Plans

National Rural Employment Guarantee Scheme (NREGS): An allocation of Rs 30,100 crore has been made for providing 100 days of wage employment to each rural household opting for it. All the districts covering rural areas have been brought under NREGS with effect from 1 April 2008.

Swaranjayanti Gram Swarozgar Yojana: Rs 2,350 crore has been allocated for establishing micro-enterprises in rural areas. At least 50 per cent of the *swarozgaries* will be SCs/STs, 40 per cent women and 3 per cent disabled.

Pradhan Mantri Gram Sadak Yojana: This project has been allocated Rs 10,000 crore for providing connectivity to eligible unconnected rural habitations through good all-weather roads.

Accelerated Rural Water Supply Programme: Rs 7,300 crore has been allocated for supplementing the states in their effort to provide safe drinking water to all rural habitations.

Rural Housing Fund: Rs 2,000 crore has been assigned for this project.

Rural Sanitation: Rs 1,200 crore has been assigned for Total Sanitation Programme.

Pradhan Mantri Adarsh Gram Yojana (PMAGY): A new scheme will be launched this year on a pilot basis for integrated development of 1,000 villages with above 50 per cent Scheduled Caste population.

Micro, small and medium enterprises:

- Rs 144 crore allocated for Credit Support Programme to provide Guarantee cover to banks for extending loans to Small/Tiny units without collateral.
- Rs 823 crore allocated for Prime Minister's Employment Generation Programme to provide subsidy to beneficiaries' meeting cost of training and to meet residual/committed liabilities under Prime Minister's Rozgar Yojana/Rural Employment Generation Programme.

Food and public distribution: Rs 45 crore has been allocated for computerisation of PDS operations in all States/Union Territories.

School education and literacy:

- Rs 13,100 crore for Sarva Shiksha Abhiyan.
- Rs 8,000 crore for National Programme of Mid-Day Meals in schools.
- Rs 1,354 crore for Rashtriya Madhyamik Shiksha Abhiyan.
- Rs 750 crore for National Means-cum-Merit Scholarship Scheme.

Women and child development:

- Rs 6,705 crore for Integrated Child Development Services (ICDS), to be extended to every child under the age of six by March 2012.
- Rs 60 crore for Integrated Child Protection Scheme (ICPS).
- Rs 100 crore for Rajiv Gandhi National Creche Scheme.

Health: Rs 11,930 crore has been allocated for National Rural Health Mission and Rs 3,650 crore for Health Sector.

Department of Pharmaceuticals: Rs 50 crore allocated for establishment of six new national institutes of pharmaceuticals education and research.

Q.24. Who has received 2009 Kluge Prize?
Q.25. Which country won the Asia Cup Hockey 2009?

Biotechnology: Rs 340 crore for Research and Development and Rs 200 crore for Autonomous R&D Institutions.

The government has proposed to bring all BPL families under the Rashtriya Swasthya Bima Yojana (RSBY). The fund allocated for this scheme has been increased by 40 per cent.

Tribal Affairs: Rs 273 crore for Post Matric Scholarships for Scheduled Tribes students.

Budget at a Glance

(In Crore Rupees)

	2007–08 Actuals	2008–09 Budget Estimates	2008–09 Revised Estimates	2009–10 Budget Estimates
1. Revenue Receipts	541864	602935	562173	614497
2. Tax Revenue (net to Centre)	439547	507150	465970	474218
3. Non-tax Revenue	102317	95785	96203	140279
4. Capital Receipts (5+6+7)$	170807	147949	338780	406341
5. Recoveries of Loans	5100	4497	9698	4225
6. Other Receipts	38795	10165	2567	1120
7. Borrowings and other Liabilities*	126912	133287	326515	400996
8. Total Receipts (1+4) $	712671	750884	900953	1020838
9. Non-plan Expenditure	507589	507498	617996	695689
10. On Revenue Account of which,	420861	448352	561790	618834
11. Interest Payments	171030	190807	192694	225511
12. On Capital Account	86728	59146	56206	76855
13. Plan Expenditure	205082	243386	282957	325149
14. On Revenue Account	173572	209767	241656	278398
15. On Capital Account	31510	33619	41301	46751
16. Total Expenditure (9+13)	712671	750884	900953	1020838
17. Revenue Expenditure (10+14)	594433	658119	803446	897232
18. Capital Expenditure (12+15)	118238	92765	97507	123606
19. Revenue Deficit (17-1)	52569 (1.1)	55184 (1.0)	241273 (4.4)	282735 (4.8)
20. Fiscal Deficit {16 – (1 + 5 + 6)}	126912 (2.7)	133287 (2.5)	326515 (6.0)	400996 (6.8)
21. Primary Deficit (20–11)	– 44118 – (0.9)	–57520 – (1.1)	133821 (2.5)	175485 (3.0)

$ Does not include receipts in respect of Market Stabilisation Scheme.
* Includes draw-down of Cash Balance.
Note: GDP for budget estimate 2009–10 has been projected at Rs 5,856,569 crore assuming 10.05 per cent growth over the revised estimates of 2008–09 (Rs 5,321,753 crore) released by CSO. Deficit indicators in RE 2008-09 have been retained on the basis of advance estimate for 2008-09 (Rs 5,426,277 crore).

Development of North-Eastern Region: Rs 60 crore allocated for North-Eastern Development Finance Corporation.

Welfare of Minorities: Rs 1,740 crore allocated for plan outlay of Ministry of Minority Affairs, which is 74 per cent increase from the budget estimate.

Sports: Rs 16,300 crore allocated for development of infrastructure, preparation of teams for holding Commonwealth Games, 2010.

Explanatory Note

- Budget estimates are presented in this document in broad aggregates to facilitate easy understanding. For this purpose certain items of receipts and expenditure have been regrouped.
- For example, the expenditure of commercial departments has been taken net of their receipts, so that increase in the volume of transactions does not inflate the figures on both sides.
- Similarly, short-term loans and advances given to the states and recovered during the same year have also been netted.
- The document shows the revenue deficit, the fiscal deficit and the primary deficit.
- **Revenue deficit** refers to the excess of revenue expenditure over revenue receipts.
- **Fiscal deficit** is the difference between the revenue receipts plus certain non-debt capital receipts and the total expenditure including loans, net of repayments. This indicates the total borrowing requirements of government from all sources.
- **Primary deficit** is measured by fiscal deficit less the interest payments.
- **Note:** Variations, if any, in the figures shown in this document and those shown in other budget documents are due to rounding.

RAILWAY BUDGET

Railway Minister Mamata Banerjee on 3 July 2009 presented the fifteenth railway budget in the Parliament. The highlights of the Railway budget 2009-10 are as follows:

Annual Plan 2009-10

- Plan outlay is Rs 40,745 crore, out of which Rs 2,921 crore will be spent on new lines, Rs 1,750 crore on gauge conversion, Rs 1,102 crore on passenger amenities, Rs 335 crore for staff quarters and Rs 424 crore for staff amenities.
- Acquisition of 18,000 wagons in 2009–10 against 11,000 in 2008-09.
- New proposals for better rail connectivity proposed to be processed; it includes 53 for new lines, three for gauge conversion works and 12 for doubling.
- Freight loading is targeted at 882 million tonnes (MT): an increment of 49 MT; number of passengers likely to grow is about six per cent.
- Gross Traffic Receipts (GTR) estimated at Rs 88,419 crore, i.e. Rs 8,557 cr more than 2008-09.
- Ordinary Working Expenses budgeted at Rs 62,900 crore to cover the full year impact of VICPC and the payment of 60 per cent arrears due in 2009-10.

Q.26. In which of the following state(s) the World Bank-assisted National Cyclone Risk Management Project (NCRMP) is being implemented?

- The dividend payable to General Revenues kept at Rs 5,479 crore.
- Budgeted Operating Ratio 92.5 per cent.

Financial Performance in 2008-09

- Freight loading at 833 million tonnes (MT) grew five per cent over 2007–08.
- Traffic receipts also increased by 11.4 per cent to reach Rs 79,862 crore cash surplus before dividend Rs 17,400 crore after disbursing Rs 13,600 crore towards implementation of Sixth Central Pay Commission.
- Railways paid full dividend liability of Rs 4,717 crore to the government.
- Investible surplus of Rs 12,681 crore generated.
- Annual Plan expenditure was Rs 36,336 crore.

Passenger Amenities

- No increase in passenger fares and freight tariffs.
- Revision in Tatkal Scheme to make it more user-friendly. Advance booking period reduced from five days to two days. Minimum charge reduced to Rs 100.
- 1000 new Passenger Reservation Stations (PRS) locations to be opened; Unreserved Ticketing Terminals services to be expanded from 5000 to 8000 locations.
- Taking ticketing to *'Maa Mati Manush'* grassroot, through issue of computerised tickets at 5000 post offices and *'Mushkil Aasaan'* mobile ticketing service vans.
- Air-conditioned double decker coaches will be rolled out for intercity commuters.
- 309 stations out of 375 across the nation to be upgraded as *'Adarsh Stations'* with basic facilities including drinking water, adequate toilets, ladies dormitories, etc.
- Toilet facilities to be introduced in DEMU/MEMU trains with journey time more than two hours.
- To launch *'janata khana'* with national and regional cuisines.

Safety and Security

- Integrated Security Scheme to be introduced at 140 vulnerable and sensitive railway stations.
- Women RPF squads for security of women passengers.

Development Work

- Target mechanised maintenance of 3,500 km in 2009–10.
- Seven nursing colleges to be set up on railway land in places including Delhi, Kolkata and Mumbai.
- Railway medical colleges to be developed along with rail hospitals on public-private partnership.
- Setting up of a new factory at Kanchrapara-Halisahar Railway Complex with annual capacity of 500 EMU/MEMU and Metro coaches in Joint Venture/Public-Private Partnership mode.
- Proposal to initiate action for setting up 1000 MW power plant with Ministry of Power, at Adra, in under-developed tribal area.
- 50 railway stations, including CST Mumbai, Nagpur, Pune, Howrah, Sealdah, Varanasi, New Delhi, Lucknow, Jaipur, Kanpur,

Q.27. What is the name of the new scheme introduced in Railway budget 2009–10, for people working in unorganised sector with an annual income up to Rs 1500?

Chennai Central, Thiruvananthapuram Central, Secunderabad, Bangalore, Byappanahalli, Ahmedabad, Bhopal, Habibganj, Agra Central, Chandigarh, Kolkata, New Jalpaiguri, Puri and Kochi, will be developed to have world-class facilities.

Trains

- Railways to introduce 57 new trains, extension of 27 trains and frequency of 13 trains to be increased across the nation.
- '*Yuva Trains*': New low-cost, air-conditioned, seated accommodation trains, dedicated specially for young generation and low-income groups to run from rural hinterland to major metros/cities; fare to range from Rs 299 up to 1500 km to Rs 399 up to 2500 km, Weekly service on pilot basis to be introduced within 3 months between Mumbai to Delhi and Delhi to Kolkata.
- 'Only ladies' EMU trains to start in Delhi, Chennai and Kolkata sub-urban during office rush hour.
- '*Duronto trains*': New non-stop, point-to-point train services introduced for the first time with 12 trains.

Concessions

- '*Izzat*': A new scheme for travelling with dignity; under this scheme concessional monthly ticket of Rs 25 will be issued to people with monthly income up to Rs 1,500, in unorganised sector, for travelling up to 100 km.
- Press correspondents to get 'photo identification cum credit cards' on certification of PIB and other competent authorities instead of existing system of coupons; concession up to 50 per cent from existing 30 per cent, 50 per cent concession for travel with spouse also to be given once a year.

ECONOMIC SURVEY

Finance Minister Shri Pranab Mukherjee on 2 July 2009 presented the Economic Survey 2008-09 in the parliament. The highlights are:

- Economic growth decelerated to 6.7 per cent in 2008–09 as compared to 8.7 per cent in 2007–08 and 9.7 per cent in 2006–07.
- Per capita growth was 4.6 per cent.
- Deceleration in growth spread across all sectors except mining and quarrying; agriculture growth fell from 4.9 per cent in 2007–08 to 1.6 per cent 2008–09; manufacturing continued to grow at 2.4 per cent; slowdown attributed to fall in exports and decline in domestic demand.
- Global financial meltdown and economic recession in developed economies are the major factors which attributed for economic slowdown in India.
- Investment remains relatively buoyant, ratio of fixed investment to GDP increased to 32.2 per cent in 2008–09 as compared to 31.6 per cent in 2007–08.
- Fiscal deficit to GDP ratio stands at 6.2 per cent.

Q.28. How many new non-stop, point-to-point train services (Duronto trains) have been introduced for the first time in Railway Budget for 2009–10?

- Credit growth declined in the later part of 2008–09 reflecting slowdown of the economy in general and the industrial sector in particular.
- Increased plan expenditure, reduction in indirect taxes, sector specific measures for textile, housing, infrastructure through stimulus packages provides support to the real economy.
- Merchandise export continued to grow at a modest 3.6 per cent in US Dollar terms while overall import growth pegged at 14.4 per cent.
- FDI investments into India went up from US$ 25.1 billion in 2007 to US$ 46.5 billion in 2008, even as global flows declined from US$ 1.9 trillion to US$ 1.7 trillion during the period.
- A large domestic market, resilient banking system and a policy of gradual liberalisation of capital account to help early mitigation of the adverse effect of global financial crisis and recession.
- Sharp dip in the growth of private consumption is a major concern at this stage.
- The banks are financially sound and well capitalised; foreign exchange position remains comfortable and the external debt position has been within comfortable zone.
- Medium to long-term capital flows likely to be lower as long as the de-leveraging process continues in the US economy.
- Revisiting the agenda of pending economic reforms imperative to renew the growth momentum.

Rate of Growth at Factor Cost at 1999–2000 prices (in %)

	2003–04	2004–05	2005–06	2006–07	2007–08	2008–09
Agriculture, forestry & fishing	10	0	5.8	4	4.9	1.6
Mining & quarrying	3.1	8.2	4.9	8.8	3.3	3.6
Manufacturing	6.6	8.7	9.1	11.8	8.2	2.4
Electricity, gas & water supply	4.8	7.9	5.1	5.3	5.3	3.4
Construction	12	16.1	16.2	11.8	10.1	7.2
Trade, hotels & restaurants	10.1	7.7	10.3	10.4	10.1	*
Transport, storage & communication	15.3	15.6	14.9	16.3	15.5	*
Financing, insurance, real estate & business services	5.6	8.7	11.4	13.8	11.7	7.8
Community, social & personal services	5.4	6.8	7.1	5.7	6.8	13.1
GDP	8.5	7.5	9.5	9.7	9	6.7

* Trade, hotels & restaurants, transport & communication (together) grew at 9%, 2008–09.
Source: *Central Statistical Organisation.*

Q.29. What is the name of the Moon mission of China to be launched in 2012?
Q.30. What was the fiscal deficit in terms of GDP in Union Budget 2009–10?

Key Indicators

Item Units	2005–06	2006–07	2007–08	2008–09
1. GDP and related indicators				
GDP (current market prices) Rs in crore	3586743	4129173	4723400	5321753 RE
Growth rate (in %)	13.9	15.1	14.4	12.7
GDP (current market prices) Rs in crore	2844942	3120029	3402716	3609425
Growth rate (in %)	9.3	9.7	9.1	6.1
Growth of GDP (factor cost, constant prices) in %	9.5	9.7	9	6.7
Savings Rate in per cent of GDP	34.2	35.7	37.7	NA
Capital formation (rate) in per cent of GDP	35.5	36.9	39.1	NA
per cap NNP (factor cost & current prices) in Rs	26003	29524	33283	37490 (in Rs)
2. Production				
Food grains mill tonne	208.6	217.3	230.8	229.9^^
Index of Industrial production (growth) in %	8.2	11.6	8.5	2.6
Electricity generation (growth) in %	5.2	7.3	6.3	2.7
3. Prices				
Inflation (WPI) (52-week average) % change	4.4	5.4	4.7	8.4
Inflation CPI (IW) % change	4.4	6.7	6.2	9.1
4. External sector				
Export growth (US$) % change	23.4	22.6	28.9	3.6
Import growth (US$) % change	33.8	24.5	35.4	14.4
Current account deficit (CAD)/GDP %	–1.2	–1.1	–1.5	–4.1^
Foreign exchange reserves US$ bn.	151.6	199.2	309.7	252.0@
Average exchange rate Rs /US$	44.27	45.28	40.26	45.99
5. Money and credit				
(M3) (Annual) % change	17	21.3	21.2	18.4
Scheduled commercial bank credit (Growth) % change	37	28.5	22.3	17.5
6. Fiscal indicators (Centre)				
Gross fiscal deficit % of GDP	4.1	3.5	2.7	6.2##
Revenue deficit % of GDP	2.6	1.9	1.1	4.6##
Primary deficit % of GDP	0.4	–0.2	-0.9	2.6##
7. Population in million	1106	1122	1138	1154

RE GDP figures for 2008–09 are Revised Estimates
NA not yet available/released for 2008–09
^^ for 2008–09 the figures are the third Advance Estimates
^ CAD to GDP ratio for 2008–09 is for the period Apr–Dec 2008
@ as of 31 March 2009
fiscal indicators for 2008–09 are based on the provisional actuals for 2008–09

Q.31. What is the new tax exemption limit for senior citizens?
Q.32. What the new Minimum Alternate Tax (MAT) is as announced in Union Budget 2009–10?

GAMES AND SPORTS

Tennis

The Australian Open, 2009: The first of the world's four Grand Slam tennis tournaments played during the year, was held in Melbourne at Melbourne Park from 19 January through to 1 February 2009.

Australian Open Champions
- **Men's Singles:** Rafael Nadal (Spain);
  Runner-up: Roger Federer (Switzerland)
- **Women's Singles:** Serena Williams (USA);
  Runner-up: Dinara Safina (Russia)
- **Men's Doubles:** Bob Bryan (USA)/Mike Bryan (USA);
  Runners-up: Mahesh Bhupathi (India)/Mark Knowles (Bahamas)
- **Women's Doubles:** Serena Williams (US)/Venus Williams (US)
  Runners-up: Daniela Hantuchova (Slovakia)/Ai Sugiyama (Japan)
- **Mixed Doubles:** Sania Mirza (India)/Mahesh Bhupati (India)
  Runners-up: Nathalie Dechy (France)/Andy Ram (Israel)
- **Boys' Singles:** Yuki Bhambri (India)
  Runner-up: Alexandros-Ferdinandos Georgoudas (Germany)
- **Girls' Singles:** Ksenia Pervak (Russia)
  Runner-up: Laura Robson (UK)

French Open 2009 (*also known as Roland Garros*)

This tournament took place at the Stade Roland Garros in Paris, France, from 24 May through to 7 June 2009.
The winners are:
- **Men's Singles:** Roger Federer (Switzerland);
  Runner-up: Robin Soderling (Sweden)
- **Women's Singles:** Svetlana Kuznetsova (Russia);
  Runner-up: Dinara Safina (Russia)
- **Men's Doubles:** Lukas Dlouhy (Czech Republic)/Leander Paes (India);
  Runner-up: Wesley Moodie (RSA)/Dick Norman (Belgium)
- **Women's Doubles:** A. Medina Garrigues (Spain)/Virginia Ruano Pascual (Spain);
  Runner-up: Victoria Azarenka (Belarus) / Elena Vesnina (Russia)
- **Mixed Doubles:** Liezel Huber (USA)/Bob Bryan (USA) ;
  Runner-up: Vania King (USA) / Marcelo Melo (Brazil)
- **Boys' Singles:** Daniel Berta (Sweden);
  Runner-up: Gianni Mina (France)
- **Girls' Singles:** Kristina Mladenovic (France);
  Runner-up: Daria Gavrilova (Russia)

Wimbledon 2009

This tournament took place at the All England Lawn Tennis and Croquet Club in Wimbledon, London, United Kingdom, from 22 June through to 5 July 2009.

Q.33. Which flagship programme has been given highest allocation in Union Budget 2009–10?

The winners are:
- **Men's Singles:** Roger Federer (Switzerland); Runner-up: Andy Roddick (USA)
- **Women's Singles:** Serena Williams (USA); Runner-up: Venus Williams (USA)
- **Men's Doubles:** Daniel Nestor (Canada)/Nenad Zimonjic (Serbia); Runner-up: Bob Bryan (USA)/Mike Bryan (USA)
- **Women's Doubles:** Venus Williams (USA)/Serena Williams (USA); Runner-up: Samantha Stosur (Australia)/Rennae Stubbs (Australia)
- **Mixed Doubles:** Mark Knowles (Bahamas)/Anna-Lena Groenefeld (Germany); Runner-up: Leander Paes (India)/Cara Black (USA)
- **Boys' Singles:** Andrey Kuznetsov (Russia); Runner-up: Jordan Cox (USA)
- **Girls' Singles:** Noppawan Lertcheewakarn (Thailand); Runner-up: Kristina Mladenovic (France)

US Open 2009

This tournament took place at the Arthur Ashe Stadium and Louis Armstrong Stadium in New York, USA, from 31 August through to 13 September 2009.

The winners are:
- **Men's Singles:** Juan Martin Del Potro (Argentina); Runner-up: Roger Federer (Switzerland)
- **Women's Singles:** Kim Clijsters (Belgium); Runner-up: Caroline Wozniacki (Denmark)
- **Men's Doubles:** Lukas Dlouhy (Czech Republic)/Leander Paes (India); Runner-up: Mahesh Bhupathi (India)/ Mark Knowles (Bahama)
- **Women's Doubles:** Venus Williams (USA)/Serena Williams (USA); Runner-up: Cara Black (Zimbabwe)/Liezel Huber (USA)
- **Mixed Doubles:** Carly Gullickson (USA)/Travis Parrott (USA); Runner-up: Leander Paes (India)/Cara Black (USA)
- **Boys' Singles:** Bernard Tomic (Australia); Runner-up: Chase Buchanan (USA)
- **Girls' Singles:** Heather Watson (UK); Runner-up: Yana Buchina (Russia)

Lexington Challenger: Indian tennis ace Sania Mirza won the USD 50,000 ITF title in Lexington, USA defeating top seed Julie Coin of France by 7–6 (5), 6–4 margin on 26 July 2009.

Hockey

Asia Cup

South Korea defeated Pakistan 1–0 in Asia Cup held at Kuantan (Malaysia) on 16 May 2009.

Sultan Azlan Shah Cup

India beat the host Malaysia by 3–1 to lift the eighteenth Sultan Azlan Shah Cup at Ipoh (Malaysia) on 12 April 2009.

Q.34. What percentage does Corporation Tax constitute of the Central Budget 2009-10?

Cricket

Women's World Cup 2009

England's beat New Zealand by four-wicket in the final of the ICC WWC 2009 held at North Sydney Oval, Sydney on 22 March 2009.

Nicky Shaw declared player of the final and Claire Taylor declared player of the tournament.

India sealed third-place at the ICC Women's World Cup after a tremendous three-wicket victory over Australia.

ICC Women Twenty20 World Cup 2009

The women team from England won the inaugural Twenty20 World Cup which was played at Lords, London on 21 June 2009, defeating New Zealand six wickets in the final. Claire Taylor of England was awarded the 'Player of the tournament' in the World T20.

Twenty20 World Cup 2009

Pakistan won the ICC World T20 Cup defeating Sri Lanka by eight wickets in the final at Lords, in London on 21 June 2009. Tillakaratne Dilshan of Sri Lanka was adjudged Man of the Tournament.

Indian tour of New Zealand 2008-09

India-New Zealand Test Series

India won a historic Test series in New Zealand after 41 years (since 1967-68) with the third and the final Test ending in a draw on 7 April 2009. India won the series 1-0.

It was also India's thirteenth overall series win overseas.

Gautam Gambhir was declared man of the match and also the man of the series.

India-New Zealand ODI Series

First match of the Series was held at McLean Park, Napier on 3 March which India won by 53 runs. Second match was held at Westpac Stadium, Wellington on 6 March, which ended in a draw. The third match of the series was held at AMI Stadium, Christchurch on 8 March and India won it by 58 runs.

Fourth match was played in Seddon Park, Hamilton on 11 March and India beat New Zealand by D/L method and the fifth match was held at Eden Park, Auckland on 14 March, which New Zealand won by 8 wickets. Virender Sehwag (India) was declared the Man of the Series.

Indian Tour of West Indies, 2009

India-West Indies ODI Series

First match of the series was held at Sabina Park, Kingston, Jamaica on 26 June which India won by 20 runs. Second match was held at Sabina Park, Kingston, Jamaica on 28 June. West Indies won the match by eight wickets. The third match of the series was held at Beausejour Stadium in St Lucia on 3 July and India won it by six wickets. Fourth match was

Q.35. Who is the Chairman of Prime Minister's Economic Advisory Council?

played in Beausejour Stadium in St. Lucia on 5 July 2009. The match was washed out due to rain and India won the series by 2–1.

M S Dhoni (India) was declared the Man of the Series.

Indian Tour of Sri Lanka, 2009

Compaq Cup, Tri Series: Indian won the Compaq Cup tri-series involving New Zealand and Sri Lanka in a day-night encounter on 14 September 2009, defeating host Sri Lanka by a 46 run margin in the final. Sachin Tendulkar of India was declared both Man of the match and Man of the series.

Indian Premier League (IPL) – 2

The second edition of the IPL was scheduled between 10 April and 24 May 2009 in South Africa. Deccan Chargers beat Bangalore Royal Challengers by six runs in the final. Mathew Hayden of Chennai Super Kings was awarded the Orange Cap for scoring most runs (572) and R P Singh of Deccan Chargers was awarded Purple cup for taking highest wickets (23) in the tournament. Adam Gilchrist, the Skipper of Deccan Chargers was adjudged the man of the series.

Deodhar Trophy

West Zone won the thirty-sixth Deodhar Trophy for the ninth time defeating East Zone by 218 runs (biggest margin of factory in the tournament) on 18 March 2009.

Ranji Trophy

The Ranji Trophy final was held at the Rajiv Gandhi Stadium, Hyderabad from 12 January to 16 between Uttar Pradesh and Mumbai, of which Mumbai won the Trophy for record thirty-eighth times beating UP by a 243 run margin.

CHESS

Asian Chess Championship

Grandmaster Surya Sekhar Ganguly of India won the Asian Chess Championship following a draw against China's Zhou Jianchao in the eleventh and final round at Subic, Philippines on 30 May 2009.

Football

Santosh Trophy 2009

Sixty-third National Football Championship for the Santosh Trophy was held in Tamil Nadu at four venues from 24 May through to 14 June. Goa won the Santosh Trophy of 2009 by defeating West Bengal 4–2.

Nehru Cup 2009

India won the ONGC Nehru Cup defeating Syria by 6–5 in the final held at Ambedkar Stadium, New Delhi on 31 August 2009.

Q.36. Which country won the Confederations Cup 2009 by defeating USA?

Q.37. Who won the Mixed Double Title in French Open 2009?

Badminton

Sudhirman Cup

China beat Korea by 3–0, held at Guangzhou (China) on 17 May 2009.

Asian Badminton Championships

The tournament took place at Suwon, Korea from 7 April to 12 April 2009.
- **Men's Singles:** Bao Chunlai (China)
  Runner Up: Chen Long (China)
- **Women's Singles:** Zhu Lin (China)
  Runner Up: Xie Xingfang (China)

Indonesian Open 2009

Saina Nehwal scripted history on 21 June 2009 by becoming the first Indian to win a Super Series tournament with a stunning victory over Chinese Lin Wang by 12–21, 21–18, 21-9 in Jakarta.

Spanish Open

Sayali Gokhale won the Women's Singles titile in the Spanish Open Badminton Championship at Madrid, defeating Liannne Tan of Belgium by 21–9, 21–18 on 24 May 2009.

Golf

Thailand Open

India's Jyoti Randhawa cruised to a comfortable two-stroke victory at Singha Thailand Open for his eighth Asian Tour victory against Rhys Davies of Wales on 8 March 2009.

Billiards and Snooker

Pankaj Advani Won World Professional Billiards Crown: Pankaj Advani (24) of India won the World Professional Billiards defeating Mike Russel of Quatar by 2030–1253 at the Northern Snooker Centre in Leeds, UK on 6 September 2009. Geet Sethi is the only Indian to have won the billiards Pro title for five times.

Archery

Indian Archers win World Cup: Ace Indian archer Jayanta Takukdar completed a golden double, winning both individual and team curve events at the archery World Cup stage II in Porec, Croatia on 9 May 2009. He defeated Italy's Athens Champion Marco Goliazzo in the final. Later Talukdar with Rahul Banerjee and Mangal Singh Chmpia beat Russian team for gold.

Shooting

World Cup

Ace Indian Shooter Gagan Narang won Bronze Medal in the first ISSF World Cup at Chongwon in South Korea on 10 April 2009. He won in the 10 meter air-rifle event and scored 696.7 points.

Q.38. Who bagged the Laureus World Sports-woman of the year 2009?

Q.39. Who is the Chairman of thirteenth Finance Commission?

Formula One

Force India's Maiden Points in Formula One: Force India's Giancanlo Fiscichella of Italy gave Indians their first ever formula one race point by finishing second in the Belgian Grand Prix on 30 August 2009.

PRIZE AND HONOURS

Nobel Prize 2009

Physics: Nobel Prize in physics was awarded half of the prize to Charles Kao (Hong Kong) *'for groundbreaking achivements in the use of glass fibers for optical communication'* and the other half jointly to Williard Boyle (a Canadian-US citizen) and George Smith (USA) *'for inventing an imaging semiconductor circuit – the charge-coupled device (CCD) sensor, which is the electronic eye of the digital camera'*.

Chemistry: Nobel Prize in chemistry was awarded to Indian born US sceintist Dr Venkatraman Ramakrishnan *'for his work on protein-producing ribosomes, and its translation of DNA information into life'*. He shared the prize with Dr Thomas Sheitz of USA and Dr Ada Yonath of Israel.

Physiology or Medicine: Nobel Prize in this category was awarded to three Americans; Australia-born Elizabeth Blackburn, Uk-born Jack Szostak and Carol Greider *'for revealing the existance and nature of telomerase, an enzyme which helps prevent the fraying of chromosomes that underlines ageing and cancer.'*

Literature: In this category, Nobel Prize was awarded to Herta Mueller of German for her work that *'with the concentration of poetry and the frankness of prose, depicts the landscape of the dispossessed'*.

Peace: US President Barack Obama was awarded the Nobel Peace Prize *'for his works in nuclear weapons elimination and international diplomacy'*.

Economics: Elinor Ostrom and Oliver Williamson of the US were awarded the prize in this category *'for their work on economic governance and the organisation of cooperation'*. Elinor Ostrom becomes the first woman to win Nobel Prize in Economics.

Pulitzer Prize 2009

Journalism

- Public Service: *The Las Vegas Sun*, notably Alexandra Berzon;
- Breaking news reporting: *The New York Times* Staff
- Investigative reporting: David Barstow of *The New York Times*
- Explanatory reporting: Bettina Boxall and Julie Cart of the *Los Angeles Times*
- Local reporting: Detroit Free Press Staff, and notably Jim Schaefer and M L Elrick and Ryan Gabrielson and Paul Giblin of the *East Valley Tribune*
- National reporting: *St Petersburg Times* Staff
- International reporting: *The New York Times* Staff
- Feature writing: Lane De Gregory of the *St Petersburg Times*
- Commentary: Eugene Robinson of *The Washington Post*
- Criticism: Holland Cotter of *The New York Times*

Q.40. National Old Age Pension (NOAP) scheme comes under which ministry?

Current Affairs

- Editorial writing: Mark Mahoney of *The Post-Star*
- Editorial cartooning: Steve Breen of *The San Diego Union-Tribune*
- Breaking news photography: Patrick Farrell of *The Miami Herald*
- Feature photography: Damon Winter of *The New York Times*
- Fiction: *Olive Kitteridge* by Elizabeth Strout (Random House)
- *Drama*: *Ruined* by Lynn Nottage (TCG)
- *History*: *The Hemingses of Monticello: An American Family* by Annette Gordon-Reed (W W Norton & Company)
- *Biography*: *American Lion: Andrew Jackson in the White House* by Jon Meacham (Random House)
- *Poetry*: *The Shadow of Sirius* by W S Merwin (Copper Canyon Press)
- General Nonfiction: *Slavery by Another Name: The Re-Enslavement of Black Americans from the Civil War to World War II* by Douglas A. Blackmon (Doubleday)
- *Music*: Double Sextet by Steve Reich (Boosey & Hawkes)

Magsaysay Award 2009

- Government Service: Krisana Kraisintu (Thailand)
- Public Service: Deep Joshi (India)
- Community Leadership: Xu Xiaogung (China)
- Journalism, Literature, and the Creative Communication Arts: Antonio Oposa, Jr (Philippines)
- Peace and International Understanding: Mr Jun (China)
- Emergent Leadership: 2009 – Ka Hsaw Wa (Burma)

Booker Prize 2009

The Man Booker Prize for Fiction 2009 was won by Hilary Mantel of UK for her fiction 'Wolf Hall'. ***Man Booker Prize International 2009:*** Alice Munro was announced as the winner of the third Man Booker International Prize on 27 May 2009.

Jawaharlal Nehru Award for International Understanding 2008: Egypt's President Hosni Mubarak was conferred the Jawaharlal Nehru Award for International Understanding in New Delhi on 18 November 2008. The award was presented to him by President Pratibha Patil.

Indira Gandhi International Prize for Peace, Disarmament and Development 2009: Microsoft founder Bill Gates received the Indira Gandhi Prize for Peace, Disarmament and Development on 25 July 2009 for the year 2007. The award was received on behalf of the Bill and Melinda Gates Foundation.

Abel Prize 2009: The Abel Prize recognises contributions of extraordinary depth and influence to the mathematical sciences and has been awarded annually by The Norwegian Academy of Science since 2003. It carries a cash award of NOK 6,000,000. The Abel Prize for 2009 was awarded to Mikhail Leonidovich Gromov, the Russian-French mathematician, 'for his revolutionary contributions to geometry.'

Mother Teresa International Humanitarian Award 2009: Fr Jacob Thadathil has been awarded this award from the Mother Teresa Foundation for Peace on 2 Feb 2009.

Nikki Asia Award 2009: Ms Kiran Mazumdar Shaw, the CMD of Biocon has been awarded this prestigious award for 2009.

Q.41. Who is the new Minister of State for Defence?
Q.42. Who won the US Open 2009 title in tennis?

Mahatma Gandhi International Peace Prize 2009: The Nobel Laureate Pro-democracy leader of Myanmar, Ms Aung San Suu Kyi was conferred the Mahatma Gandhi International Peace Prize 2009 for Peace and Reconciliation on 20 July 2009. The award was presented by the South African-based Mahatma Gandhi Foundation at Durban, South Africa.

Oscar Award (Academy Award) 2009: Eighty-first Academy Awards was announced at Kodak Theater, Los Angeles, US on 22 Feb. 2009. The winners are:

Best Picture: *Slumdog Millionaire*
Actor in a Leading Role: Sean Penn for *Milk*
Actress in a Leading Role: Kate Winslet for *The Reader*
Actor in a Supporting Role: Late. Heath Ledger for *The Dark Knight*
Actress in a Supporting Role: Penelope Cruz for *Vicky Cristina Barcelona*
Director: Danny Boyle for *Slumdog Millionaire*
Original Screenplay: Dustin Lance Black for *Milk*
Adapted Screenplay: Simon Beaufoy for *Slumdog Millionaire*
Original Score: A R Rahman for *Slumdog Millionaire*
Original Song: 'Jai Ho', A R Rahman and Gulzar for *Slumdog Millionaire*
Animated Feature Film: *Wall-E*
Foreign Language Film: *Departures* from Japan
Art Direction: *The Curious Case of Benjamin Button*
Cinematography: *Slumdog Millionaire*
Costume Design: *The Duchess*
Makeup: *The Curious Case of Benjamin Button*
Film Editing: *Slumdog Millionaire*
Documentary Feature: *Man on Wire*
Documentary Short Subject: *Smile Pinki*
Animated Short Film: *La Maison en Petits Cubes*
Live Action Short Film: *Spielzeugland*
Sound Editing: *The Dark Knight*
Sound Mixing: Resul Pookutty for *Slumdog Millionaire*
Visual Effects: *The Curious Case of Benjamin Button*
Jean Hersholt Humanitarian Award: Jerry Lewis

British Academy of Film and Television Arts (BAFTA) Awards 2009: This gala ceremony was held in London on 8 February 2009. The winners are:

Best Film: *Slumdog Millionaire*
Outstanding British Film: *Man on Wire*
Leading Actor: Mickey Rourke for *The Wrestler*
Leading Actress: Kate Winslet for *The Reader*
Supporting Actor: Late Heath Ledger for *The Dark Knight*
Supporting Actress: Penelope Cruz for *Vicky Cristina Barcelona*
Best Director: Danny Boyle for *Slumdog Millionaire*
Music: A R Rahman for *Slumdog Millionaire*
Original Screenplay: Martin McDonagh, for *In Bruges*
Adapted Screenplay: Simon Beaufoy for *Slumdog Millionaire*
Cinematography: Anthony Dod Mantle for *Slumdog Millionaire*

Q.43. Who has been appointed as the chairman of newly formed UID Authority of India (UIDAI)?

Editing: Chris Dickens for *Slumdog Millionaire*
Production Design: Donald Graham Burt, Victor J Zolfo for *The Curious Case of Benjamin Button*
Costume Design: Michael O'Connor for *The Duchess*
Sound: Glenn Freemantle, Resul Pookutty, Richard Pryke, Tom Sayers, Ian Tapp for *Slumdog Millionaire*
Special Visual Effects: Jean Black, Colleen Callaghan for *The Curious Case of Benjamin Button*
Make Up & Hair: Jean Black, Colleen Callaghan for *The Curious Case of Benjamin Button*
Film Not in the English Language: *I've Loved You So Long*
Animated Film: *Wall-E*
Short Animation: *Wallace and Gromit: A Matter of Loaf and Death*
Short Film: *September*
Rising Star: Noel Clarke
The Carl Foreman Award: Steve McQueen (Director/Writer) for *Hunger*
Academy Fellowship: Terry Gilliam

Fifty-first Grammy Awards 2009: Fifty-first Annual Grammy Awards ware held at the Staples Centre in Los Angeles on 8 February 2009. The winners are:
Album of the Year: Robert Plant and Alison Krauss – 'Raising Sand'
Record of the Year: Robert Plant and Alison Krauss – 'Please Read the Letter'
Song of the Year: Coldplay – 'Viva la Vida'
Best New Artist: Adele
Best Pop Collaboration with Vocals: Robert Plant and Alison Krauss – 'Rich Woman'
Best Female Pop Vocal Performance: Adele – 'Chasing Pavements'
Best Male Pop Vocal Performance: John Mayer – 'Say'
Best Rap Album: Lil Wayne – 'Tha Carter III'
Best Rap Song: Lil Wayne – 'Lollipop'
Best Rap Solo Performance: Lil Wayne – 'A Milli'
Best Rock Album: Coldplay – 'Viva La Vida or Death and All His Friends'
Best Rock Song: Bruce Springsteen – 'Girls in Their Summer Clothes'
Best R&B Album: Jennifer Hudson – 'Jennifer Hudson'
Best R&B Song: Ne-Yo – 'Miss Independent'
Best Male R&B Vocal Performance: Ne-Yo – 'Miss Independent'
Best Female R&B Vocal Performance: Alicia Keys – 'Superwoman'
Producer of the Year, Non-Classical: Rick Rubin

Sixty-seventh Golden Globe Awards 2009: This was taken place on 11 January 2009. The winners are:
Best Motion Picture – Drama: *Slumdog Millionaire*
Best Performance by an Actress in a Motion Picture – Drama: Kate Winslet for *Revolutionary Road*
Best Performance by an Actor in a Motion Picture – Drama: Mickey Rourke for *The Wrestler*
Best Motion Picture – Musical or Comedy: *Vicky Cristina Barcelona*

Q.44. Who were selected for Rajiv Gandhi Khel Ratna Award 2009?
Q.45. Where was the fifteenth NAM Summit held?

Best Performance by an Actress in a Motion Picture – Musical or Comedy: Sally Hawkins for Happy-Go-Lucky
Best Performance by an Actor in a Motion Picture – Musical or Comedy: Colin Farrell for *In Bruges*
Best Performance by an Actress in a Supporting Role in a Motion Picture: Kate Winslet for *The Reader*
Best Performance by an Actor in a Supporting Role in a Motion Picture: Heath Ledger for *The Dark Knight*
Best Animated Feature Film: *Wall-E*
Best Foreign Language Film: Waltz With Bashir (Israel)
Best Director – Motion Picture: Danny Boyle – *Slumdog Millionaire*
Best Screenplay – Motion Picture: *Slumdog Millionaire* – Written by Simon Beaufoy
Best Original Score – Motion Picture: *Slumdog Millionaire* – Composed by A R Rahman
Best Original Song – Motion Picture: 'The Wrestler' – *The Wrestler*; Music & Lyrics By: Bruce Springsteen
Best Television Series – Drama: Mad Men (AMC), Lionsgate
Best Performance by an Actress in a Television Series – Drama: Anna Paquin for *True Blood* (HBO)
Best Performance by an Actor in a Television Series – Drama: Gabriel Byrne for *In Treatment* (HBO)
Best Television Series – Musical Or Comedy: *30 Rock* (NBC)

Bharat Ratna: Renowned Indian classical vocalist Pandit Bhimsen Joshi was conferred with India's highest civilian award, Bharat Ratna on 10 February 2009. The honour was last received by melody queen Lata Mangeshkar and shehnai maestro Ustad Bismillah Khan in 2001.

Padma Vibhushan Award 2009: Ten recipients are:

Name	Field	State
Dr Chandrika Prasad Srivastava	Civil Service	Maharashtra
Shri Sunderlal Bahuguna	Environmental Conservation	Uttarakhand
Prof D P Chattopadhyaya	Literature and Education	West Bengal
Prof Jasbir Singh Bajaj	Medicine	Punjab
Dr Purshotam Lal	Medicine	Uttar Pradesh
Shri Govind Narain	Public Affairs	Uttar Pradesh
Dr Anil Kakodkar	Science and Engineering	Maharashtra
Dr G Madhavan Nair	Science and Engineering	Karnataka
Sister Nirmala	Social Work	West Bengal
Dr A S Ganguly	Trade and Industry	Maharashtra

Padma Bhushan Award 2009: 30 recipients are:
G Sivarama Krishna Murthy – Art, Ramanlal C Mehta – Art, Shamshad Begum – Art, V P Dhananjayan – Art, Shanta Dhananjayan – Art, Vaidyanathan Ganapathi Sthapati – Art, S K Misra – Civil Service, Shekhar Gupta – Journalism, Alappat Sreedhara Menon –

Q.46. Who is the author of **The Miracle of Democracy: India's Amazing Journey?**
Q.47. Who wrote **Jinnah: India-Partition Independence?**

Literature and Education, C K Prahlad – Literature and Education, D Jayakanthan – Literature and Education, Isher Judge Ahluwalia – Literature and Education, Kunwar Narain – Literature and Education, Minoru Hara – Literature and Education, Ramachandra Guha – Literature and Education, Brijendra Kumar Rao – Medicine, Vaidya Devendra Triguna – Medicine, Khalid Hameed – Medicine, Satish Nambiar – National Security Affairs, Inderjit Kaur Barthakur – Public Affairs, Kirit Shantilal Parikh – Public Affairs, Bhakta B Rath – Science and Engineering, Conjeevaram Srirangachari Seshadri– Science and Engineering, Gurdip Singh Randhawa – Science and Engineering, Sam Pitroda – Science and Engineering, Sarvagya Singh Katiyar – Science and Engineering, Thomas Kailath – Science and Engineering, Naganath Nayakawadi – Social Work, Sarojini Varadappan – Social Work, Abhinav Bindra – Sports, Anil Manibhai Naik – Trade and Industry.

Padma Shri Award 2009: 93 recipients are:
Thilakan – Art, A. Vivekh – Art, Aishwarya Rai Bachchan – Art, Akshay Kumar – Art, Dr Ameena Ahmed Ahuja – Art, Aruna Sairam – Art, Devayani Chaymotty – Art, Geeta Kapur – Art, Govind Ram Nirmalkar – Art, Gurumayum Gourakishor Sharma – Art, Hashmat Ullah Khan – Art, Helan Khan – Art, Hemi Bawa – Art, Pandit Hridaynath Mangeshkar – Art, Iravatham Mahadevan – Art, K P Udayabhunu – Art, Dr Kanneganti Brahmanandam – Art, Prof. Kiran Seth – Art, Kumar Sanu Bhattacharjee – Art, Prof. Dr Leela Omchery – Art, Mattannoor Sankarankutty Marar – Art, Niranjan Goswami – Art, Bhai Nirmal Singh Khalsa – Art, Penaz Masani – Art, Prakash N Dubey – Art, Dr Pratapaditya Pal – Art, Ram Kishore Chhipa – Art, Saoli Mitra – Art, Shri Skendrowell Syiemlieh (Posthumous) – Art, Dr Subrahmanyam Krishnaswamy – Art, Suresh Dutta – Art, Shri Tafazzul Ali (Posthumous) – Art, Udit Narayan – Art,Vadakka Manalath Govindan alias Kalamandalam Gopi – Art, S B Ghosh Dastidar – Civil Service, Ameen Sayani – Broadcasting, Abhay Chhajlani – Journalism, Dr A Sankara Reddy – Literature, Alok Mehta – Literature, Dr Bannanje Govindacharya – Literature, Dr Birendranath Datta – Literature, Prof. Geshe Ngawang Samten – Literature, Prof. Jalees Ahmed Khan Tareen – Literature, Jayanta Mahapatra – Literature, John Ralston Marr – Literature, Lalthangfala Sailo – Literature, Laxman Bapu Mane – Literature, Dr Mathoor Krishnamurty – Literature, Norden Tshering – Literature, Dr Panchapakesa Jayaraman – Literature, Prof. Ram Shankar Tripathi – Literature, Prof Ranbir Chander Sobti – Literature, Dr Ravindra Nath Srivastava – Literature, Shamsur Rahman Faruqi – Literature, Shashi Deshpande – Literature, Sunny Varkey – Literature, Suresh Gundu Amonkar – Literature, Dr Utpal K Banerjee – Literature, Dr A K Gupta – Medicine, Dr Alampur Saibaba Goud – Medicine, Dr Arvind Lal – Medicine, Dr Ashok K Vaid – Medicine, Dr Ashok Kumar Grover – Medicine, Dr Balswarup Choubey – Medicine, Dr D S Rana – Medicine, Dr Govindan Vijayaraghavan – Medicine, Dr Kalyan Banerjee – Medicine, P R Krishna Kumar – Medicine, Dr R Sivaraaman – Medicine, Dr Shaik Khader Noordeen – Medicine, Prof. (Dr) Thanikachalam Sadagopan – Medicine, Dr Yash Gulati – Medicine, K Asungba Sangtam – Public Affairs, Dr Shyamlha Pappu – Public Affairs, Prof. Syed Iqbal Hasnain – Research on Himalayan Glaciers, Goriparthi Narasimha Raju Yadav – Science, Prof. Pramod Tandon – Science, Bansilal Rathi – Social Work, Begum Bilkees I Latif – Social Work, Cheril Krishna Menon – Social Work, Rev. Joseph H Pereira – Social Work, K Viswanathan – Social Work, Keepu Tshering Lepcha – Social Work, Prof. Shyam Sunder Maheshwari – Social Work, Sunil Kanti Roy – Social Work, Balbir Singh

Q.48. Who is the Minister of Commerce and Industry?
Q.49. What does WADA stand for?

Khullar – Sports, Harbhajan Singh – Sports, Mahendra Singh Dhoni – Sports, Pankaj Advani – Sports, Surinder Mehta – Technology Solutions, Arunmugam Sakthivel – Trade and Industry, Dr Bavaguthu Raghuram Shetty – Trade and Industry, Shri R K Krishna Kumar – Trade and Industry.

Rajiv Khel Ratna Award, 2009: For the first time since the inception of the Rajiv Khel Ratna Award in 1991, three sportspersons – four-time world boxing champion Mangte Chungneijang Marykom, Olympic Bronze medalists: boxer, Vijender Singh and wrestler, Sushil Kumar – will receive the country's highest sporting honour.

Arjuna Award 2009: Mangal Singh Champia (Archery), K Sinimol Paukose (Atheletics), Sania Nehwal (Badminton), L Saritha Devi (Boxing), Tania Sachdeva (Chess), Gautam Gambhir (Cricket), Ignace Tirkey (Hockey), Surinder Kaur (Hockey), Pankaj Shirsat (Kabaddi), B Prabhu (Badminton – Physically challenged), Satish Joshi (Rowing), Ranjan Sodhi (Shooting), Poulami Ghatak (Table Tennis), Yogeshwar Dutt (Wrestling), G L Yadav (Yachting).

Dronacharya Award 2009: Baldev Singh (Hockey), Jaidev Bisht (Boxing), Satpal (Wrestling), Pullela Gopichand (Badminton), Udaikumar (Kabaddi).

Dhyanchand Award 2009: Ishar Singh Deol (Athletics), Satbir Singh Dahiya (Wrestling).

Gallantry Awards

Ashok Chakra 2009: This year 11 brave hearts have been awarded with Ashoka Chakra which is the highest Gallantry award given in the time of peace. They are:
Major Sandeep Unnikrishnan of Bihar Regiment, Havaldar Gajinder Singh of Parachute Regiment, Colonel Jojan Thomas of JAT Regiment, Havildar Bahadur Singh Bohra of the tenth Battalion, Delhi Police Inspector, M C Sharma, Chief of the Maharashtra Anti-Terrorist Squad (ATS) Hemant Karkare, Additional Commissioner of Maharastra Police Ashok Kamte, Senior Inspector Vijay Salaskar of Maharastra Police, Asst. Sub-Inspector Tukaram Gopal Ombale of Maharastra Police, Assistant Commandant Pramod Kumar Satapathy of Special Operation Group of the Orissa State Armed Police and R P Diengdoh of Meghalaya Police.

Kirti Chakra 2009: It is the second highest gallantry award; 13 people were chosen for this award this year. The recipients are:
N N Bora, Shashank Shinde, Brig. R D Mehta, IFS Officer V V Rao, Roop Singh of ITBP, Ajai Pathania of ITBP are among them.

Shaurya Chakra: 23 people have received this award and also 14 were awarded Param Vishisht Seva Medal. Ati Vishisht Seva Medal was awarded to 25 persons.

Sahitya Akademi Award 2008: 21 litterateurs, which include seven novelists, six poets, five short story writers and three critics, were chosen for the National Sahitya Akademi awards for 2008, which was given away on 17 February 2009.

Novel: Govind Mishra (*Kohre Mein Kaid Rang*), Rita Choudhury, Vidya Sagar Narzary, Srinivas B Vaidya, Ashok Kamat, Shyam Manohar, Mitter Sain Meet;

Poetry: Sarat Kumar Mukhopadhyay, Champa Sharma, A O Memchoubi, Pramod Kumar Mohanty, Om Prakash Pande, Jayant Parmer;

Story Writer: Suman Shah, Shri 'Kirat', Dinesh Panchal, Badal Hembam, Melanmai Ponnusamy;

Critics: K P Appan (*Madhuram Ninte Jeevitham*), Nabi Aatash and Hiro Shewkani.

Q.50. Who has been awarded Dr Adiseshiah Award 2009?

Q.51. Whom did India beat to win the Sultan Azlan Shah Cup 2009?

Fifty-fourth Filmfare Award: Winners of the Fifty-fourth Filmfare Awards 2009: Best Film – *Jodha Akbar*, Best Actor – Hritik Roshan – *Jodha Akbar*), Best Actress – Priyanka Chopra (Fashion), Best Supporting Actor – Arjun Rampal (*Rock On*), Best Supporting Actress – Kangna Ranaut (*Fashion*), Best Director – Ashutosh Gowarikar (*Jodha Akbar*), Lifetime Achievement Award – Om Puri and Bhanu Athaiya, Best Music Director – AR Rahman (*Jaane Tu Ya Jaane Na*), Best Lyricist – Javed Akhtar ('Jashn-e-Bahara' from *Jodha Akbar*), Best Story – Abhishek Kapoor (*Rock On*), Best Playback Singer (Male) – Sukhwinder Singh (*Haule Haule* – Rab Ne Bana De *Jodi*), Best Playback Singer (Female) – Shreya Ghoshal (*Singh is King*), Best Debut (Male) – Farhan Akhtar (*Rock On*) and Imraan Khan (*Jaane Tu Ya Jaane Na*), Best Debut (Female) – Asin (Ghajini), RD Burman Upcoming Talent – Benny Dayal (*Ghajini*), Best Costumes – *Oye Lucky! Lucky Oye!* Best Background Score – AR Rahman (Jodha Akbar), Best Cinematography – Jason West (*Rock On!*), Best Editing – Amit Pawar (*Mumbai Meri Jaan*), Best Choreography – Longinus (*Jaane Tu Ya Jaane Na*), Best Sound Design – Vinod Subramanyam (*Rock On*), Best Visual Effects – John Deitz (*Love Story 2050*), Best Action – Peter Heinn (*Ghajini*)

Fifty-fifth National Film Awards 2007: The winners are:
Best Film: Kanchivaram (Tamil), Best Hindi Film: *1971*, Most Popular Film: *Chak De India*, Best Actor: Prakash Raj (*Kanchivaram*), Best Actress: Umashree (*Gulabi Talkies*), Best Supporting Actor: Darshan Jariwala (*Gandhi My Father*), Best Supporting Actress: Shefali Shah (*The Last Lear*), Best Director: Adoor Gopalakrishnan (*Nalu Pennungal*), Best Lyrics: Prasoon Joshi (*Tare Zameen Par*), Jury Award: Feroz Abbas Khan (*Gandhi My Father*), Best Screenplay: *Gandhi My Father*, Indira Gandhi Award for Best First Film of a Director: Shivajee Chandrabhusan (*Frozen*), Best Childrens Film: Foto, Nargis Dutt Award for Best Feature Film on National Integration: *Dharm*

Shanti Swarup Bhatnagar Prize: The Shanti Swarup Bhatnagar (SSB) Prizes are awarded annually by the Council of Scientific and Industrial Research (CSIR).
10 leading scientists were awarded this prize for 2008.
Ravinder Goswami of All India Institute of Medical Sciences, Jaikumar Radhakrishnan of Tata Institute of Fundamental Research, Ranjan Kumar Mallik of Indian Institute of Technology (IIT) Delhi, P N Vinayachandran of Indian Institute of Science Bangalore, G P S Raghava of Institute of Microbial Technology Chandigarh, L S Shashidhara of Centre for Cellular and Molecular Biology Hyderabad, Pradeep Thalappil of IIT Madras, Jarugu Narasimha Moorthy of IIT Kanpur, Raghunathan Srianand of the Inter-University Centre for Astronomy and Astrophysics, Pune and Srikanth Sastry of Jawaharlal Nehru Centre for Advanced Scientific Research, Bangalore.

JRD Tata Young Entrepreneur Award: Mr Bhausaheb Janjire of Pune was honoured with this award on 28 April 2009 by Vice-President Mohammed Hamid Ansari.

Saraswati Samman: The noted Hindustani Classical Vocalist Pandit Jasraj was honoured with the eighty-fifth Saraswati Samman in April 2009. This award is given for excellent work in the field of Arts, Music and Dance.

WHO IS WHO

Union Government

Pratibha Devisingh Patil: President
Mohammad Hamid Ansari: Vice-President

Q.52. Who is the Attorney-General of India?
Q.53. What did UNESCO declare 2009 as?

COUNCIL OF MINISTERS

Cabinet Ministers

Dr Manmohan Singh, Prime Minister and also in-charge of the Ministries/Departments not specifically allocated to the charge of any minister, viz:
 (i) Ministry of Personnel, Public Grievances & Pensions;
 (ii) Ministry of Planning;
 (iii) Department of Atomic Energy;
 (iv) Department of Space and;
 (v) Ministry of Culture

Pranab Mukherjee	Minister of Finance
Sharad Pawar	Minister of Agriculture and Minister of Consumer Affairs, Food and Public Distribution
A K Antony	Minister of Defence
P Chidambaram	Minister of Home Affairs
Mamata Banerjee	Minister of Railways
S M Krishna	Minister of External Affairs
Virbhadra Singh	Minister of Steel
Vilasrao Deshmukh	Minister of Heavy Industries and Public Enterprises
Ghulam Nabi Azad	Minister of Health and Family Welfare
Sushil Kumar Shinde	Minister of Power
M Veerappa Moily	Minister of Law and Justice
Dr Farooq Abdullah	Minister of New and Renewable Energy
S Jaipal Reddy	Minister of Urban Development
Kamal Nath	Minister of Road Transport and Highways
Vayalar Ravi	Minister of Overseas Indian Affairs
Dayanidhi Maran	Minister of Textiles
A Raja	Minister of Communications and Information Technology
Murli Deora	Minister of Petroleum and Natural Gas
Ambika Soni	Minister of Information and Broadcasting
Mallikarjun Kharge	Minister of Labour and Employment
Kapil Sibal	Minister of Human Resource Development
B K Handique	Minister of Mines and Minister of Development of North Eastern Region
Anand Sharma	Minister of Commerce and Industry
C P Joshi	Minister of Rural Development and Minister of Panchayati Raj
Kumari Selja	Minister of Housing and Urban Poverty Alleviation and Minister of Tourism
Subodh Kant Sahay	Minister of Food Processing Industries
Dr M S Gill	Minister of Youth Affairs and Sports
G K Vasan	Minister of Shipping

Q.54. What is the name of India's first nuclear submarine?
Q.55. Who is the President of South Africa?

Pawan K Bansal   Minister of Parliamentary Affairs and Minister of Water Resources
Mukul Wasnik   Minister of Social Justice and Empowerment
Kantilal Bhuria   Minister of Tribal Affairs
MK Azhagiri   Minister of Chemicals and Fertilizers

Ministers of State (Independent Charge)

List of Ministers	Portfolio
Praful Patel	Ministry of Civil Aviation
Prithviraj Chavan	Ministry of Science and Technology; Ministry of Earth Sciences; Minister of State in the Prime Minister's Office; Minister of State in the Ministry of Personnel, Public Grievances and Pensions; and Minister of State in the Ministry of Parliamentary Affairs
Sriprakash Jaiswal	Ministry of Coal and Ministry of Statistics and Programme implementation.
Salman Khursheed	Ministry of Corporate Affairs and Ministry of Minority Affairs
Dinsha J Patel	Ministry of Micro, Small and Medium Enterprises
Krishna Tirath	Ministry of Women and Child Development
Jairam Ramesh	Ministry of Environment and Forests

Ministers of State

List of Ministers	Portfolio
Srikant Jena	Ministry of Chemicals and Fertilizers
E Ahamed	Ministry of Railways
Mullappally Ramachandran	Ministry of Home Affairs
V Narayansamy	Ministry of Planning and Minister of State in the Ministry of Parliamentary Affairs
Jyotiraditya Scindia	Ministry of Commerce and Industry
Smt D Purandeswari	Ministry of Human Resource Development
K H Muniyappa	Ministry of Railways
Ajay Maken	Ministry of Home Affairs
Smt Panabaka Lakshmi	Ministry of Textiles
Namo Narain Meena	Ministry of Finance
M M Pallam Raju	Ministry of Defence
Saugata Ray	Ministry of Urban Development
S S Palanimanickam	Ministry of Finance
Jitin Prasad	Ministry of Petroleum and Natural Gas
A Sai Prathap	Ministry of Steel
Smt Preneet Kaur	Ministry of External Affairs
Gurdas Kamat	Ministry of Communications and Information Technology
Harish Rawat	Ministry of Labour and Employment
Prof. K V Thomas	Ministry of Agriculture and Ministry of Consumer Affairs, Food and Public Distribution
Bharatsinh Solanki	Ministry of Power
Mahadev S Khandela	Ministry of Road Transport and Highways
Dinesh Trivedi	Ministry of Health and Family Welfare
Sisir Adhikari	Ministry of Rural Development

Sultan Ahmed	Ministry of Tourism
Mukul Roy	Ministry of Shipping
Choudhury Mohan Jatua	Ministry of Information and Broadcasting
D Napoleon	Ministry of Social Justice and Empowerment
Dr S Jagathrakshakan	Ministry of Information and Broadcasting
S Gandhiselvan	Ministry of Health and Family Welfare
Tusharbhai Chaudhary	Ministry of Tribal Affairs
Sachin Pilot	Ministry of Communications and Information Technology
Arun Yadav	Ministry of Heavy Industries and Public Enterprises
Pratik Prakashbapu Patil	Ministry of Youth Affairs and Sports
R P N Singh	Ministry of Road Transport and Highways
Shashi Tharoor	Ministry of External Affairs
Vincent Pala	Ministry of Water Resources
Pradeep Jain	Ministry of Rural Development
Agatha Sangma	Ministry of Rural Development

Heads of Important Offices (National)

Chief Justice:	Justice K G Balakrishnan
Speaker of Lok Sabha:	Ms Miera Kumar
Dy Speaker of Lok Sabha:	Charanjit Singh Atwal
Secretary-General of Lok Sabha:	P D T Achari
Chairman of Rajya Sabha:	Mohammad Hamid Ansari
Dy Chairman of Rajya Sabha:	K Rahman Khan
Secretary-General of Rajya Sabha:	Dr V K Agnihotri
Chairman of Planning Commission:	Dr Montek Singh Ahluwalia
Attorney General:	Goolam E Vahanvati
Solicitor General:	Gopal Subramanian
Comptroller & Auditor-General:	Vinod Rai
Chief Election Commissioner:	Navin Chawla
Election Commissioners:	S Y Quraishi and V S Sampath
Principle Secretary to the Prime Minister:	T K A Nair
National Security Adviser:	M K Narayanan
Principle Scientific Adviser to the Government:	Dr R Chidambaram
Registrar-General & Census Commissioner:	J K Banthia
Scientific Adviser to the Defence Minister:	M Natarjan
Governor of RBI:	Dr D Subbarao
Cabinet Secretary:	K M Chandrasekhar
Foreign Secretary:	Ms Nirupama Rao
Home Secretary:	Gopal Krishna Pillai
Finance Secretary:	S Narayan
Defence Secretary:	Vijay Singh
Chairman of PM Economic Advisory Council:	Suresh Tendulkar
Surveyor General of India:	Prithvish Nag
Chief Vigilance Commissioner:	N Vittal
Chairman of Prasar Bharti:	Arun Bhatnagar
CEO of Prasar Bharti:	B S Lalli
Chairman of UPSC:	Prof. D P Agarwal

Current Affairs

Chairman of Atomic Energy Commission (AEC):	Anil Kakodkar
Chairman of CBSE:	Vineet Joshi
Chairperson of NABARD:	Y S P Thorat
Chairman of NASSCOM:	Ganesh Natarajan
Chairman, IRDA:	J Harinarayanan
Chairman, LIC:	T S Vijayan
Chairman of Staff Selection Commission:	N K Raghupathy
Chairperson, Children's Film Society of India:	Nandita Das
Chairman, Press Trust of India (PTI):	Prof. E V Chitnis
Chairman, Press Council of India (PCI):	Justice G N Ray
Chairman of United News of India:	Ravindra Kumar
Chairman of Law Commission:	Justice A R Lakshmanan
Chairman of Central Board of Direct Taxes (CBDT):	S S N Moorthy
Chairperson of Central Board of Children Certification:	Sharmila Tagore
Chairman of Food Corporation of India (FCI):	V K Malhotra
Chairman of ISRO:	Dr G Madhavan Nair
Chairman of National Commission for Minorities:	Mohammed Hamid Ansari
Chairman of National Commission for SCs:	Dr Buta Singh
Chairman of National Commission for ST's:	Urmila Singh
Chairman of National Commission forBackward Classes:	Justice S Ratnavel Pandian
Chairman of National Human Rights commission (NHRC):	Justice S Rajendra Babu
Chairman of UGC:	Prof. Nazrul Islam
Chairman of Railway Board:	S S Khurana
Chairman of Sangeet Natak Academy:	Ram Niwas Mirdha
Chairperson of National Commission for Women:	Dr Girija Vyas
Chairman of Indian Banks' Association (IBA):	K C Chakrabarty
Chairman of SBI:	O P Bhat
CMD, IDBI:	V P Shetty
Chairman, SEBI:	C B Bhave
Chairman, IOC:	S Behuria
President of ASSOCHAM:	Swati Piramal
President, FICCI:	Rajeev Chandrasekhar
President of CII:	K V Kamath
President, Indian Olympic Association:	Suresh Kalmadi
President of BCCI:	Ranbir Singh Mahendra
Director of NCERT:	Prof. Krishna Kumar
Director of BARC:	Dr Srikumar Banerjee
Director of CBI:	Ashwani Kumar
Director of VSSC:	Dr B N Suresh
Director of Intelligence Bureau (IB):	Rajiv Mathur
Director of Research & Analysis Wing (RAW):	K C Verma
Director General of Doordarshan:	Aruna Sharma
Director General of Archeological Survey of India (ASI):	Anshu Vaish
Director General of AIR:	G Jayalal
Director General of BSF:	Raman Srivastava
Director General of CRPF:	A S Gill
Director General of CSIR:	Samir Brahamachari

Director General of ICMR: Dr V M Katoch
Ambassador to USA: Meera Shankar
(2009 – Present)
Ambassador to Russia: Prabhat Prakash Shukla
(2007 – Present)
Ambassador to China: Nirupama Rao
(2006 – Present)
High Commissioner to UK: Shiv Shankar Mukherjee
High Commissioner to Pakistan: Sharat Sabharwal
High Commissioner to Sri Lanka: Alok Prasad
India's Permanent member to UN: Hardeep Singh Puri

Head of Countries

	Country	President	Prime minister
1.	Afghanistan	Hamid Karzai	–
2.	Albania	Bamir Topi	Sali Berisha
3.	Algeria	Abdelaziz Bouteflika	Ahmed Ouyahia
4.	Andorra	Co-Prince Joan Enric Vives Sicília Representative Nemesi Marques Oste Co-Prince Nicolas Sarkozy Representative Christian Frémont	Jaume Bartumeu
5.	Angola	Jose Eduardo dos Santos	Paulo Kassoma
6.	Antigua and Barbuda	Queen Elizabeth II	Baldwin Spencer Governor General Louise Lake Tack
7.	Argentina	Cristina Fernandez de Kirchner	–
8.	Armenia	Serzh Sargsyan	Tigran Sargsyan
9.	Australia	Queen Elizabeth II Governor General Quentin Bryce	Kevin Rudd
10.	Austria	Heinz Fischer	Chancellor Werner Faymann
11.	Azerbaijan	Ilham Aliyev	Artur Rasizade
12.	Bahamas	Queen Elizabeth II Governor General Arthur Dion Hanna	Hubert Ingraham
13.	Bahrain	King Hamad ibn Isa Al Khalifah	Khalifah ibn Sulman Al Khalifah
14.	Bangladesh	Zillur Rahman	Hasina Wazed
15.	Barbados	Queen Elizabeth II Governor General Clifford Husbands	David Thompson
16.	Belarus	Alexander Lukashenko	Sergey Sidorsky
17.	Belgium	King Albert II	Herman Van Rompuy
18.	Belize	Queen Elizabeth II Governor General Colville Young	Dean Barrow
19.	Benin	Yayi Boni	–
20.	Bhutan	King Jigme Khesar Namgyal Wangchuck	Jigme Thinley
21.	Bolivia	Evo Morales	–

22.	Bosnia and Herzegovina	Zeljko Komsic	Nikola Spiric Presidency Member Nebojsa Radmanovic Presidency Member Haris Silajdzic
23.	Botswana	Ian Khama	–
24.	Brazil	Luiz Inacio Lula da Silva	–
25.	Brunei	Sultan Hassanal Bolkiah	–
26.	Bulgaria	Georgi Parvanov	Boyko Borisov
27.	Burkina Faso	Blaise Compaore	Tert'us Zongo
28.	Burma	–	Thein Sein
29.	Burundi	Pierre Nkurunziza	–
30.	Cambodia	King Norodom Sihamoni	Hun Sen
31.	Cameroon	Paul Biya	Philemon Yang
32.	Canada	Queen Elizabeth II Governor General Michaelle Jean	Stephen Harper
33.	Cape Verde	Pedro Pires	Jose Maria Neves
34.	Central African	Francois Bozize	Faustin-Archange Touadera Republic
35.	Chad	Idriss Deby	Youssouf Saleh Abbas
36.	Chile	Michelle Bachelet	–
37.	China	Hu Jintao	Wen Jiabao
38.	Colombia	Álvaro Uribe	–
39.	Comoros	Ahmed Abdallah Sambi	–
40.	Congo-Brazzaville	Denis Sassou-Nguesso	Isidore Mvouba
41.	Congo-Kinshasa	Joseph Kabila	Adolphe Muzito
42.	Costa Rica	Oscar Arias	–
43.	Croatia	Stjepan Mesic	Jadranka Kosor
44.	Cuba	Raul Castro	–
45.	Cyprus	Dimitris Christofias	–
46.	Czech Republic	Vaclav Klaus	Jan Fischer
47.	Denmark	Queen Margrethe II	Lars Lokke Rasmussen
48.	Djibouti	Ismail Omar Guelleh	Dileita Mohamed Dileita
49.	Dominica	Nicholas Liverpool	Roosevelt Skerrit
50.	Dominican Republic	Leonel Fernandez	
51.	East Timor	Jose Ramos-Horta	Xanana Gusmao
52.	Ecuador	Rafael Correa	–
53.	Egypt	Hosni Mubarak	Ahmed Nazif
54.	El Salvador	Mauricio Funes	.
55.	Equatorial Guinea	Teodoro Obiang Nguema Mbasogo	Ignacio Milam Tang
56.	Eritrea	Isaias Afewerki	–
57.	Estonia	Toomas Hendrik Ilves	Andrus Ansip
58.	Ethiopia	Girma Wolde-Giorgis	Meles Zenawi

59.	Fiji	Epeli Nailatukau	Frank Bainimarama
60.	Finland	Tarja Halonen	Matti Vanhanen
61.	France	Nicolas Sarkozy	Francois Fillon
62.	Gabon	Rose Francine Rogombe	Paul Biyoghe Mba
63.	Gambia	Yahya Jammeh	–
64.	Georgia	Mikheil Saakashvili	Nikoloz Gilauri
65.	Germany	Horst Kohler	Chancellor Angela Merkel
66.	Ghana	John Atta Mills	–
67.	Greece	Karolos Papoulias	Kostas Karamanlis
68.	Grenada	Queen Elizabeth II Governor General Carlyle Glean	Tillman Thomas
69.	Guatemala	Alvaro Colom	–
70.	Guinea	Moussa Dadis Camara	Kabine Komara
71.	Guinea-Bissau	Malam Bacai Sanha	Carlos Gomes Junior
72.	Guyana	Bharrat Jagdeo	Sam Hinds
73.	Haiti	Rene Preval	Michele Pierre-Louis
74.	Honduras	Roberto Micheletti	–
75.	Hungary	Laszlo Solyom	Gordon Bajnai
76.	Iceland	Olafur Ragnar Grímsson	Johanna Siguroardottir
77.	India	Pratibha Patil	Dr Manmohan Singh
78.	Indonesia	Susilo Bambang Yudhoyono	–
79.	Iran	Supreme Leader Ali Khamenei Mahmoud Ahmadinejad	–
80.	Iraq	Jalal Talabani (Pres.)	Nouri al-Maliki
81.	Ireland	Mary McAleese	Taoiseach Brian Cowen
82.	Israel	Shimon Peres	Benjamin Netanyahu
83.	Italy	Giorgio Napolitano	Silvio Berlusconi
84.	Ivory Coast	Laurent Gbagbo	Guillaume Soro
85.	Jamaica	Queen Elizabeth II Governor General Patrick Allen	Bruce Golding
86.	Japan	Emperor Akihito	Yokio Hatoyama
87.	Jordan	King Abdullah II	Nader al-Dahabi
88.	Kazakhstan	Nursultan Nazarbayev	Karim Massimov
89.	Kenya	Mwai Kibaki	Raila Odinga
90.	Kiribati	Anote Tong	–
91.	Kuwait	Emir Sabah Al-Ahmad Al-Jaber Al-Sabah	Nasser Al-Mohammed Al-Ahmed Al-Sabah
92.	Kyrgyzstan	Kurmanbek Bakiyev	Igor Chudinov
93.	Laos	Choummaly Sayasone	Bouasone Bouphavanh
94.	Latvia	Valdis Zatlers	Valdis Dombrovskis
95.	Lebanon	Michel Sleiman	Fouad Siniora
96.	Lesotho	King Letsie III	Pakalitha Mosisili
97.	Liberia	Ellen Johnson-Sirleaf	–
98.	Libya	–	Baghdadi Mahmudi
99.	Liechtenstein	Prince Hans-Adam II Prince-Regent Alois	Klaus Tschütscher
100.	Lithuania	Dalia Grybauskaite	Andrius Kubilius

101.	Luxembourg	Grand Duke Henri	Jean-Claude Juncker
102.	Macedonia	Gjorge Ivanov	Nikola Gruevski
103.	Madagascar	President of the High Authority of Transition Andry Rajoelina	Monja Roindefo
104.	Malawi	Bingu wa Mutharika	
105.	Malaysia	Yang di-Pertuan Agong Mizan	Najib Razak Zainal Abidin
106.	Maldives	Mohamed Nasheed	–
107.	Mali	Amadou Toumani Toure	Modibo Sidibe
108.	Malta	George Abela	Lawrence Gonzi
109.	Marshall Islands	Litokwa Tomeing	
110.	Mauritania	Mohamed Ould Abdel Aziz	Moulaye Ould Mohamed Laghdaf ý
111.	Mauritius	Anerood Jugnauth	Navin Ramgoolam
112.	Mexico	Felipe Calderon	–
113.	Micronesia	Manny Mori	–
114.	Moldova	Mihai Ghimpu	Vitalie Pirlog
115.	Monaco	Prince Albert II	Minister of State Jean-Paul Proust
116.	Mongolia	Tsakhiaagiin Elbegdorj	Sanjaagiin Bayar
117.	Montenegro	Filip Vujanovic	Milo Dukanovic
118.	Morocco	King Muhammad VI	Abbas El Fassi
119.	Mozambique	Armando Guebuza	Luisa Diogo
120.	Namibia	Hifikepunye Pohamba	Nahas Angula
121.	Nauru	Marcus Stephen	–
122.	Nepal	Ram Baran Yadav	Madhav Kumar Nepal
123.	Netherlands	Queen Beatrix	Jan Peter Balkenende
124.	New Zealand	Queen Elizabeth II Governor General Anand Satyanand	John Key
125.	Nicaragua	Daniel Ortega	–
126.	Niger	Tandja Mamadou	Seyni Oumarou
127.	Nigeria	Umaru Yar'Adua	–
128.	North Korea	Kim Jong-il	· Kim Yong-il
129.	Norway	King Harald V	Jens Stoltenberg
130.	Oman	Sultan Qaboos	–
131.	Pakistan	Asif Ali Zardari	Yousaf Raza Gillani
132.	Palau	Johnson Toribiong	–
133.	Panama	Ricardo Martinelli	–
134.	Papua New Guinea	Queen Elizabeth II Governor General Paulias Matane	Michael Somare
135.	Paraguay	Fernando Lugo	
136.	Peru	Alan Garcia	Javier Velasquez
137.	Philippines	Gloria Macapagal-Arroyo	–
138.	Poland	Lech Kaczynski	Donald Tusk
139.	Portugal	Anibal Cavaco Silva	Jose Socrates
140.	Qatar	Emir Hamad bin Khalifa	Hamad ibn Jaber Al Thani

#	Country	Head of State	Head of Government
141.	Romania	Traian Basescu	Emil Boc
142.	Russia	Dmitry Medvedev	Vladimir Putin
143.	Rwanda	Paul Kagame	Bernard Makuza
144.	Saint Kitts and Nevis	Queen Elizabeth II Governor General Cuthbert Sebastian	Denzil Douglas
145.	Saint Lucia	Queen Elizabeth II Governor General Pearlette Louisy	Stephenson King
146.	Saint Vincent and the Grenadines	Queen Elizabeth II Governor General Frederick Ballantyne	Ralph Gonsalves
147.	Samoa	O le Ao o le Malo Tufuga Efi	Tuilaepa Aiono Sailele Malielegaoi
148.	San Marino	Captain Regent Massimo Cenciý	Captain Regent Oscar Minaý
149.	Saudi Arabia	King Abdullah	–
150.	Senegal	Abdoulaye Wade	Souleymane Ndene Ndiaye
151.	Serbia	Boris Tadic	Mirko Cvetkovic
152.	Seychelles	James Michel	–
153.	Sierra Leone	Ernest Bai Koroma	–
154.	Singapore	Sellapan Ramanathan	Lee Hsien Loong
155.	Slovakia	Ivan Gasparovic	Robert Fico
156.	Slovenia	Danilo Türk	Borut Pahor
157.	Somalia	Sharif Ahmed	Omar Abdirashid Ali Sharmarke
158.	South Africa	Jacob Zuma	–
159.	South Korea	Lee Myung-bak	Han Seung-soo
160.	Spain	King Juan Carlos I	José Luis Rodriguez Zapatero
161.	Sri Lanka	Mahinda Rajapaksa	Ratnasiri Wickremanayake
162.	Sudan	Omar al-Bashir	–
163.	Suriname	Ronald Venetiaan	–
164.	Swaziland	King Mswati III	Barnabas Sibusiso Dlamini
165.	Sweden	King Carl XVI Gustaf	Fredrik Reinfeldt
166.	Switzerland	Hans-Rudolf Merz	–
167.	Syria	Bashar al-Assad	Muhammad Naji al-Otari
168.	Tajikistan	Emomalii Rahmon	Oqil Oqilov
169.	Tanzania	Jakaya Kikwete	Mizengo Pinda
170.	Thailand	King Bhumibol Adulyadej	Abhisit Vejjajiva
171.	Togo	Faure Gnassingbe	Gilbert Houngbo
172.	Tonga	King George Tupou V	Feleti Sevele
173.	Trinidad and Tobago	George Maxwell Richards	Patrick Manning
174.	Tunisia	Zine El Abidine Ben Ali	Mohamed Ghannouchi

175. Turkey	Abdullah Gül	Recep Tayyip Erdoðan
176. Turkmenistan	Gurbanguly Berdimuhamedow	–
177. Tuvalu	Queen Elizabeth II Governor General Filoimea Telito	Apisai Ielemia
178. Uganda	Yoweri Museveni	Apolo Nsibambi
179. Ukraine	Viktor Yushchenko	Yulia Tymoshenko
180. United Arab Emirates	Khalifa bin Zayed Al Nahyan	Mohammed bin Rashid Al Maktoum
181. United Kingdom	Queen Elizabeth II	Gordon Brown
182. United States	Barack Obama	–
183. Uruguay	Tabare Vazquez	–
184. Uzbekistan	Islam Karimov	Shavkat Mirziyoyev
185. Vanuatu	Lolu Abil	Edward Natapei
186. Vatican City	Sovereign Benedict XVI Giovanni Lajolo	–
187. Venezuela	Hugo Chavez	–
188. Vietnam	Nguyen Minh Tri?t	Nguyen Tan Dung
189. Yemen	Ali Abdullah Saleh	Ali Muhammad Mujawar
190. Zambia	Rupiah Banda	–
191. Zimbabwe	Robert Mugabe	Morgan Tsvangirai

Heads of Important Offices (International)

Secretary-General, United Nations Organisation:	Ban Ki-moon
First Deputy Secretary-General, UN:	Asha-Rose Migiro
President, World Bank (or IBRD):	Robert Zoellick
President, International Court of Justice (ICJ):	Rosalyn Higgins
President, Asian Development Bank (ADB):	Haruhiko Kuroda
President, African Development Bank (AFD):	Donald Kaberuka
President, International Olympic Committee (IOC):	Jacques Rogge
President, European Commission:	Jose Manuel Durao Barroso
President, South- West African People's Organisation (SWAPO):	Hitikepunge Pohamba
President, International Amateur Athletic Federation (IAAF):	Lamine Diack
Acting President, International Cricket Council:	David Morgan
Managing Director, International Monetary Fund (IMF):	Dominique Strauss Kahn
Director-General, UNESCO:	Koichiro Matsuura
Director-General, World Health Organisation (WHO):	Dr Margaret Chan
Director-General, Food and Agricultural Organisation (FAO):	Jacques Diouf
Director-General, World Trade Organisation (WTO):	Pascal Lamy
Deputy Director General, World Trade Organisation (WTO):	Harshvardhana Singh
Director-General, International Labour Organisation (ILO):	Juan Somavia
Director-General, United Nations Development Programme (UNDP):	Mark M Brown

Q.56. Who is the Secretary-General of SAARC?
Q.57. What does UNCCC stand for?

Director-General, UNIDO: Kandeh K Yumkelia
Director-General, International Atomic Energy
  Agency (IAEA): Yukiya Amano
Executive Director, United Nations International Children's: Ann M Veneman
Emergency Fund (UNICEF) Executive Director, UNFPA: Thoraya Ahmed Obaid
UN High Commissioner for Refugees (UNHCR): Antonio Guterres
High Commissioner, UN High Commission for
  Human Rights: Navi Pillay
Secretary-General, Commonwealth: Kamlesh Sharma
Secretary-General, African Union (AU): Amara Essy
Secretary General, United Nations Conference on Dr Supachai Panitchpakdi
  Trade and Development (UNCTAD):
Secretary-General, Organisation of Economic
  Cooperation and Development (OECD): Angel Gurria
Secretary-General, Gulf Co-operation Council: Jammel Al Hujilan
Secretary-General, Organisation of Islamic Conference: Ekmeleddin Ihsanoglu
Secretary-General, Organisation of Petroleum
  Exporting Countries (OPEC): Abdalla Salem El-Badri
Secretary-General, ASEAN: Dr Surin Pitsuwan
Secretary-General, SAARC: Sheel Kant Sharma
Secretary-General, Amnesty International (AI): Irene Zubaida Khan
Secretary-General, North Atlantic Treaty
  Organisation (NATO): Jaap de Hoop Scheffer
Chairman, African Union (AU): Prof. Alpha Oumar Konare
Chairman, Non-Aligned Movement (NAM): Hosni Mubarak
Chairman, Organisation of American States (OAS): Cesar Gaviria Trujilo
Chairman, Commonwealth Parliamentary Association: Hashim Abdul Halim
Director, Commonwealth of Learning: Dr Abdul Waheed Khan
Military Adviser to UN Dept of Peace-keeping Operations: Major Gen. Randhir Mehta

APPOINTMENTS

- Radha Vinod Raju, a 1975-batch Indian Police Service officer of Jammu and Kashmir cadre took over as the first head of National Investigation Agency (NIA) on 19 January 2009.
- S S Khurana has taken over as the new Chairman, Railway Board on 4 February 2009.
- Venu Srinivasan, Managing Director of Sundaram-Clayton and Chairman-cum-Managing Director of TVS Motor Company, on 27 March 2009 took over as the President of the Confederation of Indian Industry (CII) for 2009–10.
- Nirupam Sen has been appointed Special Senior Advisor to the President of UN General Assembly on 31 March 2009.
- Pramod Bhasin took over as Chairman of NASSCOM on 2 April 2009.
- Senior Election Commissioner Navin Chawla took over as the 16th Chief Election Commissioner (CEC) of India on 21 April 2009.

Q.58. Which is the other name of Yuva Bharti Stadium?

Q.59. Up to what age of the children are covered under Integrated Child Development Services (ICDS)?